What The Duck

What The Duck

A W.T. Duck Collection

by Aaron Johnson

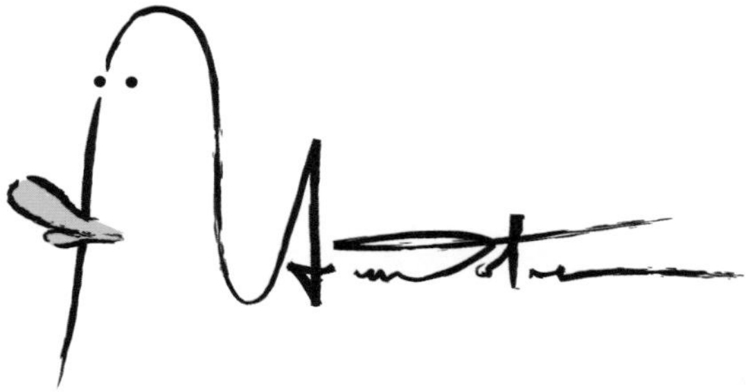

Andrews McMeel Publishing, LLC

Kansas City • Sydney • London

W.T. Duck is distributed internationally by Universal Press Syndicate.

What the Duck copyright © 2009 by Aaron Johnson. All rights reserved. Printed in China. No part of this book may be used or reproduced in any manner whatsoever without written permission except in the case of reprints in the context of reviews. For information, write Andrews McMeel Publishing, LLC, an Andrews McMeel Universal company, 1130 Walnut, Kansas City, Missouri 64106.

09 10 11 12 13 TEN 10 9 8 7 6 5 4 3 2 1

ISBN-13: 978-0-7407-8096-7
ISBN-10: 0-7407-8096-4

Library of Congress Control Number: 2008936249

www.andrewsmcmeel.com
www.whattheduck.net

**To my free time and sunlight.
Oh, how I miss thee . . .**

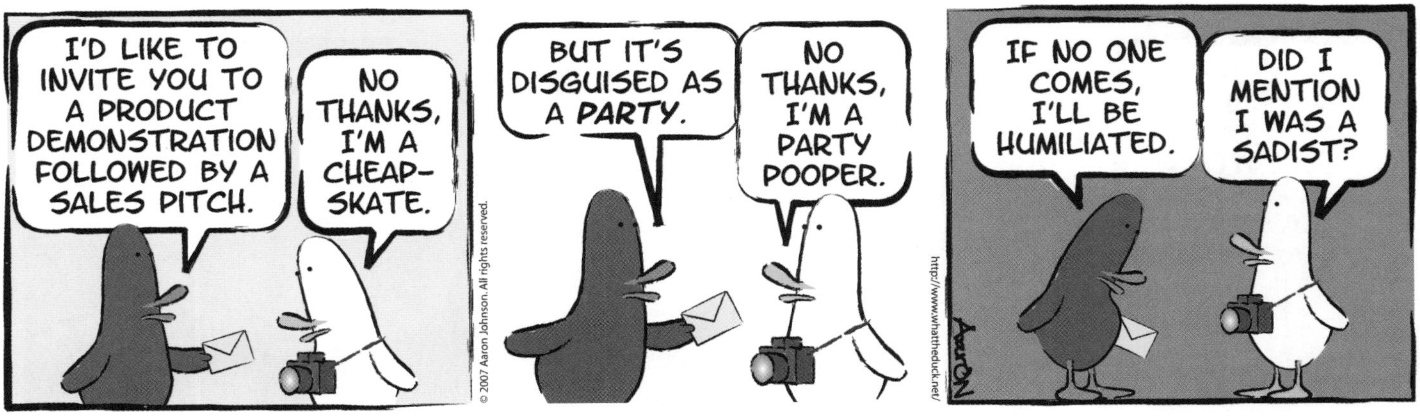
I'D LIKE TO INVITE YOU TO A PRODUCT DEMONSTRATION FOLLOWED BY A SALES PITCH.
NO THANKS, I'M A CHEAP-SKATE.
BUT IT'S DISGUISED AS A **PARTY**.
NO THANKS, I'M A PARTY POOPER.
IF NO ONE COMES, I'LL BE HUMILIATED.
DID I MENTION I WAS A SADIST?
© 2007 Aaron Johnson. All rights reserved.
http://www.whattheduck.net/
AARON

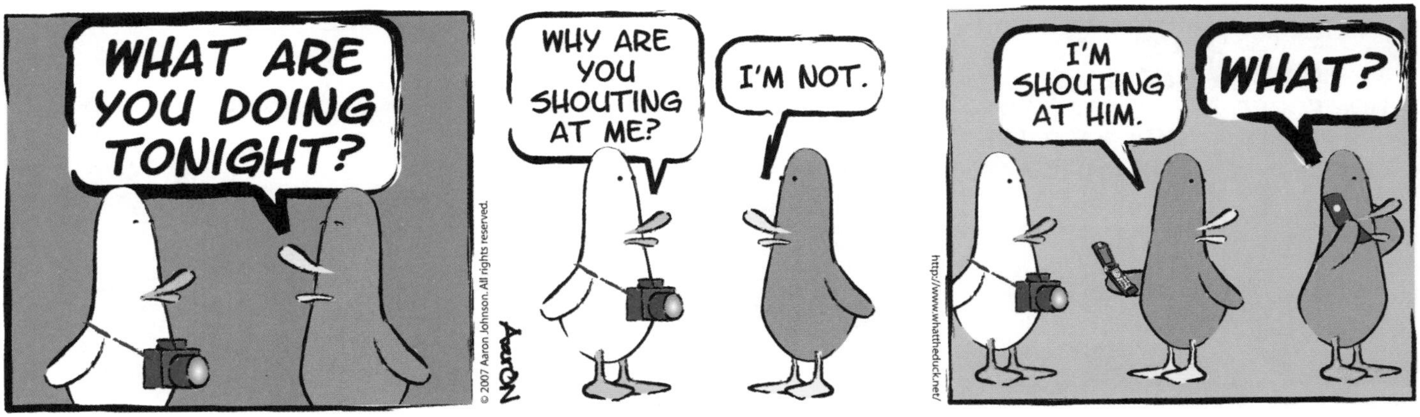
WHAT ARE YOU DOING TONIGHT?
WHY ARE YOU SHOUTING AT ME?
I'M NOT.
I'M SHOUTING AT HIM.
WHAT?
© 2007 Aaron Johnson. All rights reserved.
http://www.whattheduck.net/
AARON

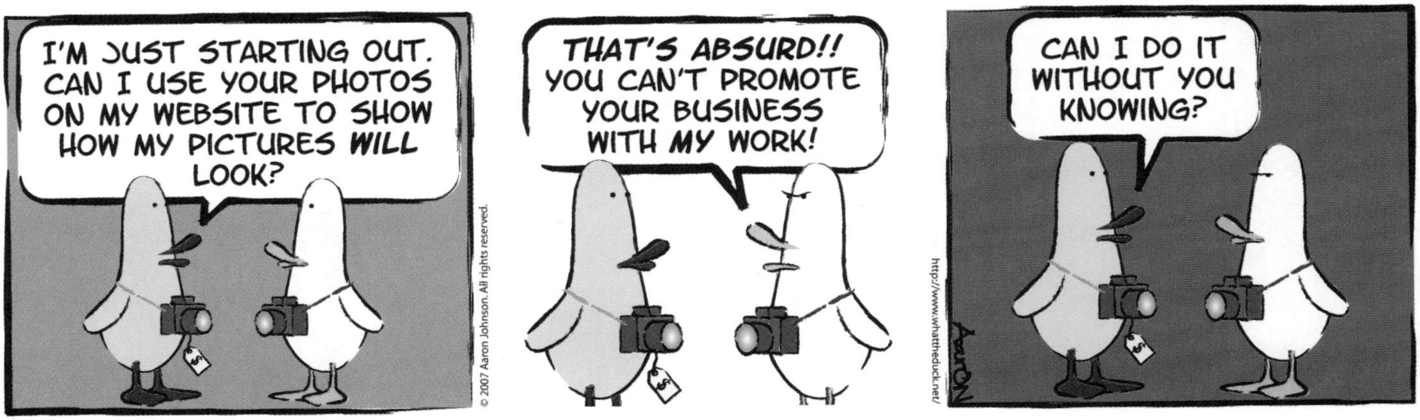
I'M JUST STARTING OUT. CAN I USE YOUR PHOTOS ON MY WEBSITE TO SHOW HOW MY PICTURES **WILL** LOOK?
THAT'S ABSURD!! YOU CAN'T PROMOTE YOUR BUSINESS WITH **MY** WORK!
CAN I DO IT WITHOUT YOU KNOWING?
© 2007 Aaron Johnson. All rights reserved.
http://www.whattheduck.net/
AARON

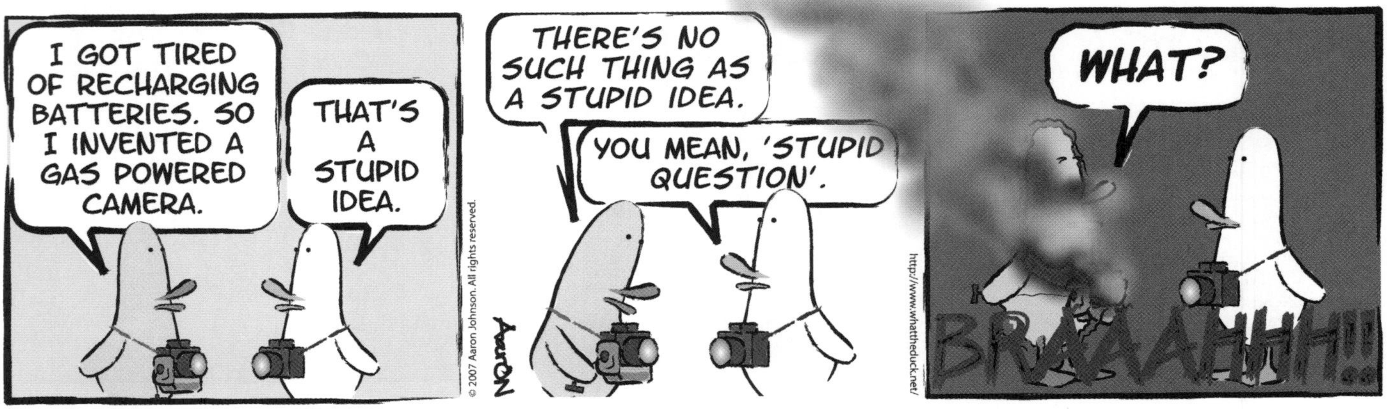
I GOT TIRED OF RECHARGING BATTERIES. SO I INVENTED A GAS POWERED CAMERA.
THAT'S A STUPID IDEA.
© 2007 Aaron Johnson. All rights reserved.
THERE'S NO SUCH THING AS A STUPID IDEA.
YOU MEAN, 'STUPID QUESTION'.
http://www.whattheduck.net/
WHAT?
BRAAAHHH!!

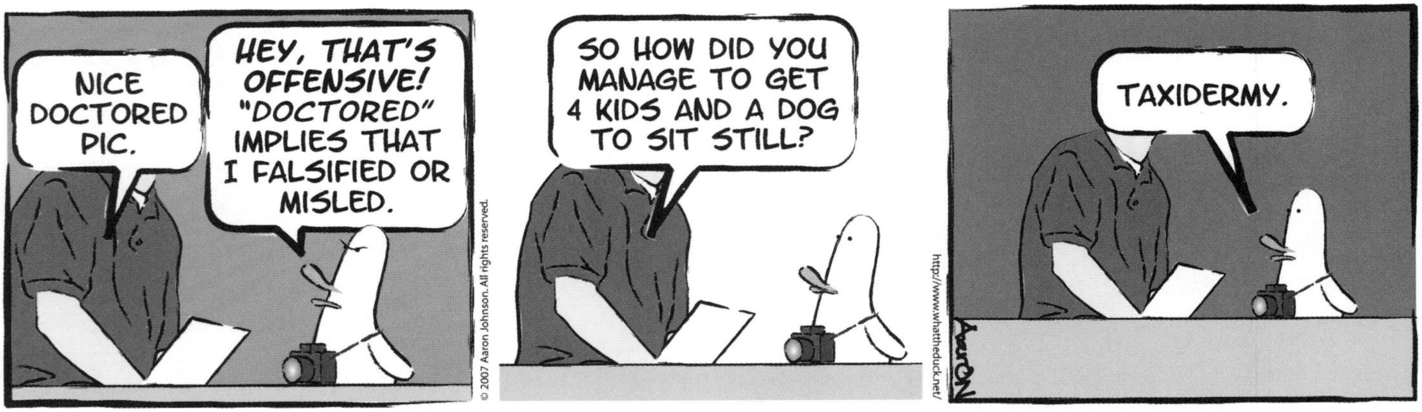
NICE DOCTORED PIC.
HEY, THAT'S OFFENSIVE! "DOCTORED" IMPLIES THAT I FALSIFIED OR MISLED.
© 2007 Aaron Johnson. All rights reserved.
SO HOW DID YOU MANAGE TO GET 4 KIDS AND A DOG TO SIT STILL?
http://www.whattheduck.net/
TAXIDERMY.

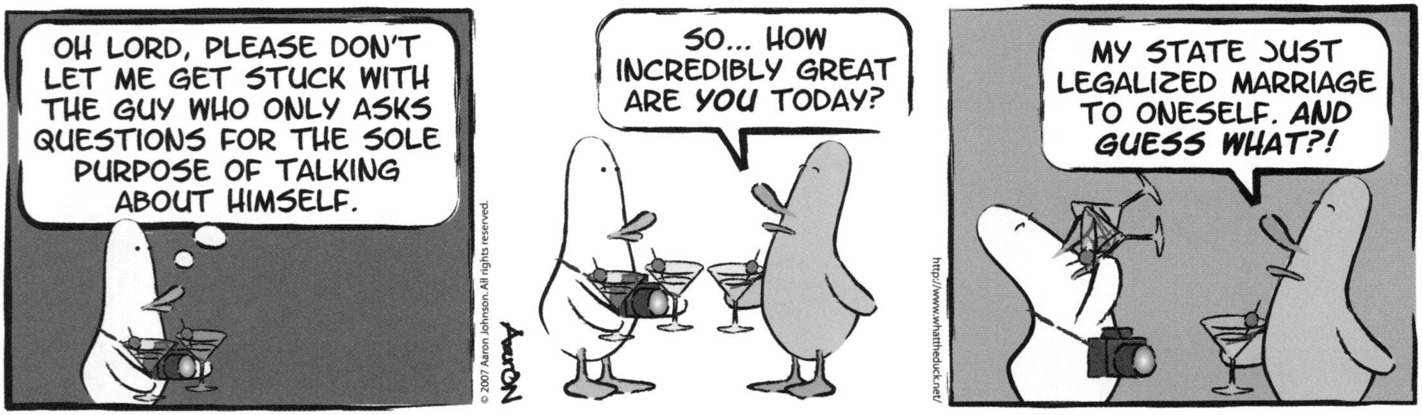
OH LORD, PLEASE DON'T LET ME GET STUCK WITH THE GUY WHO ONLY ASKS QUESTIONS FOR THE SOLE PURPOSE OF TALKING ABOUT HIMSELF.
© 2007 Aaron Johnson. All rights reserved.
SO... HOW INCREDIBLY GREAT ARE YOU TODAY?
http://www.whattheduck.net/
MY STATE JUST LEGALIZED MARRIAGE TO ONESELF. AND GUESS WHAT?!

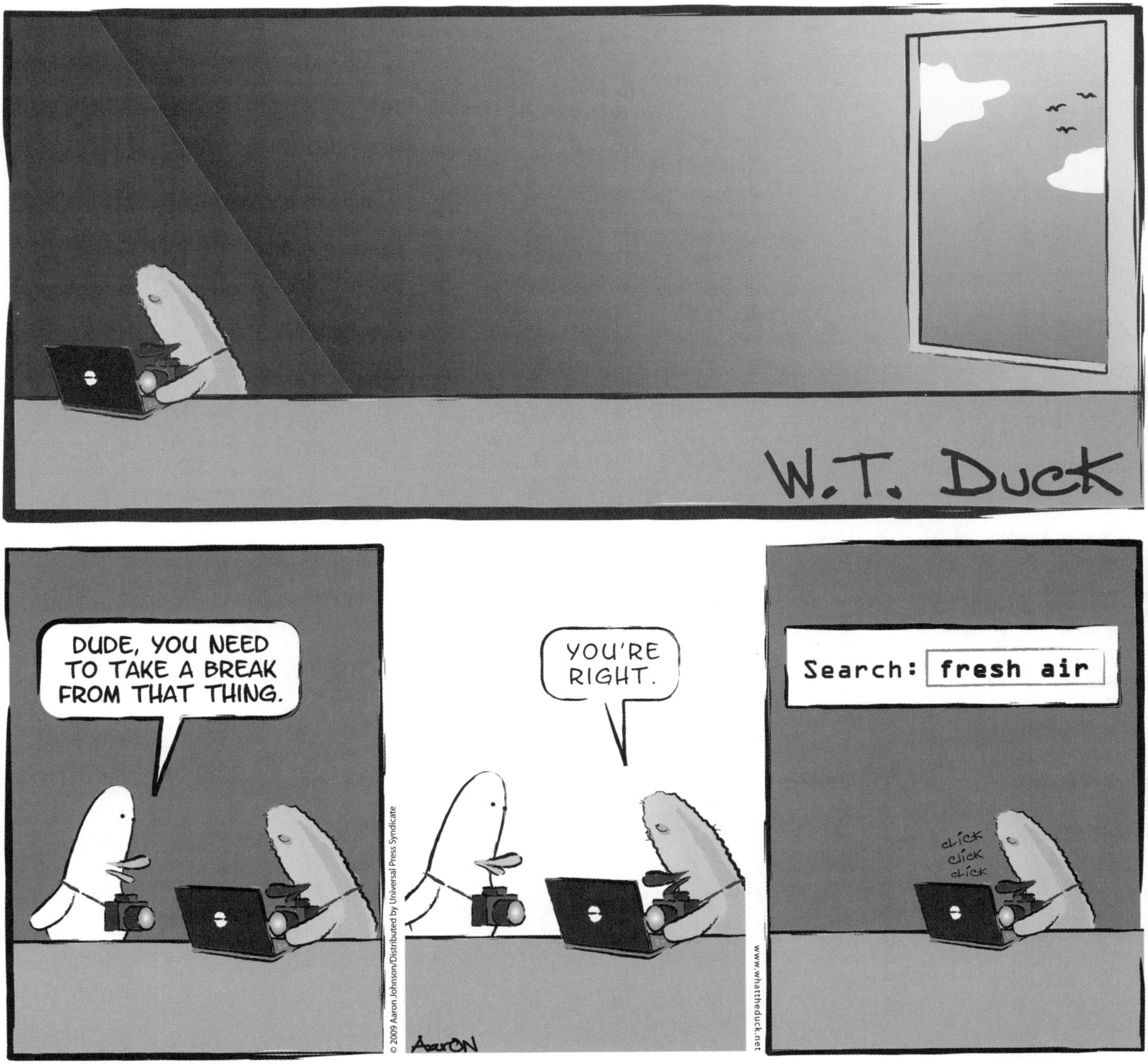
W.T. Duck
DUDE, YOU NEED TO TAKE A BREAK FROM THAT THING.
YOU'RE RIGHT.
Search: fresh air
click click click
© 2009 Aaron Johnson/Distributed by Universal Press Syndicate
AarON
www.whattheduck.net

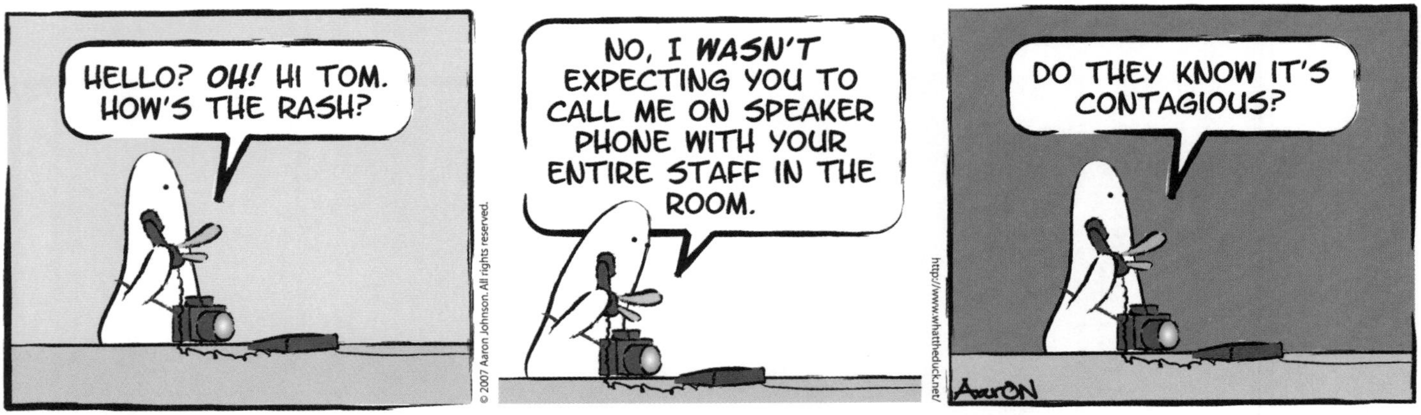
HELLO? OH! HI TOM. HOW'S THE RASH?
© 2007 Aaron Johnson. All rights reserved.
NO, I WASN'T EXPECTING YOU TO CALL ME ON SPEAKER PHONE WITH YOUR ENTIRE STAFF IN THE ROOM.
http://www.whattheduck.net/
DO THEY KNOW IT'S CONTAGIOUS?
AarON

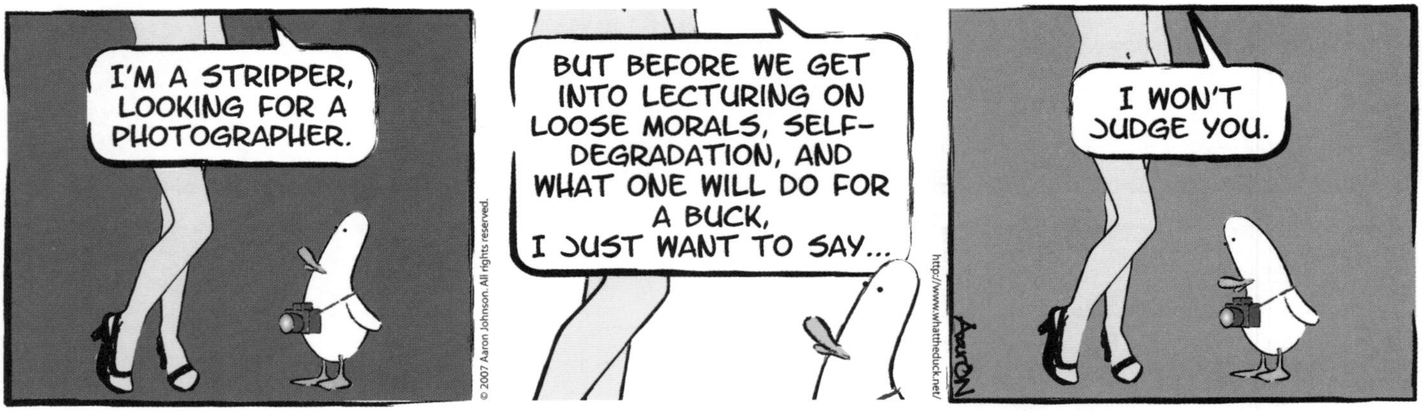
I'M A STRIPPER, LOOKING FOR A PHOTOGRAPHER.
© 2007 Aaron Johnson. All rights reserved.
BUT BEFORE WE GET INTO LECTURING ON LOOSE MORALS, SELF-DEGRADATION, AND WHAT ONE WILL DO FOR A BUCK, I JUST WANT TO SAY...
http://www.whattheduck.net/
AarON
I WON'T JUDGE YOU.

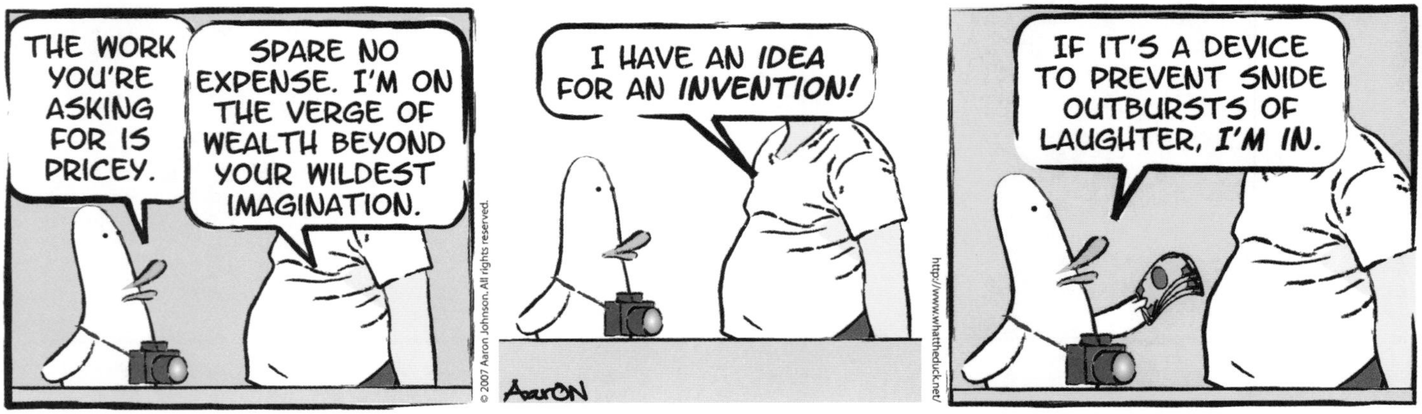
THE WORK YOU'RE ASKING FOR IS PRICEY.
SPARE NO EXPENSE. I'M ON THE VERGE OF WEALTH BEYOND YOUR WILDEST IMAGINATION.
© 2007 Aaron Johnson. All rights reserved.
I HAVE AN IDEA FOR AN INVENTION!
AarON
http://www.whattheduck.net/
IF IT'S A DEVICE TO PREVENT SNIDE OUTBURSTS OF LAUGHTER, I'M IN.

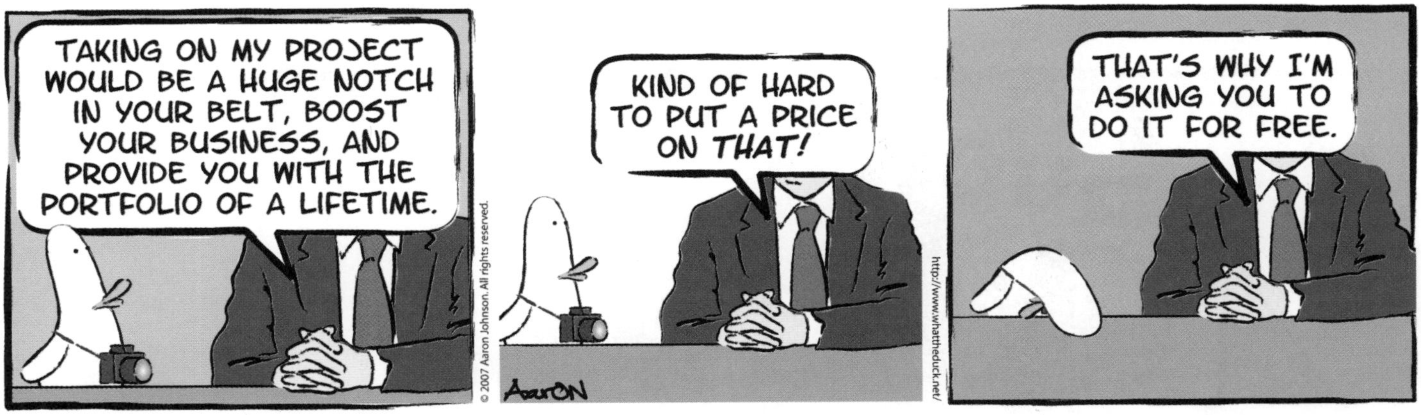
TAKING ON MY PROJECT WOULD BE A HUGE NOTCH IN YOUR BELT, BOOST YOUR BUSINESS, AND PROVIDE YOU WITH THE PORTFOLIO OF A LIFETIME.
KIND OF HARD TO PUT A PRICE ON THAT!
THAT'S WHY I'M ASKING YOU TO DO IT FOR FREE.
© 2007 Aaron Johnson. All rights reserved.
http://www.whattheduck.net/

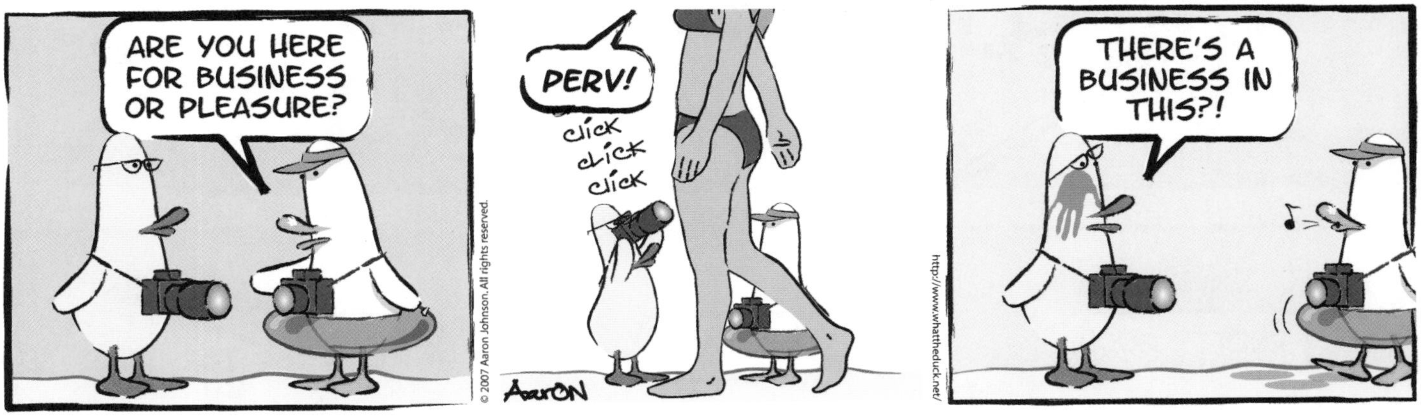
ARE YOU HERE FOR BUSINESS OR PLEASURE?
PERV!
click click click
THERE'S A BUSINESS IN THIS?!
© 2007 Aaron Johnson. All rights reserved.
http://www.whattheduck.net/

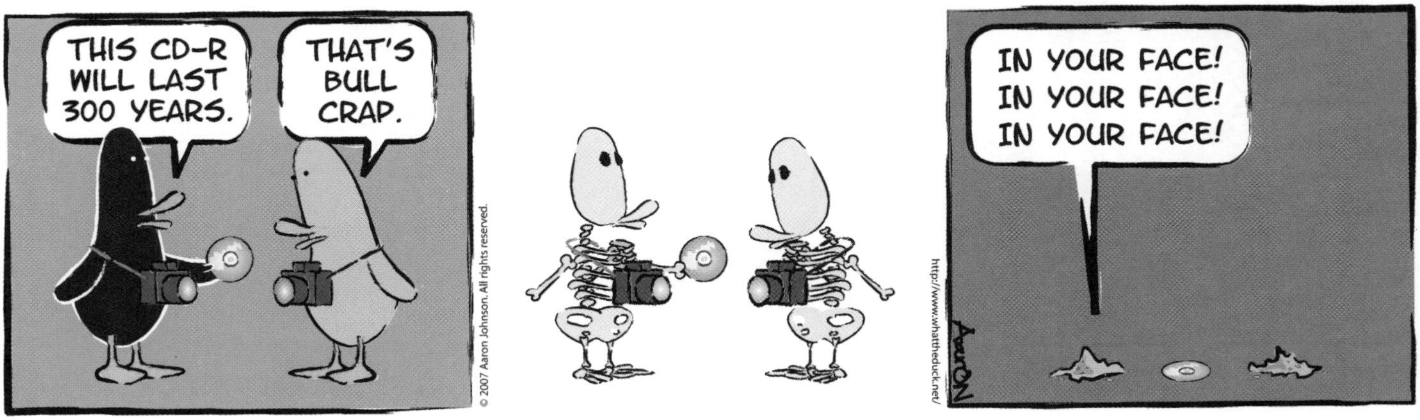
THIS CD-R WILL LAST 300 YEARS.
THAT'S BULL CRAP.
IN YOUR FACE! IN YOUR FACE! IN YOUR FACE!
© 2007 Aaron Johnson. All rights reserved.
http://www.whattheduck.net/

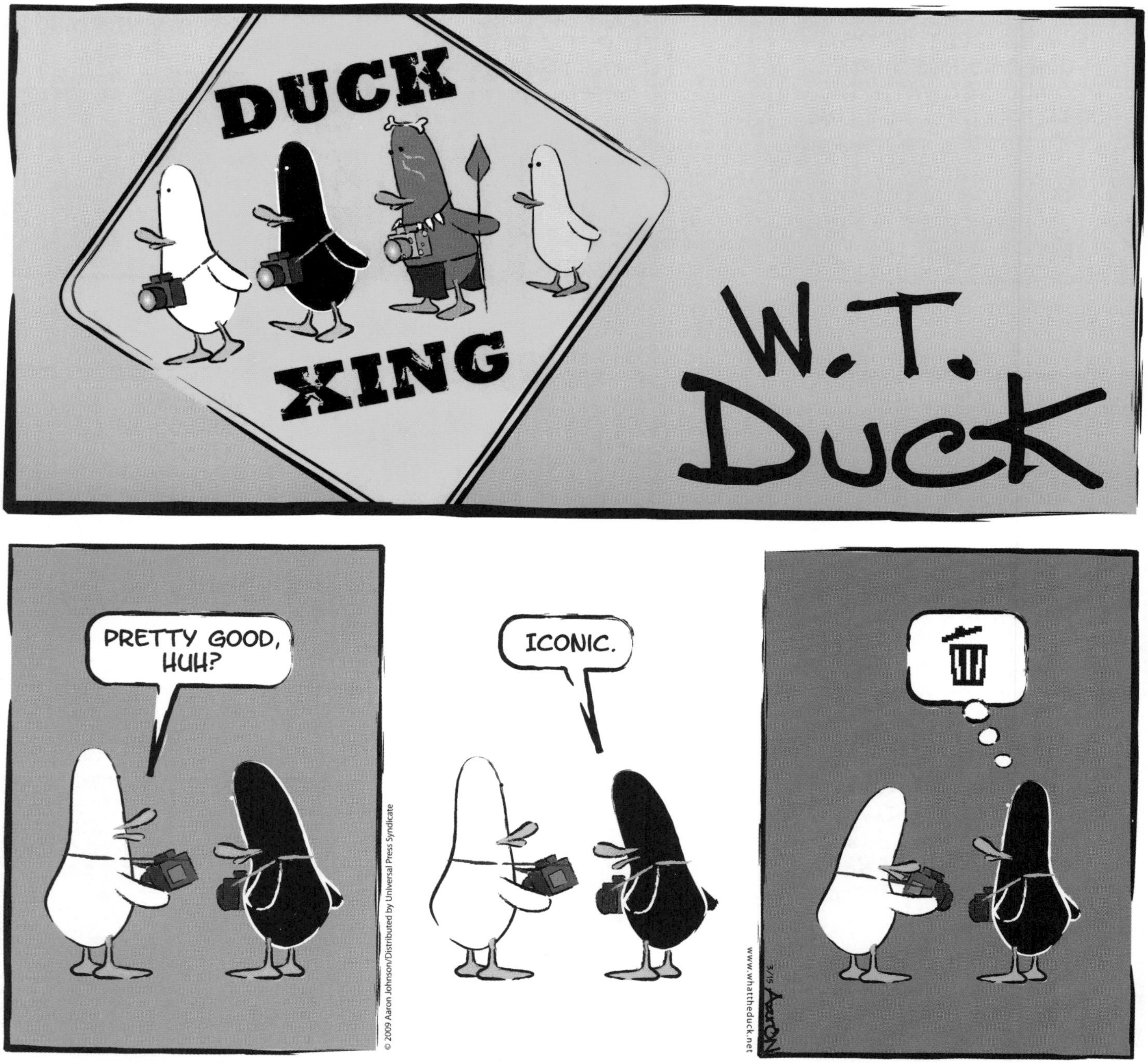
DUCK
XING
W.T. Duck
PRETTY GOOD, HUH?
ICONIC.
© 2009 Aaron Johnson/Distributed by Universal Press Syndicate
www.whattheduck.net
AARON
3/15

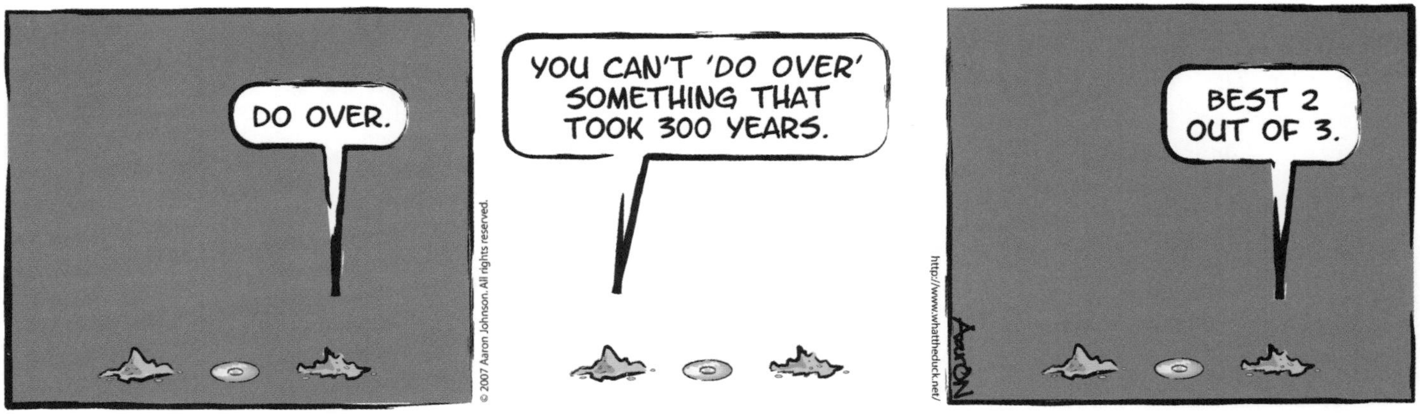
DO OVER.
YOU CAN'T 'DO OVER' SOMETHING THAT TOOK 300 YEARS.
BEST 2 OUT OF 3.
© 2007 Aaron Johnson. All rights reserved.
http://www.whattheduck.net/
AARON

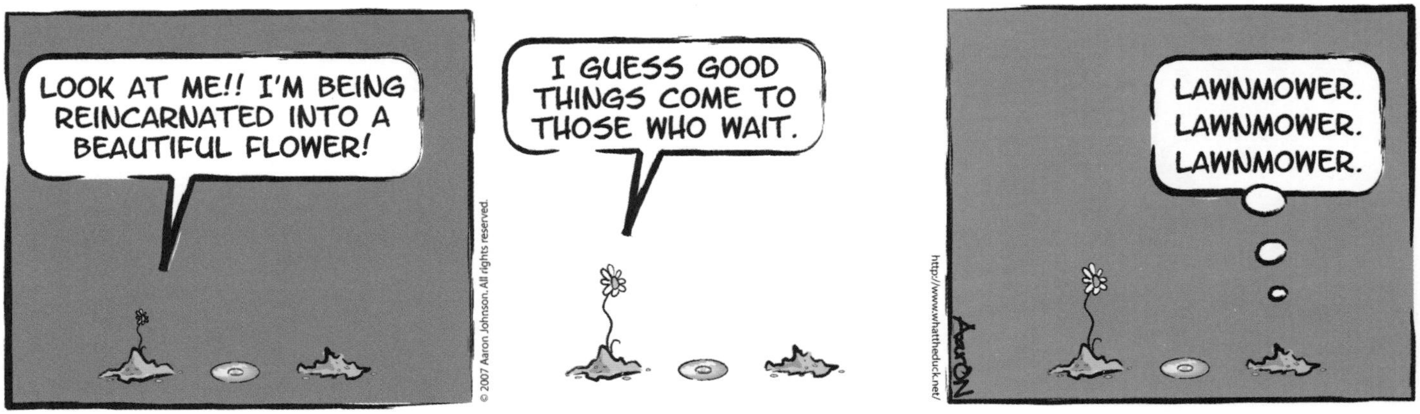
LOOK AT ME!! I'M BEING REINCARNATED INTO A BEAUTIFUL FLOWER!
I GUESS GOOD THINGS COME TO THOSE WHO WAIT.
LAWNMOWER. LAWNMOWER. LAWNMOWER.
© 2007 Aaron Johnson. All rights reserved.
http://www.whattheduck.net/
AARON

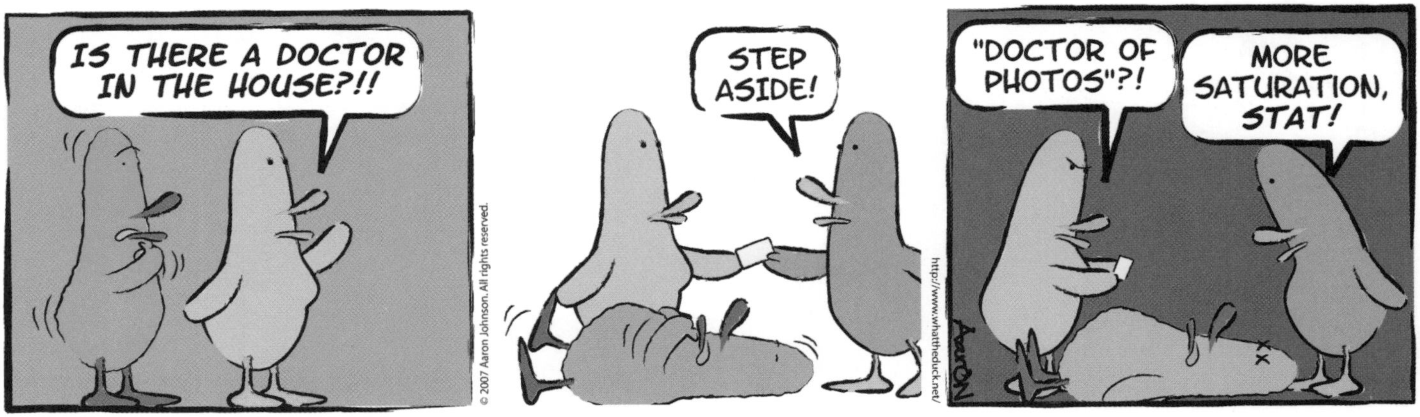
IS THERE A DOCTOR IN THE HOUSE?!!
STEP ASIDE!
"DOCTOR OF PHOTOS"?!
MORE SATURATION, STAT!
© 2007 Aaron Johnson. All rights reserved.
http://www.whattheduck.net/
AARON

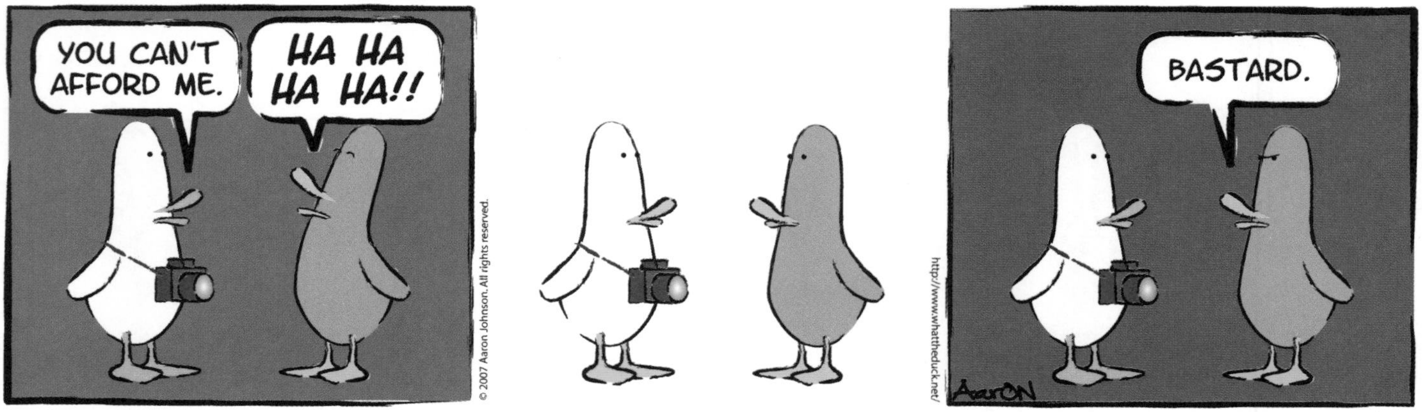
YOU CAN'T AFFORD ME.
HA HA HA HA!!
BASTARD.
© 2007 Aaron Johnson. All rights reserved.
http://www.whattheduck.net/
AarON

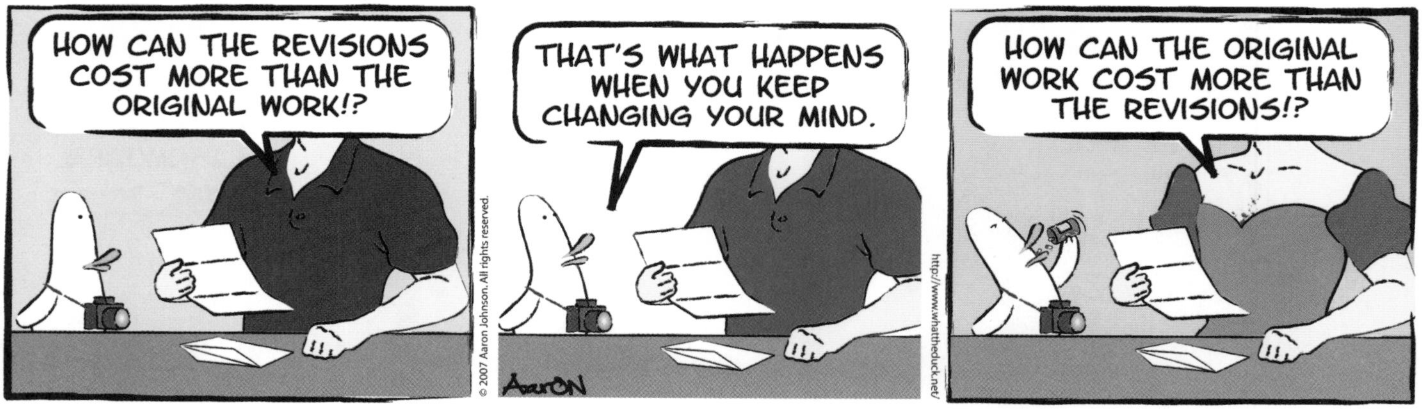
HOW CAN THE REVISIONS COST MORE THAN THE ORIGINAL WORK!?
THAT'S WHAT HAPPENS WHEN YOU KEEP CHANGING YOUR MIND.
HOW CAN THE ORIGINAL WORK COST MORE THAN THE REVISIONS!?
© 2007 Aaron Johnson. All rights reserved.
http://www.whattheduck.net/
AarON

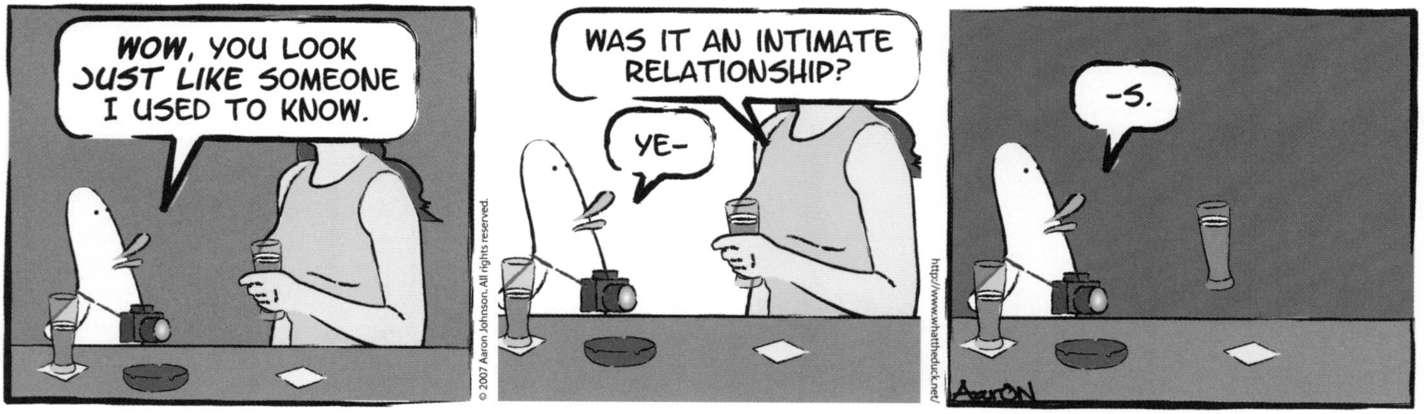
WOW, YOU LOOK JUST LIKE SOMEONE I USED TO KNOW.
WAS IT AN INTIMATE RELATIONSHIP?
YE-
-S.
© 2007 Aaron Johnson. All rights reserved.
http://www.whattheduck.net/
AarON

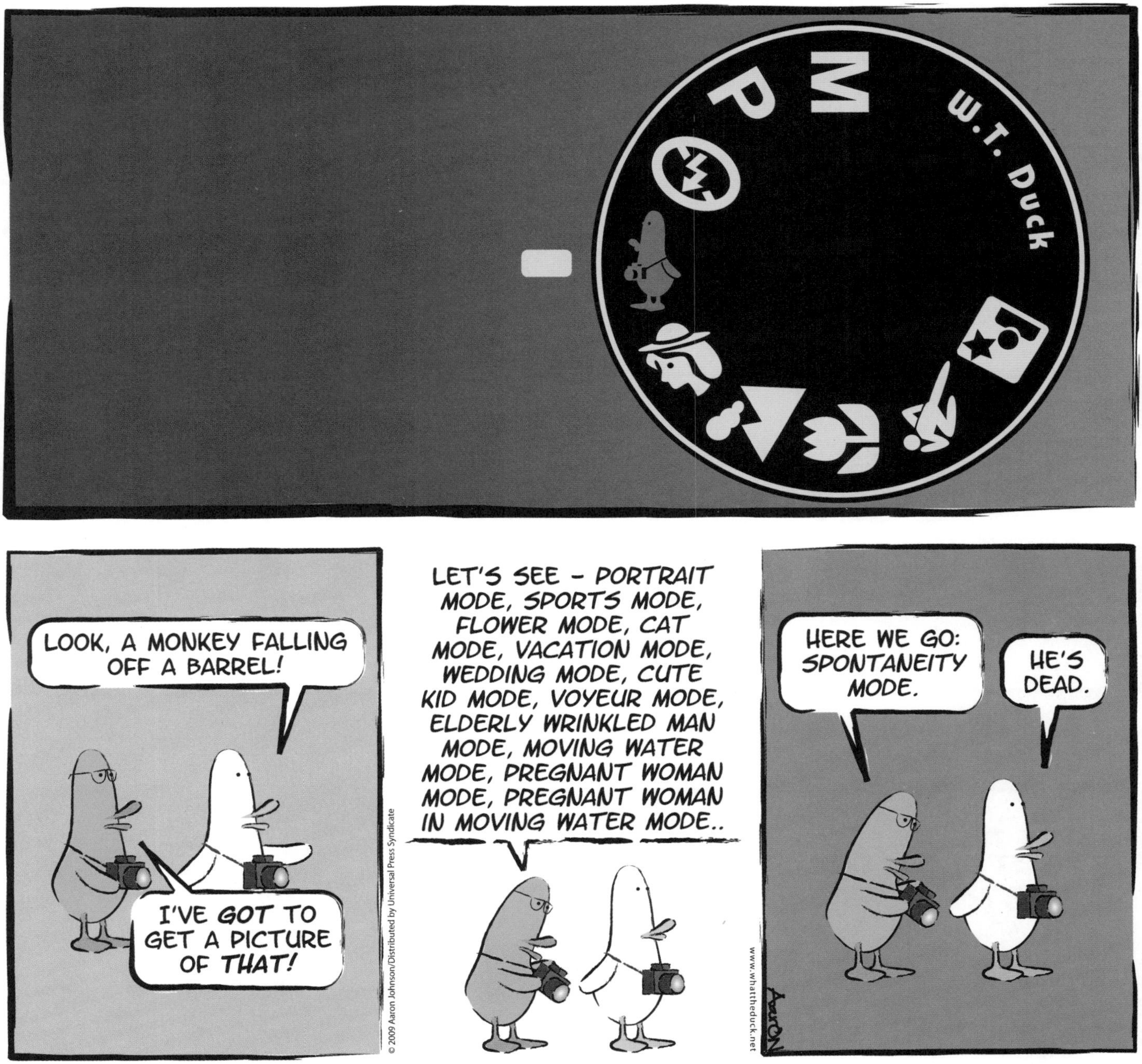

M
P
W.T. Duck
LOOK, A MONKEY FALLING OFF A BARREL!
I'VE GOT TO GET A PICTURE OF THAT!
© 2009 Aaron Johnson/Distributed by Universal Press Syndicate
LET'S SEE - PORTRAIT MODE, SPORTS MODE, FLOWER MODE, CAT MODE, VACATION MODE, WEDDING MODE, CUTE KID MODE, VOYEUR MODE, ELDERLY WRINKLED MAN MODE, MOVING WATER MODE, PREGNANT WOMAN MODE, PREGNANT WOMAN IN MOVING WATER MODE..
www.whattheduck.net
HERE WE GO: SPONTANEITY MODE.
HE'S DEAD.
AARON

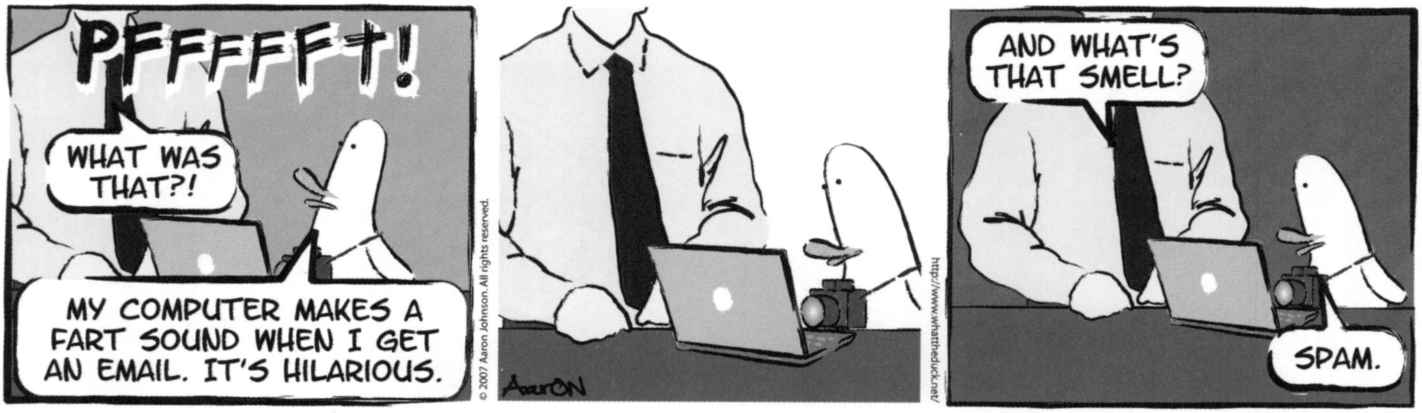
PFFFFFT!
WHAT WAS THAT?!
MY COMPUTER MAKES A FART SOUND WHEN I GET AN EMAIL. IT'S HILARIOUS.
© 2007 Aaron Johnson. All rights reserved.
AARON
http://www.whattheduck.net/
AND WHAT'S THAT SMELL?
SPAM.

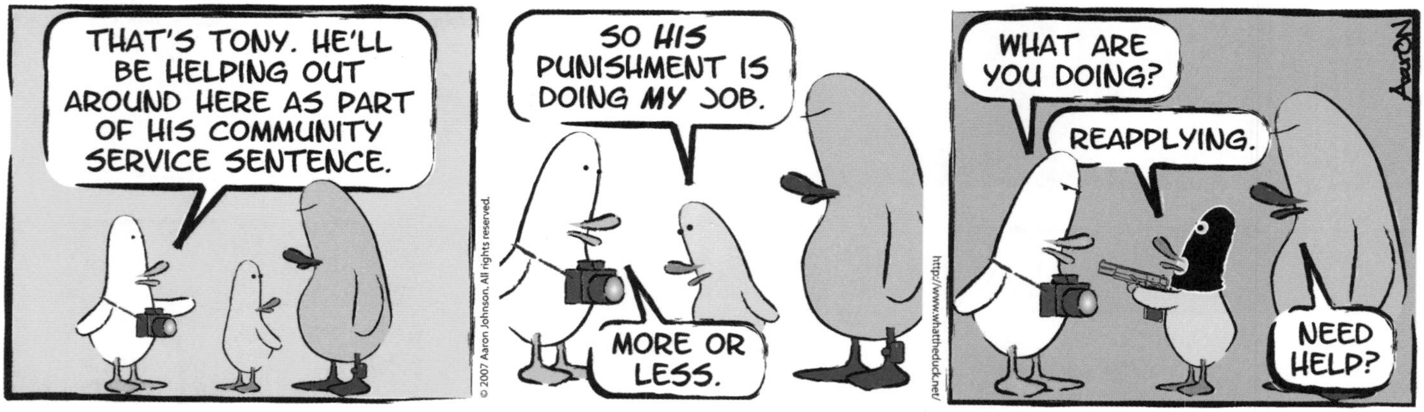
THAT'S TONY. HE'LL BE HELPING OUT AROUND HERE AS PART OF HIS COMMUNITY SERVICE SENTENCE.
© 2007 Aaron Johnson. All rights reserved.
SO HIS PUNISHMENT IS DOING MY JOB.
MORE OR LESS.
http://www.whattheduck.net/
WHAT ARE YOU DOING?
REAPPLYING.
NEED HELP?
AARON

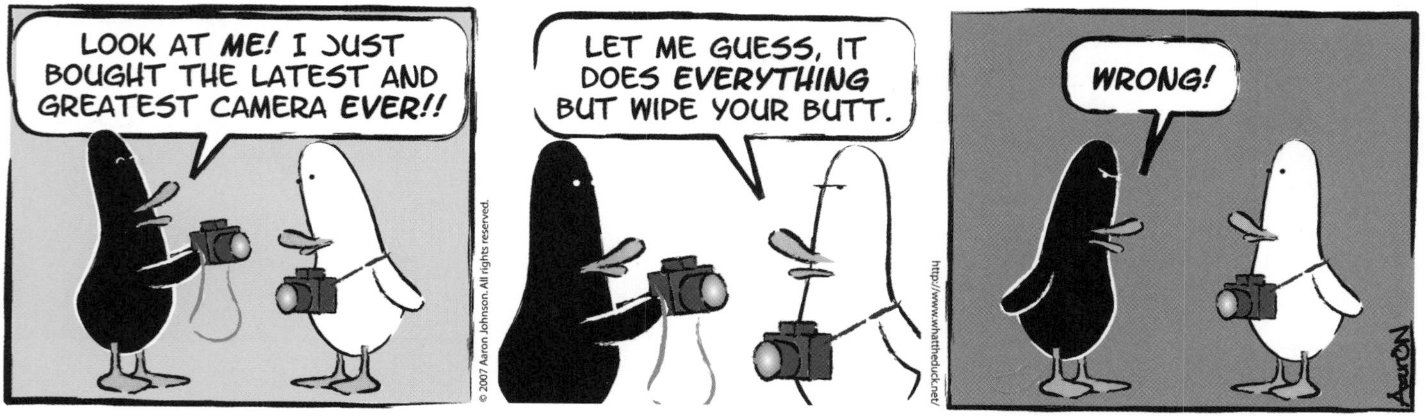
LOOK AT ME! I JUST BOUGHT THE LATEST AND GREATEST CAMERA EVER!!
© 2007 Aaron Johnson. All rights reserved.
LET ME GUESS, IT DOES EVERYTHING BUT WIPE YOUR BUTT.
http://www.whattheduck.net/
WRONG!
AARON

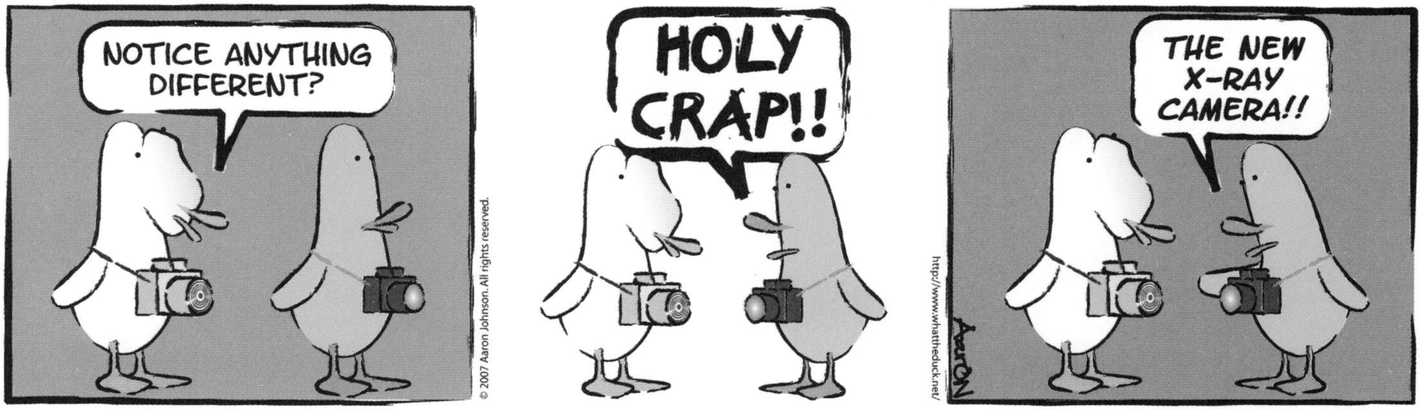
NOTICE ANYTHING DIFFERENT?
HOLY CRAP!!
THE NEW X-RAY CAMERA!!
© 2007 Aaron Johnson. All rights reserved.
http://www.whattheduck.net/
AARON

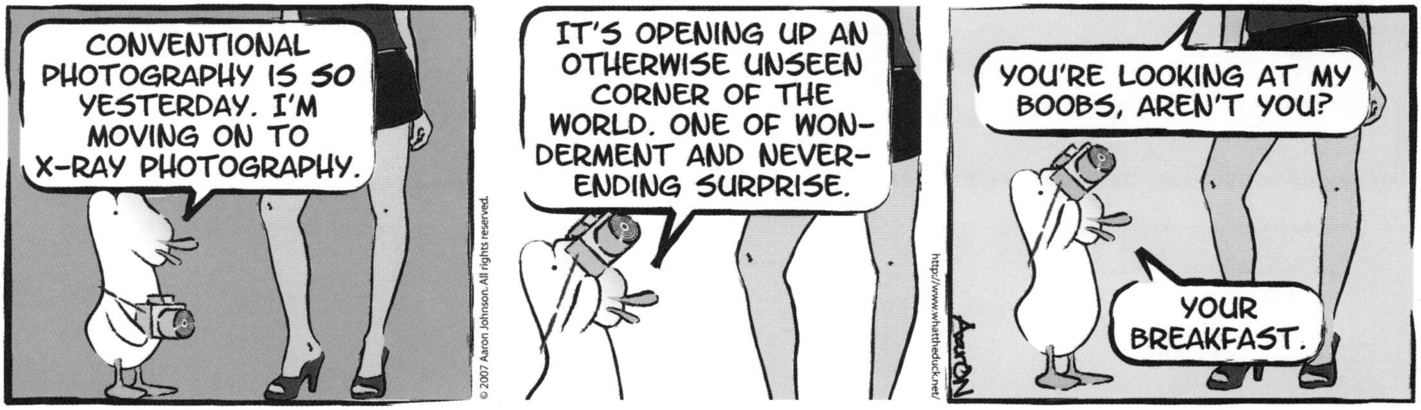
CONVENTIONAL PHOTOGRAPHY IS SO YESTERDAY. I'M MOVING ON TO X-RAY PHOTOGRAPHY.
IT'S OPENING UP AN OTHERWISE UNSEEN CORNER OF THE WORLD. ONE OF WONDERMENT AND NEVER-ENDING SURPRISE.
YOU'RE LOOKING AT MY BOOBS, AREN'T YOU?
YOUR BREAKFAST.
© 2007 Aaron Johnson. All rights reserved.
http://www.whattheduck.net/
AARON

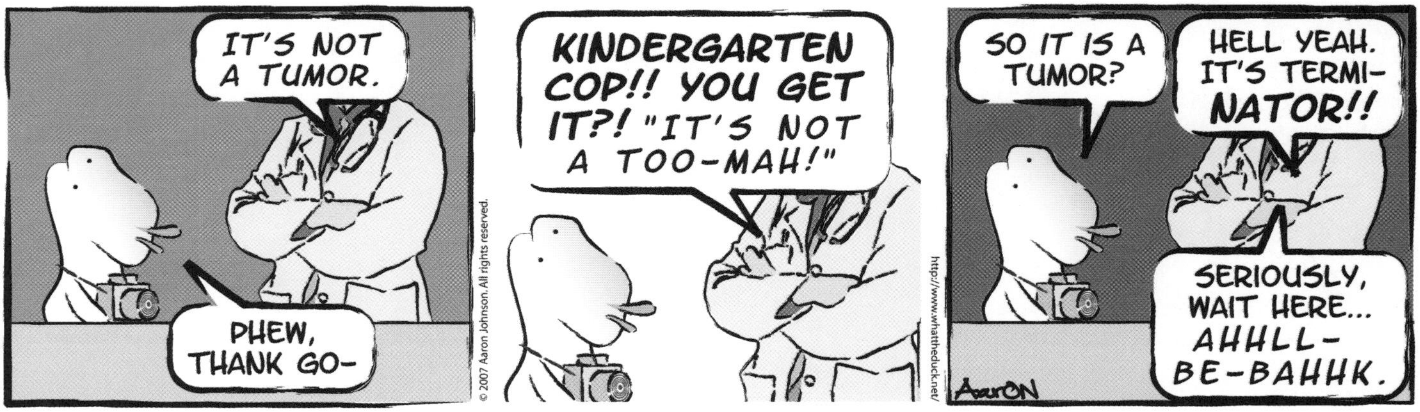
IT'S NOT A TUMOR.
PHEW, THANK GO-
KINDERGARTEN COP!! YOU GET IT?! "IT'S NOT A TOO-MAH!"
SO IT IS A TUMOR?
HELL YEAH. IT'S TERMI-NATOR!!
SERIOUSLY, WAIT HERE... AHHLL-BE-BAHHK.
© 2007 Aaron Johnson. All rights reserved.
http://www.whattheduck.net/
AARON

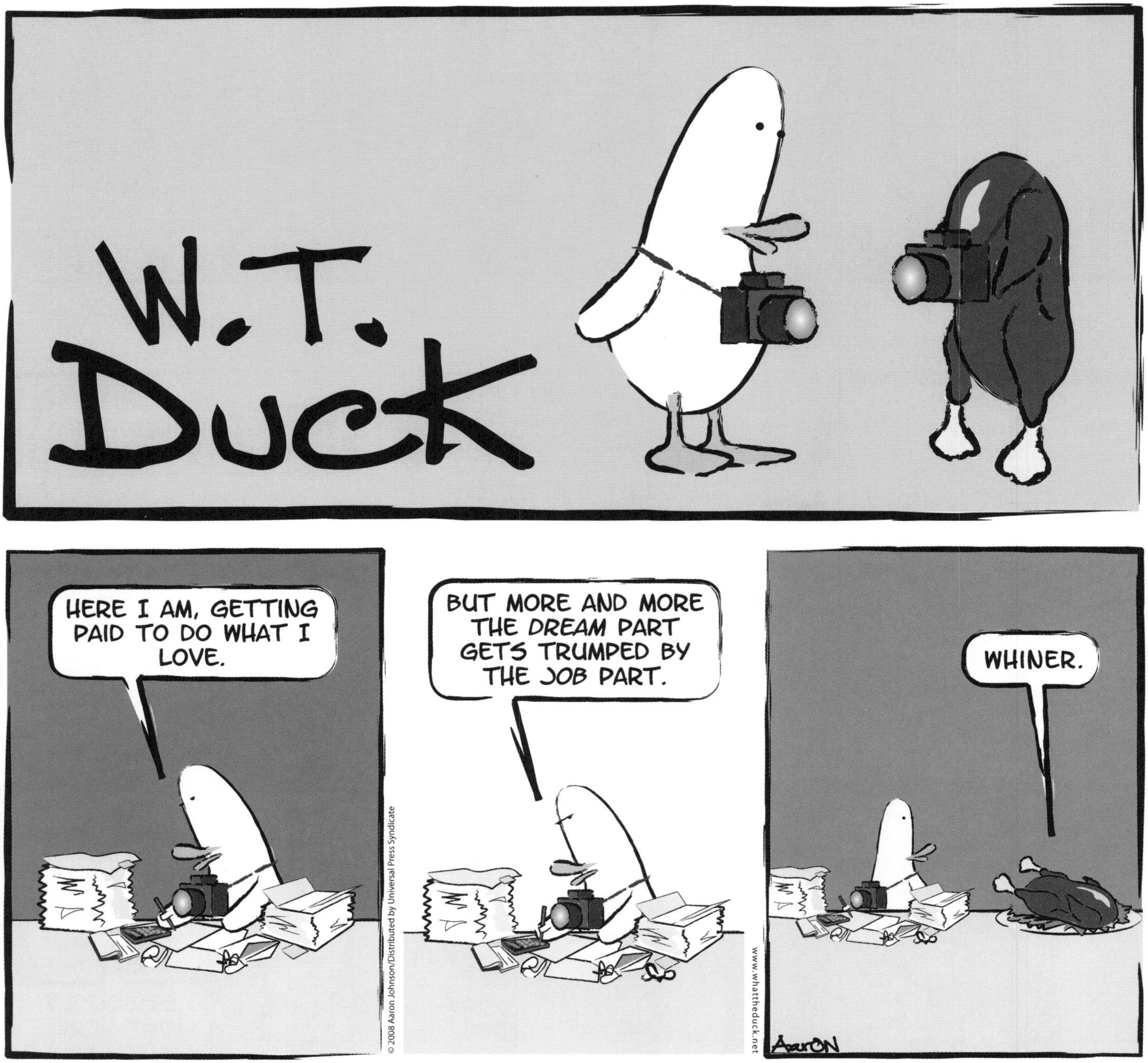
W.T. DUCK
HERE I AM, GETTING PAID TO DO WHAT I LOVE.
BUT MORE AND MORE THE *DREAM* PART GETS TRUMPED BY THE *JOB* PART.
WHINER.
© 2008 Aaron Johnson/Distributed by Universal Press Syndicate
www.whattheduck.net
AARON

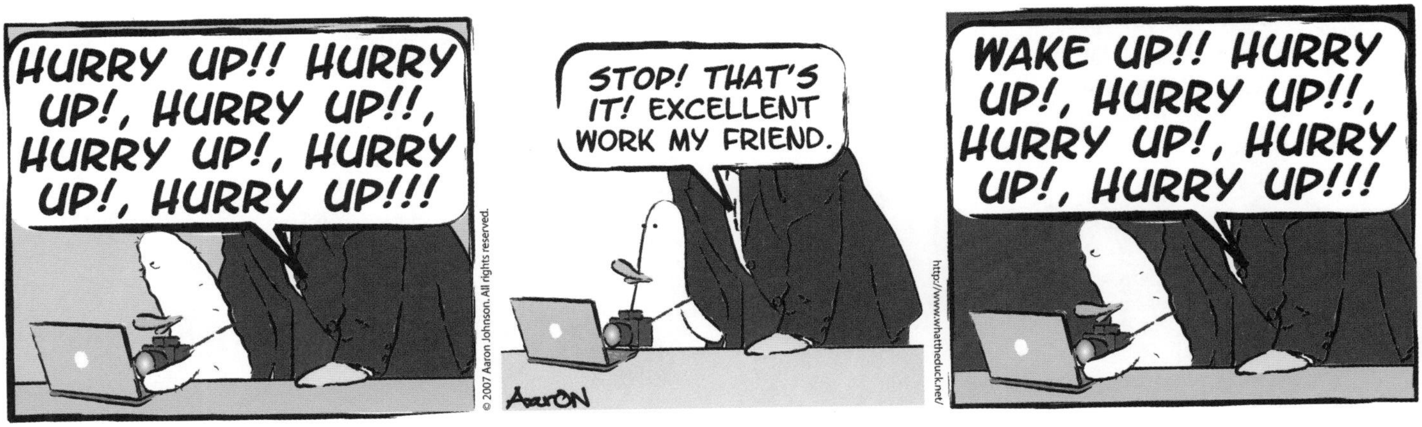
HURRY UP!! HURRY UP!, HURRY UP!!, HURRY UP!, HURRY UP!, HURRY UP!!!
© 2007 Aaron Johnson. All rights reserved.
STOP! THAT'S IT! EXCELLENT WORK MY FRIEND.
AARON
http://www.whattheduck.net/
WAKE UP!! HURRY UP!, HURRY UP!!, HURRY UP!, HURRY UP!, HURRY UP!!!

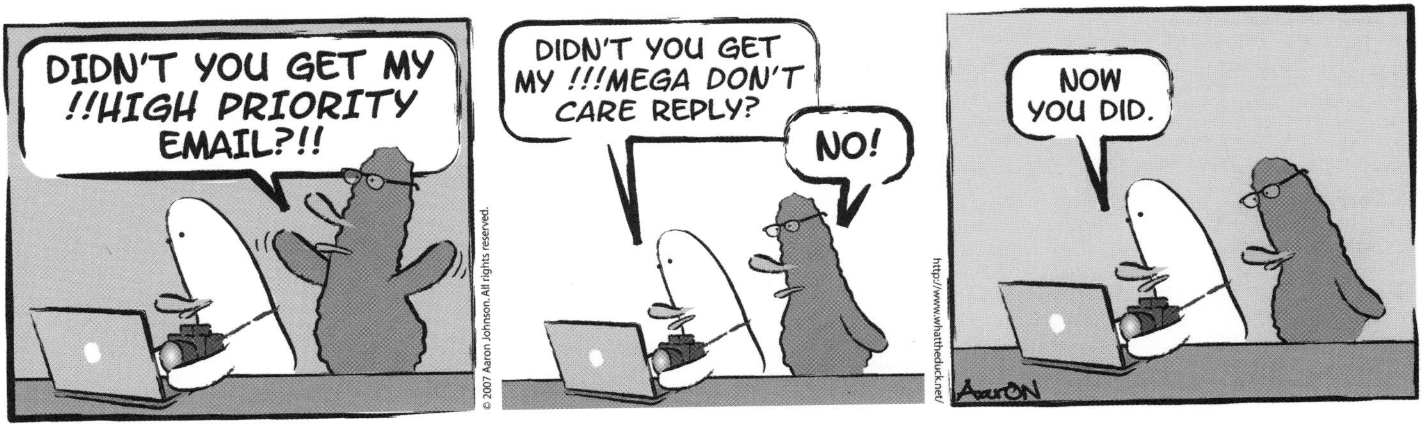
DIDN'T YOU GET MY !!HIGH PRIORITY EMAIL?!!
© 2007 Aaron Johnson. All rights reserved.
DIDN'T YOU GET MY !!!MEGA DON'T CARE REPLY?
NO!
http://www.whattheduck.net/
NOW YOU DID.
AARON

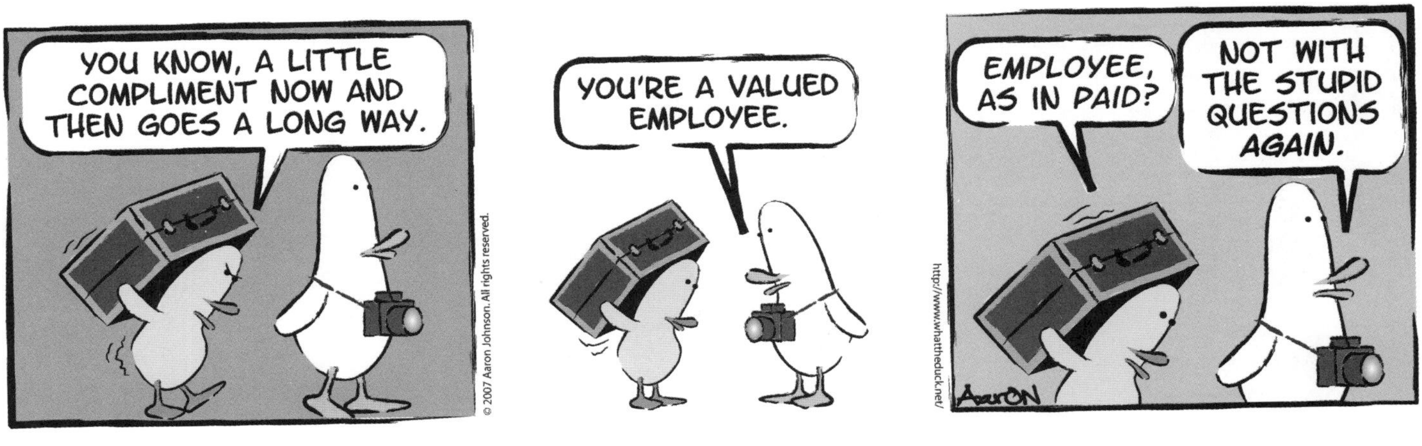
YOU KNOW, A LITTLE COMPLIMENT NOW AND THEN GOES A LONG WAY.
© 2007 Aaron Johnson. All rights reserved.
YOU'RE A VALUED EMPLOYEE.
http://www.whattheduck.net/
EMPLOYEE, AS IN PAID?
NOT WITH THE STUPID QUESTIONS AGAIN.
AARON

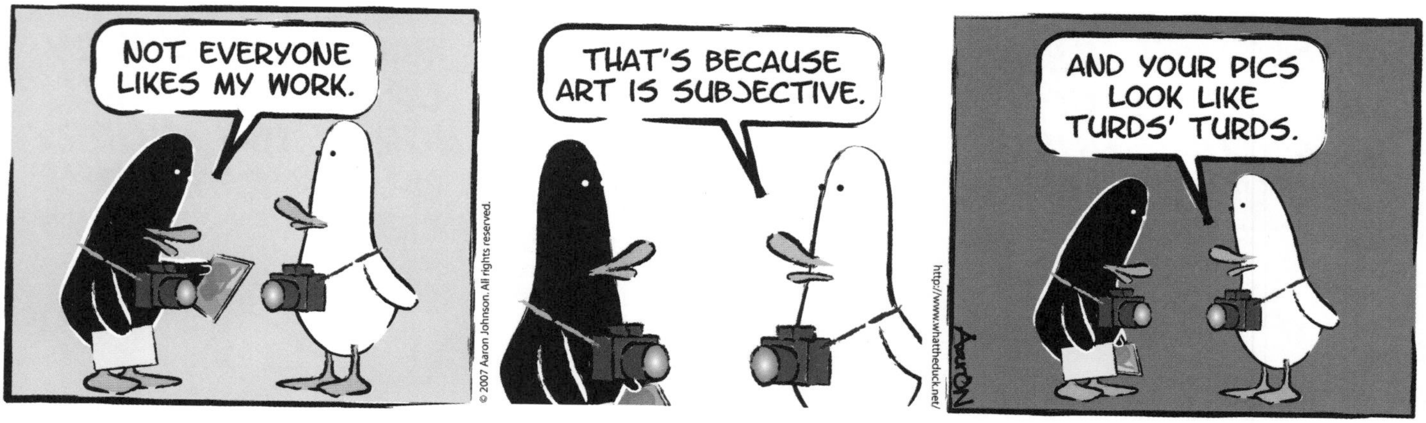
NOT EVERYONE LIKES MY WORK.
THAT'S BECAUSE ART IS SUBJECTIVE.
AND YOUR PICS LOOK LIKE TURDS' TURDS.
© 2007 Aaron Johnson. All rights reserved.
http://www.whattheduck.net/
AARON

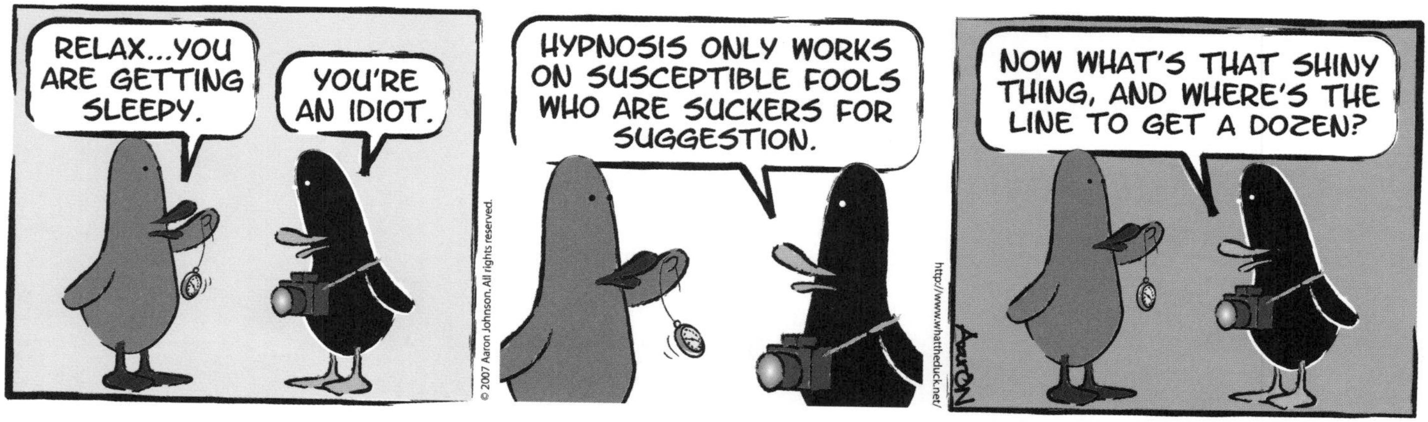
RELAX...YOU ARE GETTING SLEEPY.
YOU'RE AN IDIOT.
HYPNOSIS ONLY WORKS ON SUSCEPTIBLE FOOLS WHO ARE SUCKERS FOR SUGGESTION.
NOW WHAT'S THAT SHINY THING, AND WHERE'S THE LINE TO GET A DOZEN?
© 2007 Aaron Johnson. All rights reserved.
http://www.whattheduck.net/
AARON

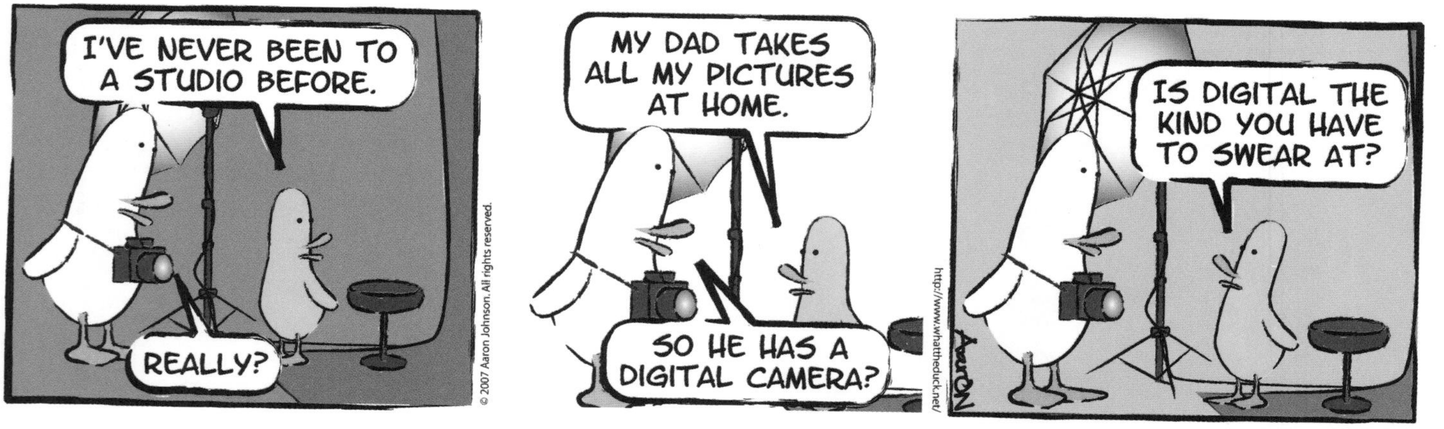
I'VE NEVER BEEN TO A STUDIO BEFORE.
REALLY?
MY DAD TAKES ALL MY PICTURES AT HOME.
SO HE HAS A DIGITAL CAMERA?
IS DIGITAL THE KIND YOU HAVE TO SWEAR AT?
© 2007 Aaron Johnson. All rights reserved.
http://www.whattheduck.net/
AARON

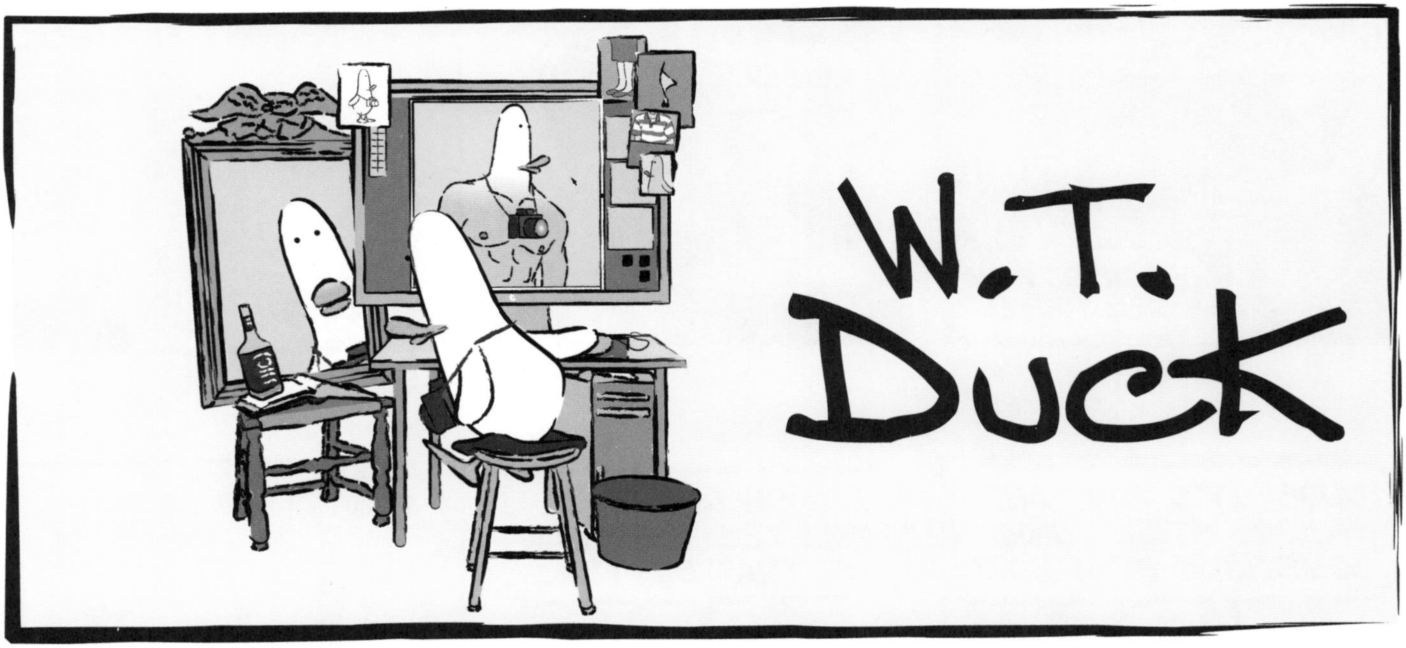
W.T. Duck

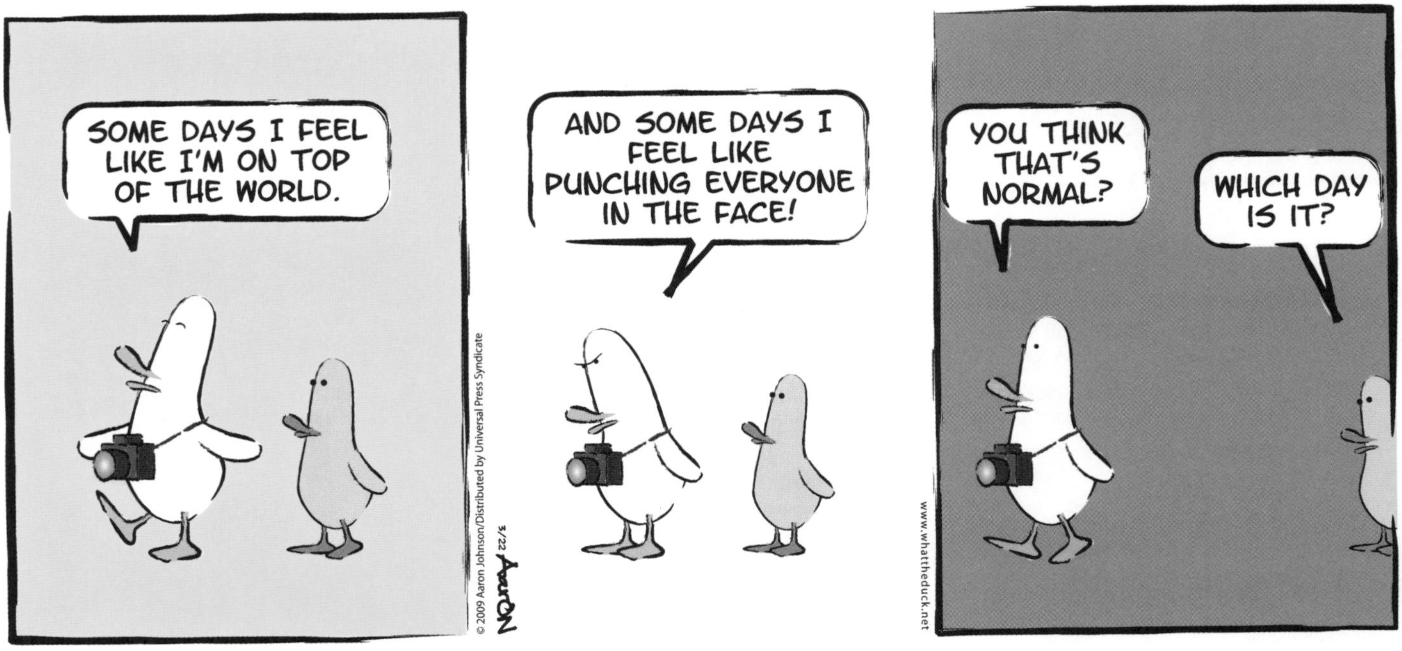
SOME DAYS I FEEL LIKE I'M ON TOP OF THE WORLD.
AND SOME DAYS I FEEL LIKE PUNCHING EVERYONE IN THE FACE!
YOU THINK THAT'S NORMAL?
WHICH DAY IS IT?
© 2009 Aaron Johnson/Distributed by Universal Press Syndicate
3/22 AARON
www.whattheduck.net

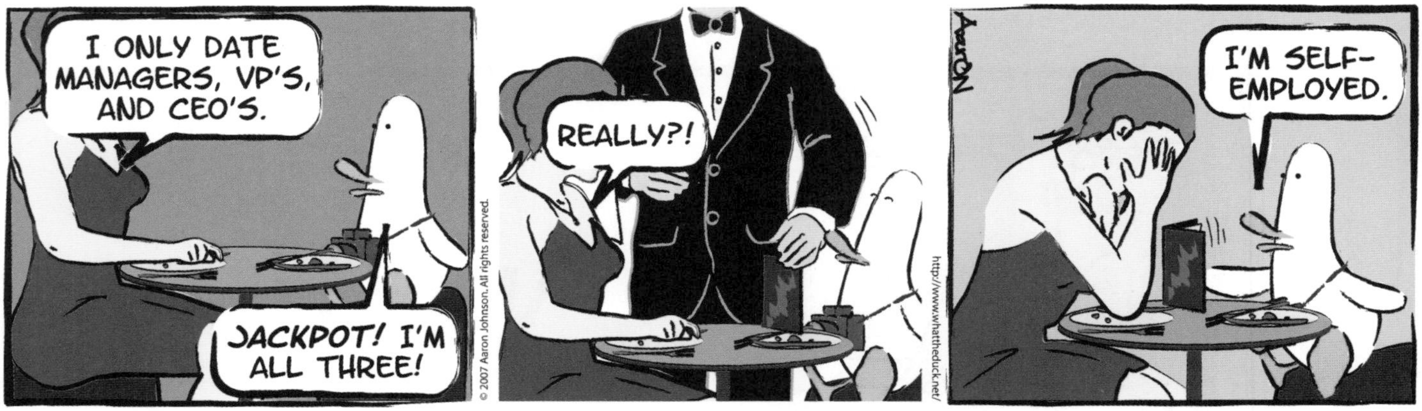
I ONLY DATE MANAGERS, VP'S, AND CEO'S.
JACKPOT! I'M ALL THREE!
REALLY?!
I'M SELF-EMPLOYED.
© 2007 Aaron Johnson. All rights reserved.
http://www.whattheduck.net/

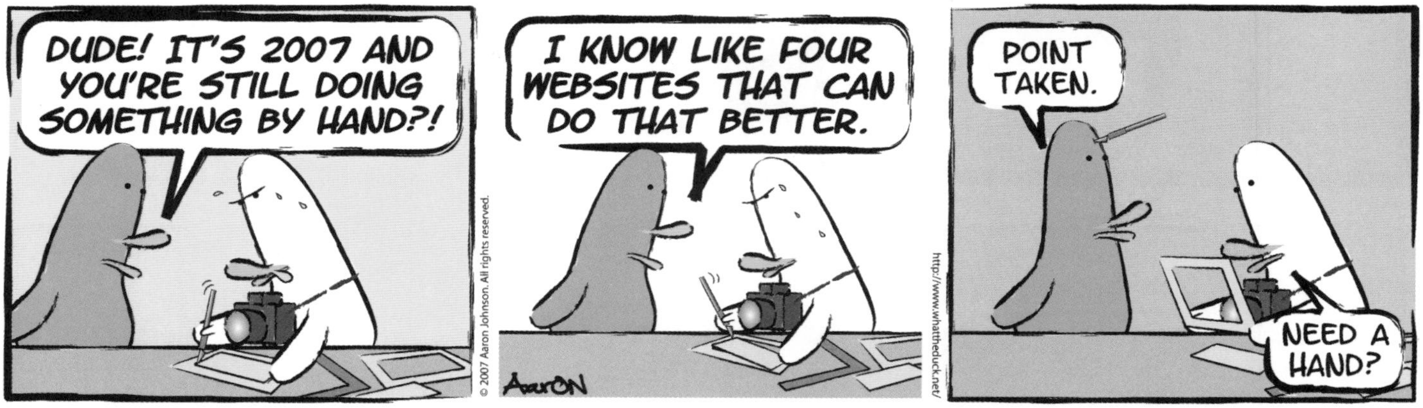
DUDE! IT'S 2007 AND YOU'RE STILL DOING SOMETHING BY HAND?!
I KNOW LIKE FOUR WEBSITES THAT CAN DO THAT BETTER.
POINT TAKEN.
NEED A HAND?
© 2007 Aaron Johnson. All rights reserved.
http://www.whattheduck.net/

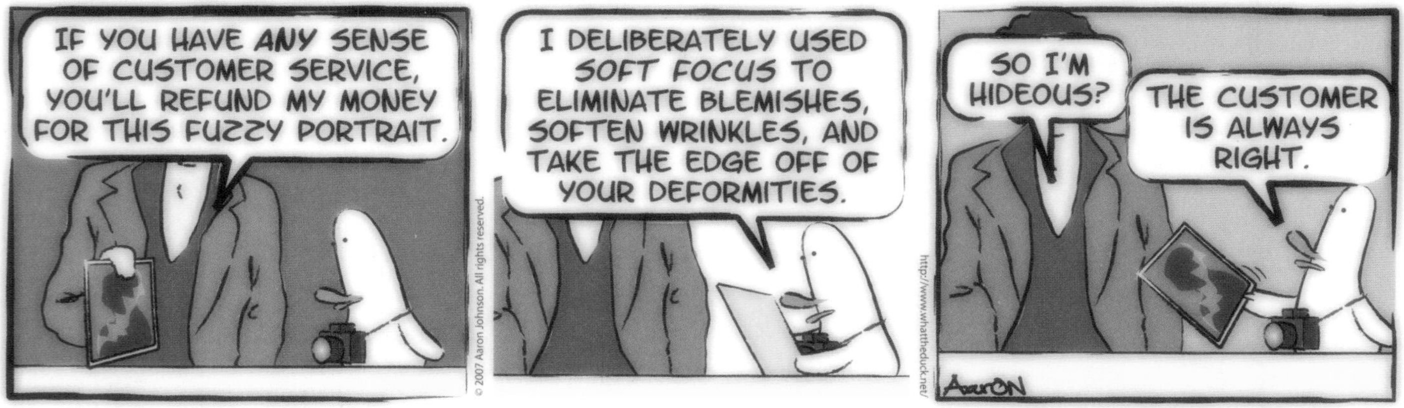
IF YOU HAVE ANY SENSE OF CUSTOMER SERVICE, YOU'LL REFUND MY MONEY FOR THIS FUZZY PORTRAIT.
I DELIBERATELY USED SOFT FOCUS TO ELIMINATE BLEMISHES, SOFTEN WRINKLES, AND TAKE THE EDGE OFF OF YOUR DEFORMITIES.
SO I'M HIDEOUS?
THE CUSTOMER IS ALWAYS RIGHT.
© 2007 Aaron Johnson. All rights reserved.
http://www.whattheduck.net/

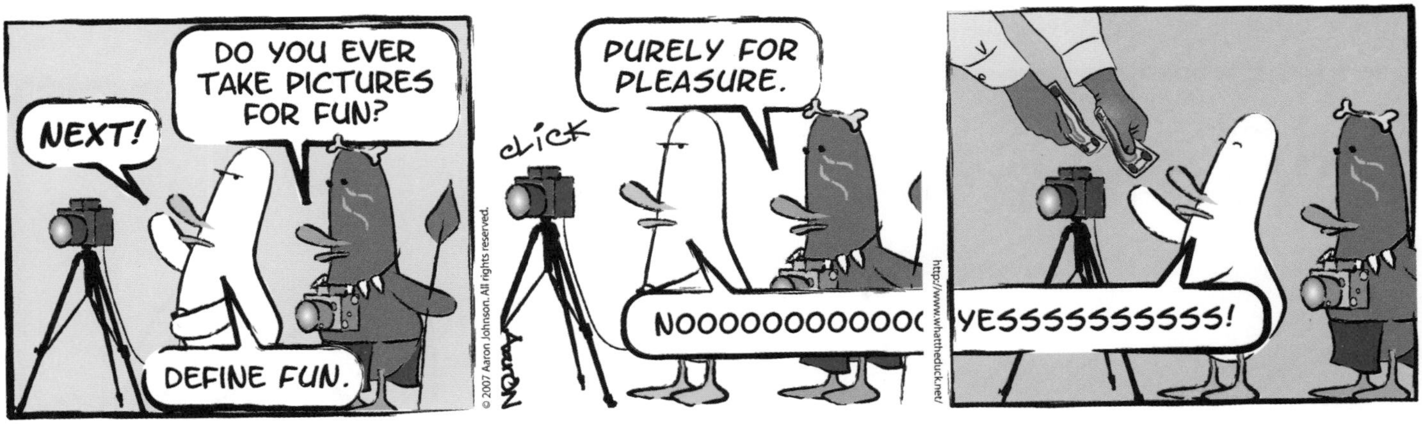
DO YOU EVER TAKE PICTURES FOR FUN?
DEFINE FUN.
NEXT!
© 2007 Aaron Johnson. All rights reserved.
AARON
CLICK
PURELY FOR PLEASURE.
http://www.whattheduck.net/
NOOOOOOOOOOOO
YESSSSSSSSSSS!

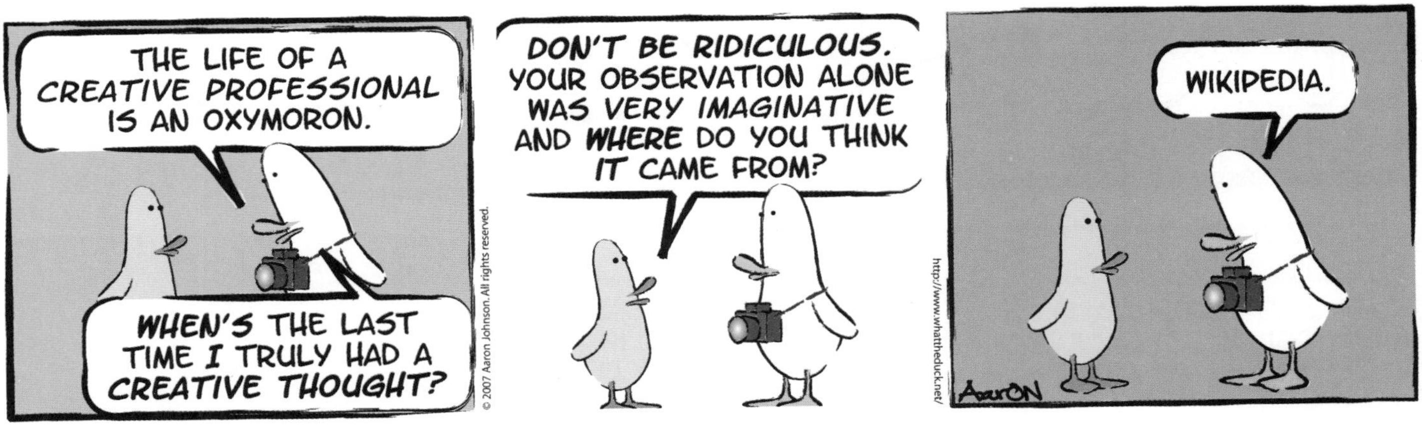
THE LIFE OF A CREATIVE PROFESSIONAL IS AN OXYMORON.
WHEN'S THE LAST TIME I TRULY HAD A CREATIVE THOUGHT?
© 2007 Aaron Johnson. All rights reserved.
DON'T BE RIDICULOUS. YOUR OBSERVATION ALONE WAS VERY IMAGINATIVE AND WHERE DO YOU THINK IT CAME FROM?
http://www.whattheduck.net/
WIKIPEDIA.
AARON

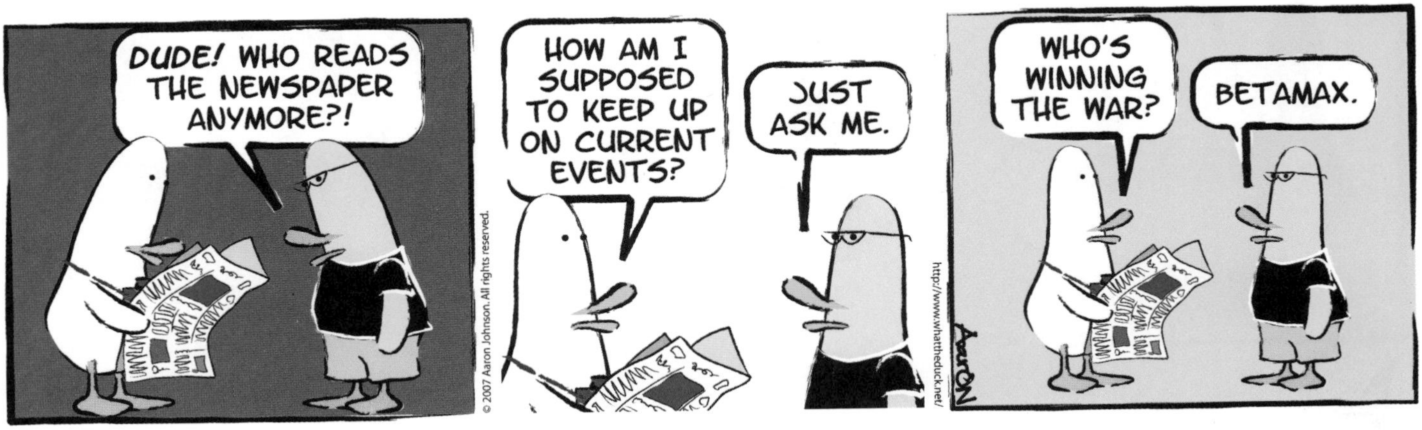
DUDE! WHO READS THE NEWSPAPER ANYMORE?!
© 2007 Aaron Johnson. All rights reserved.
HOW AM I SUPPOSED TO KEEP UP ON CURRENT EVENTS?
JUST ASK ME.
http://www.whattheduck.net/
WHO'S WINNING THE WAR?
BETAMAX.
AARON

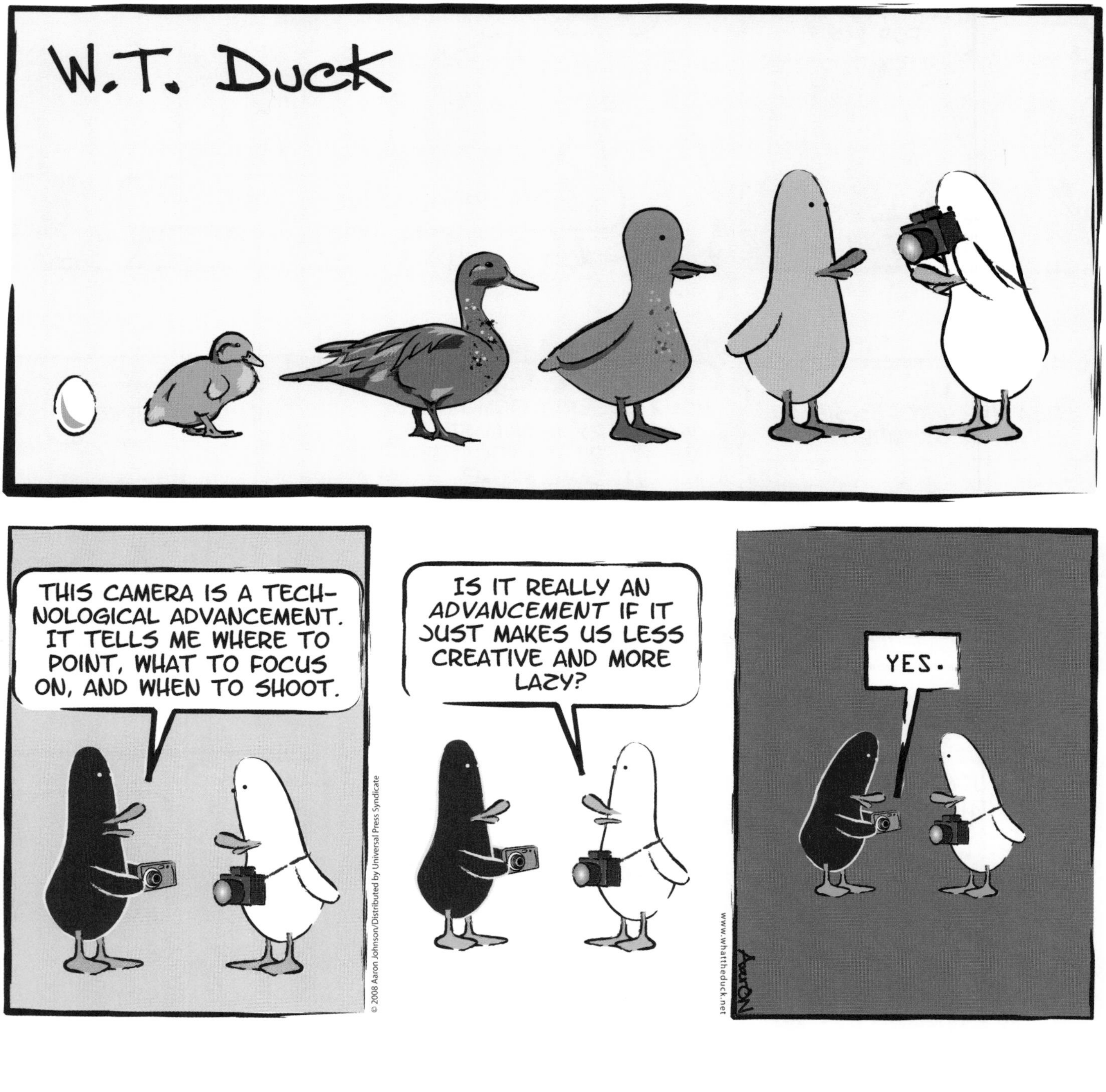
W.T. Duck
THIS CAMERA IS A TECHNOLOGICAL ADVANCEMENT. IT TELLS ME WHERE TO POINT, WHAT TO FOCUS ON, AND WHEN TO SHOOT.
IS IT REALLY AN *ADVANCEMENT* IF IT JUST MAKES US LESS CREATIVE AND MORE LAZY?
YES.
© 2008 Aaron Johnson/Distributed by Universal Press Syndicate
www.whattheduck.net
AARON

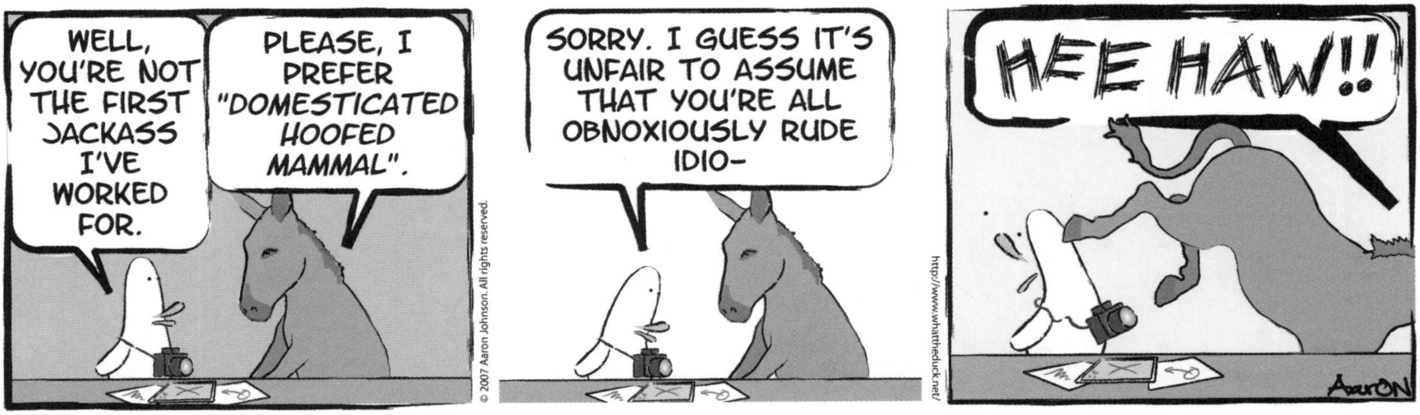
WELL, YOU'RE NOT THE FIRST JACKASS I'VE WORKED FOR.
PLEASE, I PREFER "DOMESTICATED HOOFED MAMMAL".
© 2007 Aaron Johnson. All rights reserved.
SORRY. I GUESS IT'S UNFAIR TO ASSUME THAT YOU'RE ALL OBNOXIOUSLY RUDE IDIO-
http://www.whattheduck.net/
HEE HAW!!
AarON

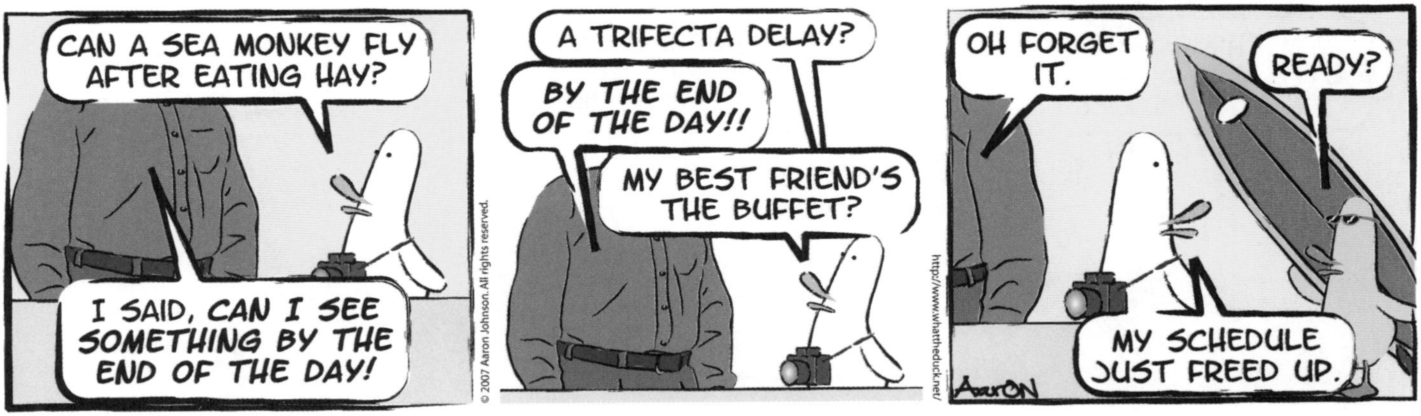
CAN A SEA MONKEY FLY AFTER EATING HAY?
I SAID, CAN I SEE SOMETHING BY THE END OF THE DAY!
© 2007 Aaron Johnson. All rights reserved.
A TRIFECTA DELAY?
BY THE END OF THE DAY!!
MY BEST FRIEND'S THE BUFFET?
http://www.whattheduck.net/
OH FORGET IT.
READY?
MY SCHEDULE JUST FREED UP.
AarON

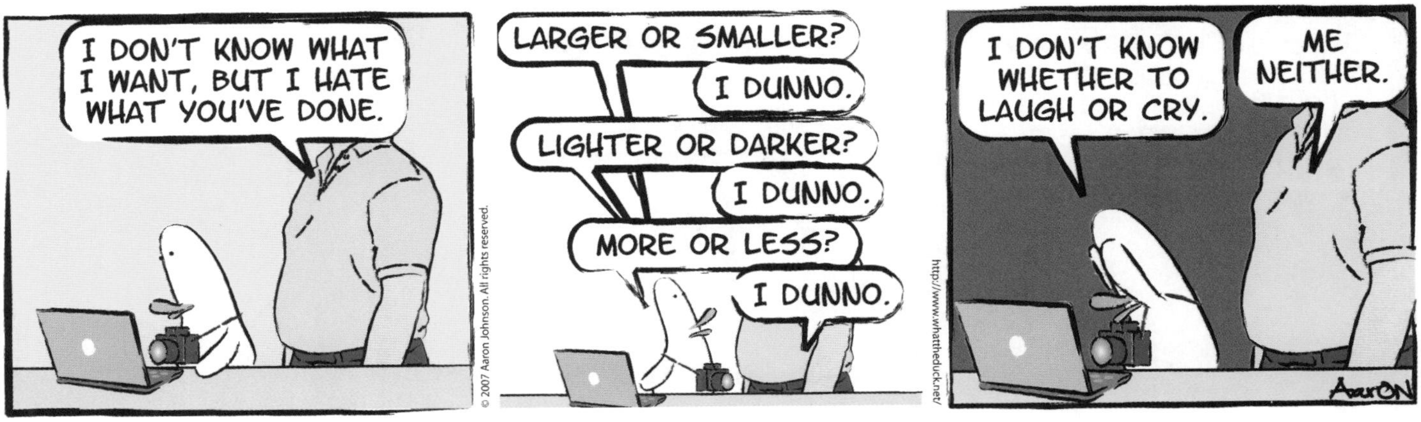
I DON'T KNOW WHAT I WANT, BUT I HATE WHAT YOU'VE DONE.
© 2007 Aaron Johnson. All rights reserved.
LARGER OR SMALLER?
I DUNNO.
LIGHTER OR DARKER?
I DUNNO.
MORE OR LESS?
I DUNNO.
http://www.whattheduck.net/
I DON'T KNOW WHETHER TO LAUGH OR CRY.
ME NEITHER.
AarON

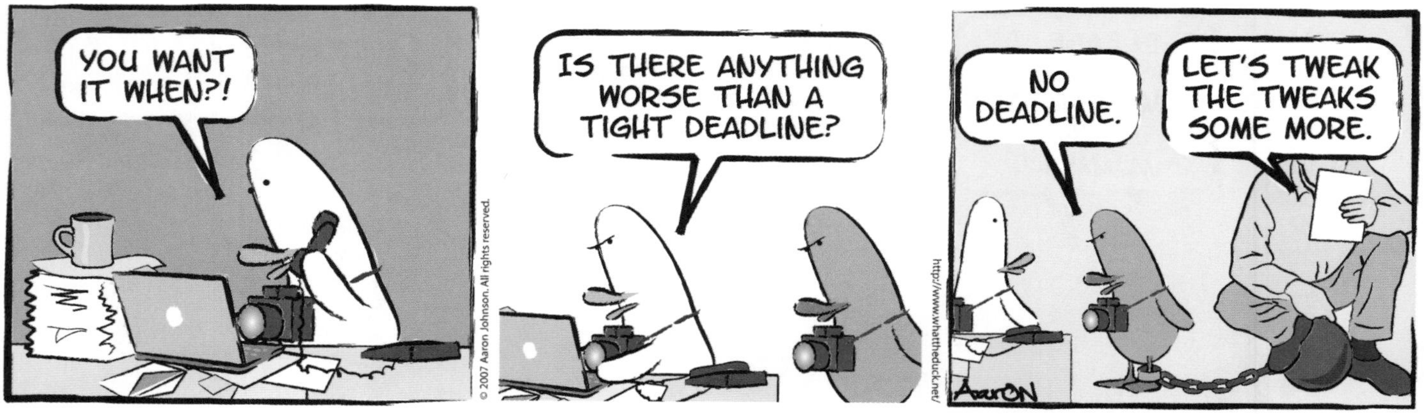
YOU WANT IT WHEN?!
IS THERE ANYTHING WORSE THAN A TIGHT DEADLINE?
NO DEADLINE.
LET'S TWEAK THE TWEAKS SOME MORE.
© 2007 Aaron Johnson. All rights reserved.
http://www.whattheduck.net/
AARON

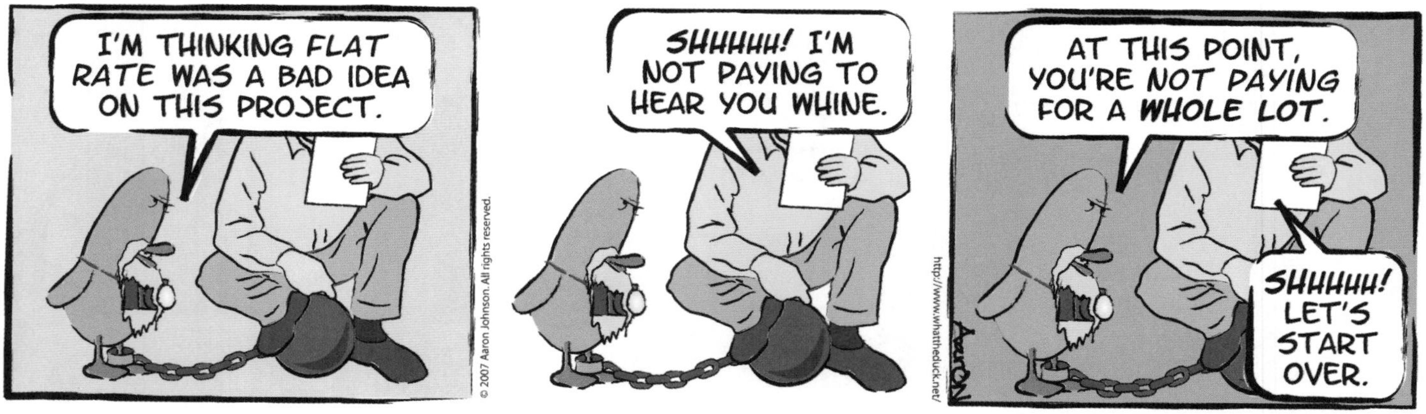
I'M THINKING FLAT RATE WAS A BAD IDEA ON THIS PROJECT.
SHHHHH! I'M NOT PAYING TO HEAR YOU WHINE.
AT THIS POINT, YOU'RE NOT PAYING FOR A WHOLE LOT.
SHHHHH! LET'S START OVER.
© 2007 Aaron Johnson. All rights reserved.
http://www.whattheduck.net/
AARON

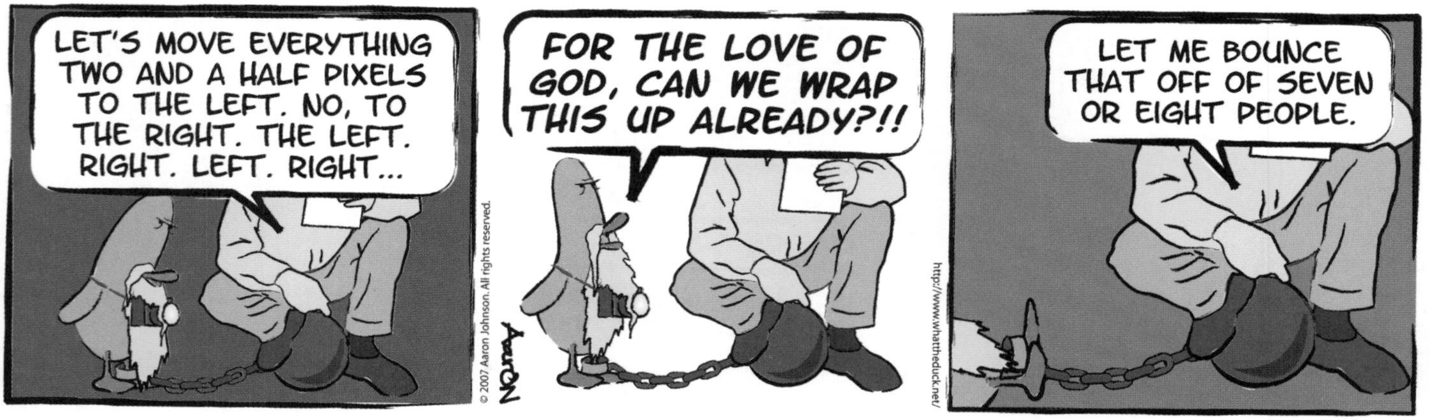
LET'S MOVE EVERYTHING TWO AND A HALF PIXELS TO THE LEFT. NO, TO THE RIGHT. THE LEFT. RIGHT. LEFT. RIGHT...
FOR THE LOVE OF GOD, CAN WE WRAP THIS UP ALREADY?!!
LET ME BOUNCE THAT OFF OF SEVEN OR EIGHT PEOPLE.
© 2007 Aaron Johnson. All rights reserved.
http://www.whattheduck.net/
AARON

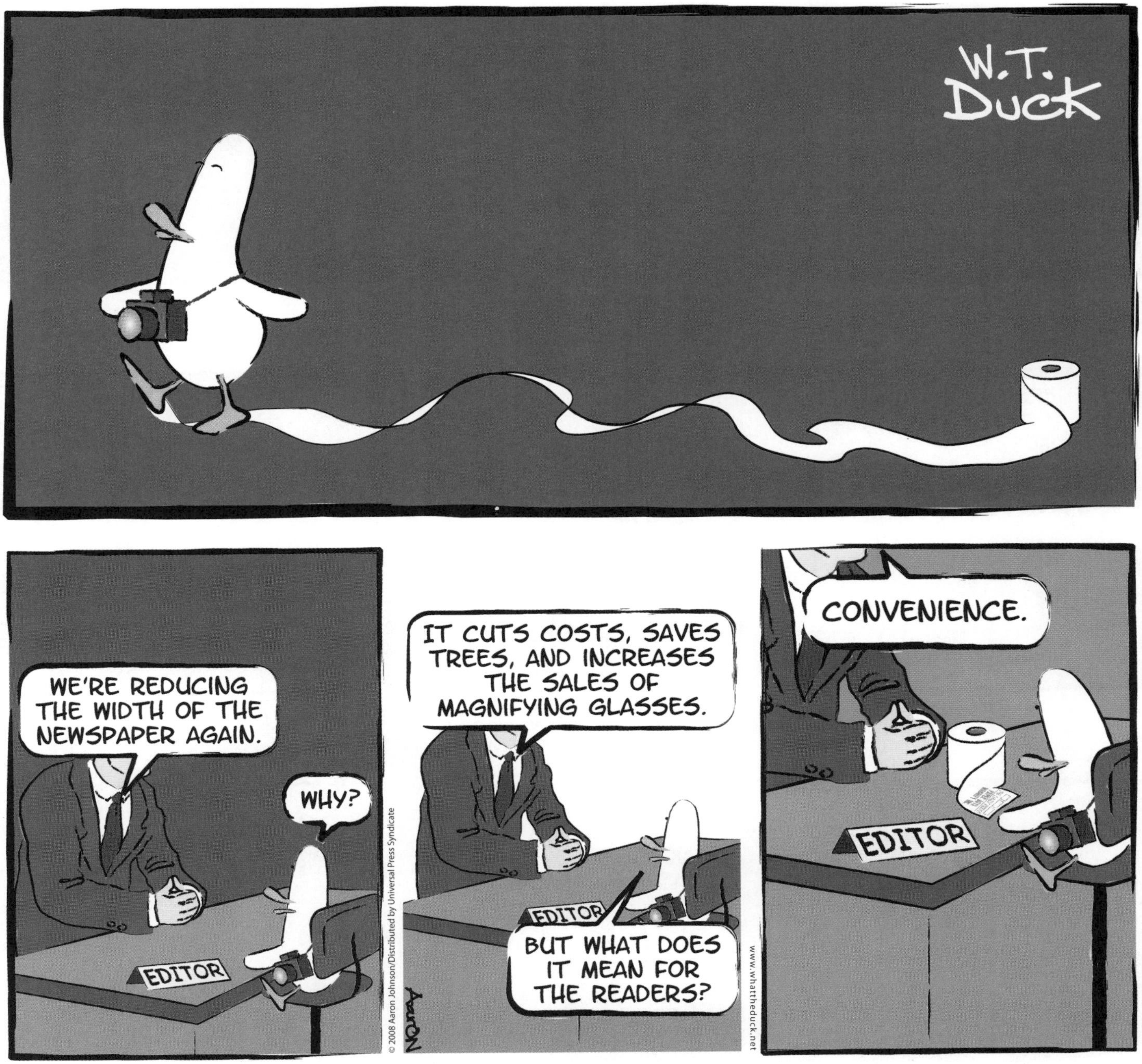
W.T. DUCK
WE'RE REDUCING THE WIDTH OF THE NEWSPAPER AGAIN.
WHY?
EDITOR
IT CUTS COSTS, SAVES TREES, AND INCREASES THE SALES OF MAGNIFYING GLASSES.
BUT WHAT DOES IT MEAN FOR THE READERS?
EDITOR
CONVENIENCE.
EDITOR
© 2008 Aaron Johnson/Distributed by Universal Press Syndicate
AARON
www.whattheduck.net

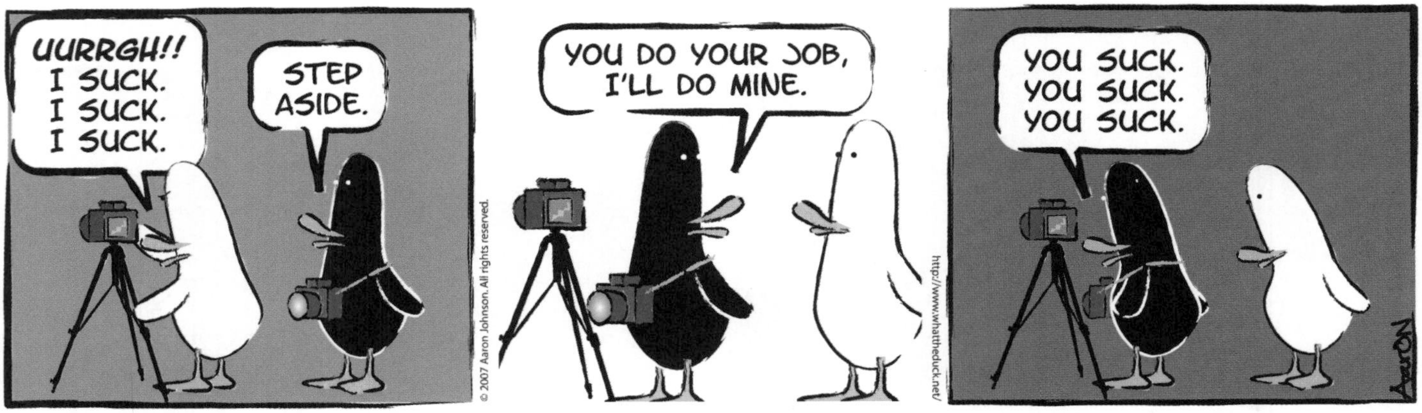
UURRGH!! I SUCK. I SUCK. I SUCK.
STEP ASIDE.
© 2007 Aaron Johnson. All rights reserved.
YOU DO YOUR JOB, I'LL DO MINE.
http://www.whattheduck.net/
YOU SUCK. YOU SUCK. YOU SUCK.
AARON

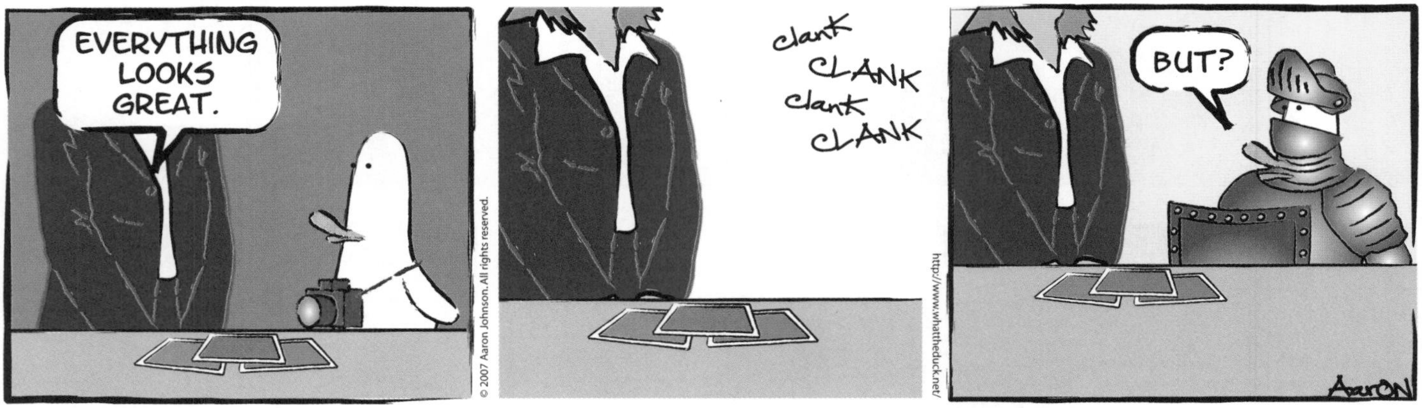
EVERYTHING LOOKS GREAT.
© 2007 Aaron Johnson. All rights reserved.
clank CLANK clank CLANK
http://www.whattheduck.net/
BUT?
AARON

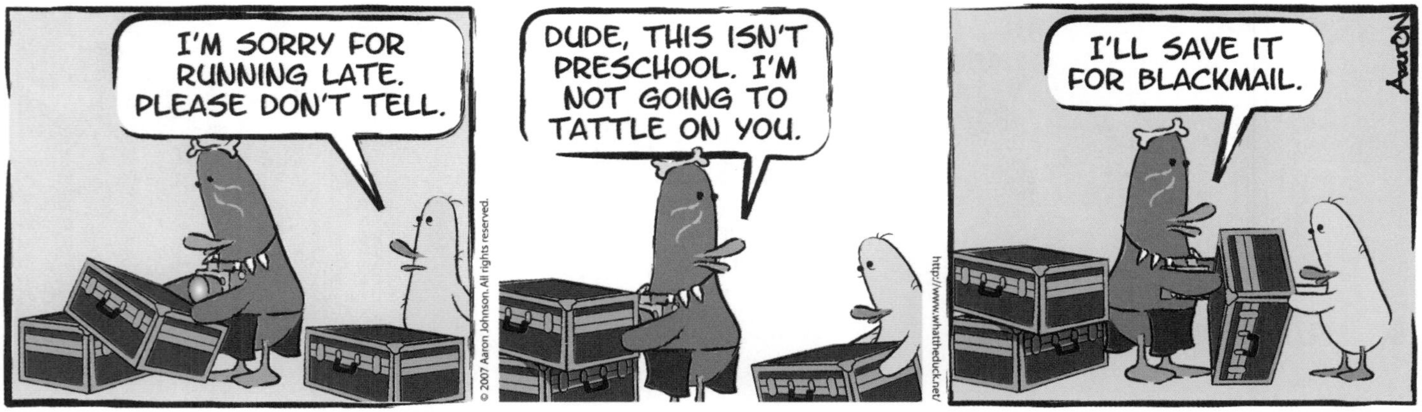
I'M SORRY FOR RUNNING LATE. PLEASE DON'T TELL.
© 2007 Aaron Johnson. All rights reserved.
DUDE, THIS ISN'T PRESCHOOL. I'M NOT GOING TO TATTLE ON YOU.
http://www.whattheduck.net/
I'LL SAVE IT FOR BLACKMAIL.
AARON

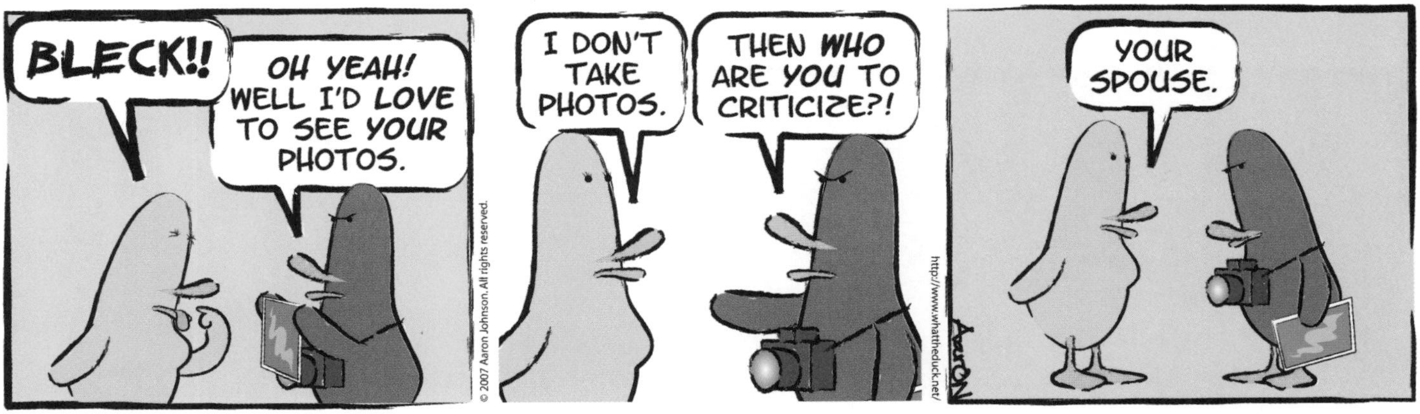
BLECK!!
OH YEAH! WELL I'D LOVE TO SEE YOUR PHOTOS.
© 2007 Aaron Johnson. All rights reserved.
I DON'T TAKE PHOTOS.
THEN WHO ARE YOU TO CRITICIZE?!
http://www.whattheduck.net/
YOUR SPOUSE.
AARON

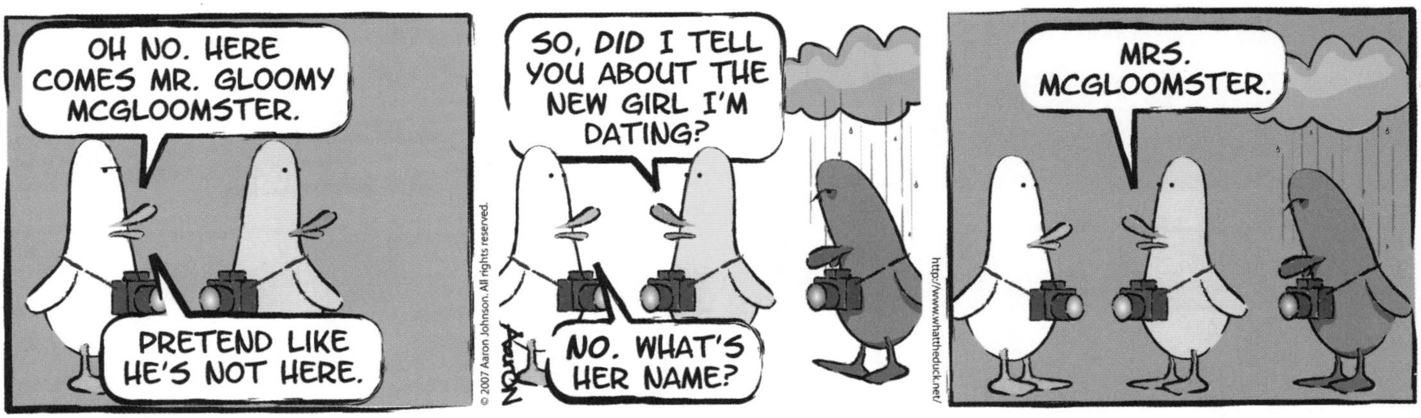
OH NO. HERE COMES MR. GLOOMY MCGLOOMSTER.
PRETEND LIKE HE'S NOT HERE.
© 2007 Aaron Johnson. All rights reserved.
AARON
SO, DID I TELL YOU ABOUT THE NEW GIRL I'M DATING?
NO. WHAT'S HER NAME?
http://www.whattheduck.net/
MRS. MCGLOOMSTER.

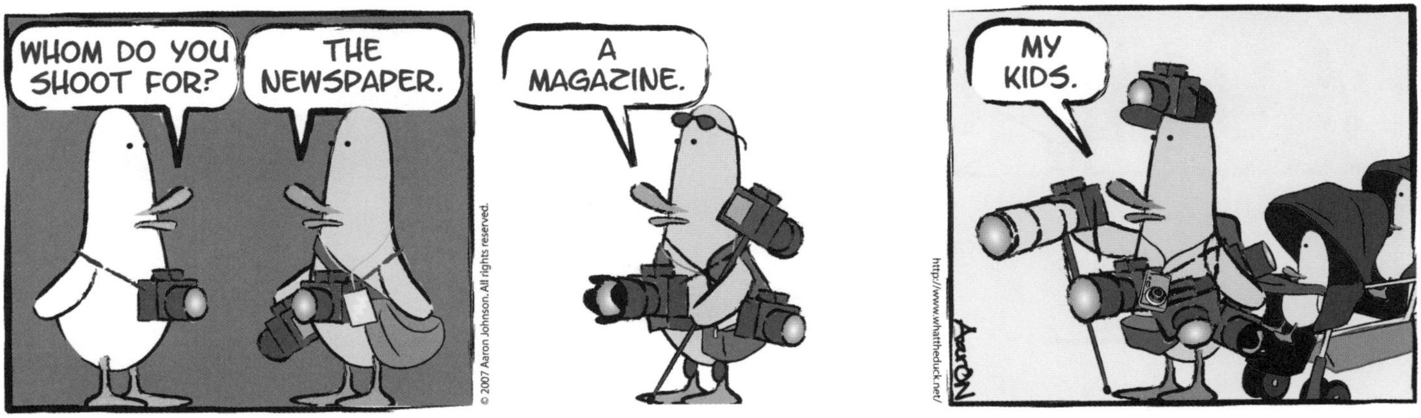
WHOM DO YOU SHOOT FOR?
THE NEWSPAPER.
© 2007 Aaron Johnson. All rights reserved.
A MAGAZINE.
http://www.whattheduck.net/
MY KIDS.
AARON

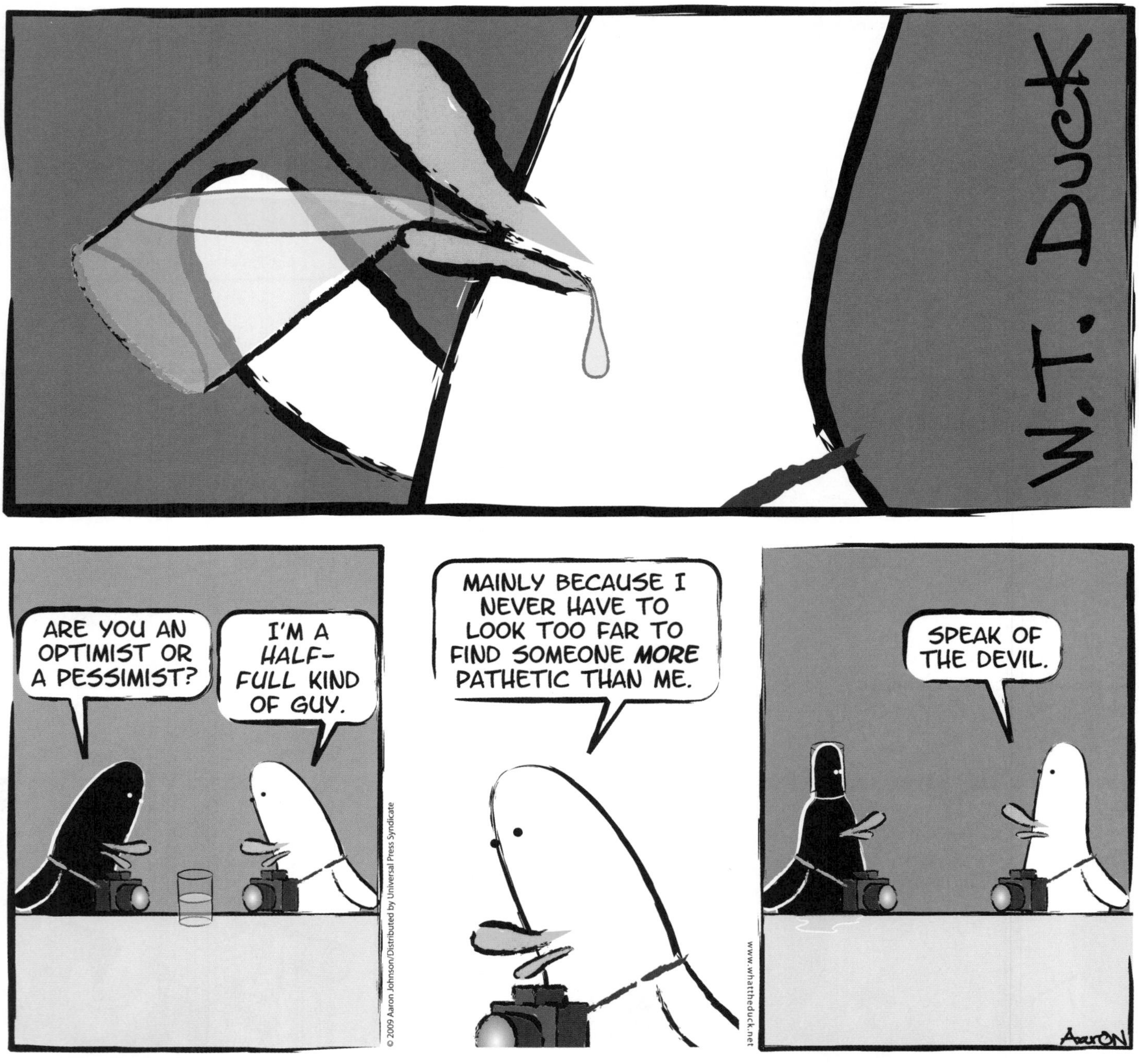
W.T. Duck
ARE YOU AN OPTIMIST OR A PESSIMIST?
I'M A HALF-FULL KIND OF GUY.
© 2009 Aaron Johnson/Distributed by Universal Press Syndicate
MAINLY BECAUSE I NEVER HAVE TO LOOK TOO FAR TO FIND SOMEONE **MORE** PATHETIC THAN ME.
www.whattheduck.net
SPEAK OF THE DEVIL.
AARON

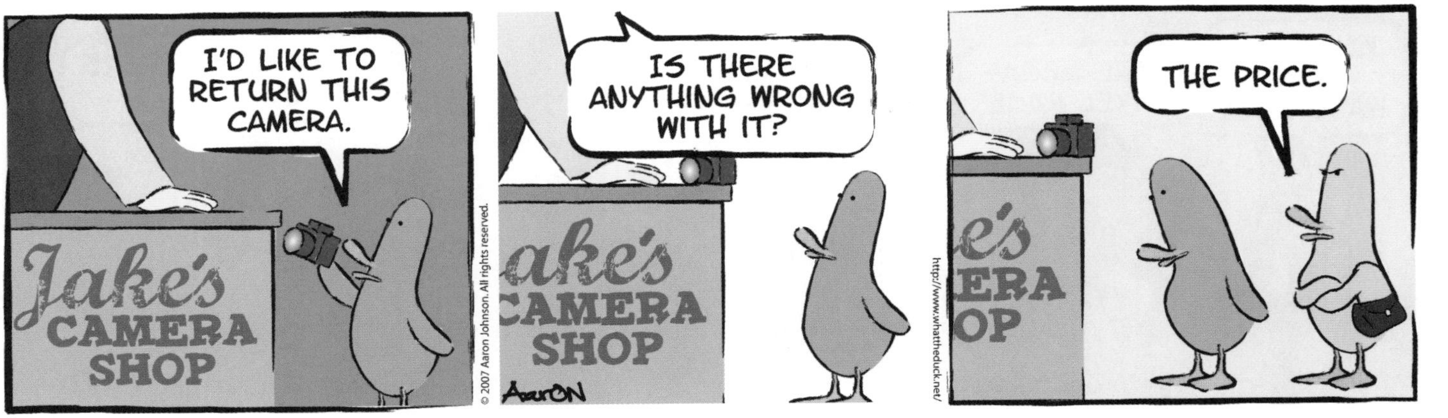
Jake's
CAMERA
SHOP
I'D LIKE TO RETURN THIS CAMERA.
IS THERE ANYTHING WRONG WITH IT?
THE PRICE.
© 2007 Aaron Johnson. All rights reserved.
http://www.whattheduck.net/
AARON

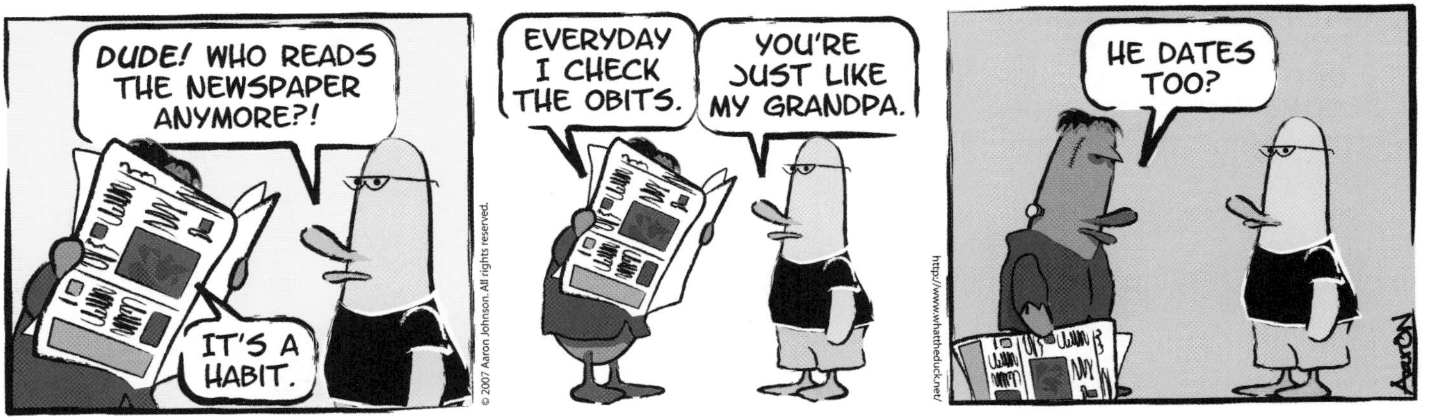
DUDE! WHO READS THE NEWSPAPER ANYMORE?!
IT'S A HABIT.
EVERYDAY I CHECK THE OBITS.
YOU'RE JUST LIKE MY GRANDPA.
HE DATES TOO?
© 2007 Aaron Johnson. All rights reserved.
http://www.whattheduck.net/
AARON

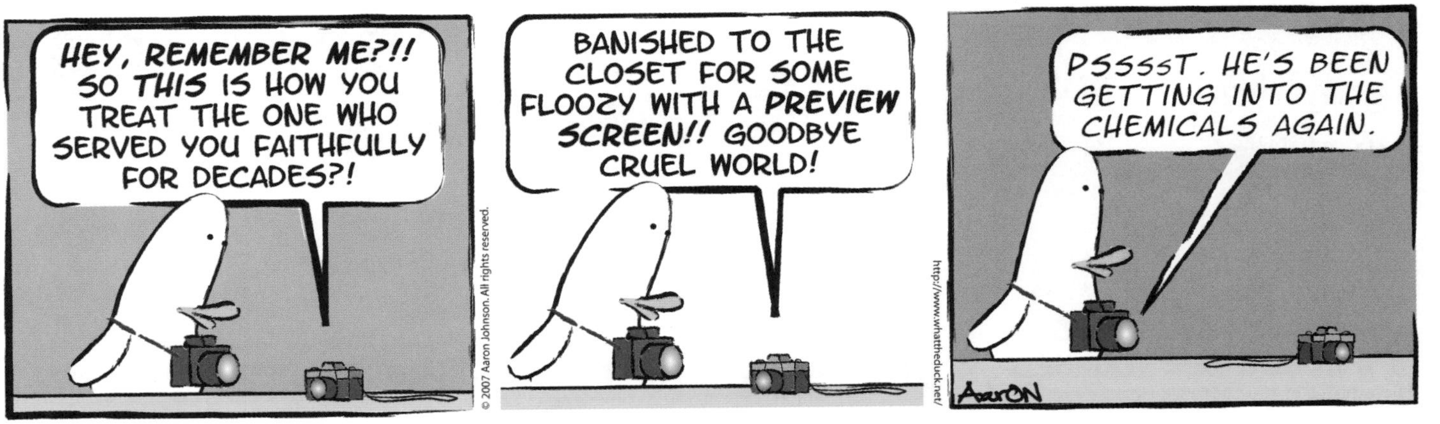
HEY, REMEMBER ME?!! SO THIS IS HOW YOU TREAT THE ONE WHO SERVED YOU FAITHFULLY FOR DECADES?!
BANISHED TO THE CLOSET FOR SOME FLOOZY WITH A PREVIEW SCREEN!! GOODBYE CRUEL WORLD!
PSSSST. HE'S BEEN GETTING INTO THE CHEMICALS AGAIN.
© 2007 Aaron Johnson. All rights reserved.
http://www.whattheduck.net/
AARON

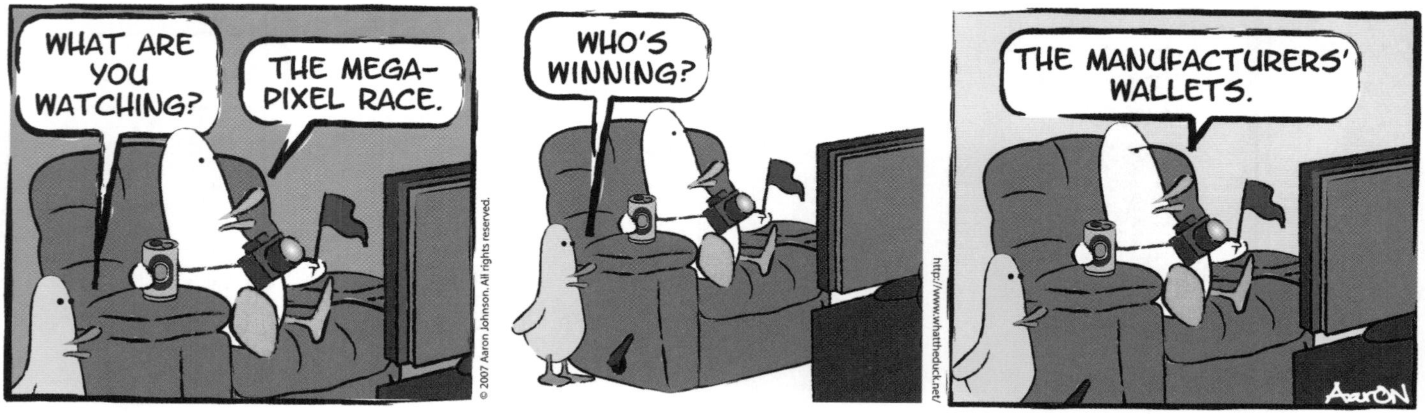
WHAT ARE YOU WATCHING?
THE MEGA-PIXEL RACE.
WHO'S WINNING?
THE MANUFACTURERS' WALLETS.
© 2007 Aaron Johnson. All rights reserved.
http://www.whattheduck.net/

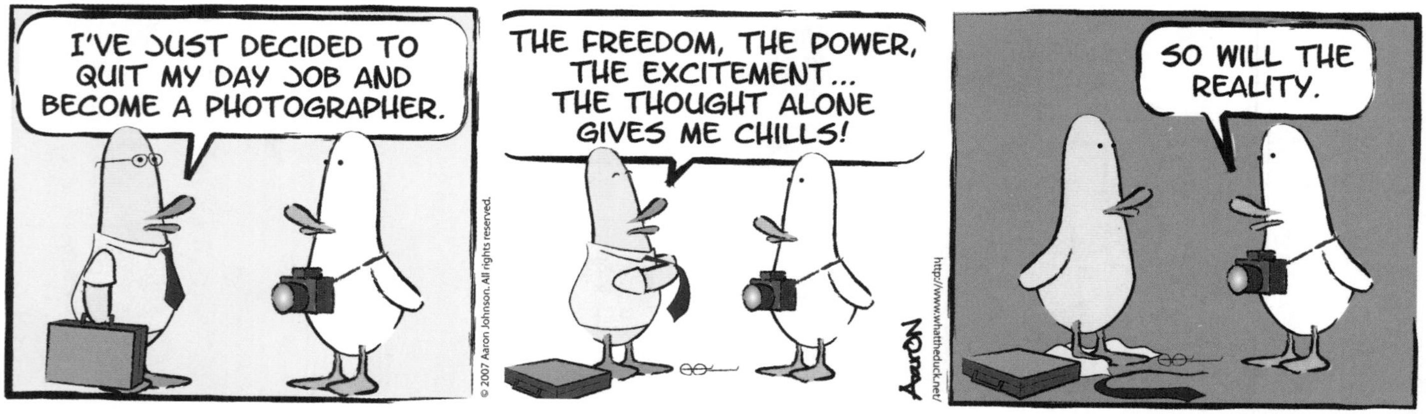
I'VE JUST DECIDED TO QUIT MY DAY JOB AND BECOME A PHOTOGRAPHER.
THE FREEDOM, THE POWER, THE EXCITEMENT... THE THOUGHT ALONE GIVES ME CHILLS!
SO WILL THE REALITY.
© 2007 Aaron Johnson. All rights reserved.
http://www.whattheduck.net/

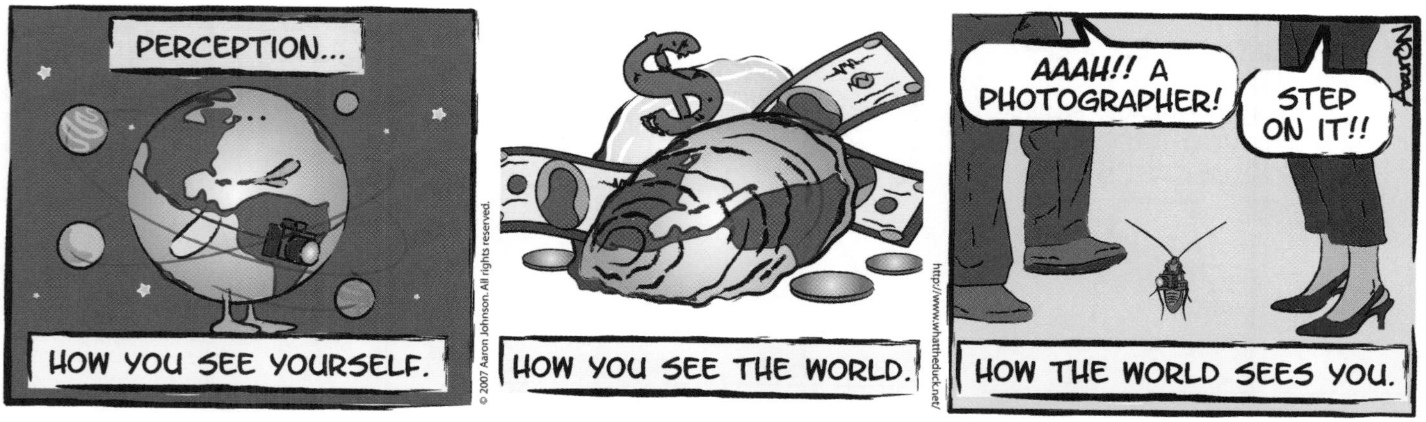
PERCEPTION...
HOW YOU SEE YOURSELF.
HOW YOU SEE THE WORLD.
AAAH!! A PHOTOGRAPHER!
STEP ON IT!!
HOW THE WORLD SEES YOU.
© 2007 Aaron Johnson. All rights reserved.
http://www.whattheduck.net/

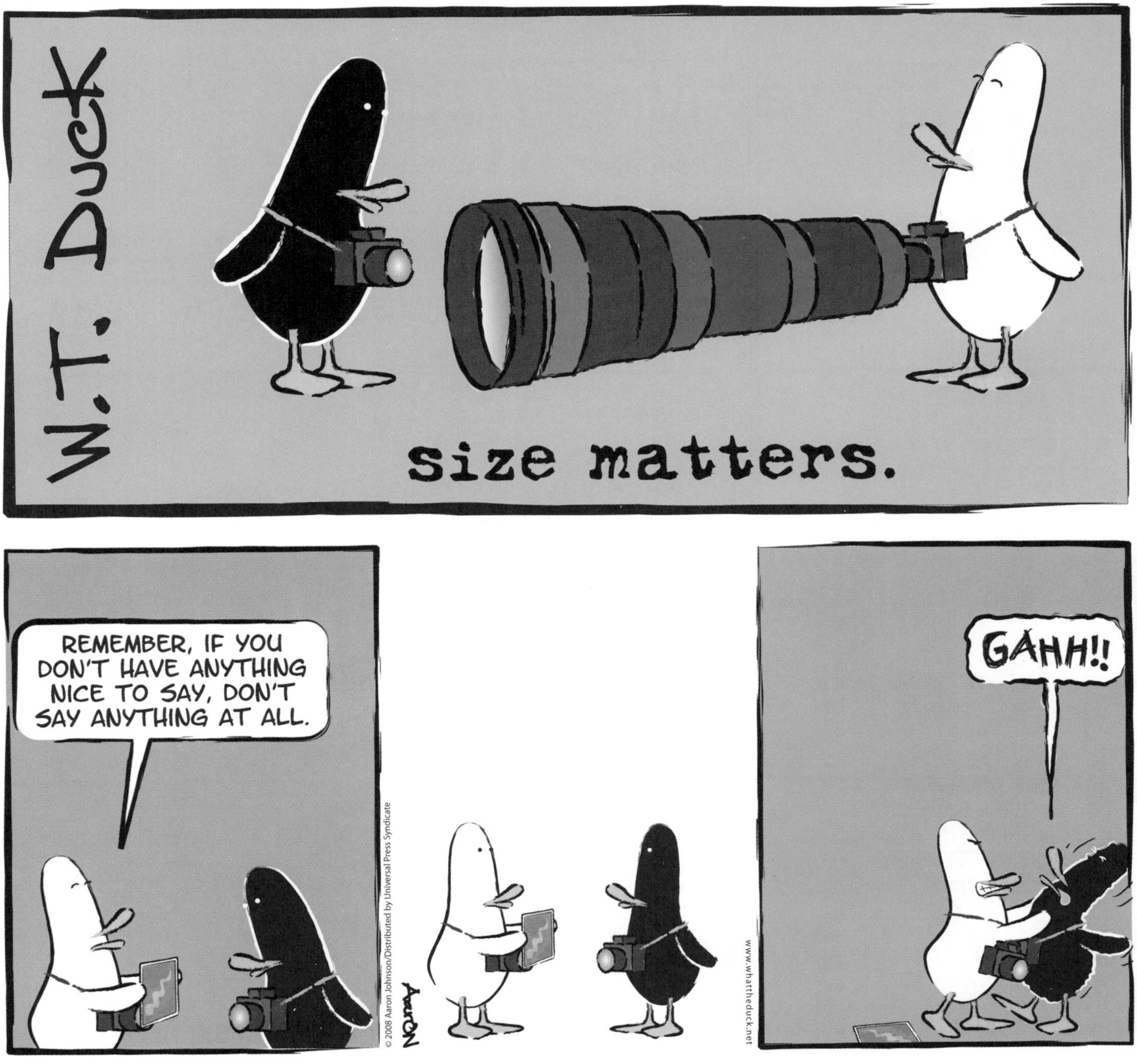
W.T. Duck
size matters.
REMEMBER, IF YOU DON'T HAVE ANYTHING NICE TO SAY, DON'T SAY ANYTHING AT ALL.
© 2008 Aaron Johnson/Distributed by Universal Press Syndicate
AARON
www.whattheduck.net
GAHH!!

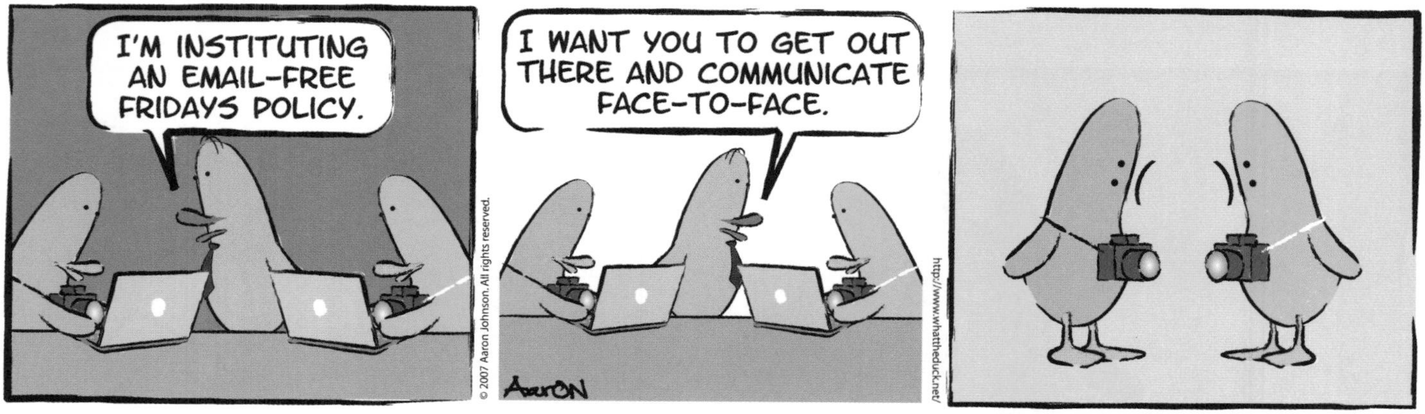
I'M INSTITUTING AN EMAIL-FREE FRIDAYS POLICY.
I WANT YOU TO GET OUT THERE AND COMMUNICATE FACE-TO-FACE.
© 2007 Aaron Johnson. All rights reserved.
http://www.whattheduck.net/

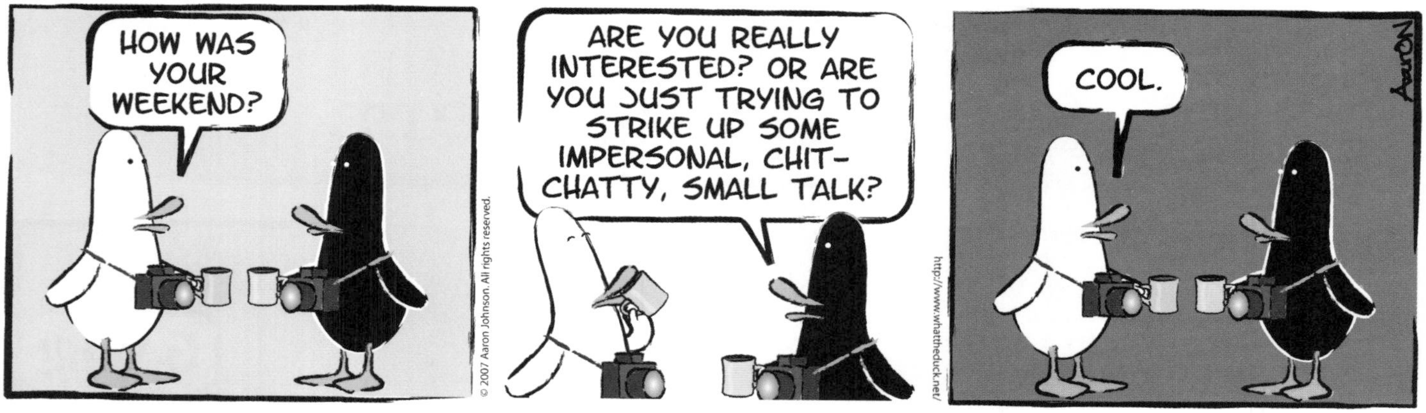
HOW WAS YOUR WEEKEND?
ARE YOU REALLY INTERESTED? OR ARE YOU JUST TRYING TO STRIKE UP SOME IMPERSONAL, CHIT-CHATTY, SMALL TALK?
COOL.
© 2007 Aaron Johnson. All rights reserved.
http://www.whattheduck.net/

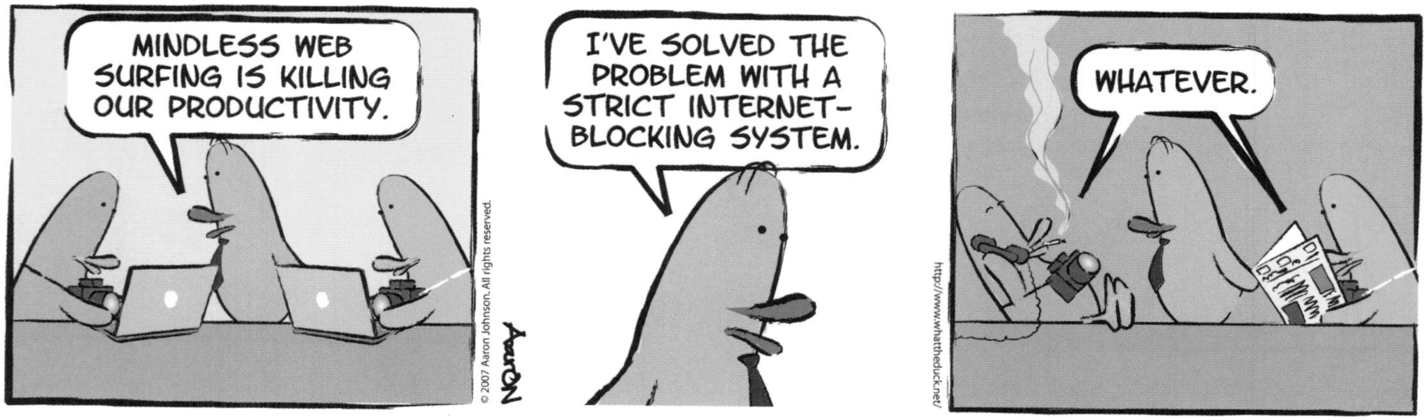
MINDLESS WEB SURFING IS KILLING OUR PRODUCTIVITY.
I'VE SOLVED THE PROBLEM WITH A STRICT INTERNET-BLOCKING SYSTEM.
WHATEVER.
© 2007 Aaron Johnson. All rights reserved.
http://www.whattheduck.net/

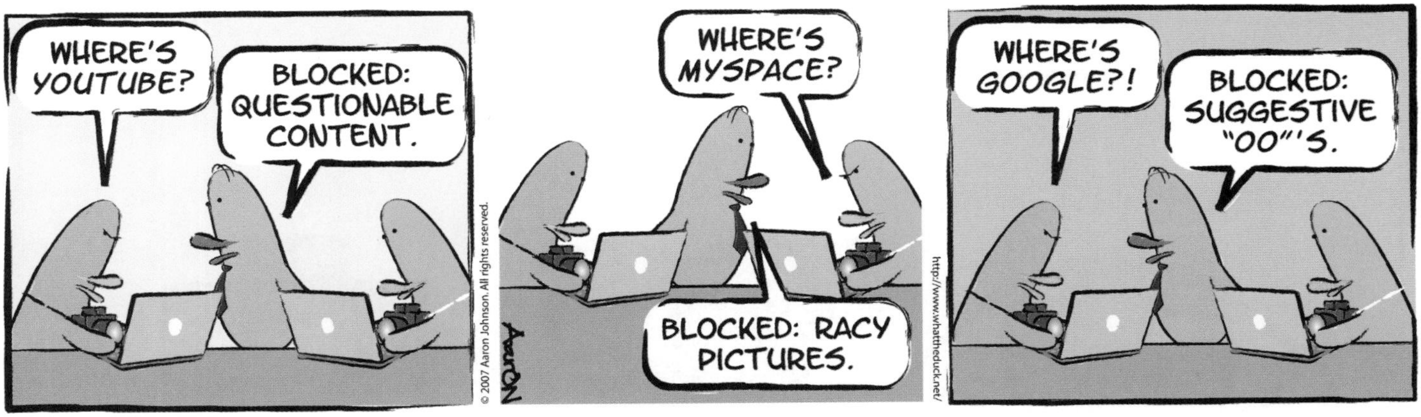
WHERE'S YOUTUBE?
BLOCKED: QUESTIONABLE CONTENT.
© 2007 Aaron Johnson. All rights reserved.
AARON
WHERE'S MYSPACE?
BLOCKED: RACY PICTURES.
http://www.whattheduck.net/
WHERE'S GOOGLE?!
BLOCKED: SUGGESTIVE "OO"'S.

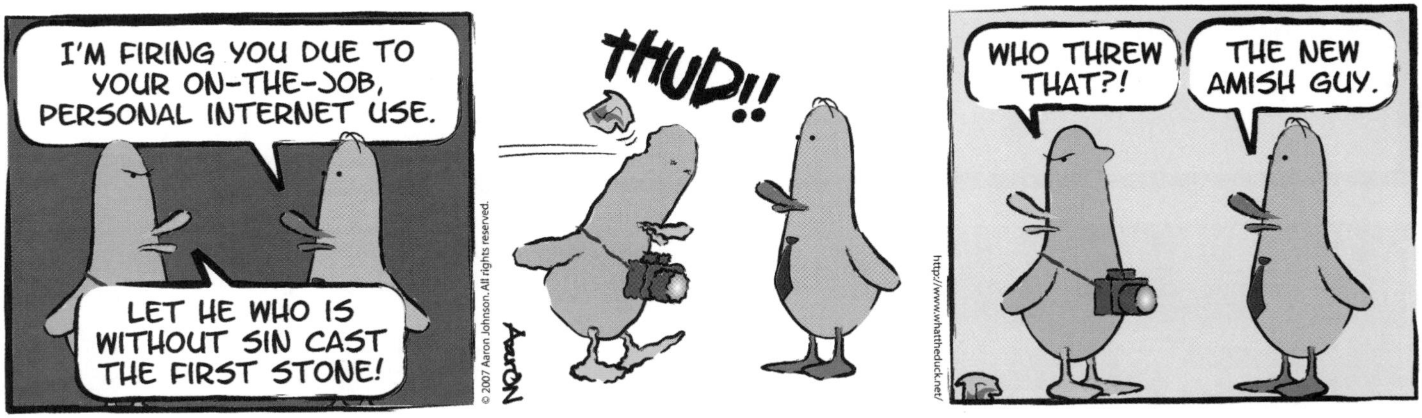
I'M FIRING YOU DUE TO YOUR ON-THE-JOB, PERSONAL INTERNET USE.
LET HE WHO IS WITHOUT SIN CAST THE FIRST STONE!
© 2007 Aaron Johnson. All rights reserved.
AARON
THUD!!
http://www.whattheduck.net/
WHO THREW THAT?!
THE NEW AMISH GUY.

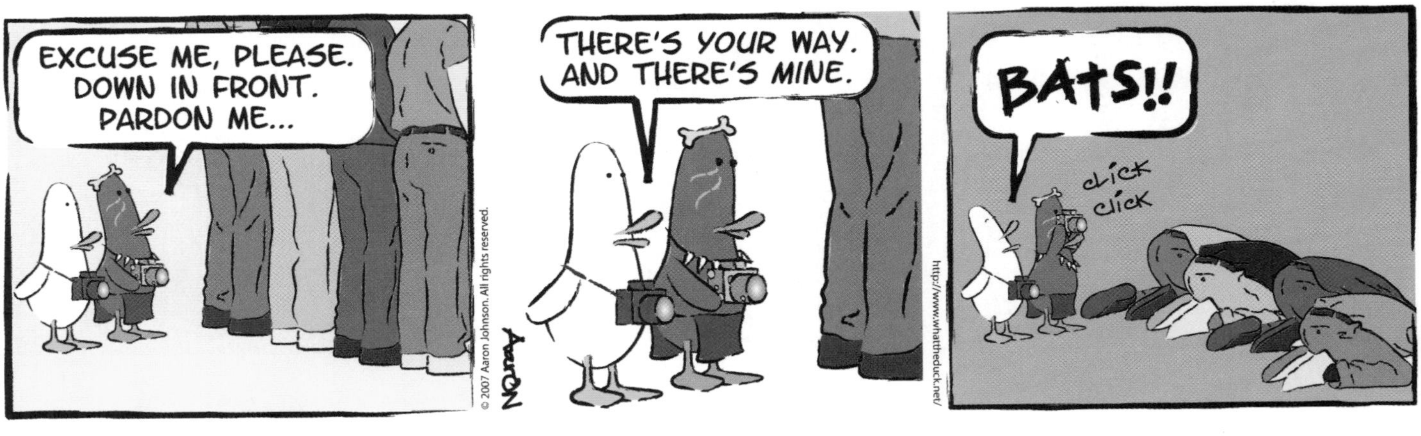
EXCUSE ME, PLEASE. DOWN IN FRONT. PARDON ME...
© 2007 Aaron Johnson. All rights reserved.
AARON
THERE'S YOUR WAY. AND THERE'S MINE.
http://www.whattheduck.net/
BATS!!
click click

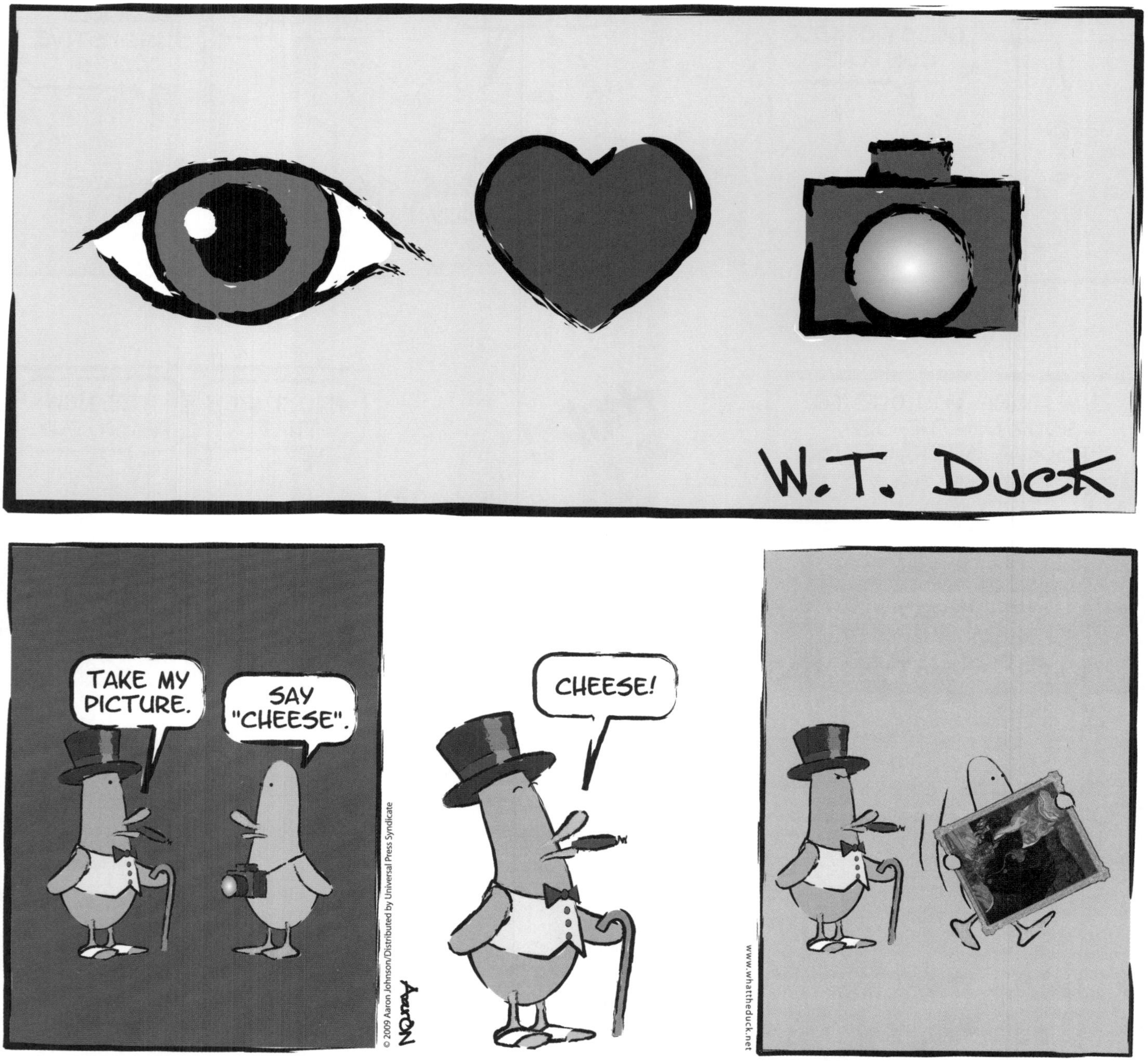
W.T. Duck
TAKE MY PICTURE.
SAY "CHEESE".
CHEESE!
© 2009 Aaron Johnson/Distributed by Universal Press Syndicate
AARON
www.whattheduck.net

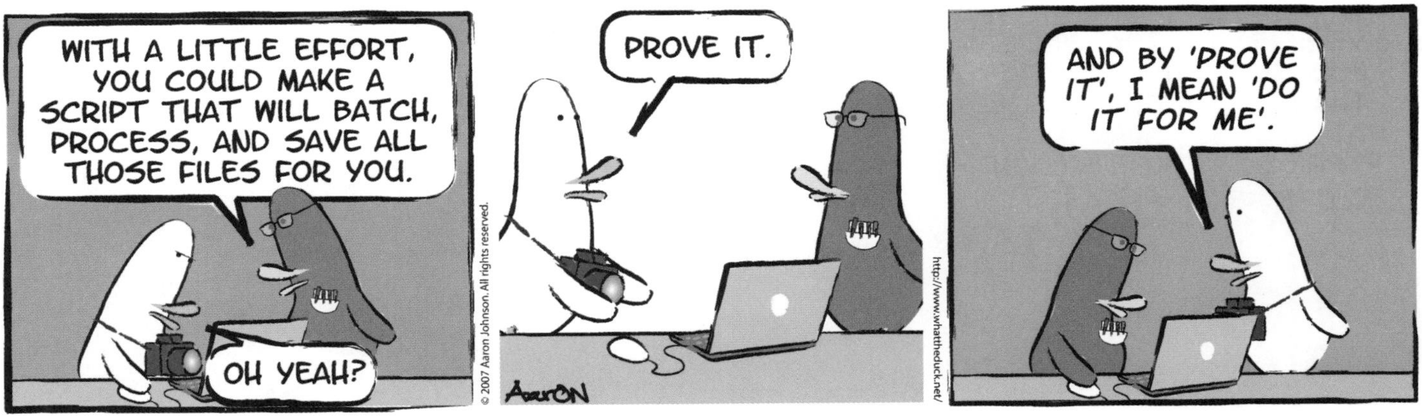
WITH A LITTLE EFFORT, YOU COULD MAKE A SCRIPT THAT WILL BATCH, PROCESS, AND SAVE ALL THOSE FILES FOR YOU.
OH YEAH?
PROVE IT.
AND BY 'PROVE IT', I MEAN 'DO IT FOR ME'.
© 2007 Aaron Johnson. All rights reserved.
http://www.whattheduck.net/

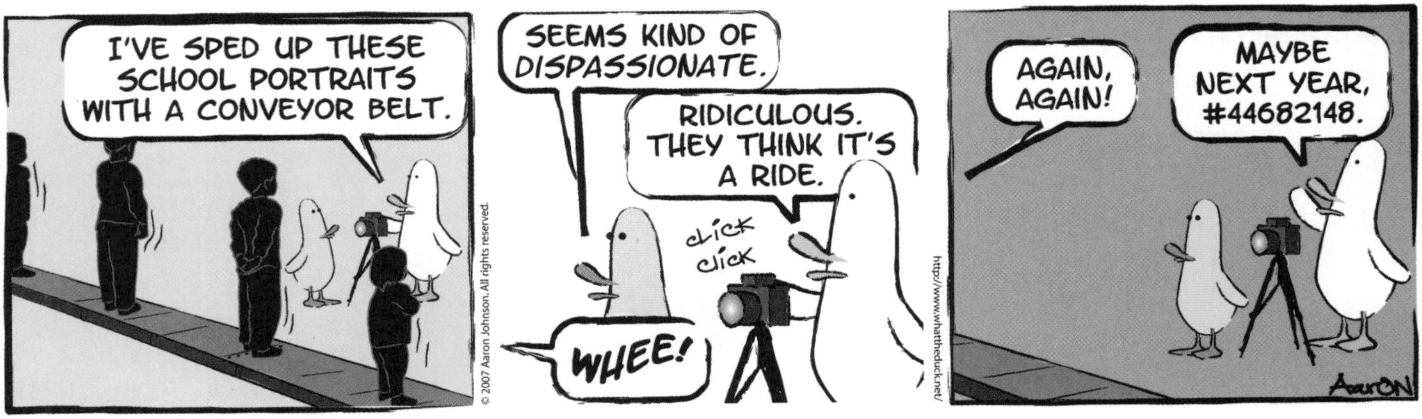
I'VE SPED UP THESE SCHOOL PORTRAITS WITH A CONVEYOR BELT.
SEEMS KIND OF DISPASSIONATE.
RIDICULOUS. THEY THINK IT'S A RIDE.
click click
WHEE!
AGAIN, AGAIN!
MAYBE NEXT YEAR, #44682148.
© 2007 Aaron Johnson. All rights reserved.
http://www.whattheduck.net/

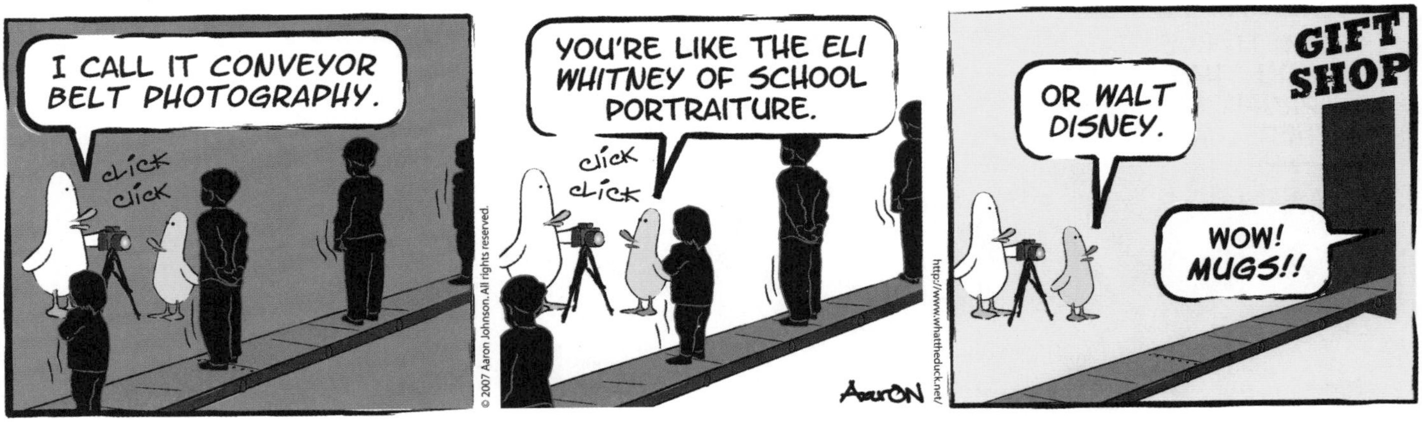
I CALL IT CONVEYOR BELT PHOTOGRAPHY.
click click
YOU'RE LIKE THE ELI WHITNEY OF SCHOOL PORTRAITURE.
click click
OR WALT DISNEY.
GIFT SHOP
WOW! MUGS!!
© 2007 Aaron Johnson. All rights reserved.
http://www.whattheduck.net/

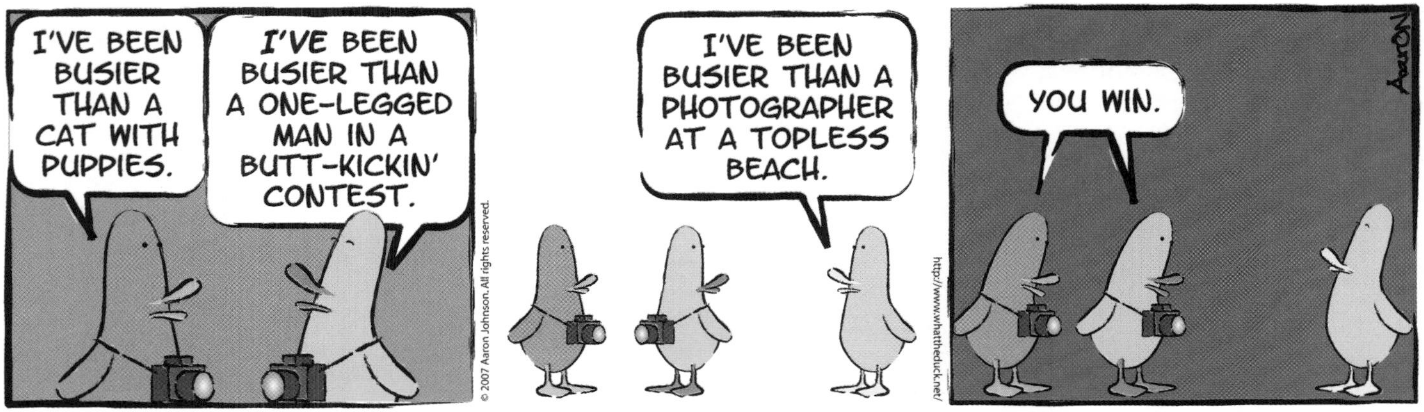
I'VE BEEN BUSIER THAN A CAT WITH PUPPIES.
I'VE BEEN BUSIER THAN A ONE-LEGGED MAN IN A BUTT-KICKIN' CONTEST.
I'VE BEEN BUSIER THAN A PHOTOGRAPHER AT A TOPLESS BEACH.
YOU WIN.
© 2007 Aaron Johnson. All rights reserved.
http://www.whattheduck.net/
AarON

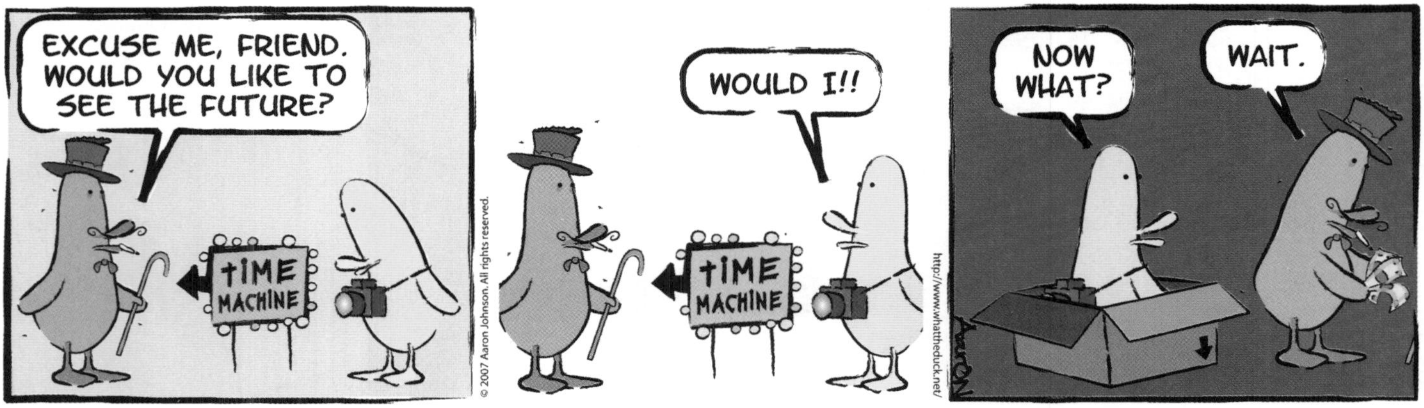
EXCUSE ME, FRIEND. WOULD YOU LIKE TO SEE THE FUTURE?
TIME MACHINE
WOULD I!!
TIME MACHINE
NOW WHAT?
WAIT.
© 2007 Aaron Johnson. All rights reserved.
http://www.whattheduck.net/
AarON

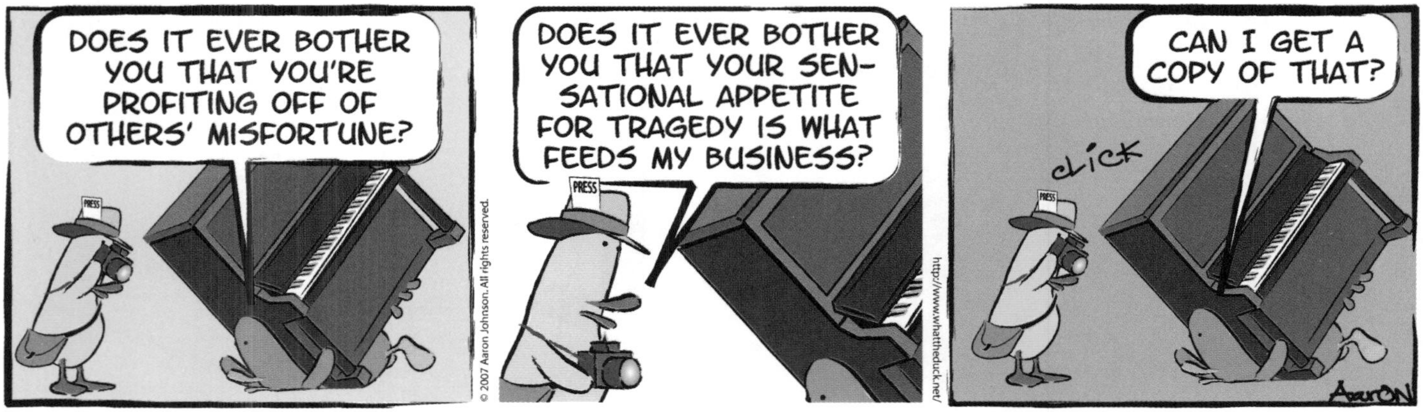
DOES IT EVER BOTHER YOU THAT YOU'RE PROFITING OFF OF OTHERS' MISFORTUNE?
DOES IT EVER BOTHER YOU THAT YOUR SEN-SATIONAL APPETITE FOR TRAGEDY IS WHAT FEEDS MY BUSINESS?
PRESS
CLICK
CAN I GET A COPY OF THAT?
© 2007 Aaron Johnson. All rights reserved.
http://www.whattheduck.net/
AarON

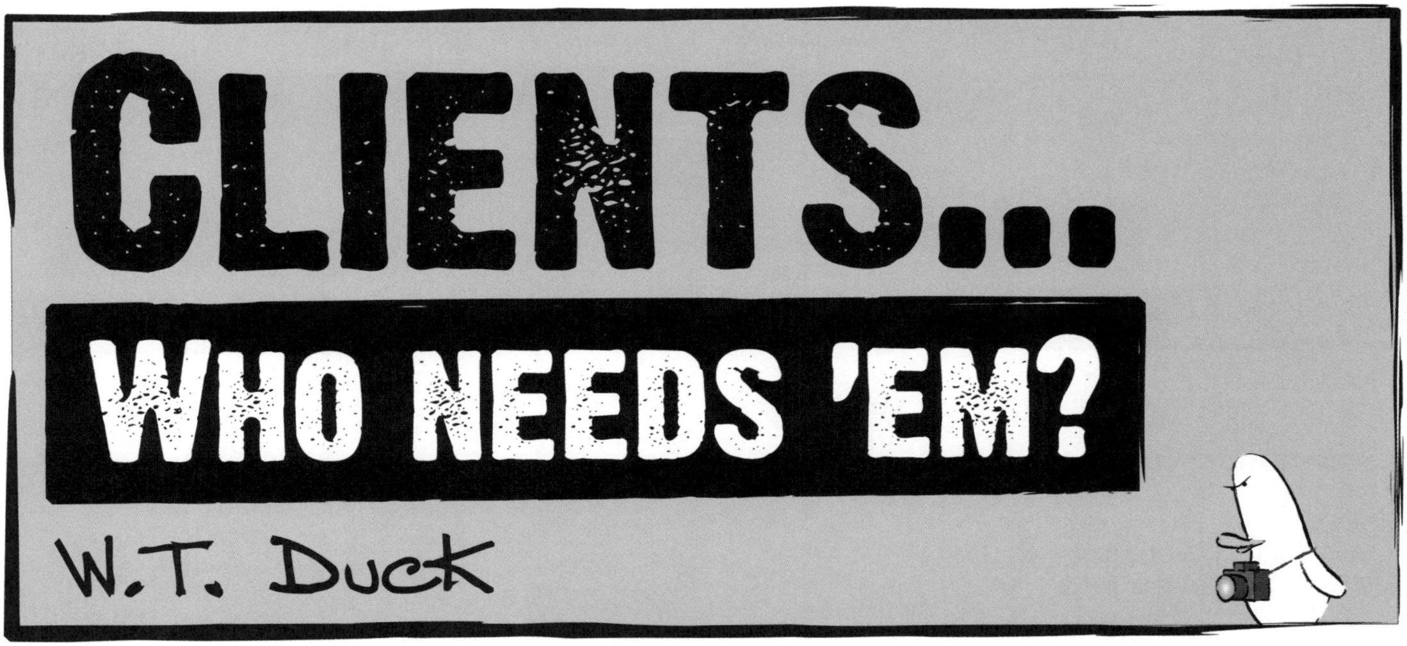
CLIENTS...
WHO NEEDS 'EM?
W.T. Duck

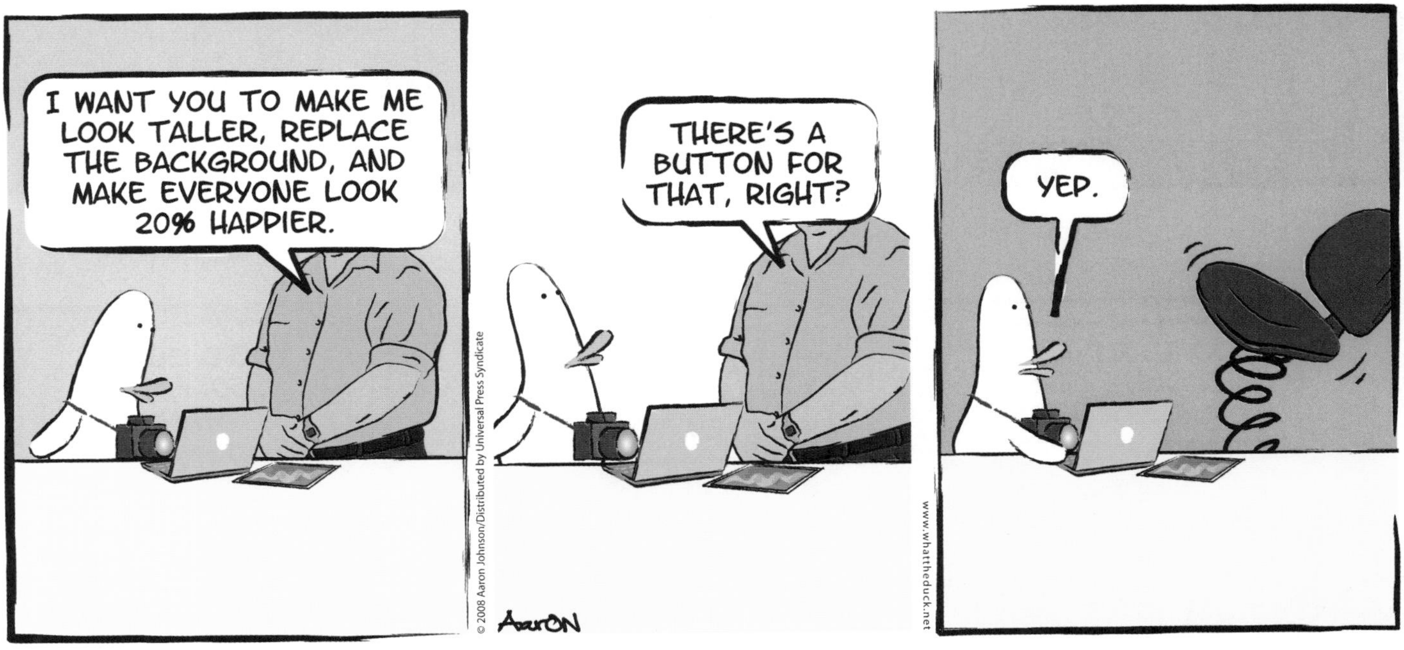
I WANT YOU TO MAKE ME LOOK TALLER, REPLACE THE BACKGROUND, AND MAKE EVERYONE LOOK 20% HAPPIER.
THERE'S A BUTTON FOR THAT, RIGHT?
YEP.
© 2008 Aaron Johnson/Distributed by Universal Press Syndicate
AarON
www.whattheduck.net

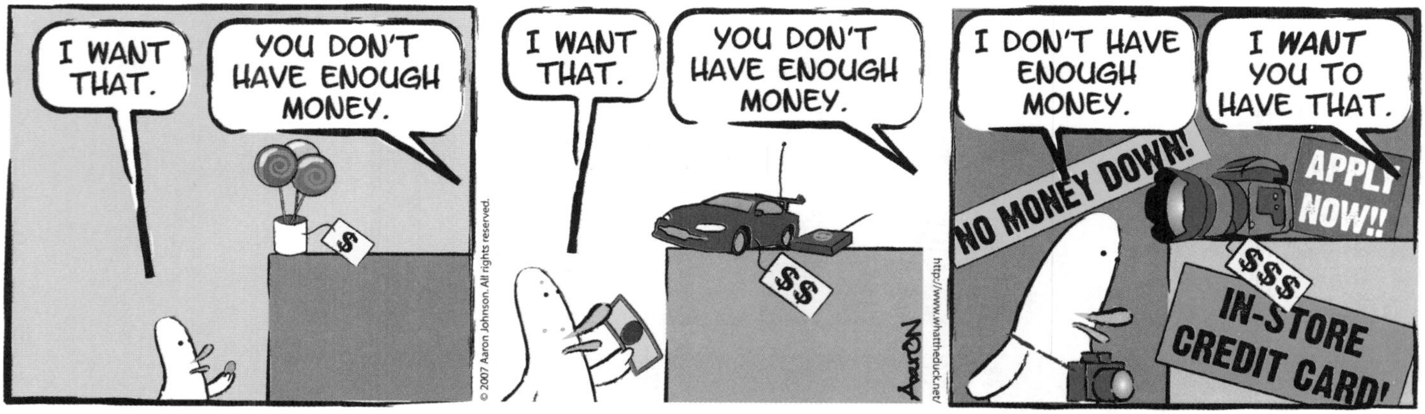
I WANT THAT.
YOU DON'T HAVE ENOUGH MONEY.
$
© 2007 Aaron Johnson. All rights reserved.
I WANT THAT.
YOU DON'T HAVE ENOUGH MONEY.
$$
AARON
http://www.whattheduck.net/
I DON'T HAVE ENOUGH MONEY.
I WANT YOU TO HAVE THAT.
NO MONEY DOWN!
APPLY NOW!!
$$$
IN-STORE CREDIT CARD!

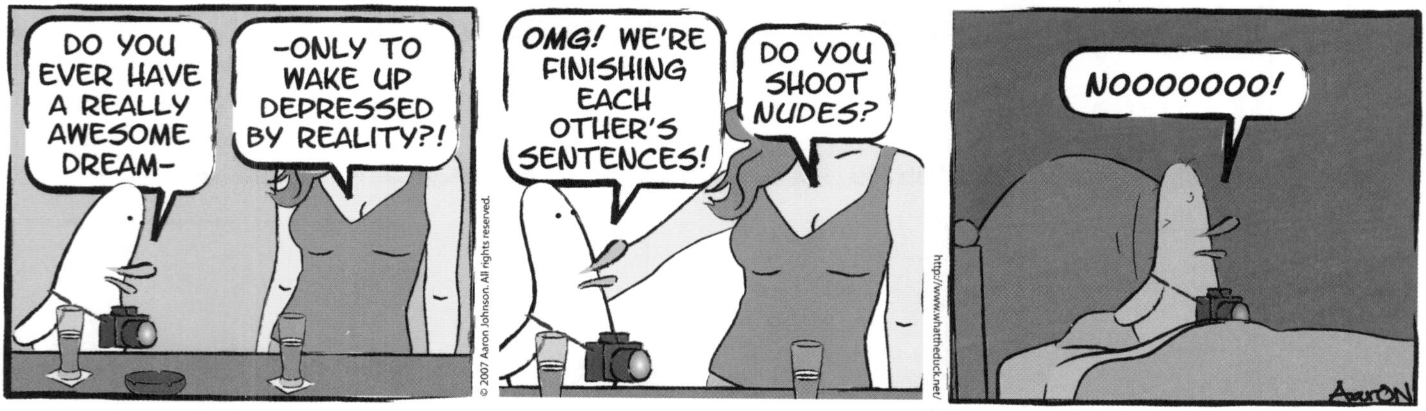
DO YOU EVER HAVE A REALLY AWESOME DREAM-
-ONLY TO WAKE UP DEPRESSED BY REALITY?!
© 2007 Aaron Johnson. All rights reserved.
OMG! WE'RE FINISHING EACH OTHER'S SENTENCES!
DO YOU SHOOT NUDES?
http://www.whattheduck.net/
NOOOOOOO!
AARON

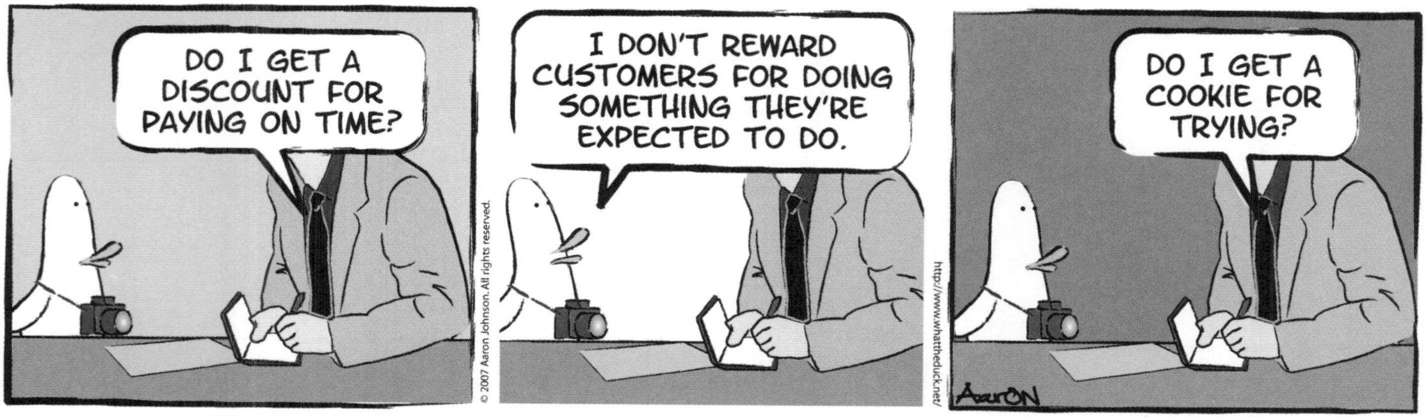
DO I GET A DISCOUNT FOR PAYING ON TIME?
© 2007 Aaron Johnson. All rights reserved.
I DON'T REWARD CUSTOMERS FOR DOING SOMETHING THEY'RE EXPECTED TO DO.
http://www.whattheduck.net/
DO I GET A COOKIE FOR TRYING?
AARON

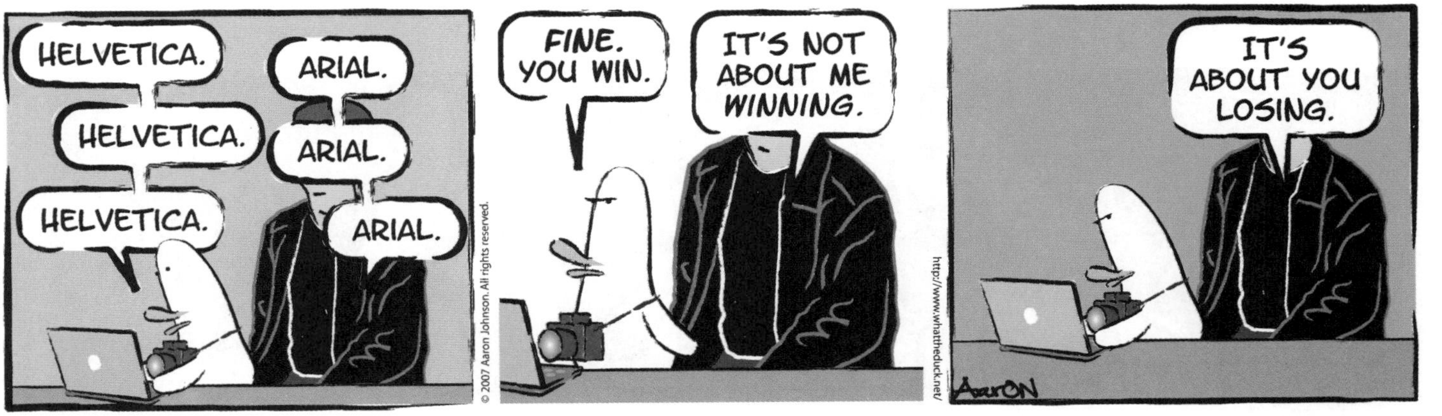
HELVETICA.
ARIAL.
HELVETICA.
ARIAL.
HELVETICA.
ARIAL.
© 2007 Aaron Johnson. All rights reserved.
FINE. YOU WIN.
IT'S NOT ABOUT ME WINNING.
http://www.whattheduck.net/
IT'S ABOUT YOU LOSING.
AARON

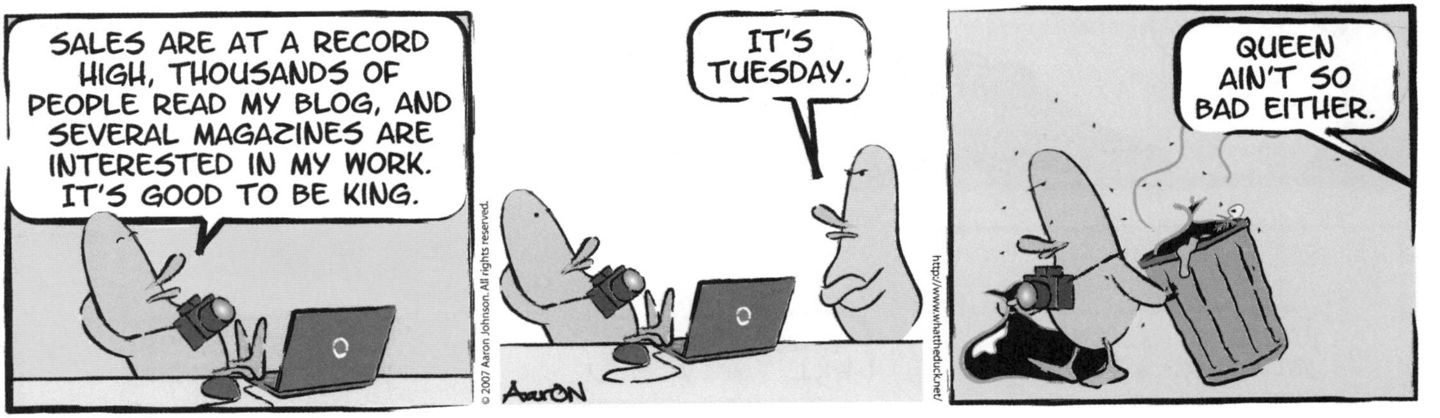
SALES ARE AT A RECORD HIGH, THOUSANDS OF PEOPLE READ MY BLOG, AND SEVERAL MAGAZINES ARE INTERESTED IN MY WORK. IT'S GOOD TO BE KING.
© 2007 Aaron Johnson. All rights reserved.
IT'S TUESDAY.
AARON
http://www.whattheduck.net/
QUEEN AIN'T SO BAD EITHER.

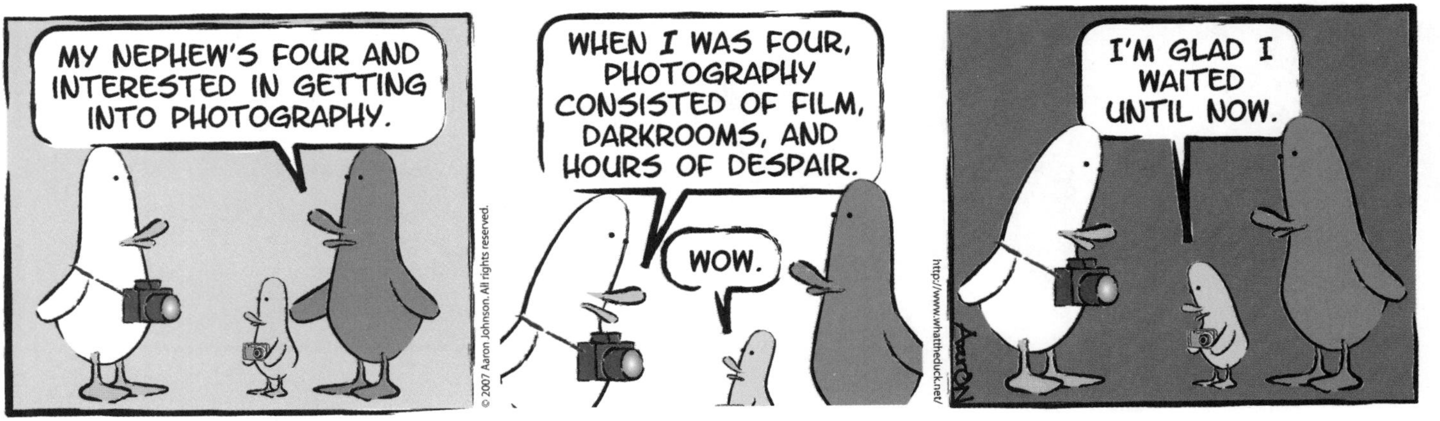
MY NEPHEW'S FOUR AND INTERESTED IN GETTING INTO PHOTOGRAPHY.
© 2007 Aaron Johnson. All rights reserved.
WHEN I WAS FOUR, PHOTOGRAPHY CONSISTED OF FILM, DARKROOMS, AND HOURS OF DESPAIR.
WOW.
http://www.whattheduck.net/
I'M GLAD I WAITED UNTIL NOW.
AARON

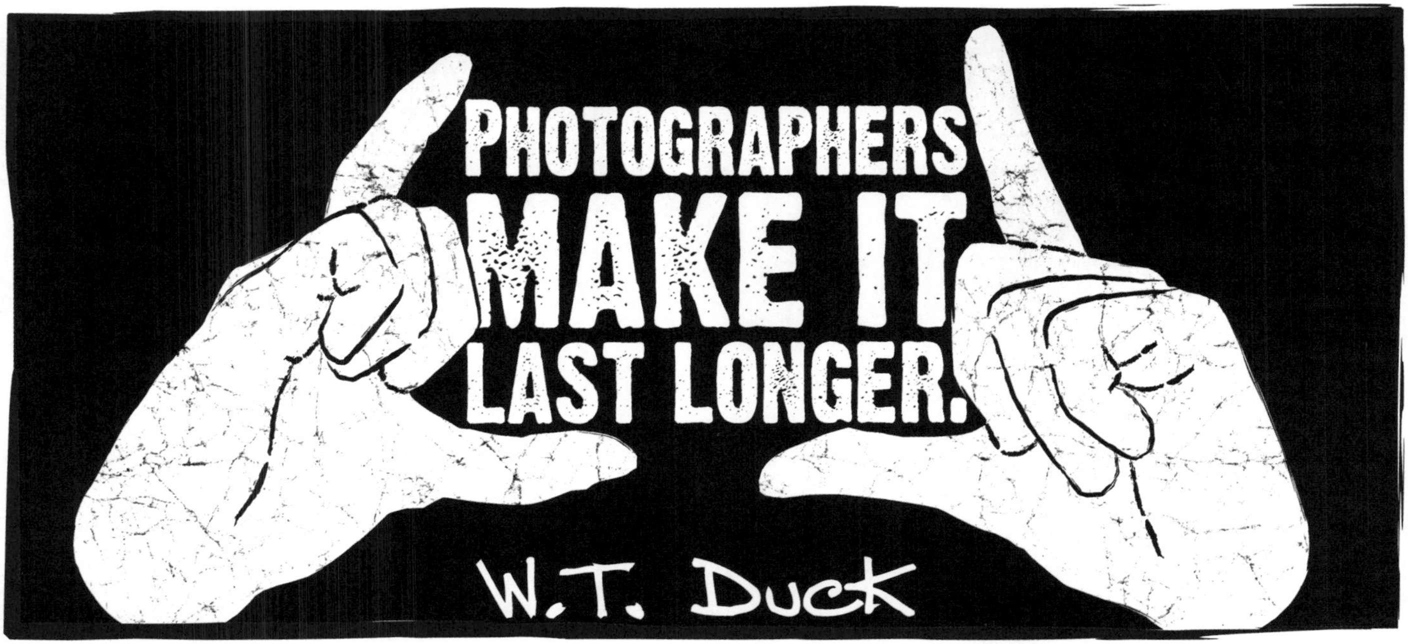
PHOTOGRAPHERS
MAKE IT
LAST LONGER.
W.T. DUCK

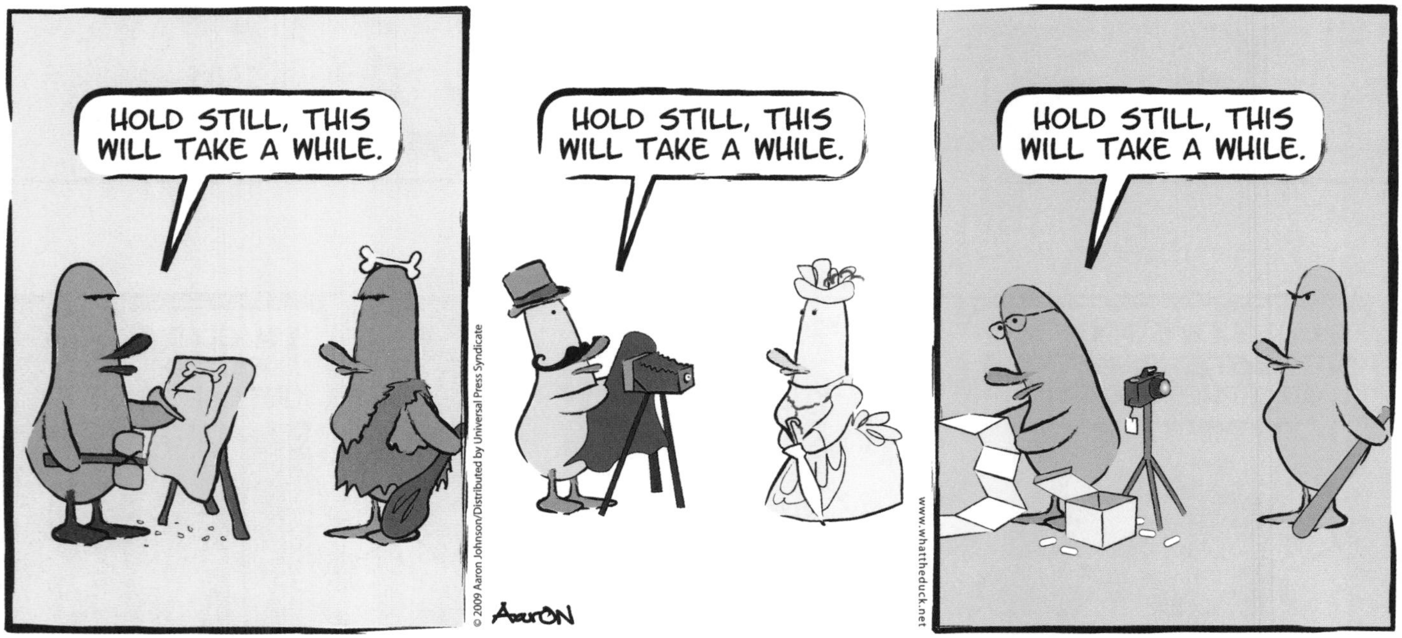
HOLD STILL, THIS WILL TAKE A WHILE.
HOLD STILL, THIS WILL TAKE A WHILE.
HOLD STILL, THIS WILL TAKE A WHILE.
© 2009 Aaron Johnson/Distributed by Universal Press Syndicate
AARON
www.whattheduck.net

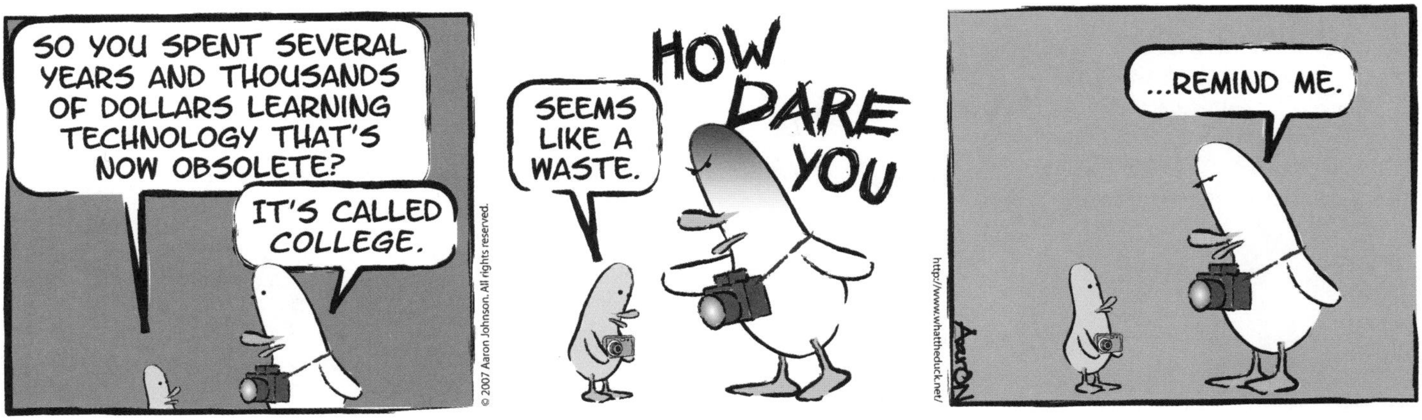
SO YOU SPENT SEVERAL YEARS AND THOUSANDS OF DOLLARS LEARNING TECHNOLOGY THAT'S NOW OBSOLETE?
IT'S CALLED COLLEGE.
© 2007 Aaron Johnson. All rights reserved.
SEEMS LIKE A WASTE.
HOW DARE YOU
...REMIND ME.
http://www.whattheduck.net/
AARON

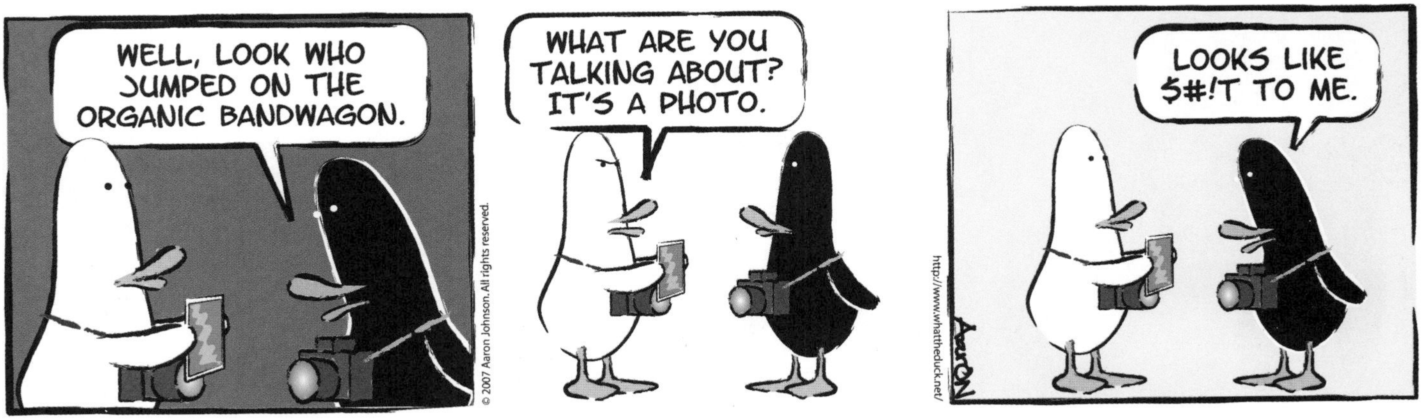
WELL, LOOK WHO JUMPED ON THE ORGANIC BANDWAGON.
© 2007 Aaron Johnson. All rights reserved.
WHAT ARE YOU TALKING ABOUT? IT'S A PHOTO.
LOOKS LIKE $#!T TO ME.
http://www.whattheduck.net/
AARON

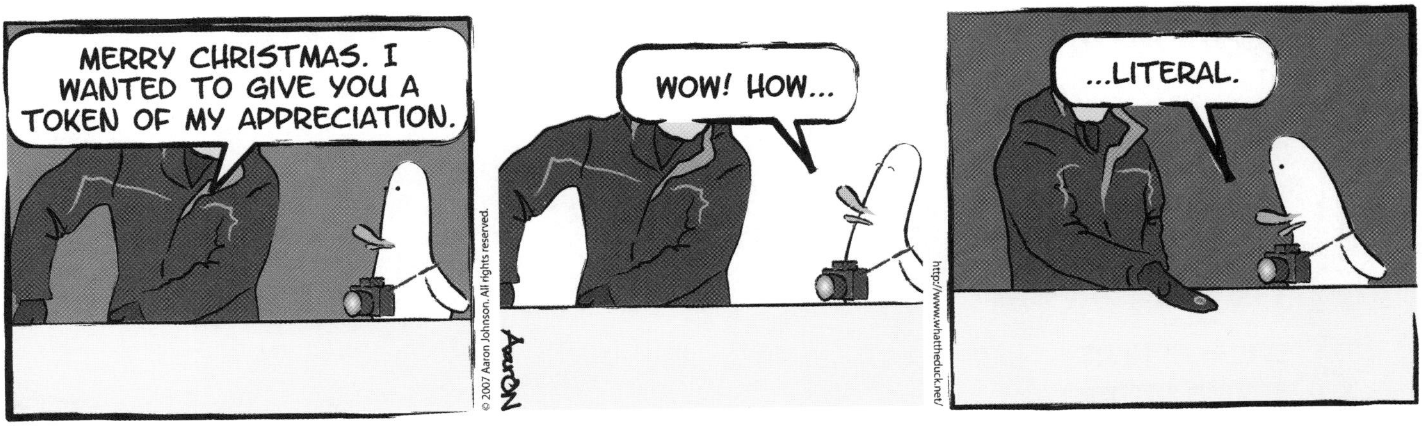
MERRY CHRISTMAS. I WANTED TO GIVE YOU A TOKEN OF MY APPRECIATION.
© 2007 Aaron Johnson. All rights reserved.
AARON
WOW! HOW...
...LITERAL.
http://www.whattheduck.net/

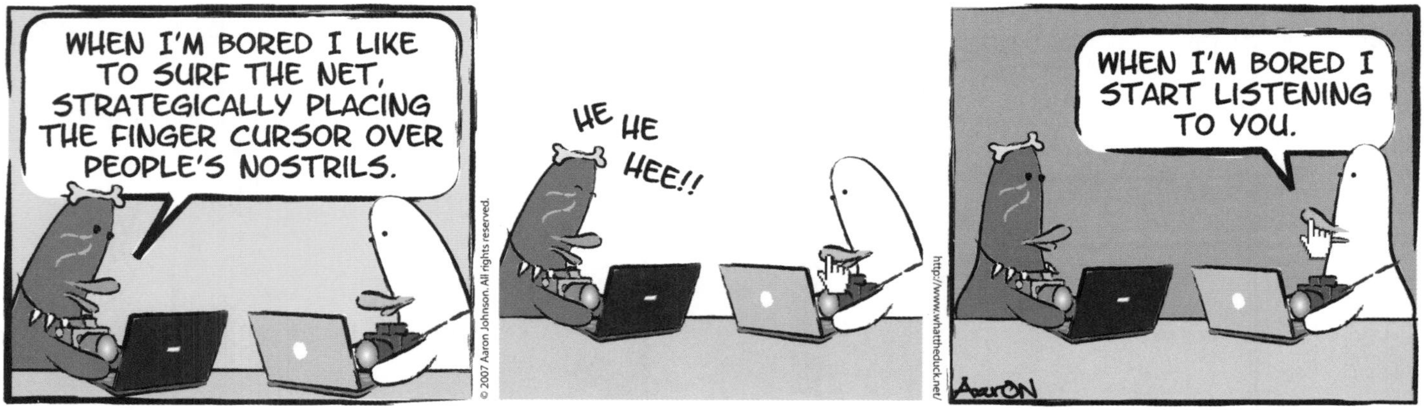
WHEN I'M BORED I LIKE TO SURF THE NET, STRATEGICALLY PLACING THE FINGER CURSOR OVER PEOPLE'S NOSTRILS.
HE HE HEE!!
WHEN I'M BORED I START LISTENING TO YOU.
AaronN

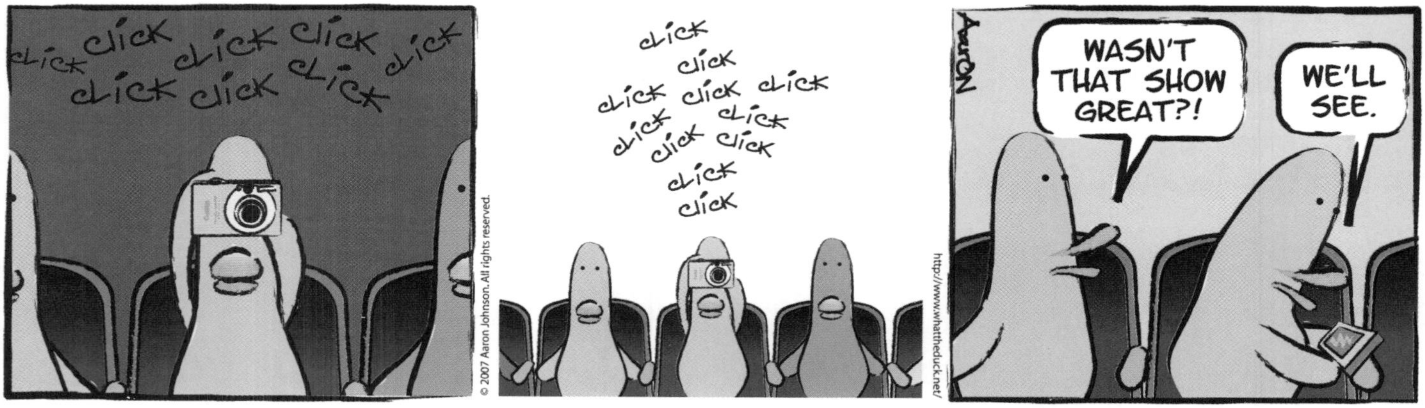
click click click click click click click click click
click click click click click click click click click click click
WASN'T THAT SHOW GREAT?!
WE'LL SEE.
AaronN

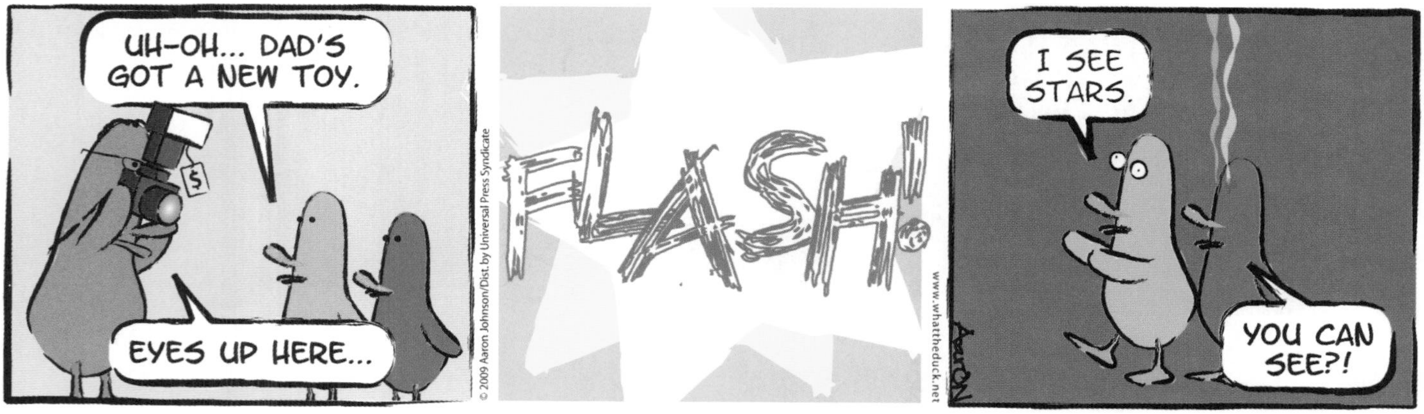
UH-OH... DAD'S GOT A NEW TOY.
EYES UP HERE...
FLASH!
I SEE STARS.
YOU CAN SEE?!
AaronN

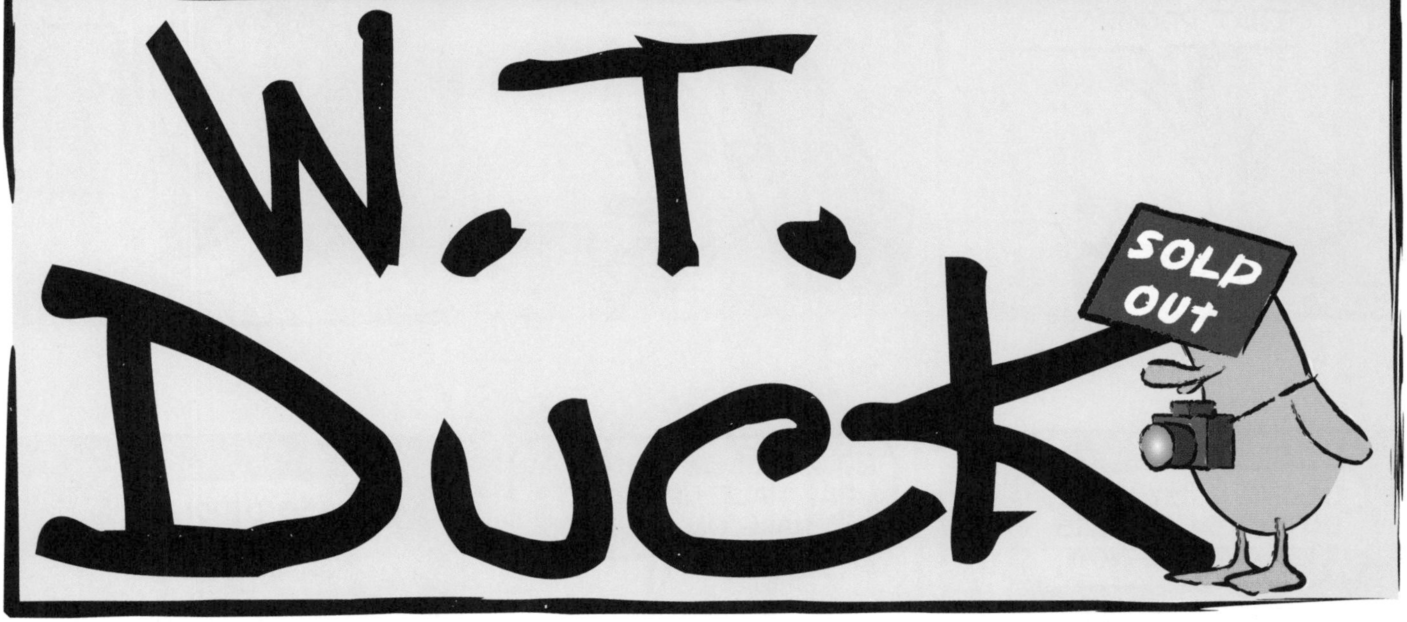
W.T. Duck
SOLD OUT

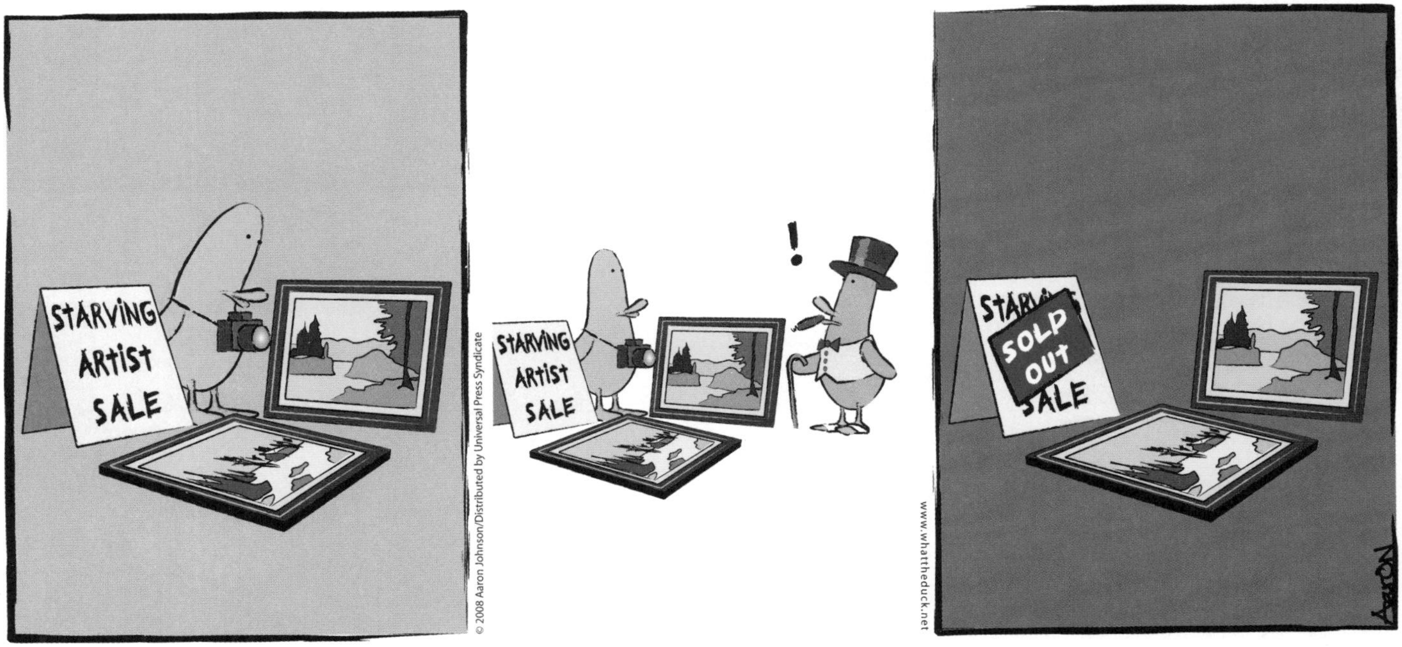
STARVING ARTIST SALE
STARVING ARTIST SALE
!
© 2008 Aaron Johnson/Distributed by Universal Press Syndicate
www.whattheduck.net
SOLD OUT
SALE
AARON

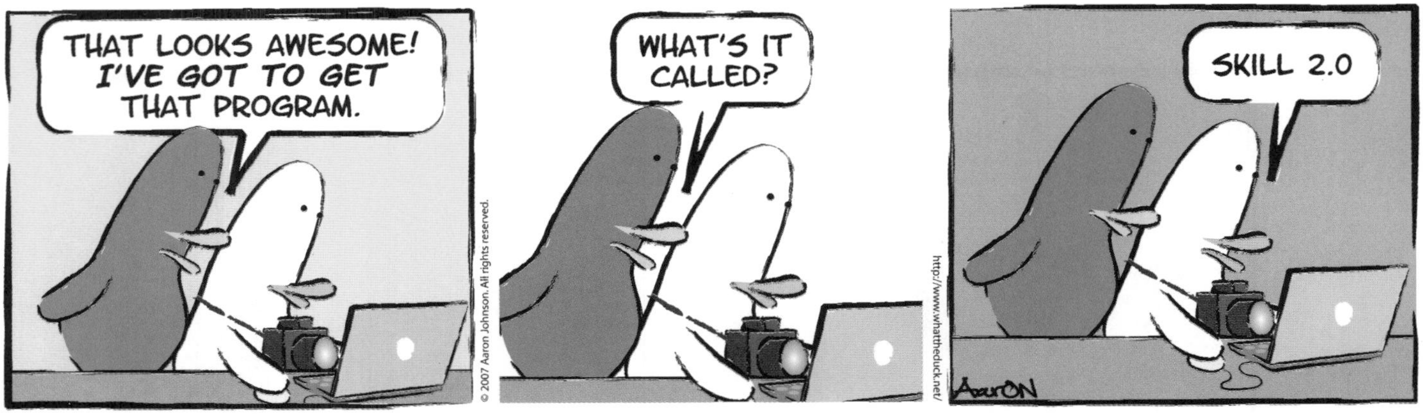
THAT LOOKS AWESOME! I'VE GOT TO GET THAT PROGRAM.
WHAT'S IT CALLED?
SKILL 2.0
© 2007 Aaron Johnson. All rights reserved.
http://www.whattheduck.net/
AarON

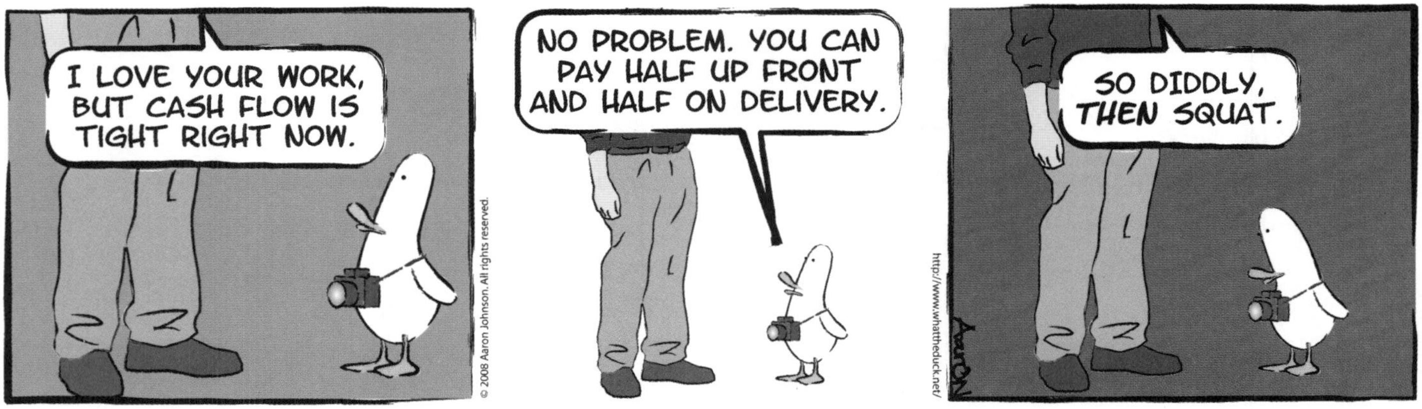
I LOVE YOUR WORK, BUT CASH FLOW IS TIGHT RIGHT NOW.
NO PROBLEM. YOU CAN PAY HALF UP FRONT AND HALF ON DELIVERY.
SO DIDDLY, THEN SQUAT.
© 2008 Aaron Johnson. All rights reserved.
http://www.whattheduck.net/
AarON

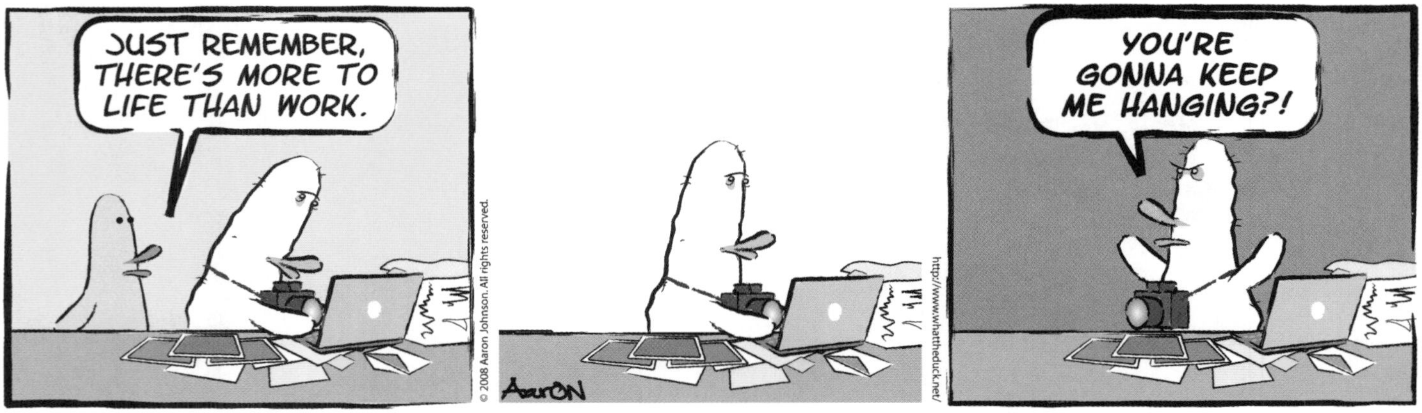
JUST REMEMBER, THERE'S MORE TO LIFE THAN WORK.
YOU'RE GONNA KEEP ME HANGING?!
© 2008 Aaron Johnson. All rights reserved.
http://www.whattheduck.net/
AarON

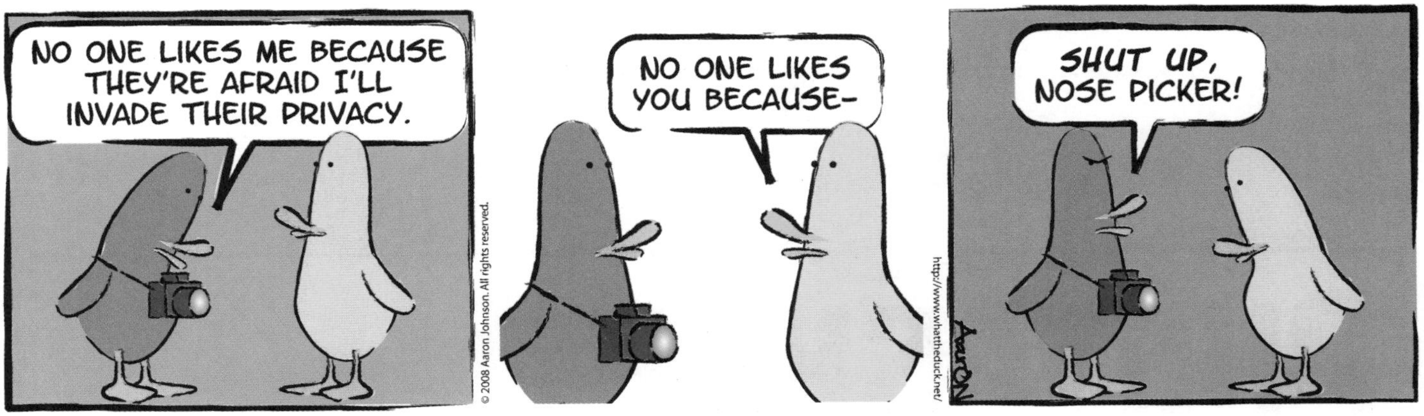
NO ONE LIKES ME BECAUSE THEY'RE AFRAID I'LL INVADE THEIR PRIVACY.
NO ONE LIKES YOU BECAUSE-
SHUT UP, NOSE PICKER!
© 2008 Aaron Johnson. All rights reserved.
http://www.whattheduck.net/
AARON

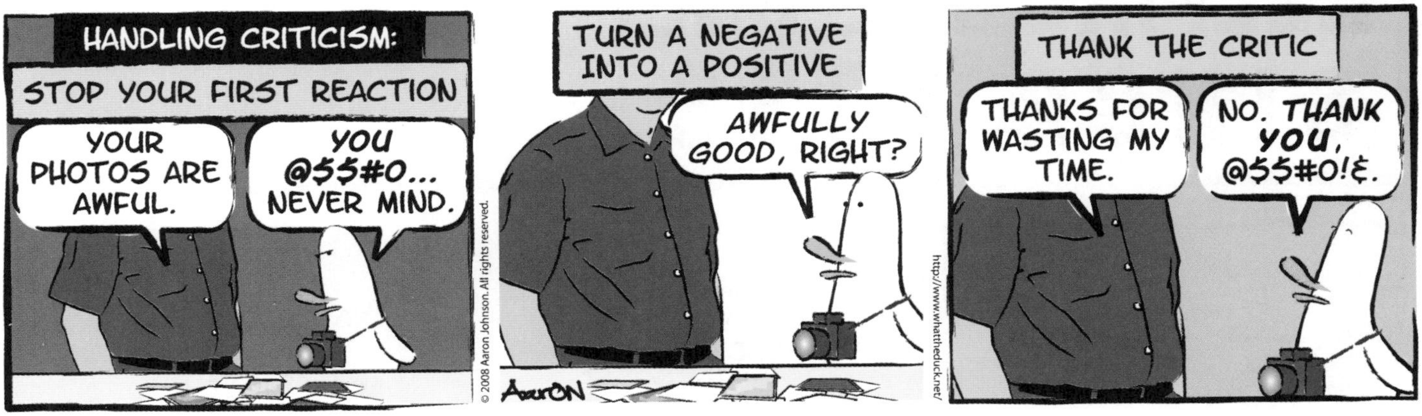
HANDLING CRITICISM:
STOP YOUR FIRST REACTION
YOUR PHOTOS ARE AWFUL.
YOU @$$#O... NEVER MIND.
TURN A NEGATIVE INTO A POSITIVE
AWFULLY GOOD, RIGHT?
THANK THE CRITIC
THANKS FOR WASTING MY TIME.
NO. THANK YOU, @$$#O!&.
© 2008 Aaron Johnson. All rights reserved.
http://www.whattheduck.net/
AARON

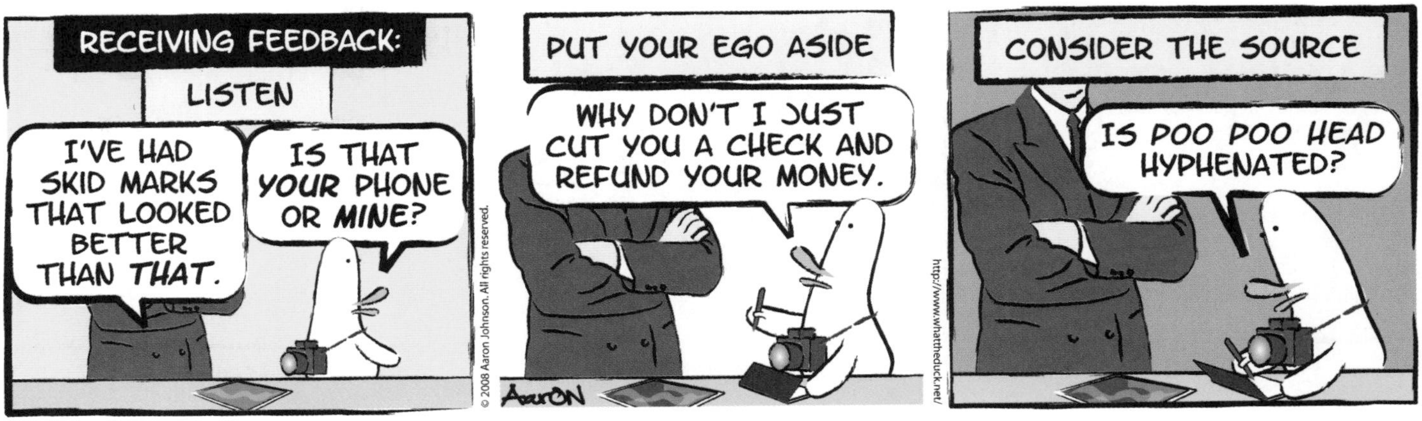
RECEIVING FEEDBACK:
LISTEN
I'VE HAD SKID MARKS THAT LOOKED BETTER THAN THAT.
IS THAT YOUR PHONE OR MINE?
PUT YOUR EGO ASIDE
WHY DON'T I JUST CUT YOU A CHECK AND REFUND YOUR MONEY.
CONSIDER THE SOURCE
IS POO POO HEAD HYPHENATED?
© 2008 Aaron Johnson. All rights reserved.
http://www.whattheduck.net/
AARON

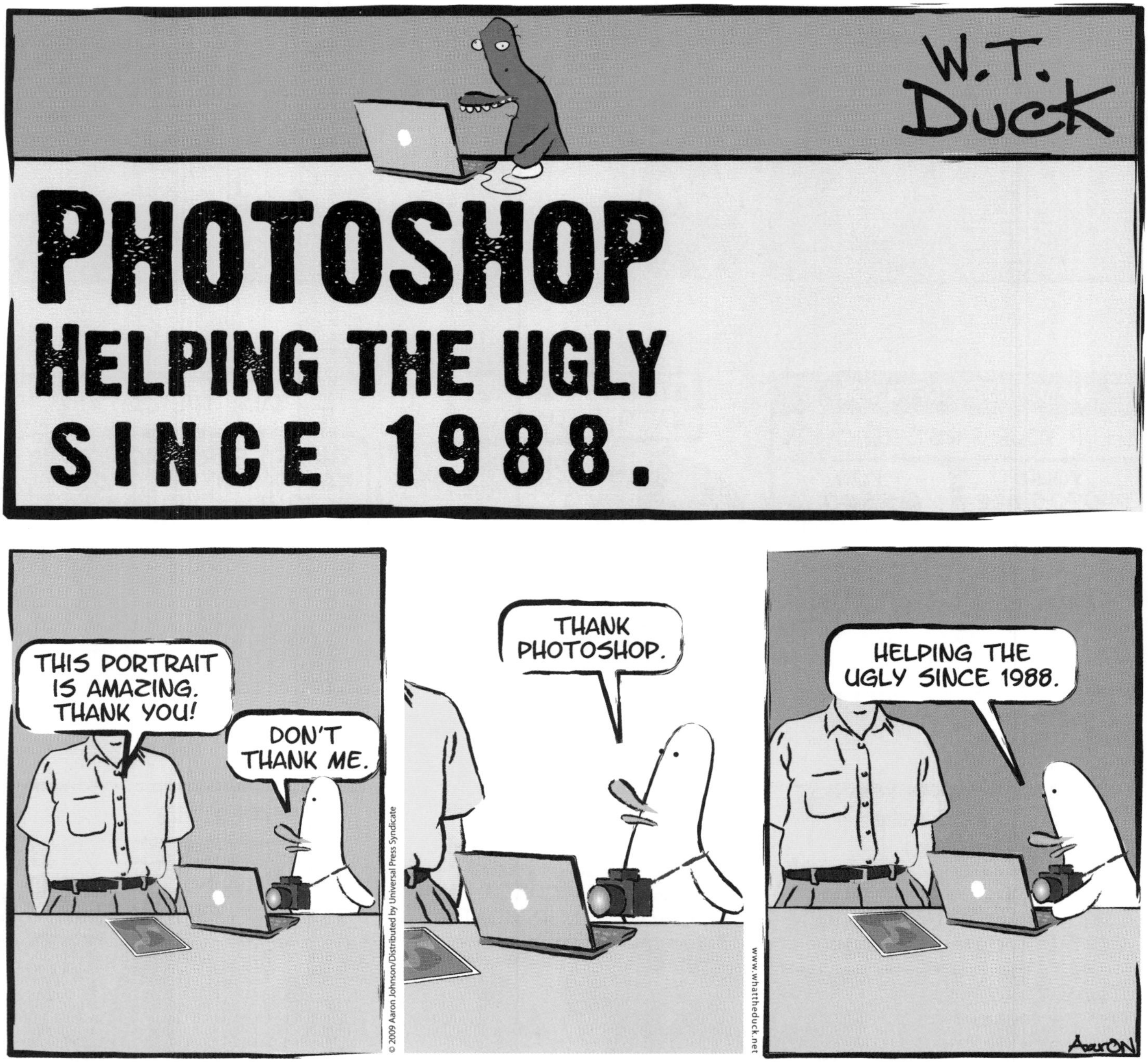
W.T. Duck
PHOTOSHOP
HELPING THE UGLY
SINCE 1988.
THIS PORTRAIT IS AMAZING. THANK YOU!
DON'T THANK ME.
© 2009 Aaron Johnson/Distributed by Universal Press Syndicate
THANK PHOTOSHOP.
www.whattheduck.net
HELPING THE UGLY SINCE 1988.
AaRON

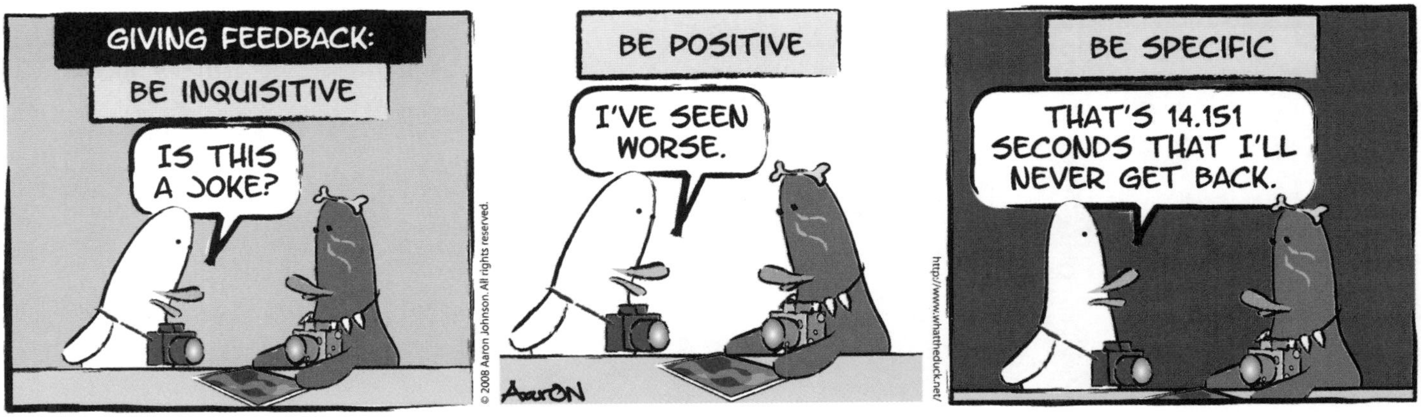
GIVING FEEDBACK:
BE INQUISITIVE
IS THIS A JOKE?
© 2008 Aaron Johnson. All rights reserved.
BE POSITIVE
I'VE SEEN WORSE.
AARON
BE SPECIFIC
THAT'S 14.151 SECONDS THAT I'LL NEVER GET BACK.
http://www.whattheduck.net/

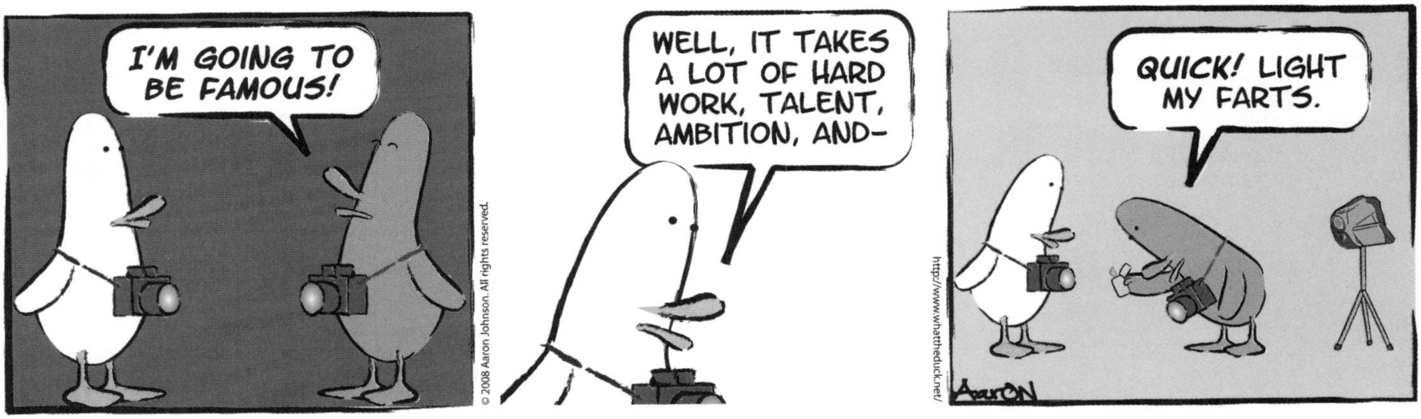
I'M GOING TO BE FAMOUS!
© 2008 Aaron Johnson. All rights reserved.
WELL, IT TAKES A LOT OF HARD WORK, TALENT, AMBITION, AND-
http://www.whattheduck.net/
QUICK! LIGHT MY FARTS.
AARON

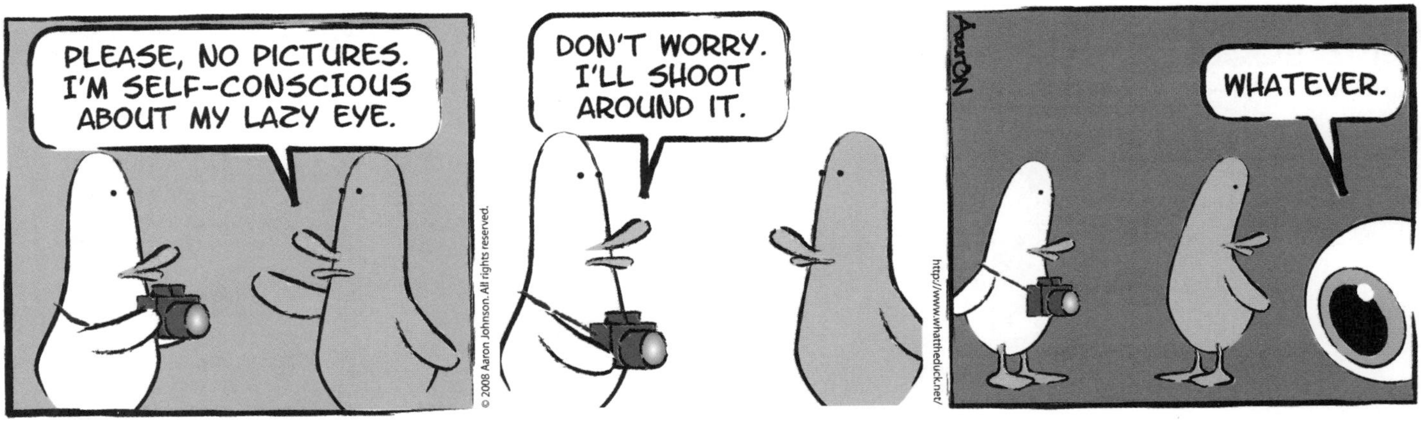
PLEASE, NO PICTURES. I'M SELF-CONSCIOUS ABOUT MY LAZY EYE.
© 2008 Aaron Johnson. All rights reserved.
DON'T WORRY. I'LL SHOOT AROUND IT.
http://www.whattheduck.net/
AARON
WHATEVER.

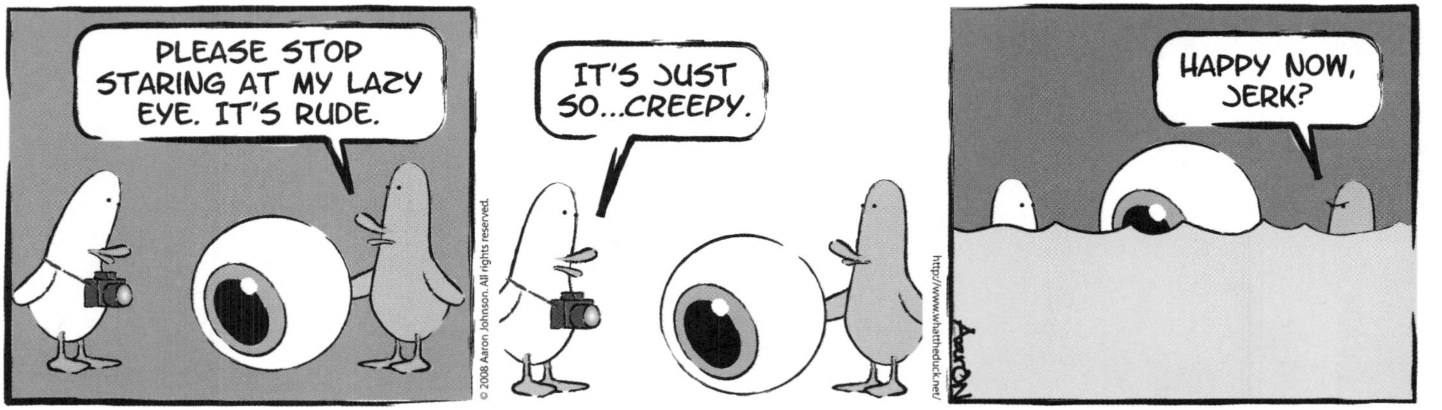
PLEASE STOP STARING AT MY LAZY EYE. IT'S RUDE.
IT'S JUST SO...CREEPY.
HAPPY NOW, JERK?
© 2008 Aaron Johnson. All rights reserved.
http://www.whattheduck.net/
AARON

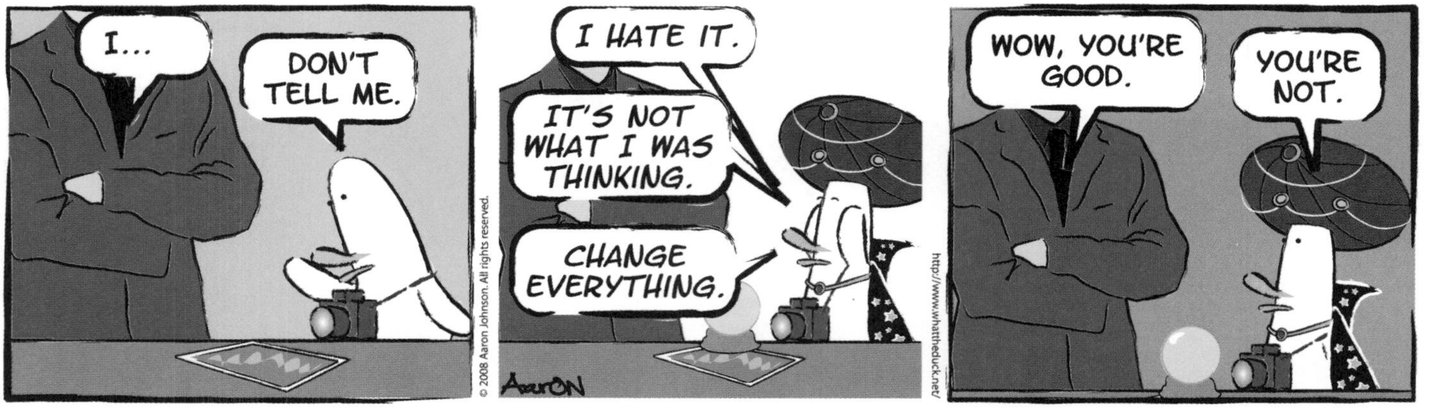
I...
DON'T TELL ME.
I HATE IT.
IT'S NOT WHAT I WAS THINKING.
CHANGE EVERYTHING.
WOW, YOU'RE GOOD.
YOU'RE NOT.
© 2008 Aaron Johnson. All rights reserved.
http://www.whattheduck.net/
AARON

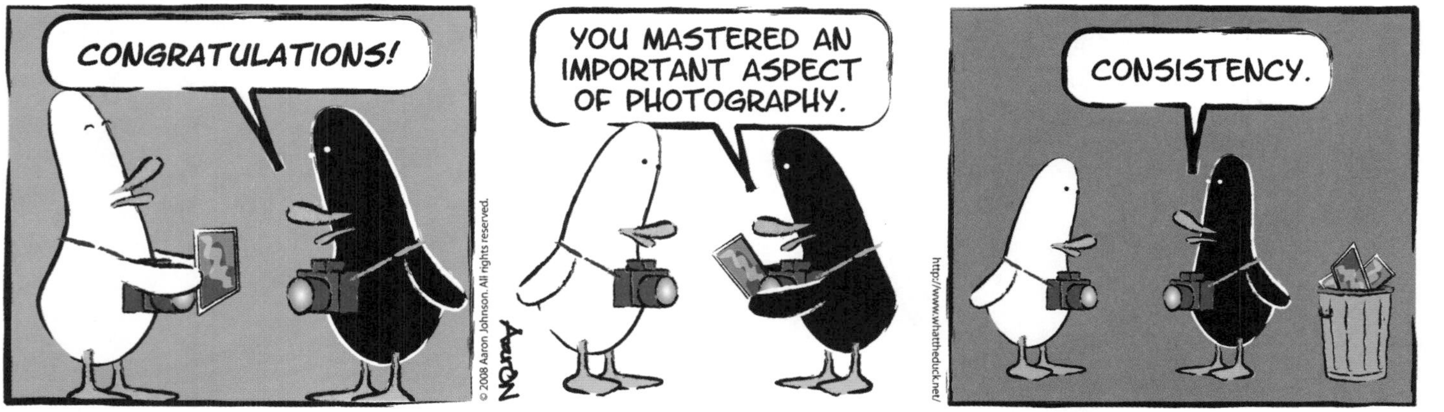
CONGRATULATIONS!
YOU MASTERED AN IMPORTANT ASPECT OF PHOTOGRAPHY.
CONSISTENCY.
© 2008 Aaron Johnson. All rights reserved.
http://www.whattheduck.net/
AARON

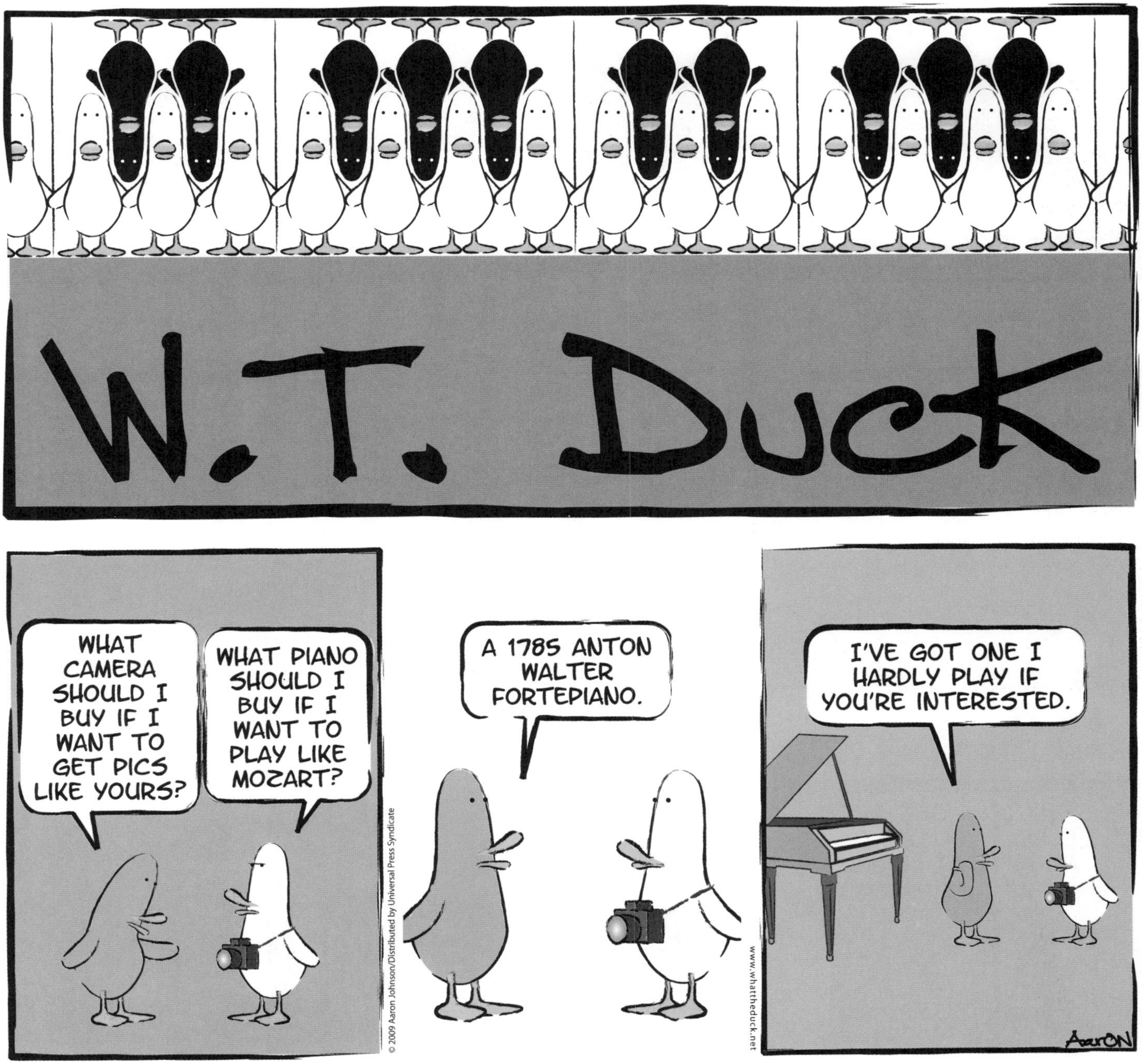
W.T. DUCK
WHAT CAMERA SHOULD I BUY IF I WANT TO GET PICS LIKE YOURS?
WHAT PIANO SHOULD I BUY IF I WANT TO PLAY LIKE MOZART?
© 2009 Aaron Johnson/Distributed by Universal Press Syndicate
A 1785 ANTON WALTER FORTEPIANO.
www.whattheduck.net
I'VE GOT ONE I HARDLY PLAY IF YOU'RE INTERESTED.
AARON

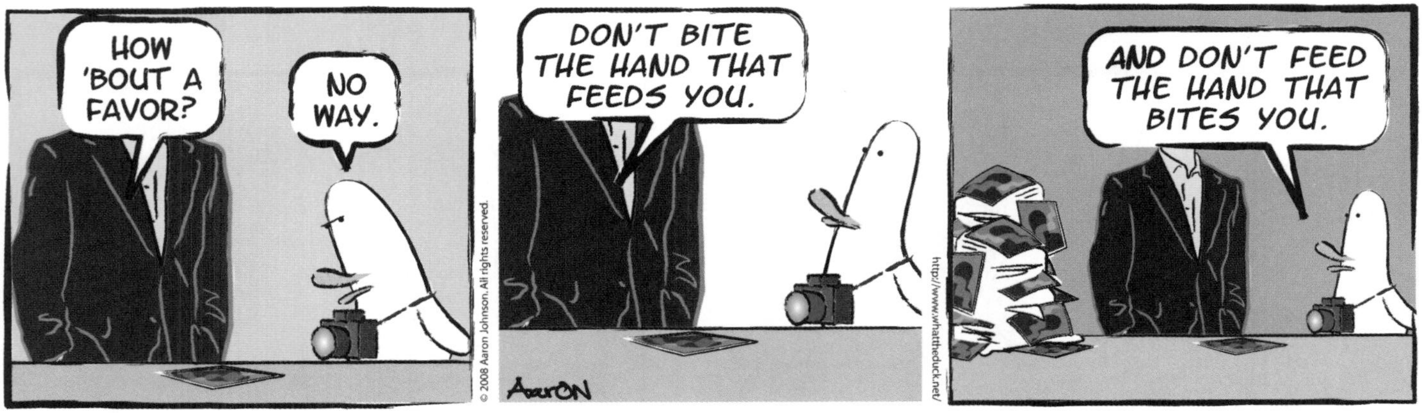
HOW 'BOUT A FAVOR?
NO WAY.
© 2008 Aaron Johnson. All rights reserved.
DON'T BITE THE HAND THAT FEEDS YOU.
AaronN
http://www.whattheduck.net/
AND DON'T FEED THE HAND THAT BITES YOU.

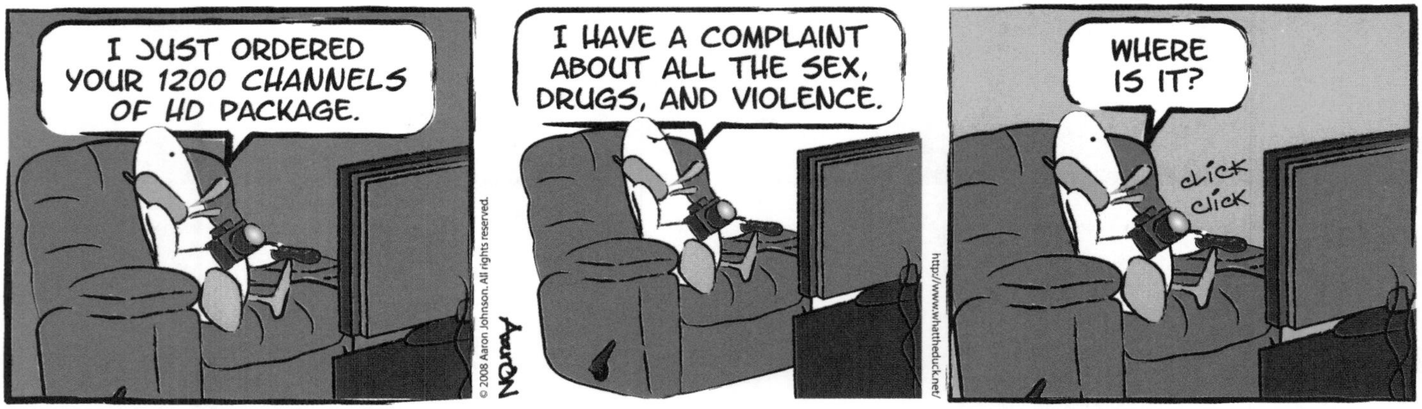
I JUST ORDERED YOUR 1200 CHANNELS OF HD PACKAGE.
© 2008 Aaron Johnson. All rights reserved.
AaronN
I HAVE A COMPLAINT ABOUT ALL THE SEX, DRUGS, AND VIOLENCE.
http://www.whattheduck.net/
WHERE IS IT?
click click

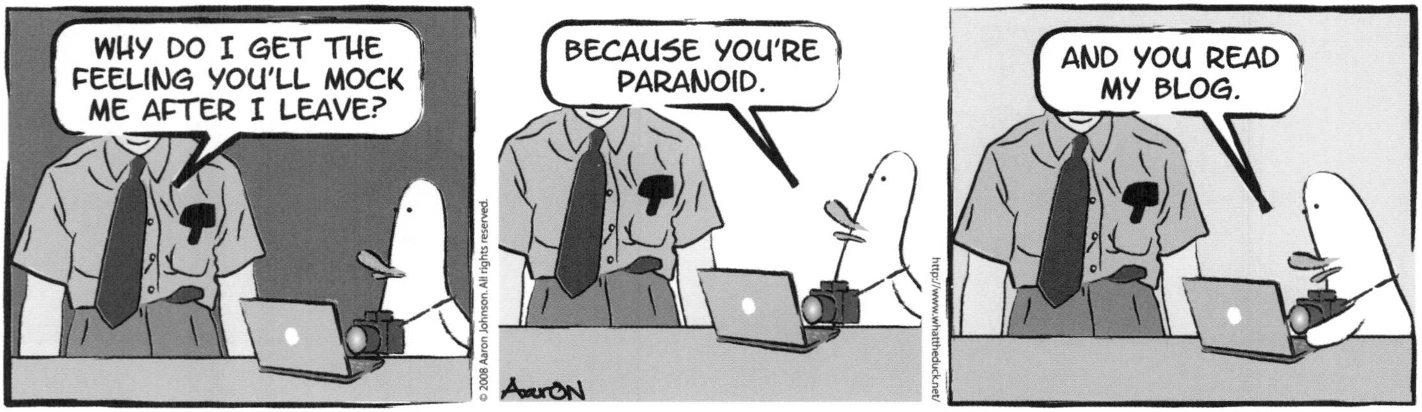
WHY DO I GET THE FEELING YOU'LL MOCK ME AFTER I LEAVE?
© 2008 Aaron Johnson. All rights reserved.
BECAUSE YOU'RE PARANOID.
AaronN
http://www.whattheduck.net/
AND YOU READ MY BLOG.

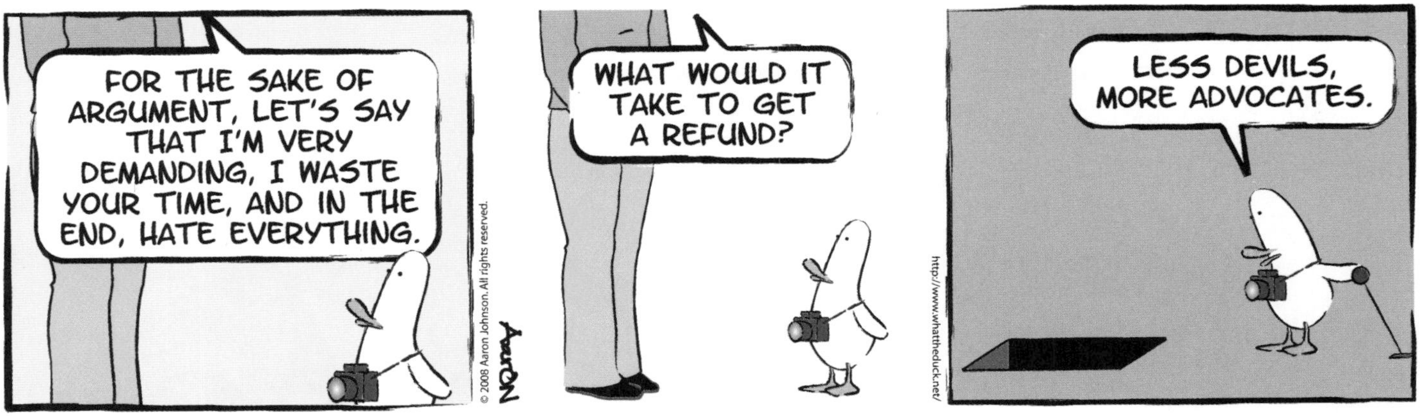
FOR THE SAKE OF ARGUMENT, LET'S SAY THAT I'M VERY DEMANDING, I WASTE YOUR TIME, AND IN THE END, HATE EVERYTHING.
WHAT WOULD IT TAKE TO GET A REFUND?
LESS DEVILS, MORE ADVOCATES.
© 2008 Aaron Johnson. All rights reserved.
http://www.whattheduck.net/

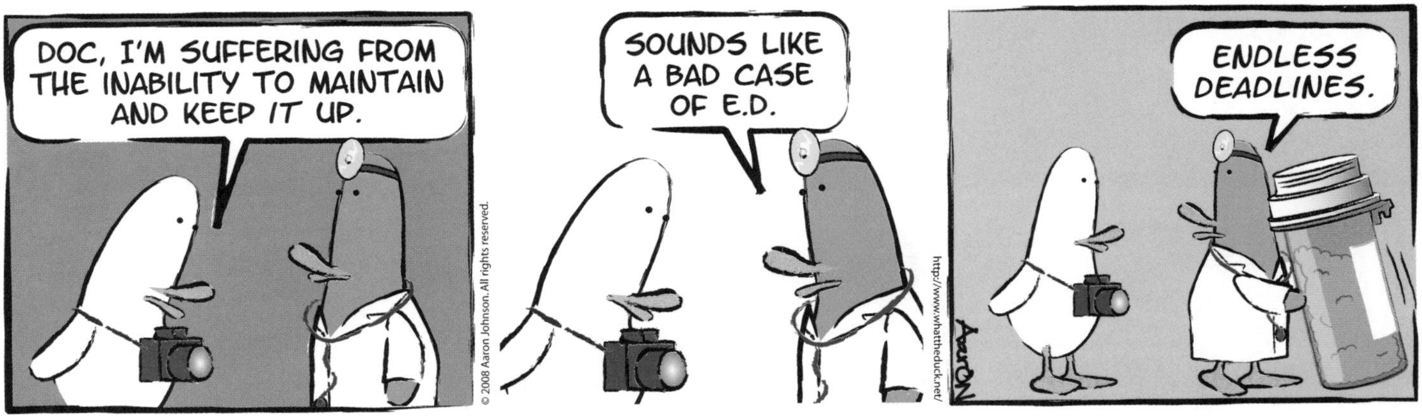
DOC, I'M SUFFERING FROM THE INABILITY TO MAINTAIN AND KEEP IT UP.
SOUNDS LIKE A BAD CASE OF E.D.
ENDLESS DEADLINES.
© 2008 Aaron Johnson. All rights reserved.
http://www.whattheduck.net/

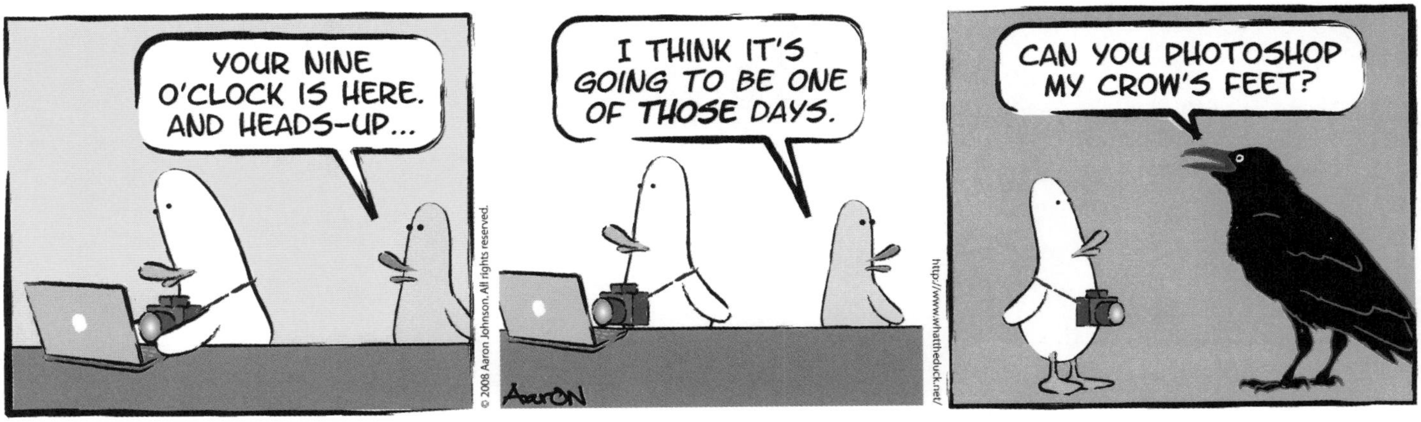
YOUR NINE O'CLOCK IS HERE. AND HEADS-UP...
I THINK IT'S GOING TO BE ONE OF THOSE DAYS.
CAN YOU PHOTOSHOP MY CROW'S FEET?
© 2008 Aaron Johnson. All rights reserved.
http://www.whattheduck.net/

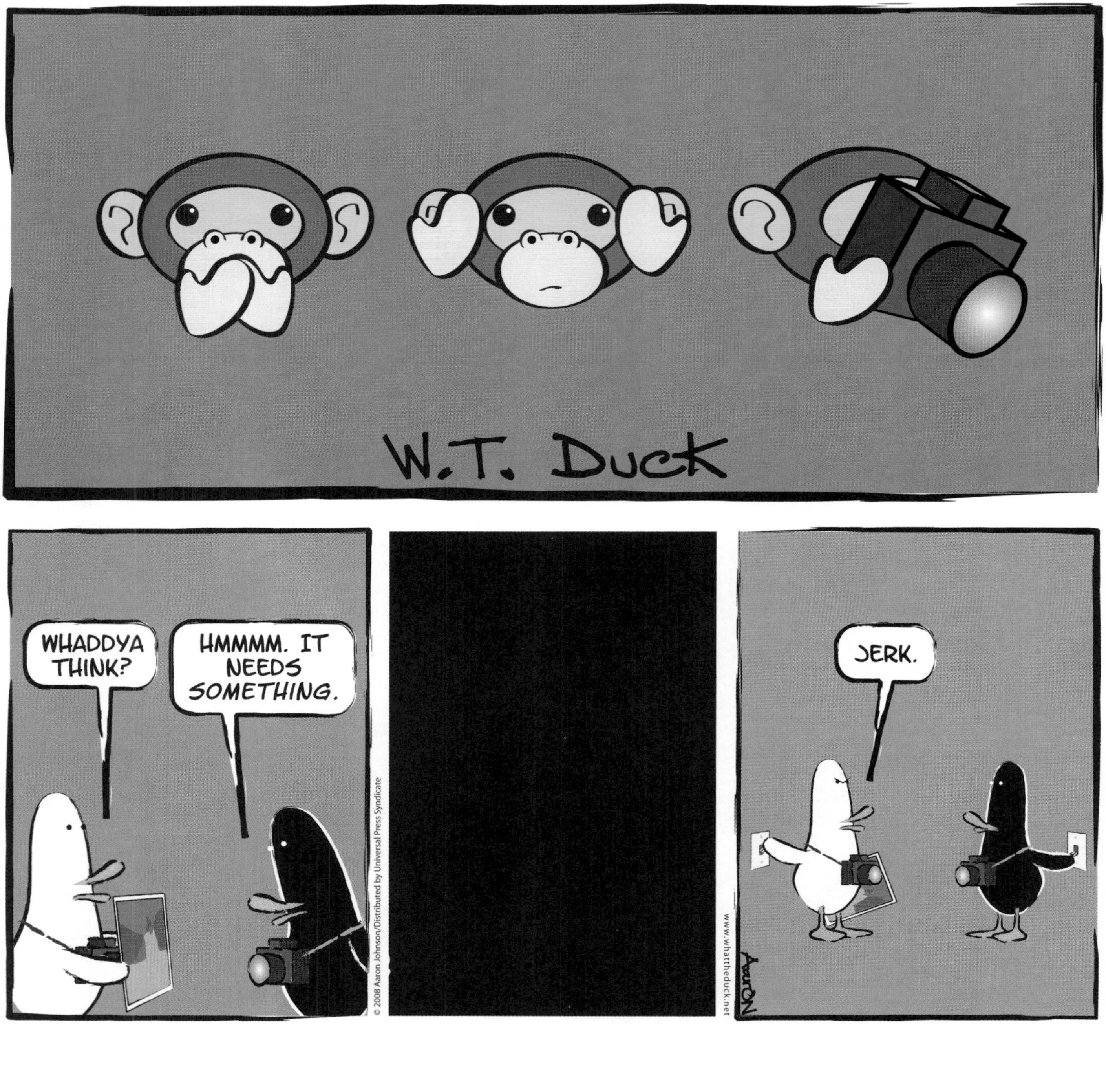
W.T. Duck
WHADDYA THINK?
HMMMM. IT NEEDS SOMETHING.
© 2008 Aaron Johnson/Distributed by Universal Press Syndicate
www.whattheduck.net
JERK.
AARON

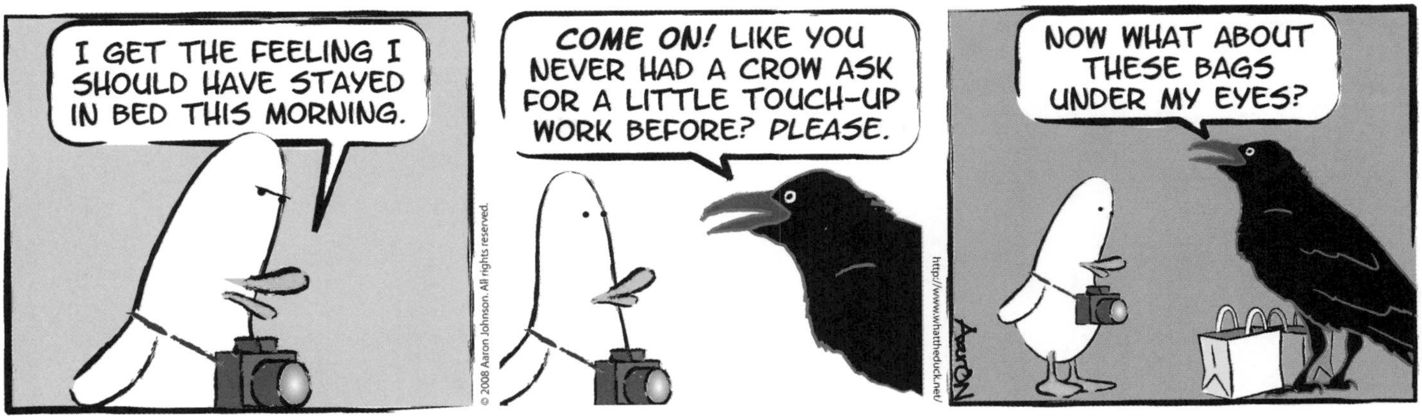
I GET THE FEELING I SHOULD HAVE STAYED IN BED THIS MORNING.
COME ON! LIKE YOU NEVER HAD A CROW ASK FOR A LITTLE TOUCH-UP WORK BEFORE? PLEASE.
NOW WHAT ABOUT THESE BAGS UNDER MY EYES?
© 2008 Aaron Johnson. All rights reserved.
http://www.whattheduck.net/
AarON

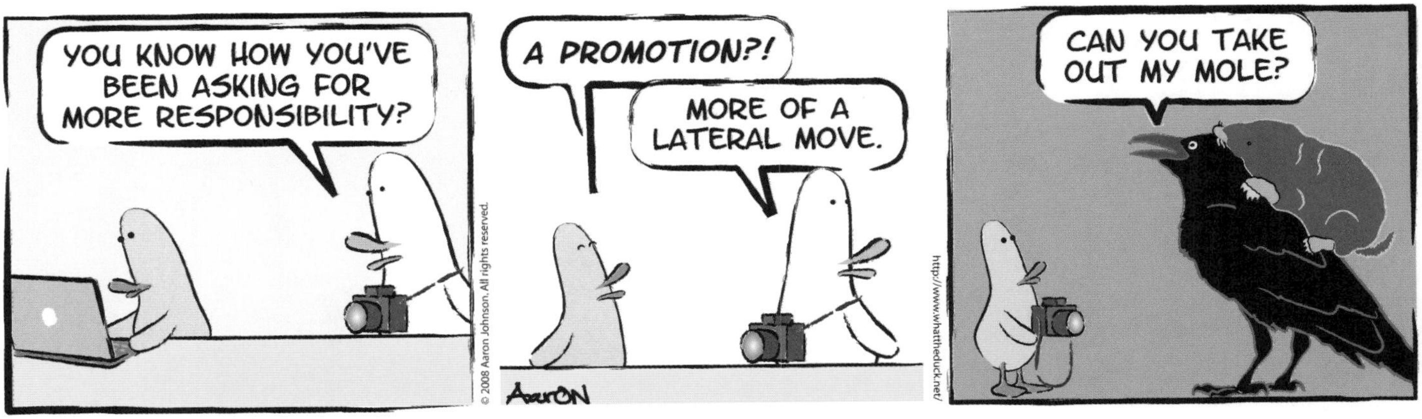
YOU KNOW HOW YOU'VE BEEN ASKING FOR MORE RESPONSIBILITY?
A PROMOTION?!
MORE OF A LATERAL MOVE.
CAN YOU TAKE OUT MY MOLE?
© 2008 Aaron Johnson. All rights reserved.
http://www.whattheduck.net/
AarON

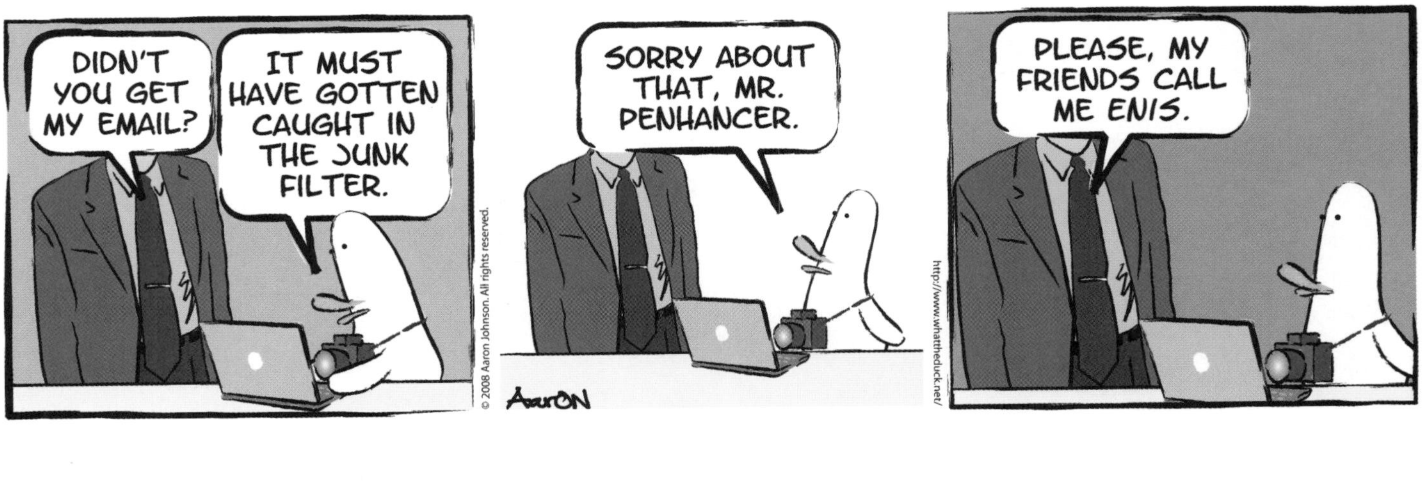
DIDN'T YOU GET MY EMAIL?
IT MUST HAVE GOTTEN CAUGHT IN THE JUNK FILTER.
SORRY ABOUT THAT, MR. PENHANCER.
PLEASE, MY FRIENDS CALL ME ENIS.
© 2008 Aaron Johnson. All rights reserved.
http://www.whattheduck.net/
AarON

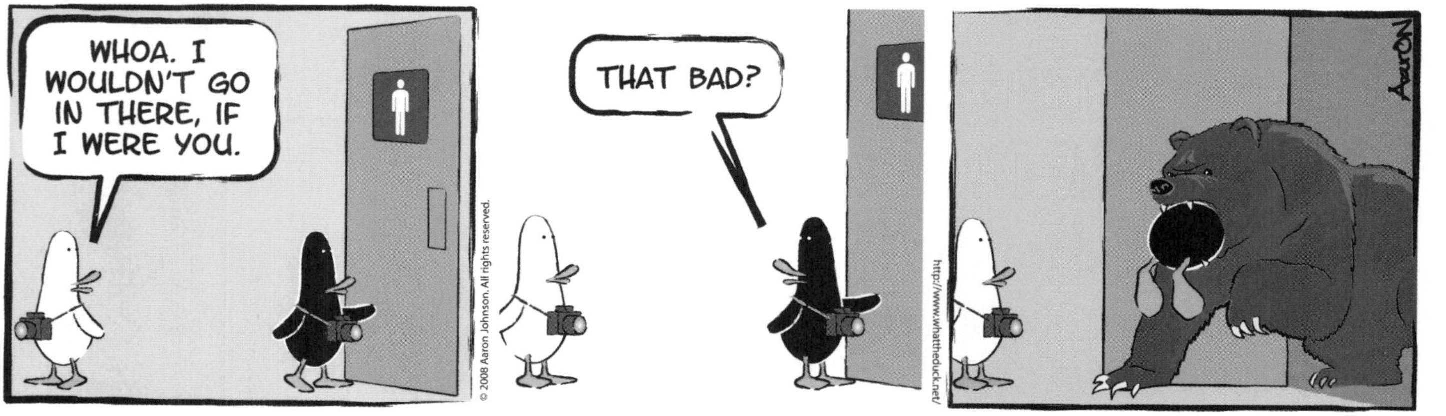
WHOA. I WOULDN'T GO IN THERE, IF I WERE YOU.
© 2008 Aaron Johnson. All rights reserved.
THAT BAD?
http://www.whattheduck.net/
AarON

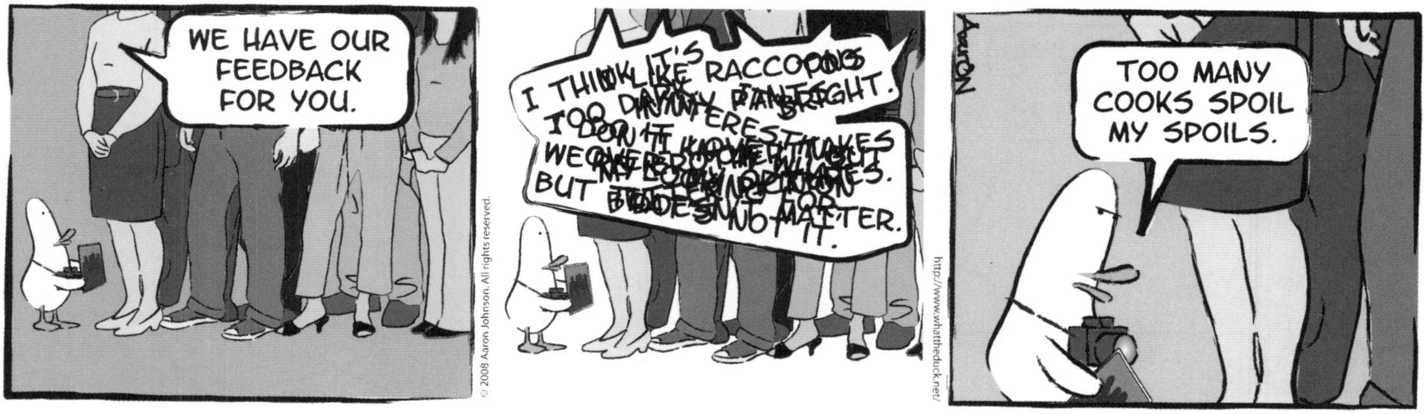
WE HAVE OUR FEEDBACK FOR YOU.
© 2008 Aaron Johnson. All rights reserved.
http://www.whattheduck.net/
AarON
TOO MANY COOKS SPOIL MY SPOILS.

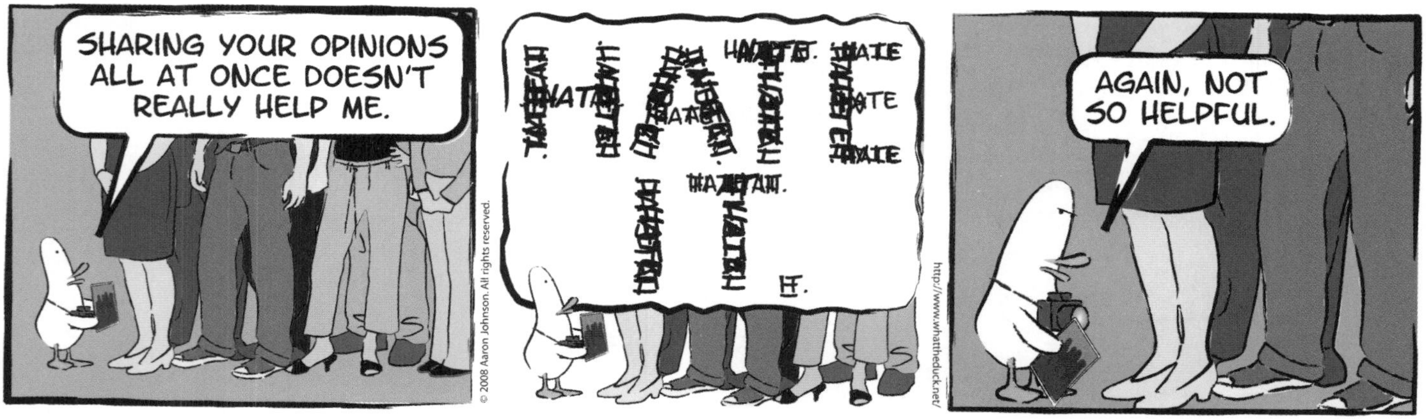
SHARING YOUR OPINIONS ALL AT ONCE DOESN'T REALLY HELP ME.
© 2008 Aaron Johnson. All rights reserved.
HATE IT
http://www.whattheduck.net/
AGAIN, NOT SO HELPFUL.

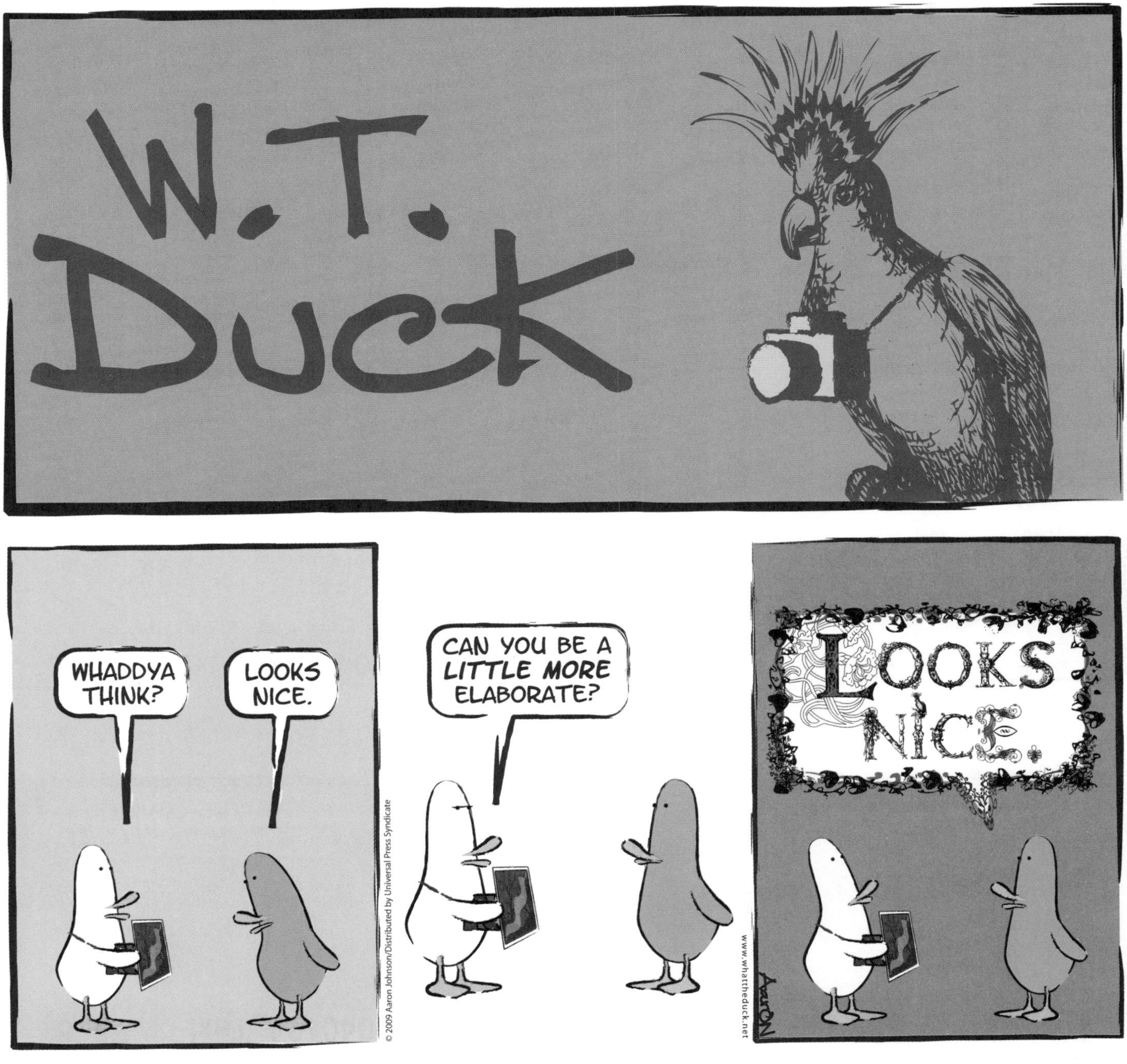
W.T. DUCK
WHADDYA THINK?
LOOKS NICE.
© 2009 Aaron Johnson/Distributed by Universal Press Syndicate
CAN YOU BE A *LITTLE MORE* ELABORATE?
www.whattheduck.net
AARON
LOOKS NICE.

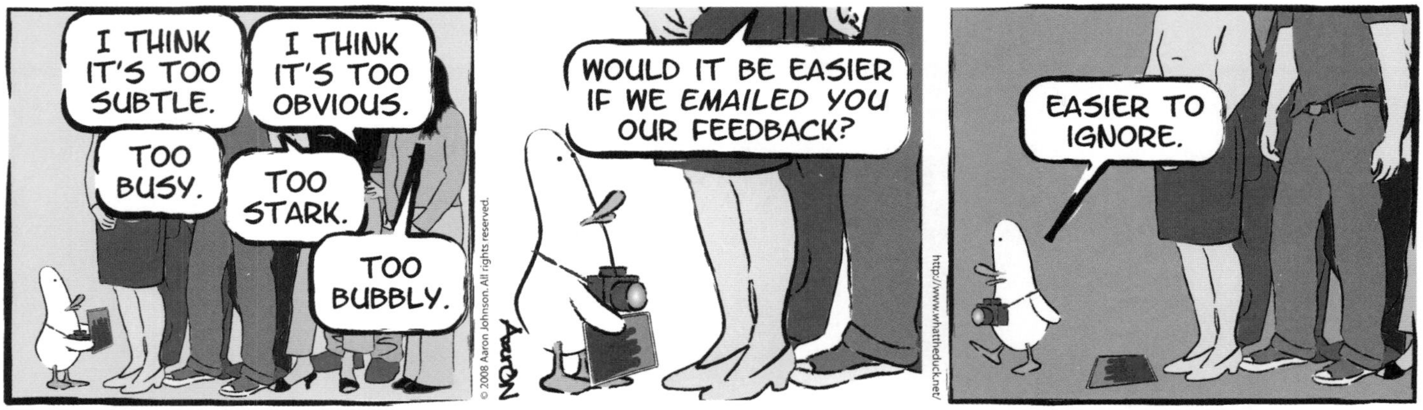
I THINK IT'S TOO SUBTLE.
I THINK IT'S TOO OBVIOUS.
TOO BUSY.
TOO STARK.
TOO BUBBLY.
WOULD IT BE EASIER IF WE EMAILED YOU OUR FEEDBACK?
EASIER TO IGNORE.
© 2008 Aaron Johnson. All rights reserved.
AARON
http://www.whattheduck.net/

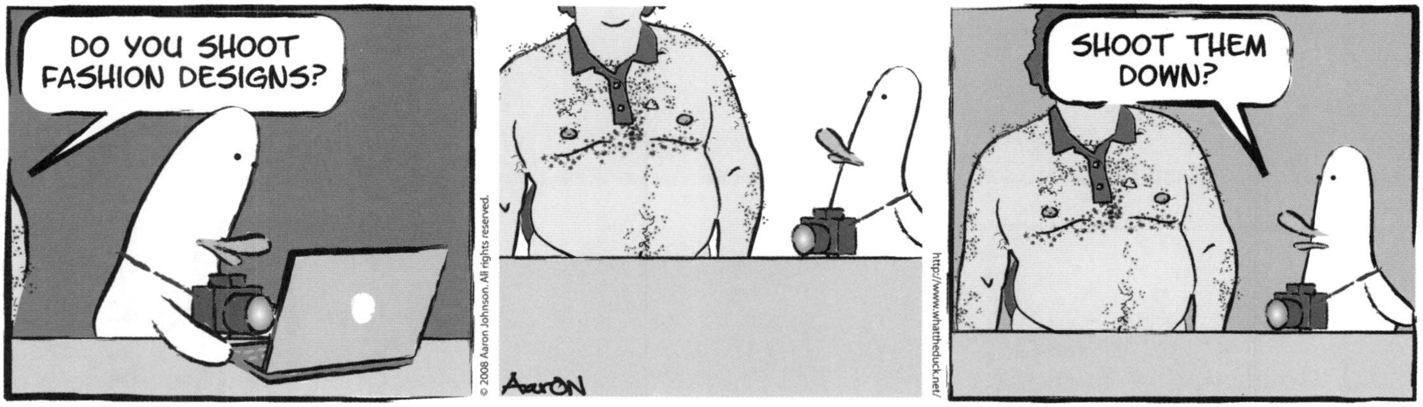
DO YOU SHOOT FASHION DESIGNS?
SHOOT THEM DOWN?
© 2008 Aaron Johnson. All rights reserved.
AARON
http://www.whattheduck.net/

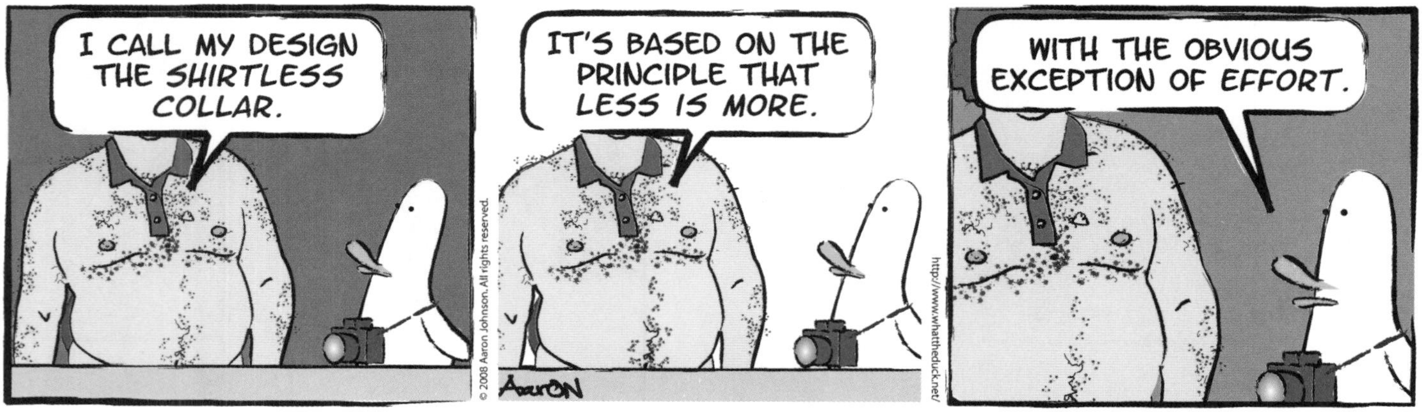
I CALL MY DESIGN THE SHIRTLESS COLLAR.
IT'S BASED ON THE PRINCIPLE THAT LESS IS MORE.
WITH THE OBVIOUS EXCEPTION OF EFFORT.
© 2008 Aaron Johnson. All rights reserved.
AARON
http://www.whattheduck.net/

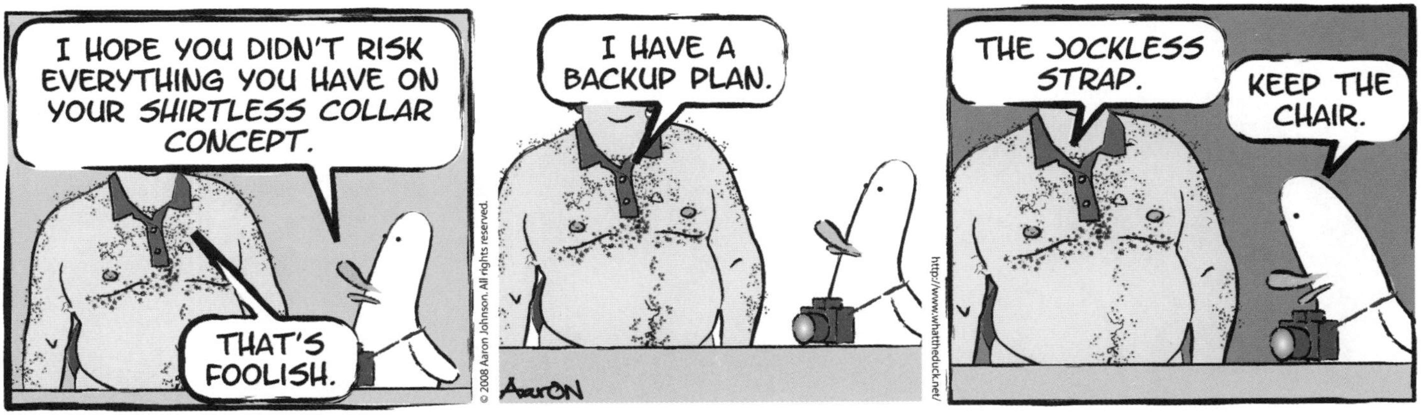
I HOPE YOU DIDN'T RISK EVERYTHING YOU HAVE ON YOUR SHIRTLESS COLLAR CONCEPT.
THAT'S FOOLISH.
I HAVE A BACKUP PLAN.
THE JOCKLESS STRAP.
KEEP THE CHAIR.
© 2008 Aaron Johnson. All rights reserved.
http://www.whattheduck.net/

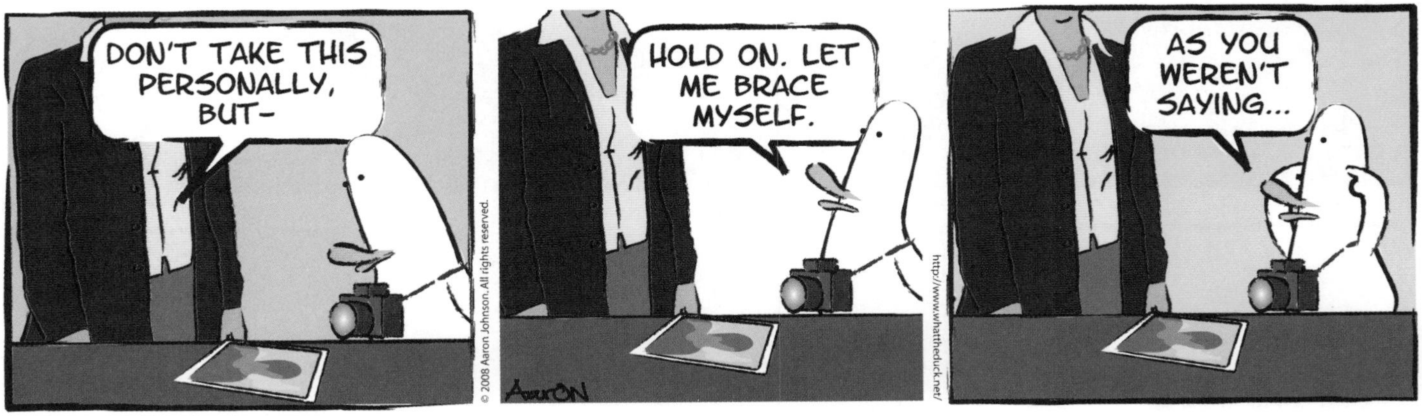
DON'T TAKE THIS PERSONALLY, BUT-
HOLD ON. LET ME BRACE MYSELF.
AS YOU WEREN'T SAYING...
© 2008 Aaron Johnson. All rights reserved.
http://www.whattheduck.net/

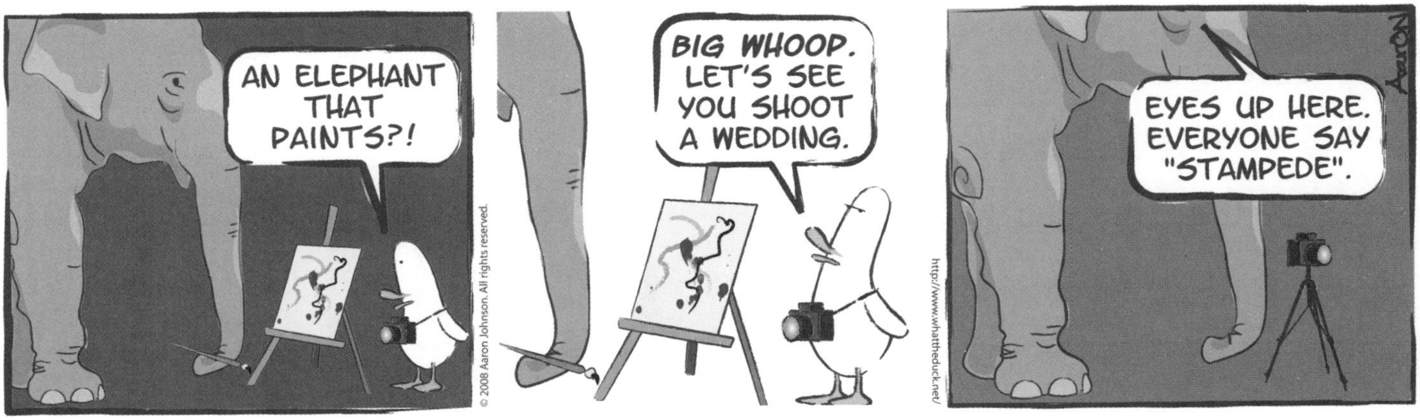
AN ELEPHANT THAT PAINTS?!
BIG WHOOP. LET'S SEE YOU SHOOT A WEDDING.
EYES UP HERE. EVERYONE SAY "STAMPEDE".
© 2008 Aaron Johnson. All rights reserved.
http://www.whattheduck.net/

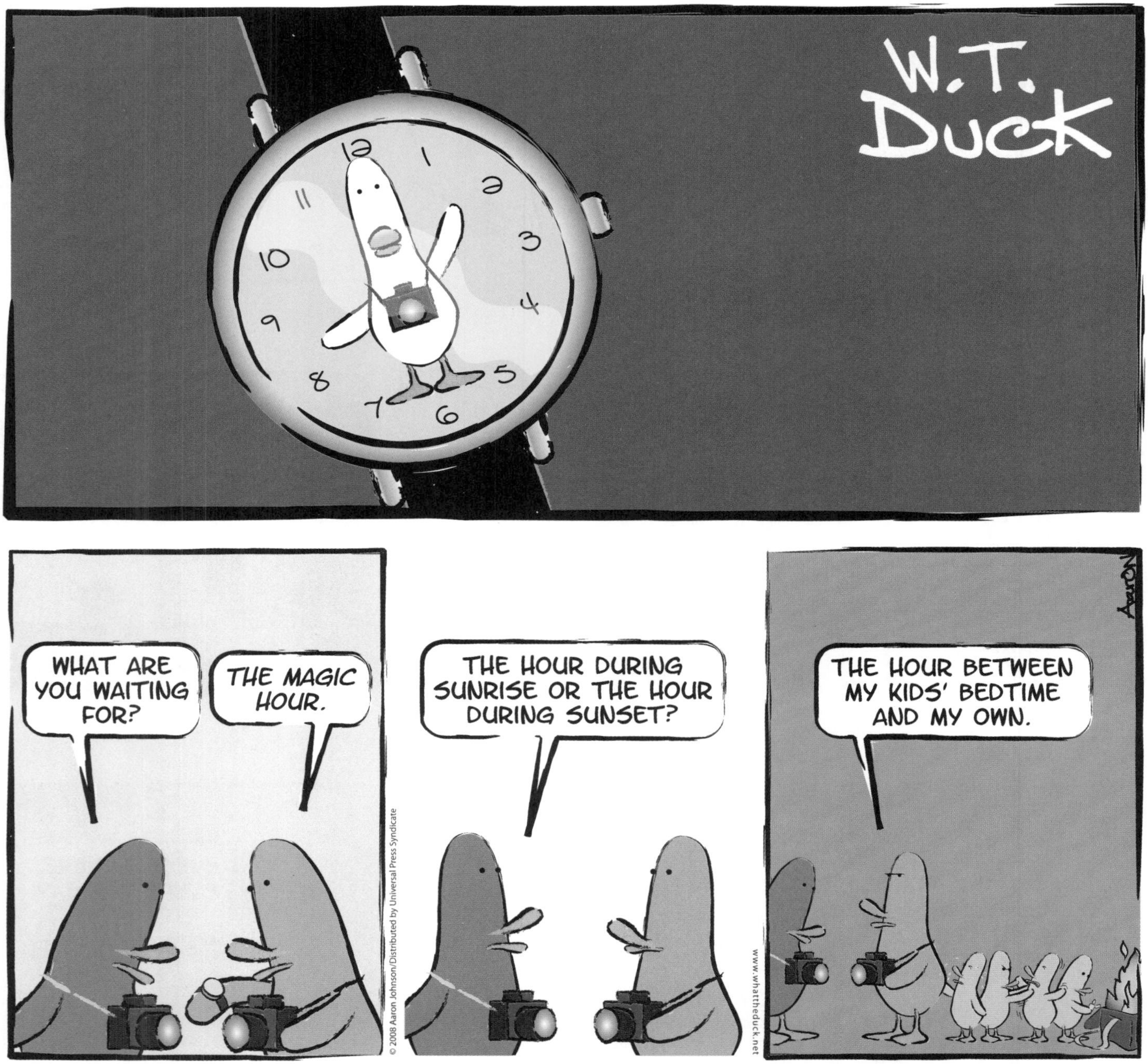
W.T. DUCK
WHAT ARE YOU WAITING FOR?
THE MAGIC HOUR.
THE HOUR DURING SUNRISE OR THE HOUR DURING SUNSET?
THE HOUR BETWEEN MY KIDS' BEDTIME AND MY OWN.
AARON
© 2008 Aaron Johnson/Distributed by Universal Press Syndicate
www.whattheduck.net

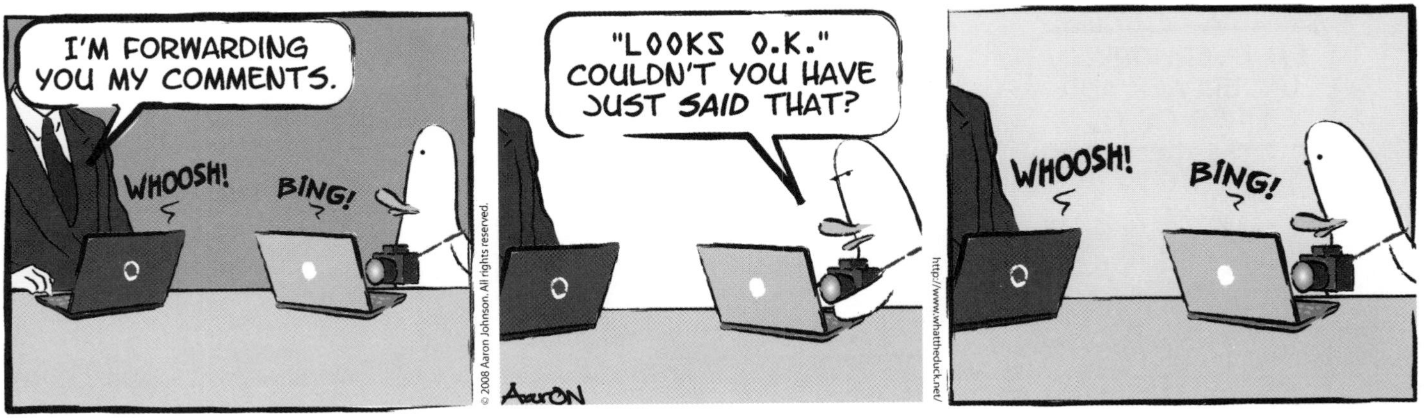
I'M FORWARDING YOU MY COMMENTS.
WHOOSH!
BING!
"LOOKS O.K." COULDN'T YOU HAVE JUST SAID THAT?
WHOOSH!
BING!
© 2008 Aaron Johnson. All rights reserved.
http://www.whattheduck.net/

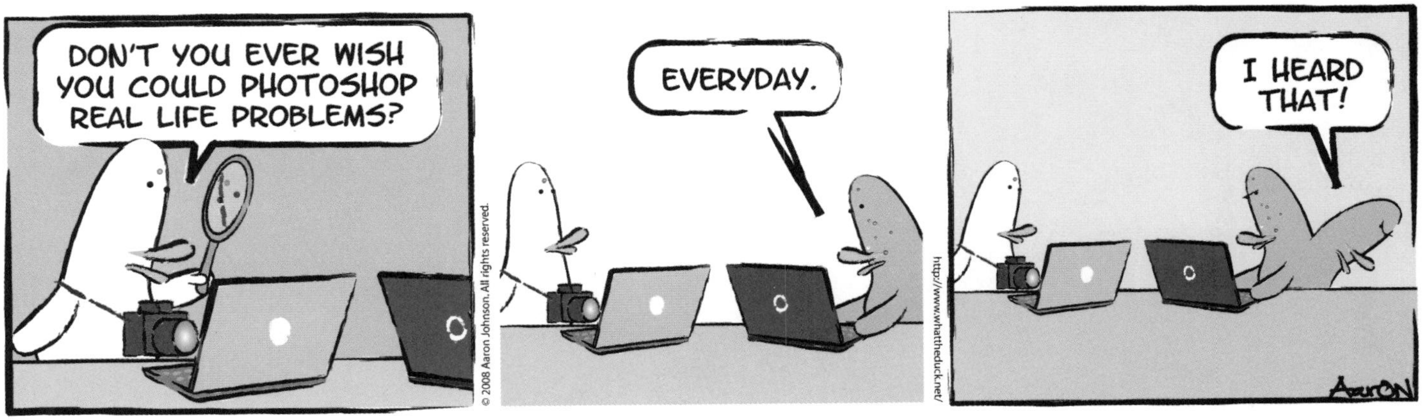
DON'T YOU EVER WISH YOU COULD PHOTOSHOP REAL LIFE PROBLEMS?
EVERYDAY.
I HEARD THAT!
© 2008 Aaron Johnson. All rights reserved.
http://www.whattheduck.net/

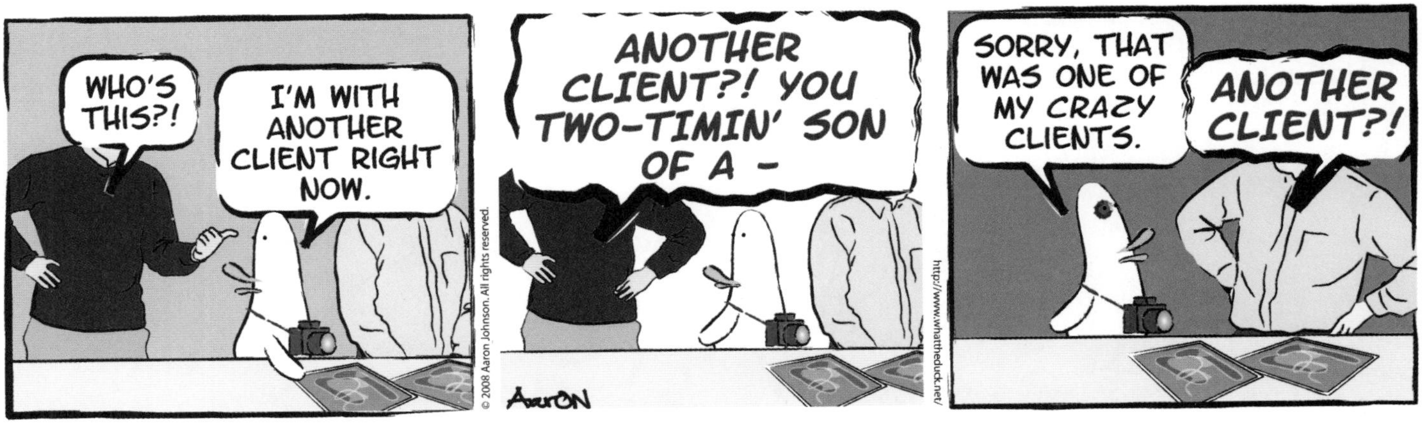
WHO'S THIS?!
I'M WITH ANOTHER CLIENT RIGHT NOW.
ANOTHER CLIENT?! YOU TWO-TIMIN' SON OF A -
SORRY, THAT WAS ONE OF MY CRAZY CLIENTS.
ANOTHER CLIENT?!
© 2008 Aaron Johnson. All rights reserved.
http://www.whattheduck.net/

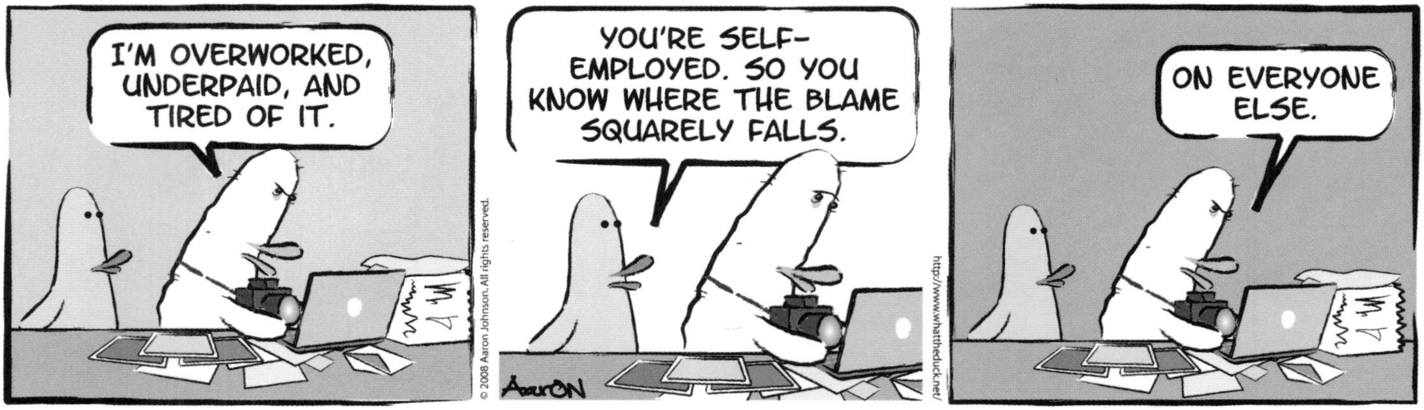
I'M OVERWORKED, UNDERPAID, AND TIRED OF IT.
YOU'RE SELF-EMPLOYED. SO YOU KNOW WHERE THE BLAME SQUARELY FALLS.
ON EVERYONE ELSE.
© 2008 Aaron Johnson. All rights reserved.
http://www.whattheduck.net/
AARON

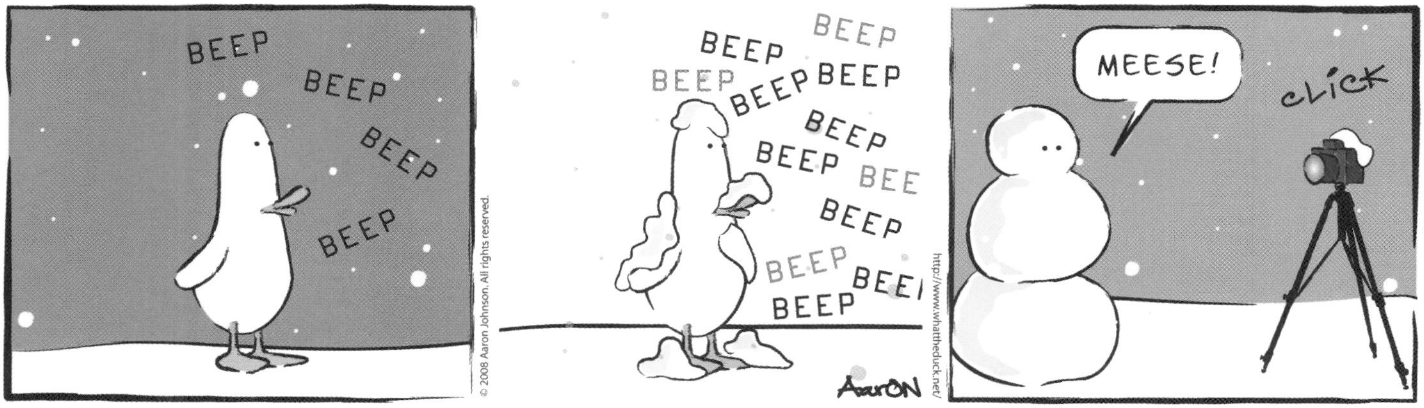
BEEP
BEEP
BEEP
BEEP
BEEP BEEP BEEP BEEP BEEP BEEP BEEP BEE BEEP BEEP BEE BEEP
MEESE!
CLICK
© 2008 Aaron Johnson. All rights reserved.
http://www.whattheduck.net/
AARON

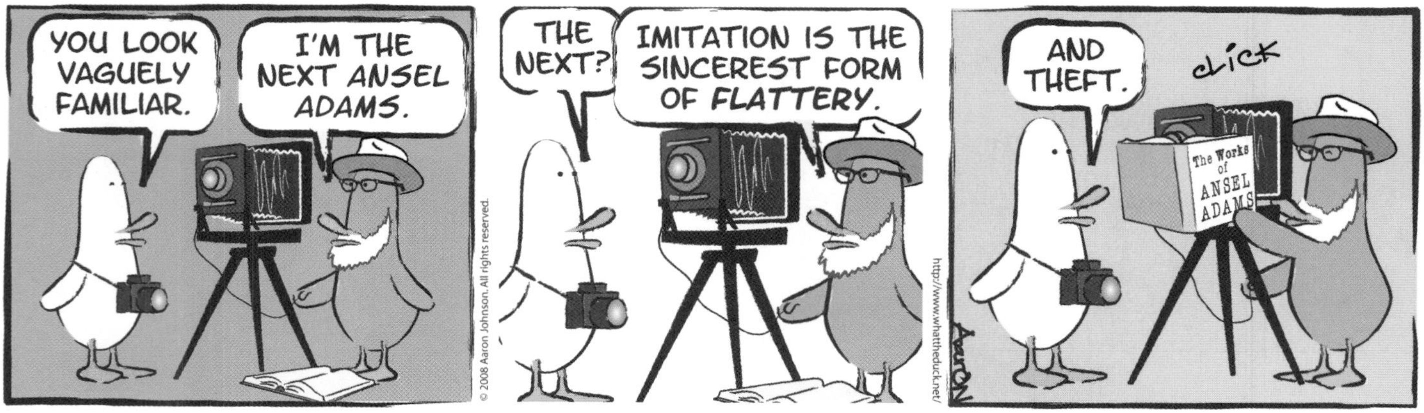
YOU LOOK VAGUELY FAMILIAR.
I'M THE NEXT ANSEL ADAMS.
THE NEXT?
IMITATION IS THE SINCEREST FORM OF FLATTERY.
AND THEFT.
CLICK
The Works of ANSEL ADAMS
© 2008 Aaron Johnson. All rights reserved.
http://www.whattheduck.net/
AARON

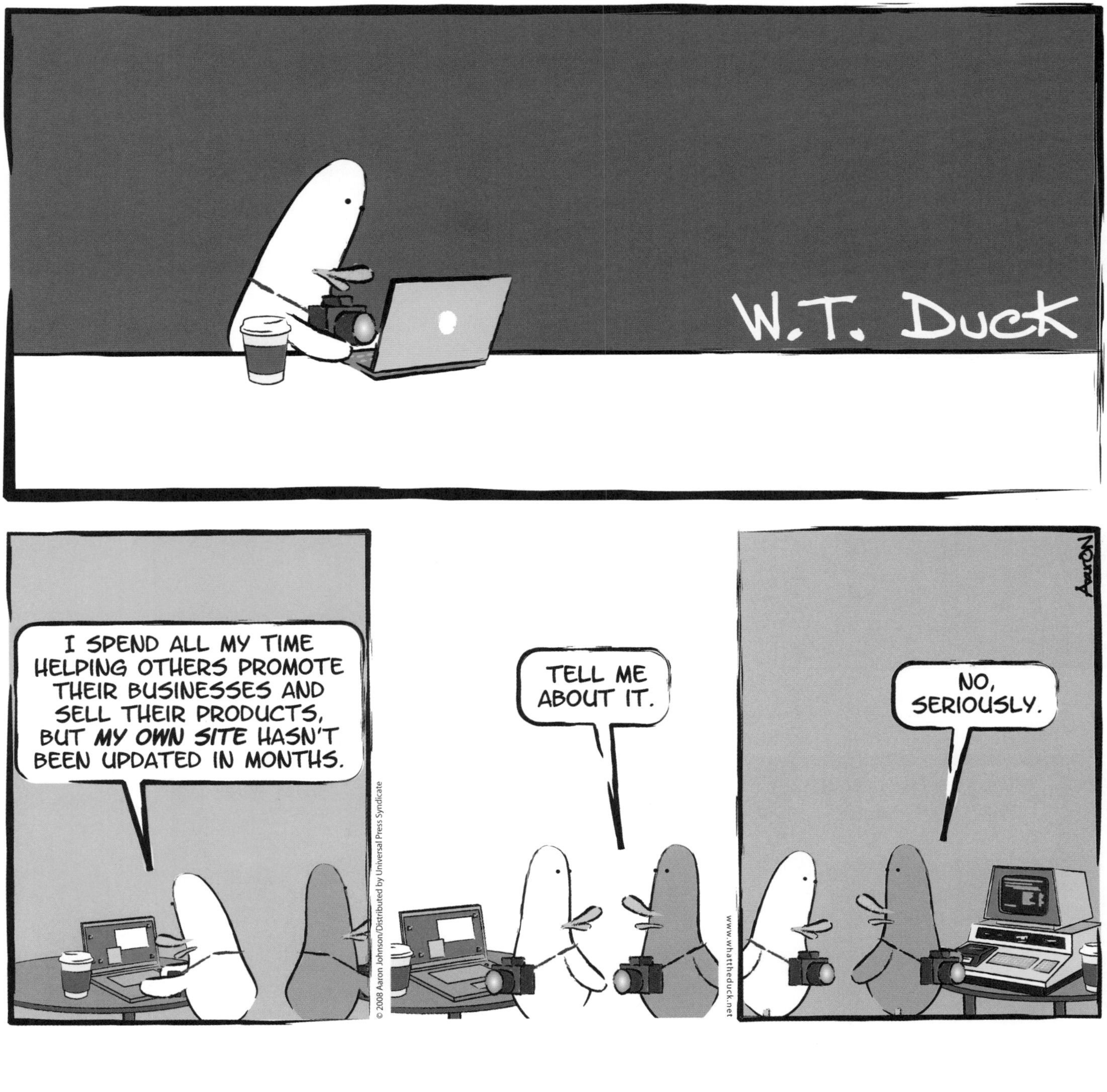
W.T. Duck
I SPEND ALL MY TIME HELPING OTHERS PROMOTE THEIR BUSINESSES AND SELL THEIR PRODUCTS, BUT MY OWN SITE HASN'T BEEN UPDATED IN MONTHS.
© 2008 Aaron Johnson/Distributed by Universal Press Syndicate
TELL ME ABOUT IT.
www.whattheduck.net
NO, SERIOUSLY.
AARON

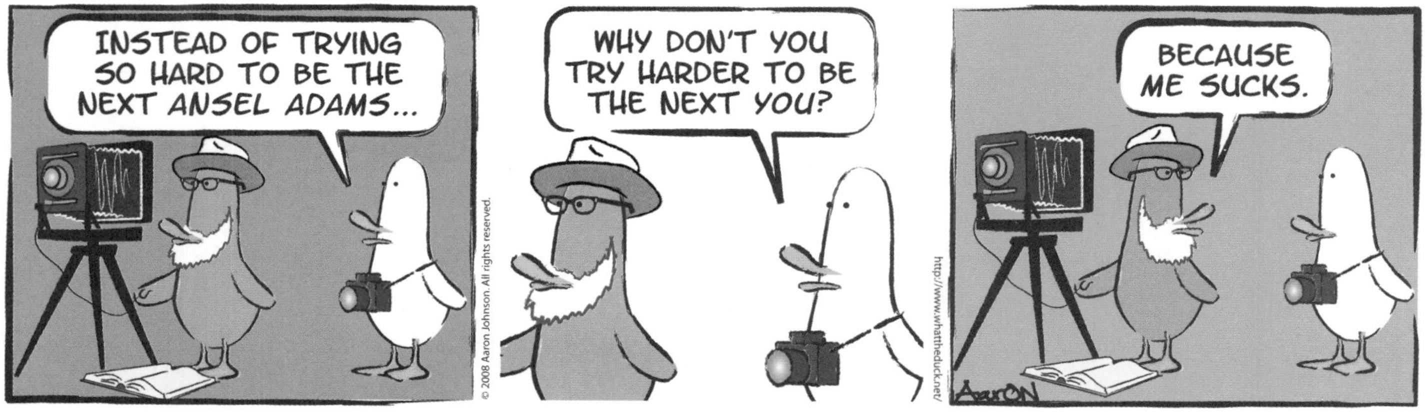
INSTEAD OF TRYING SO HARD TO BE THE NEXT ANSEL ADAMS...
WHY DON'T YOU TRY HARDER TO BE THE NEXT YOU?
BECAUSE ME SUCKS.
© 2008 Aaron Johnson. All rights reserved.
http://www.whattheduck.net/

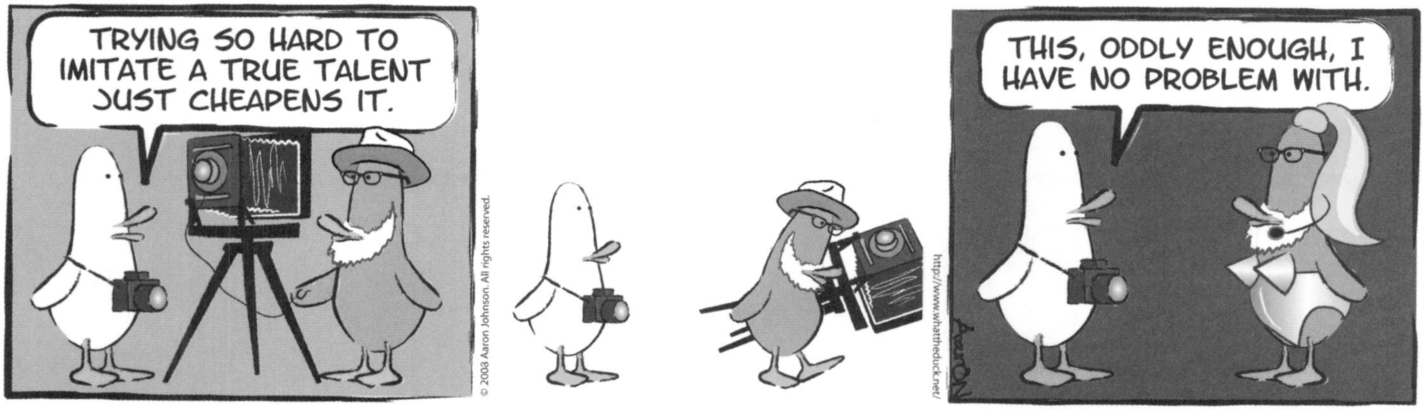
TRYING SO HARD TO IMITATE A TRUE TALENT JUST CHEAPENS IT.
THIS, ODDLY ENOUGH, I HAVE NO PROBLEM WITH.
© 2008 Aaron Johnson. All rights reserved.
http://www.whattheduck.net/

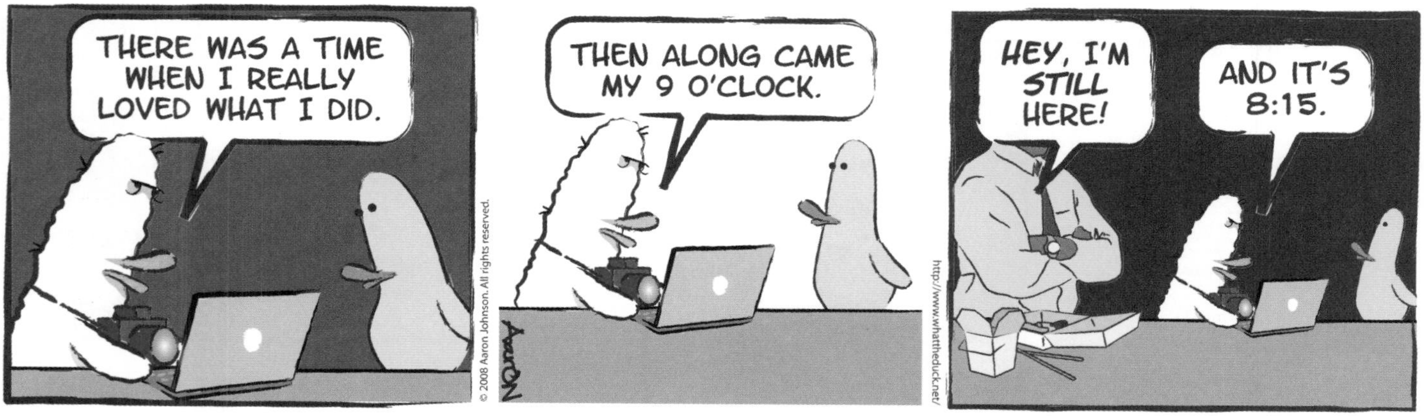
THERE WAS A TIME WHEN I REALLY LOVED WHAT I DID.
THEN ALONG CAME MY 9 O'CLOCK.
HEY, I'M STILL HERE!
AND IT'S 8:15.
© 2008 Aaron Johnson. All rights reserved.
http://www.whattheduck.net/

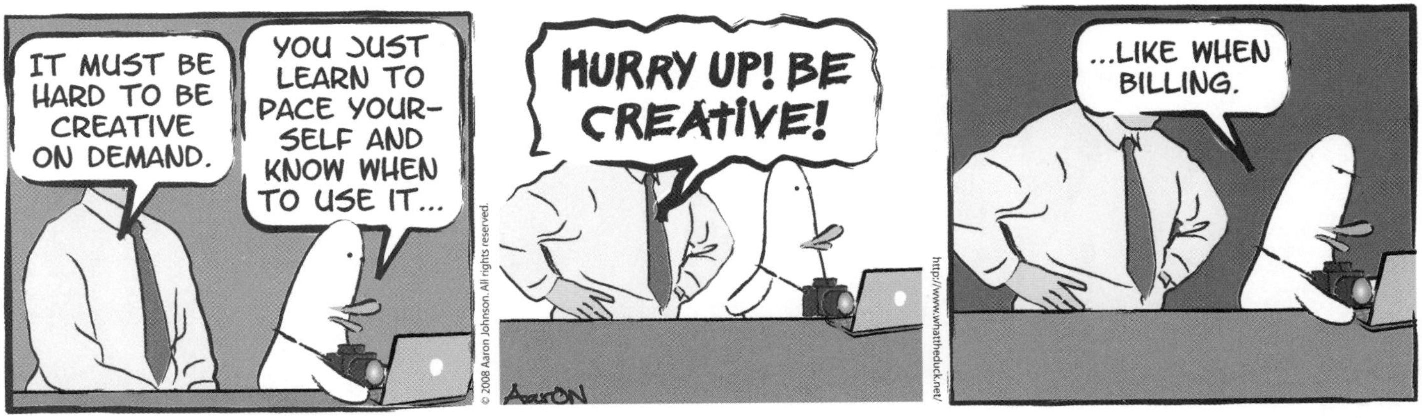
IT MUST BE HARD TO BE CREATIVE ON DEMAND.
YOU JUST LEARN TO PACE YOURSELF AND KNOW WHEN TO USE IT...
HURRY UP! BE CREATIVE!
...LIKE WHEN BILLING.
© 2008 Aaron Johnson. All rights reserved.
AARON
http://www.whattheduck.net/

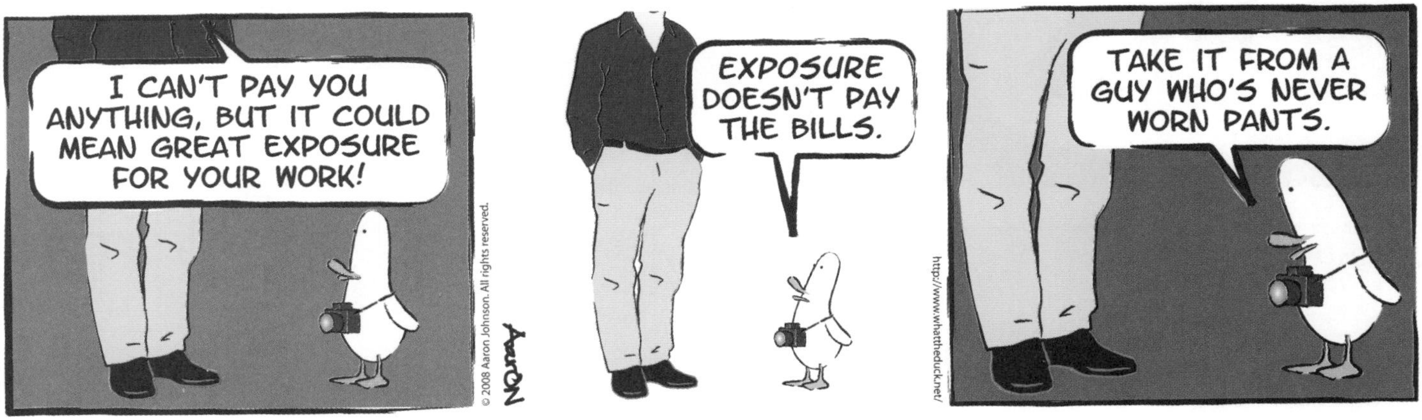
I CAN'T PAY YOU ANYTHING, BUT IT COULD MEAN GREAT EXPOSURE FOR YOUR WORK!
EXPOSURE DOESN'T PAY THE BILLS.
TAKE IT FROM A GUY WHO'S NEVER WORN PANTS.
© 2008 Aaron Johnson. All rights reserved.
AARON
http://www.whattheduck.net/

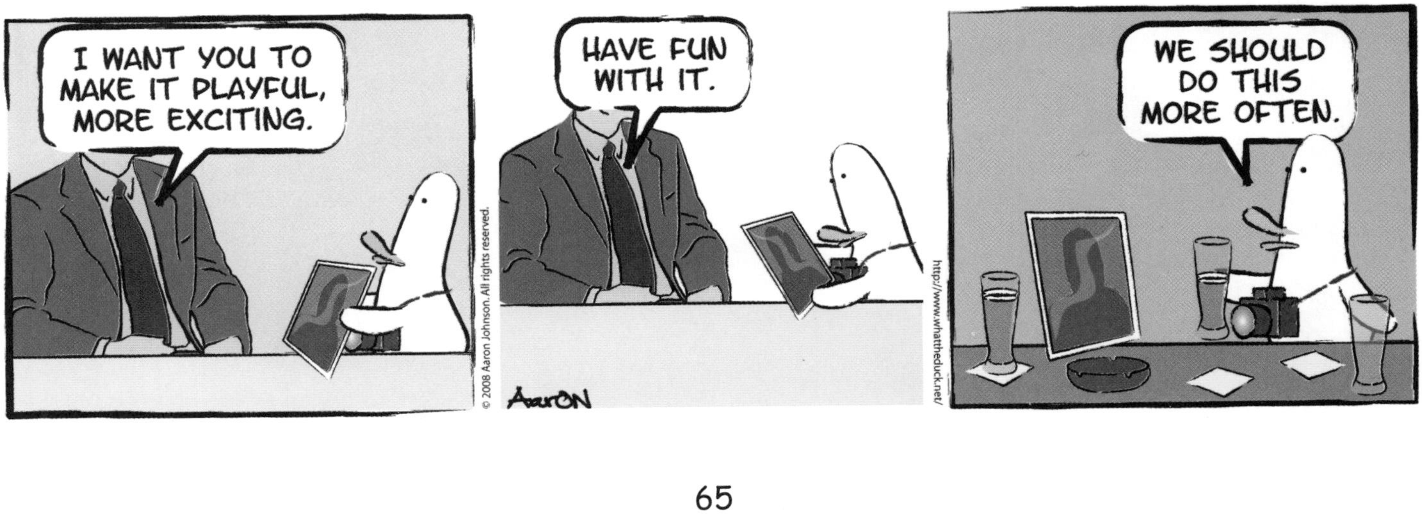
I WANT YOU TO MAKE IT PLAYFUL, MORE EXCITING.
HAVE FUN WITH IT.
WE SHOULD DO THIS MORE OFTEN.
© 2008 Aaron Johnson. All rights reserved.
AARON
http://www.whattheduck.net/

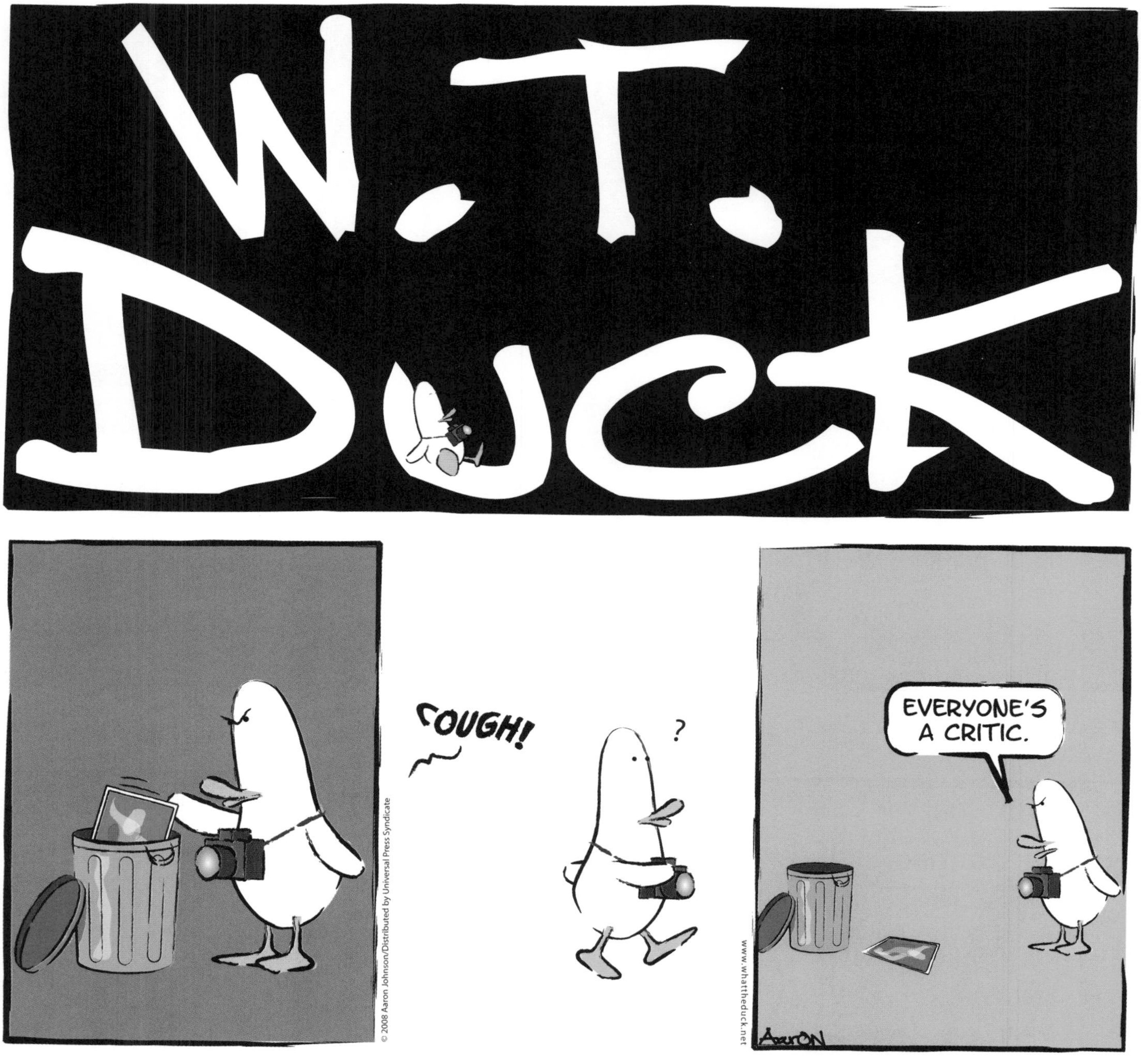
W.T. Duck
COUGH!
?
EVERYONE'S A CRITIC.
© 2008 Aaron Johnson/Distributed by Universal Press Syndicate
www.whattheduck.net
AarON

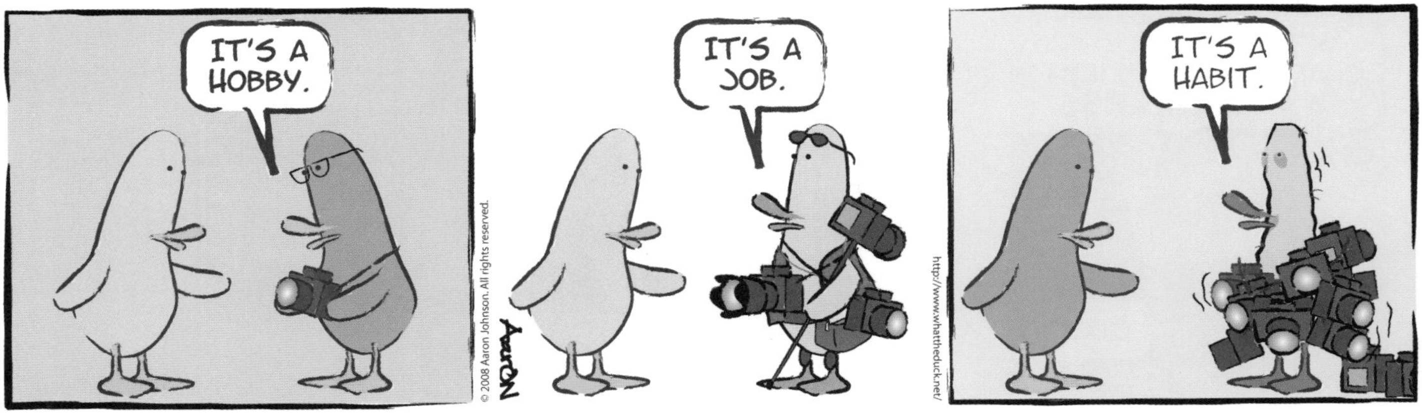
IT'S A HOBBY.
© 2008 Aaron Johnson. All rights reserved.
IT'S A JOB.
http://www.whattheduck.net/
IT'S A HABIT.

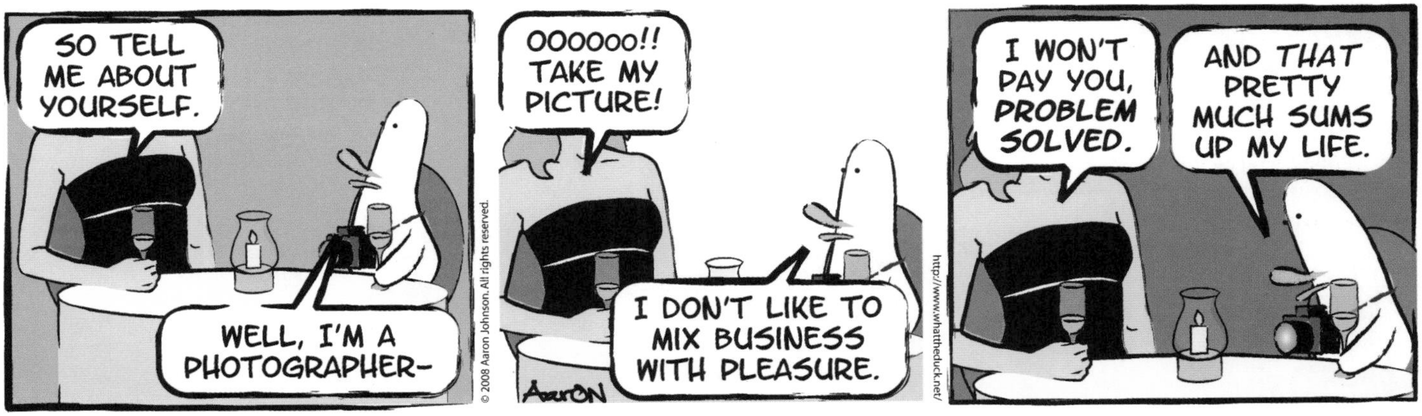
SO TELL ME ABOUT YOURSELF.
WELL, I'M A PHOTOGRAPHER-
© 2008 Aaron Johnson. All rights reserved.
OOOOOO!! TAKE MY PICTURE!
I DON'T LIKE TO MIX BUSINESS WITH PLEASURE.
http://www.whattheduck.net/
I WON'T PAY YOU, PROBLEM SOLVED.
AND THAT PRETTY MUCH SUMS UP MY LIFE.

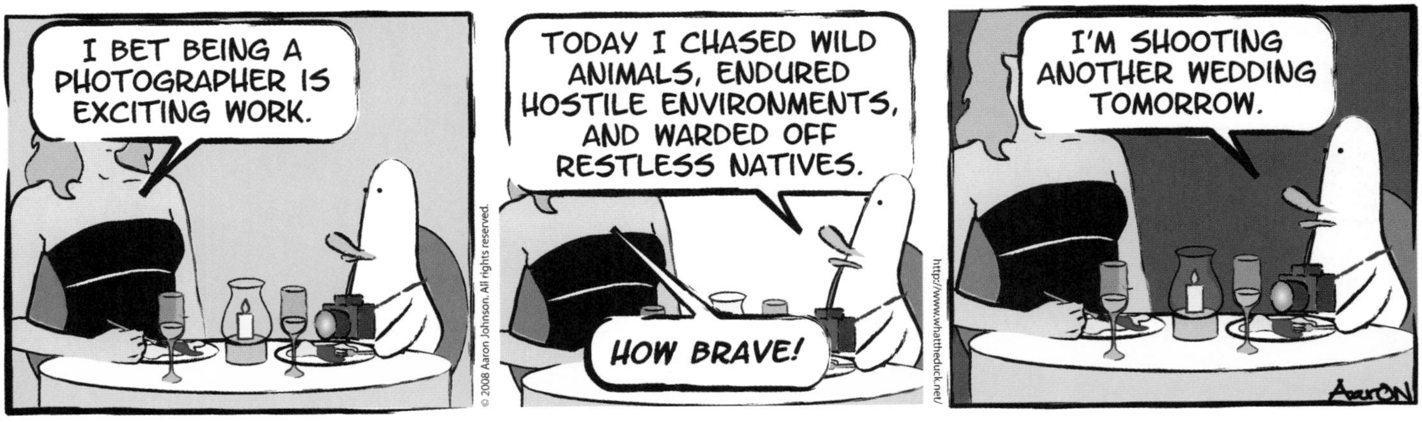
I BET BEING A PHOTOGRAPHER IS EXCITING WORK.
© 2008 Aaron Johnson. All rights reserved.
TODAY I CHASED WILD ANIMALS, ENDURED HOSTILE ENVIRONMENTS, AND WARDED OFF RESTLESS NATIVES.
HOW BRAVE!
http://www.whattheduck.net/
I'M SHOOTING ANOTHER WEDDING TOMORROW.

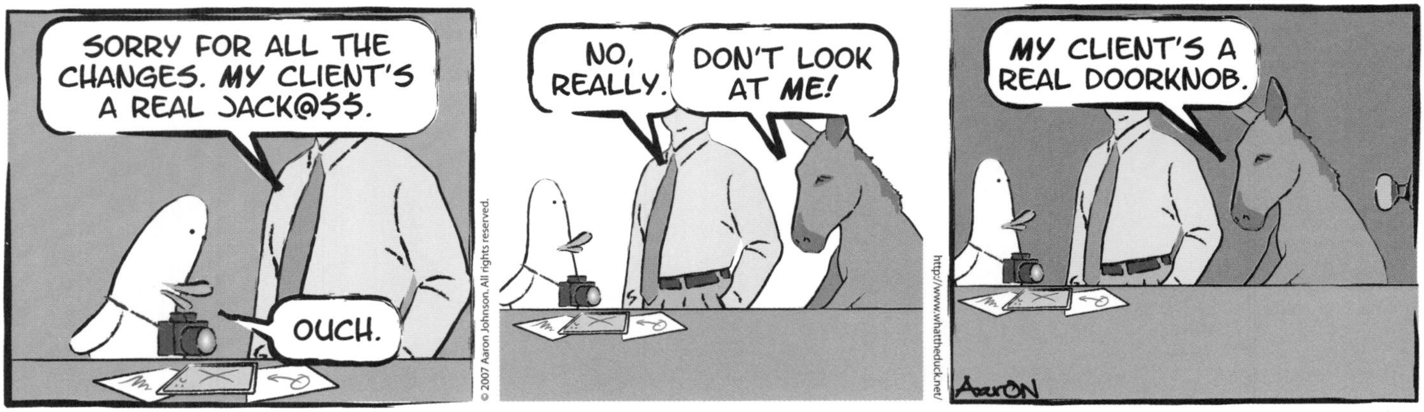
SORRY FOR ALL THE CHANGES. MY CLIENT'S A REAL JACK@$$.
OUCH.
NO, REALLY.
DON'T LOOK AT ME!
MY CLIENT'S A REAL DOORKNOB.
© 2007 Aaron Johnson. All rights reserved.
http://www.whattheduck.net/
AARON

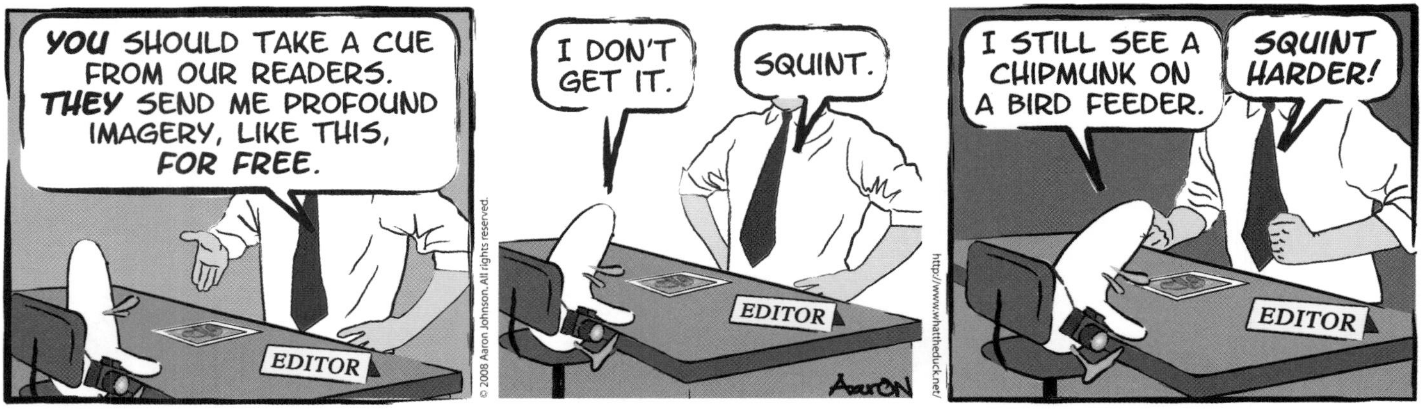
YOU SHOULD TAKE A CUE FROM OUR READERS. THEY SEND ME PROFOUND IMAGERY, LIKE THIS, FOR FREE.
EDITOR
I DON'T GET IT.
SQUINT.
I STILL SEE A CHIPMUNK ON A BIRD FEEDER.
SQUINT HARDER!
© 2008 Aaron Johnson. All rights reserved.
http://www.whattheduck.net/
AARON

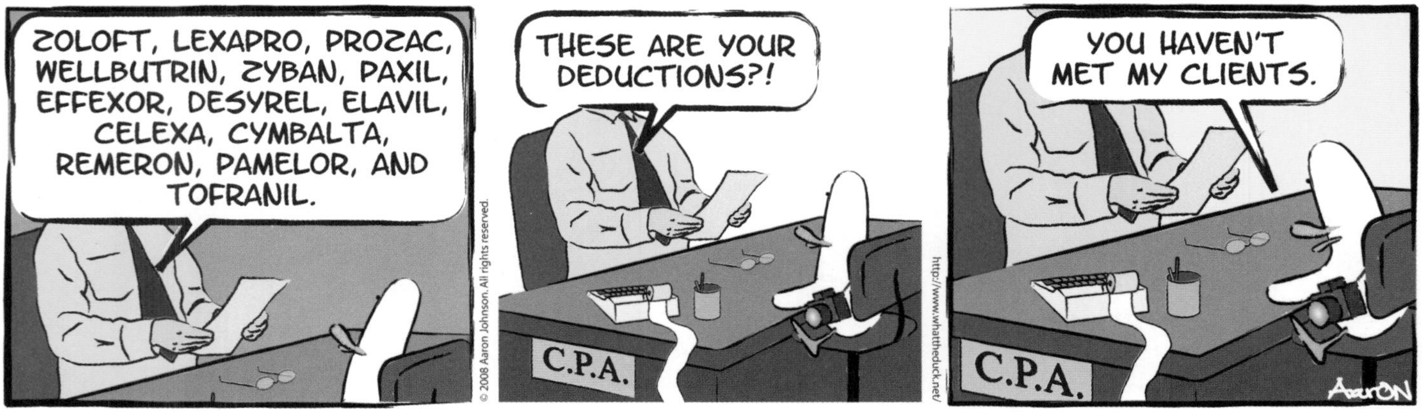
ZOLOFT, LEXAPRO, PROZAC, WELLBUTRIN, ZYBAN, PAXIL, EFFEXOR, DESYREL, ELAVIL, CELEXA, CYMBALTA, REMERON, PAMELOR, AND TOFRANIL.
THESE ARE YOUR DEDUCTIONS?!
C.P.A.
YOU HAVEN'T MET MY CLIENTS.
© 2008 Aaron Johnson. All rights reserved.
http://www.whattheduck.net/
AARON

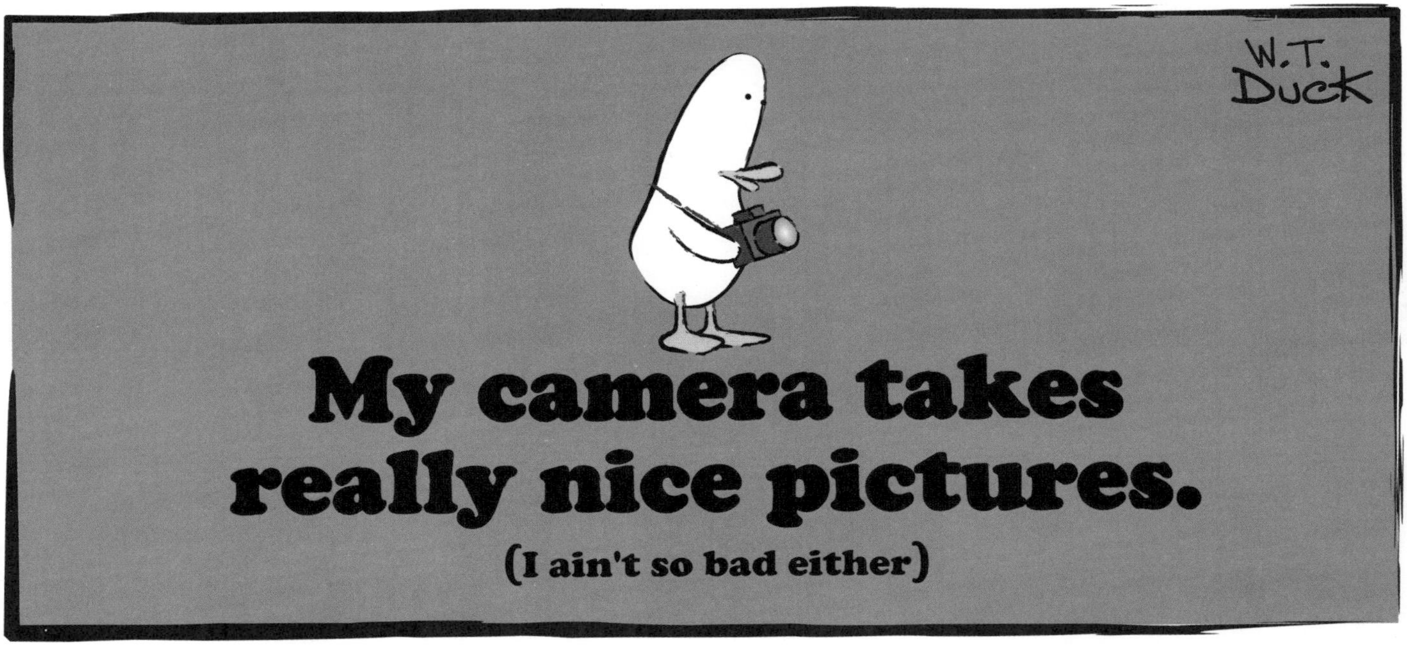
W.T. DUCK
My camera takes really nice pictures.
(I ain't so bad either)

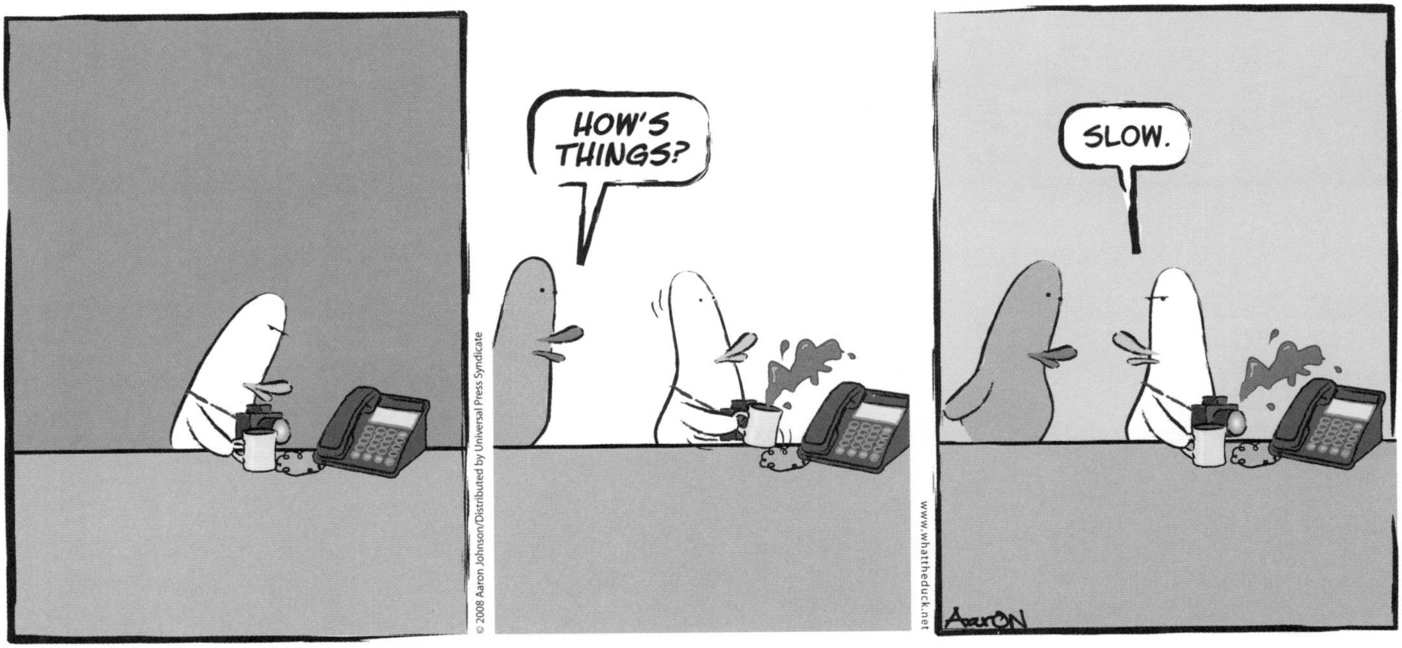
HOW'S THINGS?
SLOW.
© 2008 Aaron Johnson/Distributed by Universal Press Syndicate
www.whattheduck.net
AARON

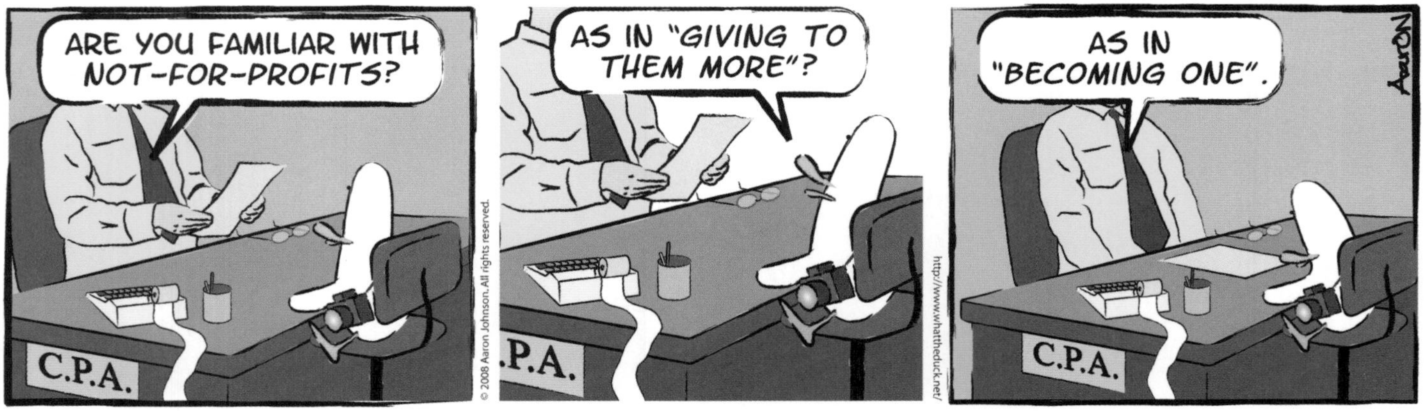
ARE YOU FAMILIAR WITH NOT-FOR-PROFITS?
AS IN "GIVING TO THEM MORE"?
AS IN "BECOMING ONE".
C.P.A.
© 2008 Aaron Johnson. All rights reserved.
http://www.whattheduck.net/

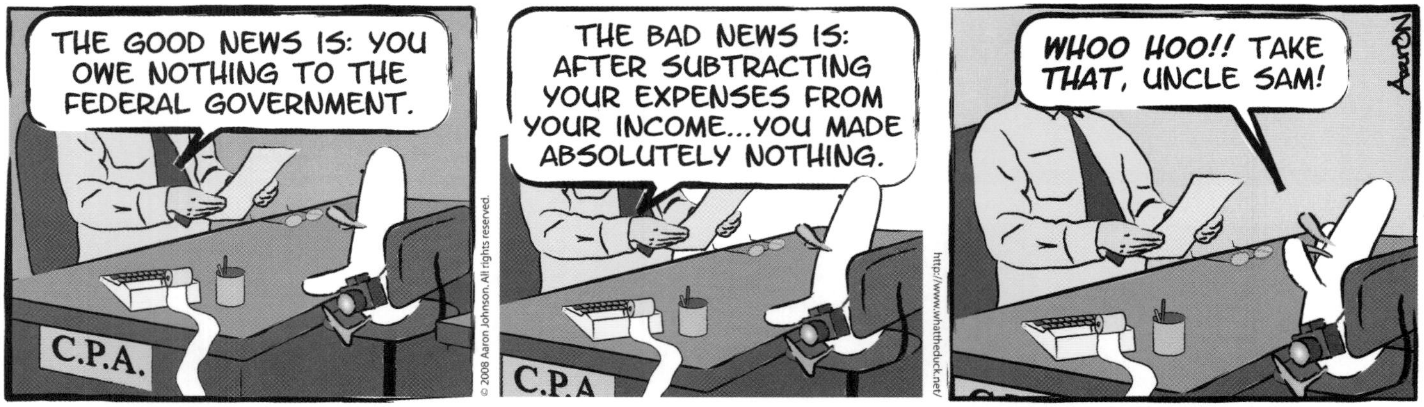
THE GOOD NEWS IS: YOU OWE NOTHING TO THE FEDERAL GOVERNMENT.
THE BAD NEWS IS: AFTER SUBTRACTING YOUR EXPENSES FROM YOUR INCOME...YOU MADE ABSOLUTELY NOTHING.
WHOO HOO!! TAKE THAT, UNCLE SAM!
C.P.A.
© 2008 Aaron Johnson. All rights reserved.
http://www.whattheduck.net/

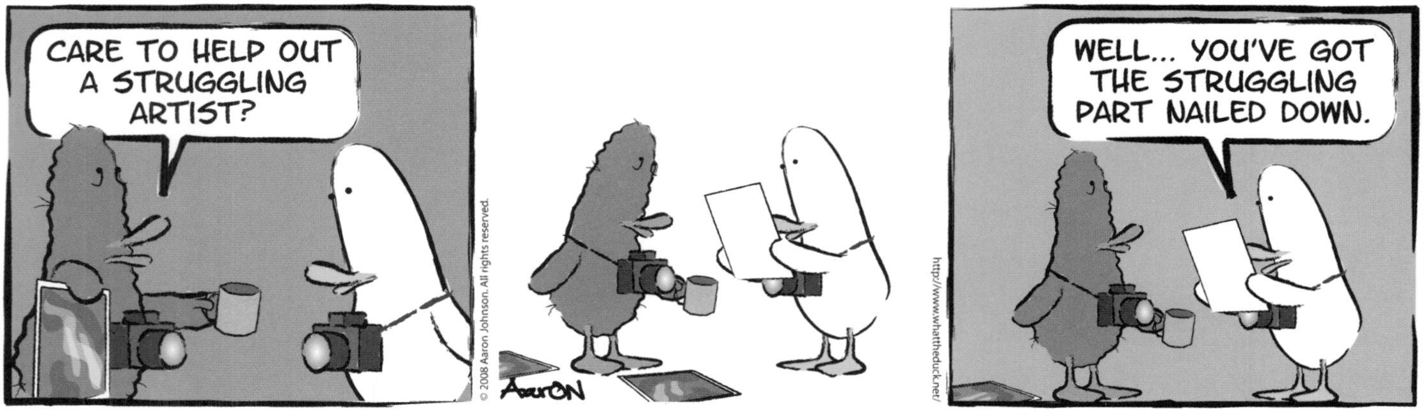
CARE TO HELP OUT A STRUGGLING ARTIST?
WELL... YOU'VE GOT THE STRUGGLING PART NAILED DOWN.
© 2008 Aaron Johnson. All rights reserved.
http://www.whattheduck.net/

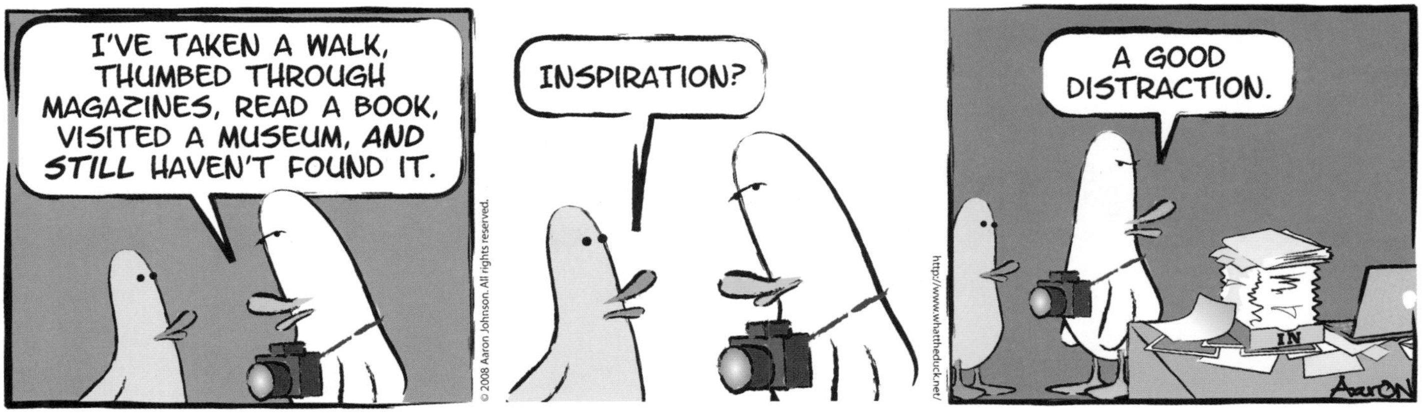
I'VE TAKEN A WALK, THUMBED THROUGH MAGAZINES, READ A BOOK, VISITED A MUSEUM, AND STILL HAVEN'T FOUND IT.
INSPIRATION?
A GOOD DISTRACTION.
IN
AaroN
© 2008 Aaron Johnson. All rights reserved.
http://www.whattheduck.net/

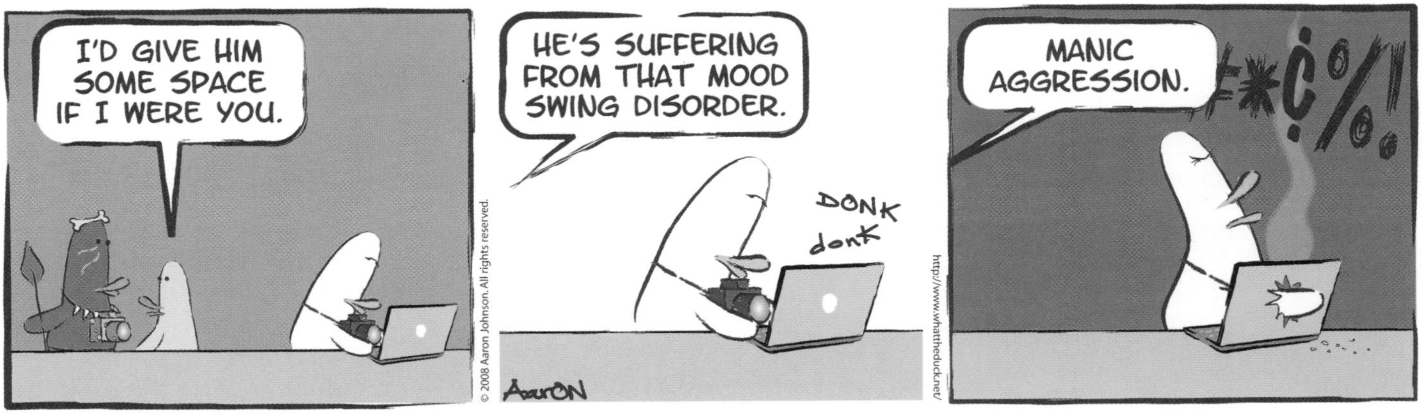
I'D GIVE HIM SOME SPACE IF I WERE YOU.
HE'S SUFFERING FROM THAT MOOD SWING DISORDER.
DONK
donk
MANIC AGGRESSION.
AaroN
© 2008 Aaron Johnson. All rights reserved.
http://www.whattheduck.net/

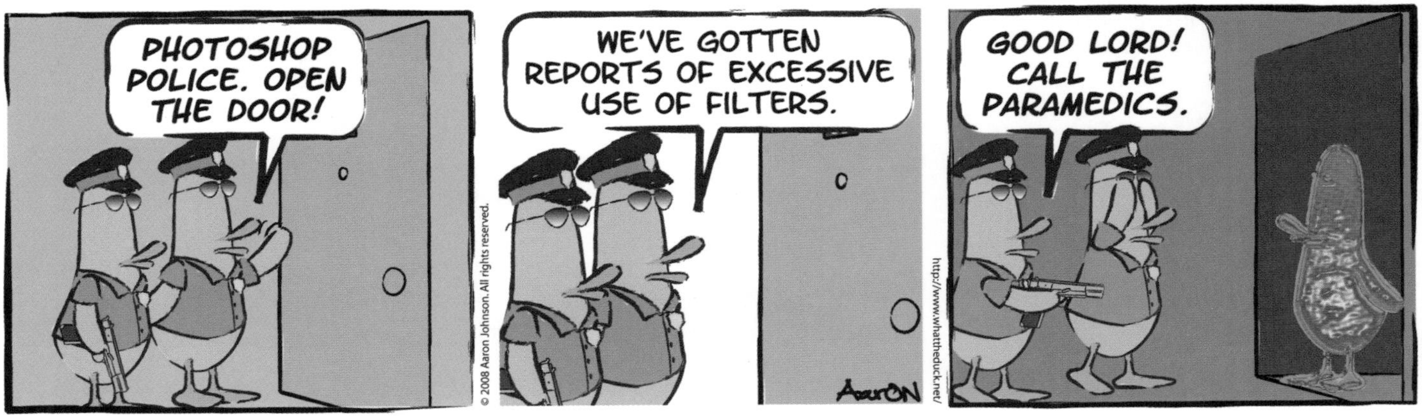
PHOTOSHOP POLICE. OPEN THE DOOR!
WE'VE GOTTEN REPORTS OF EXCESSIVE USE OF FILTERS.
GOOD LORD! CALL THE PARAMEDICS.
AaroN
© 2008 Aaron Johnson. All rights reserved.
http://www.whattheduck.net/

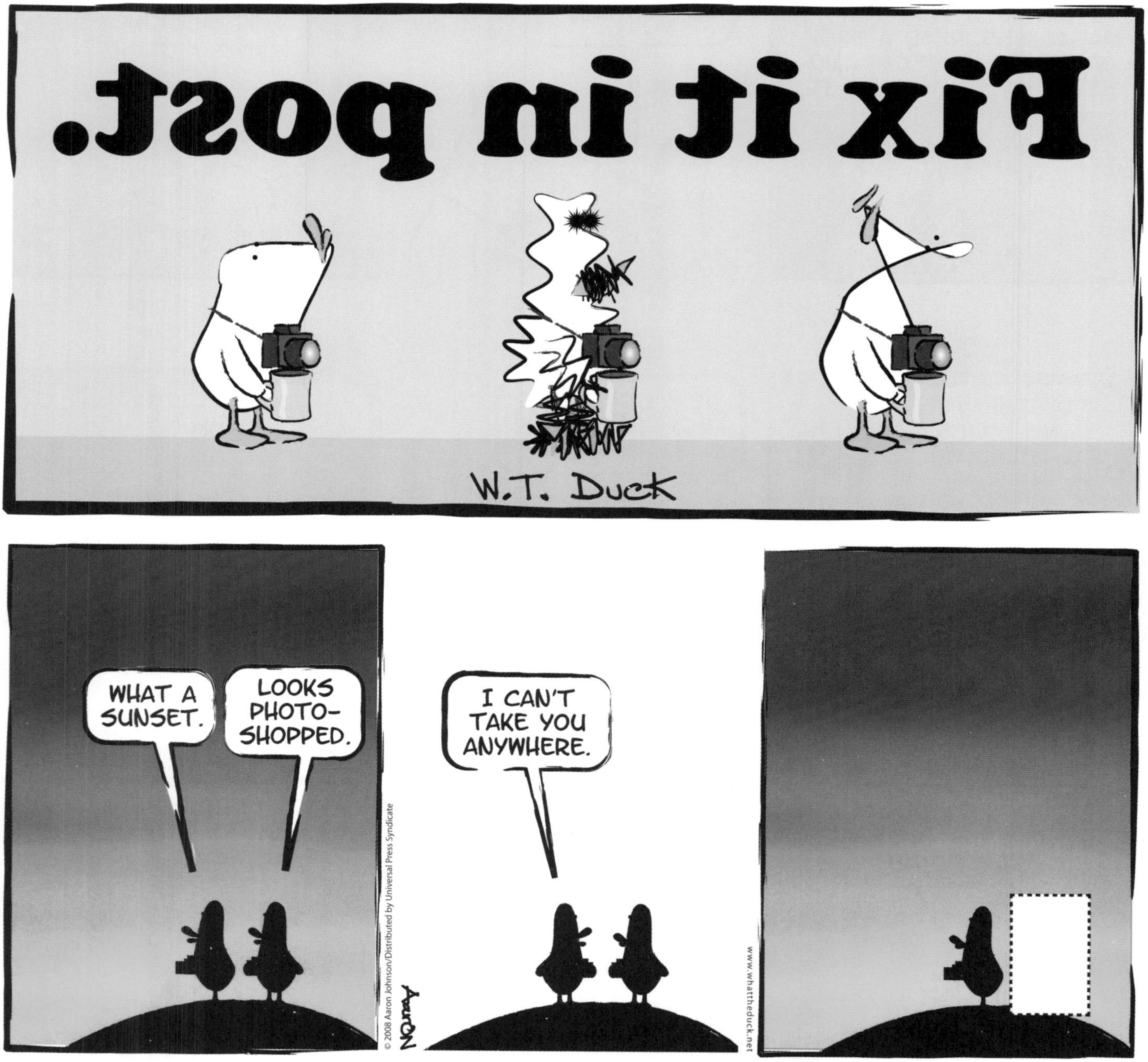
Fix it in post.
W.T. Duck
WHAT A SUNSET.
LOOKS PHOTO-SHOPPED.
I CAN'T TAKE YOU ANYWHERE.
AARON
© 2008 Aaron Johnson/Distributed by Universal Press Syndicate
www.whattheduck.net

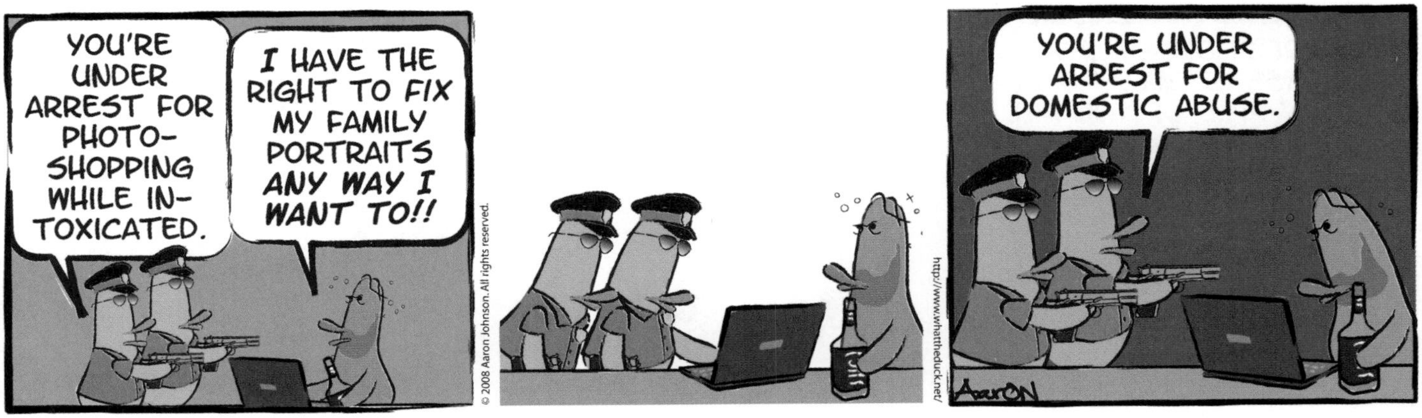
YOU'RE UNDER ARREST FOR PHOTO-SHOPPING WHILE IN-TOXICATED.
I HAVE THE RIGHT TO FIX MY FAMILY PORTRAITS ANY WAY I WANT TO!!
© 2008 Aaron Johnson. All rights reserved.
YOU'RE UNDER ARREST FOR DOMESTIC ABUSE.
http://www.whattheduck.net/
AARON

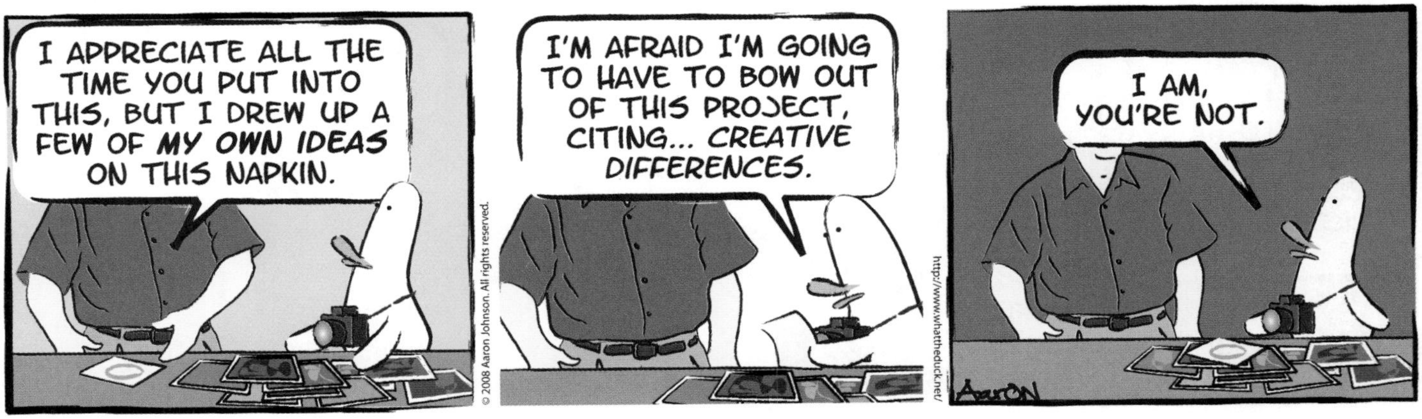
I APPRECIATE ALL THE TIME YOU PUT INTO THIS, BUT I DREW UP A FEW OF MY OWN IDEAS ON THIS NAPKIN.
© 2008 Aaron Johnson. All rights reserved.
I'M AFRAID I'M GOING TO HAVE TO BOW OUT OF THIS PROJECT, CITING... CREATIVE DIFFERENCES.
I AM, YOU'RE NOT.
http://www.whattheduck.net/
AARON

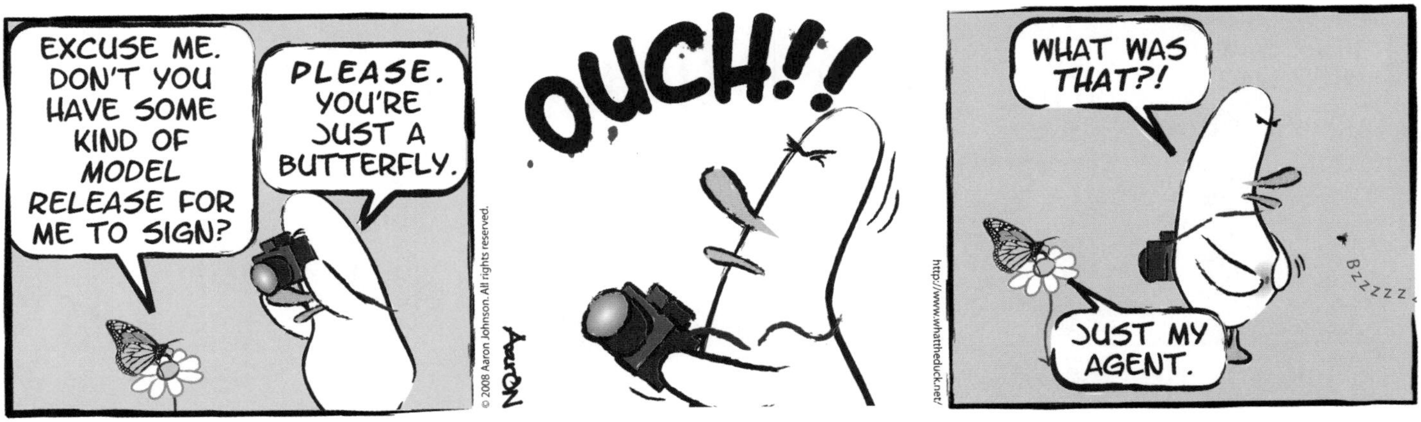
EXCUSE ME. DON'T YOU HAVE SOME KIND OF MODEL RELEASE FOR ME TO SIGN?
PLEASE. YOU'RE JUST A BUTTERFLY.
© 2008 Aaron Johnson. All rights reserved.
AARON
OUCH!!
WHAT WAS THAT?!
BZZZZZ
JUST MY AGENT.
http://www.whattheduck.net/

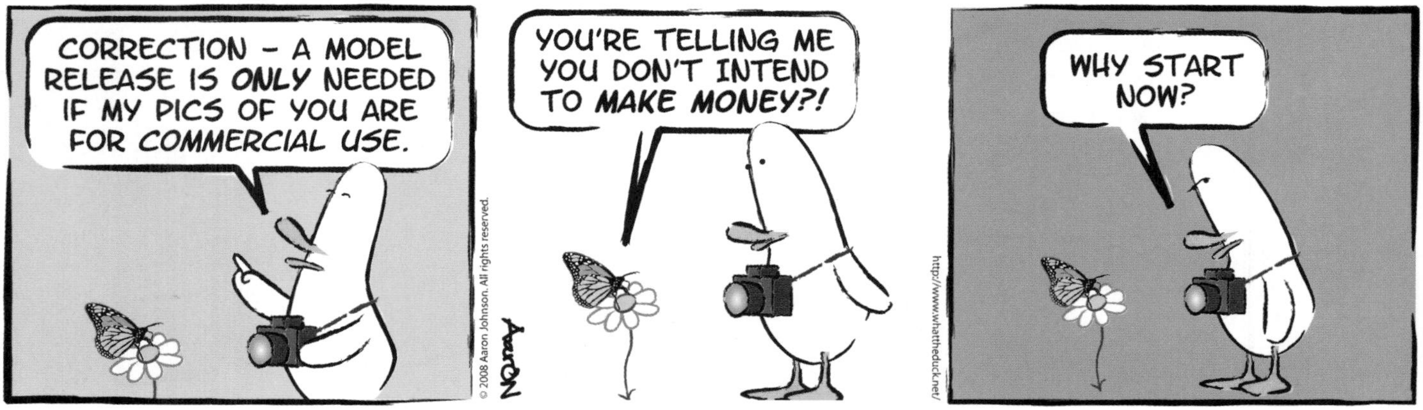
CORRECTION - A MODEL RELEASE IS ONLY NEEDED IF MY PICS OF YOU ARE FOR COMMERCIAL USE.
YOU'RE TELLING ME YOU DON'T INTEND TO MAKE MONEY?!
WHY START NOW?
© 2008 Aaron Johnson. All rights reserved.
AarON
http://www.whattheduck.net/

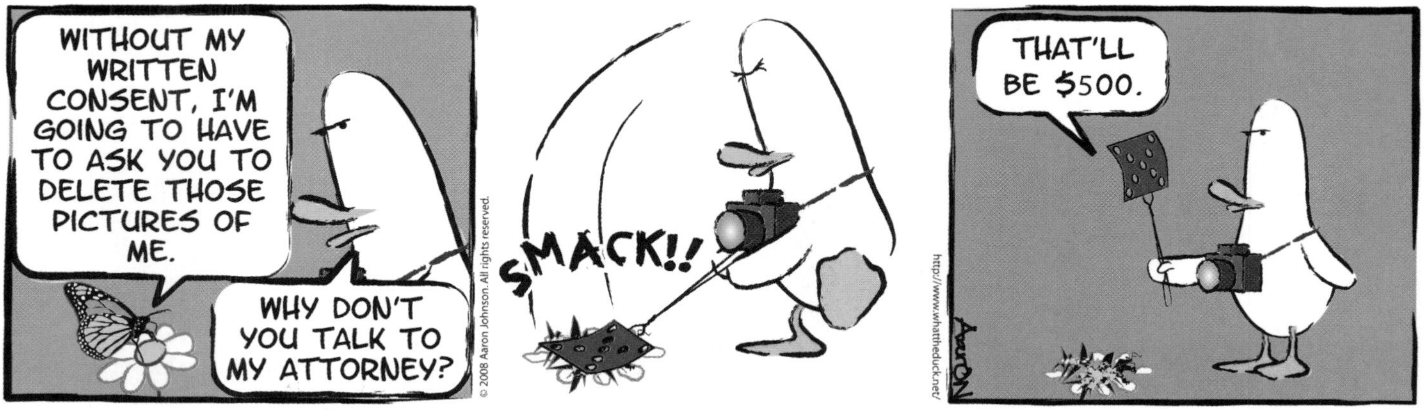
WITHOUT MY WRITTEN CONSENT, I'M GOING TO HAVE TO ASK YOU TO DELETE THOSE PICTURES OF ME.
WHY DON'T YOU TALK TO MY ATTORNEY?
© 2008 Aaron Johnson. All rights reserved.
SMACK!!
THAT'LL BE $500.
http://www.whattheduck.net/
AarON

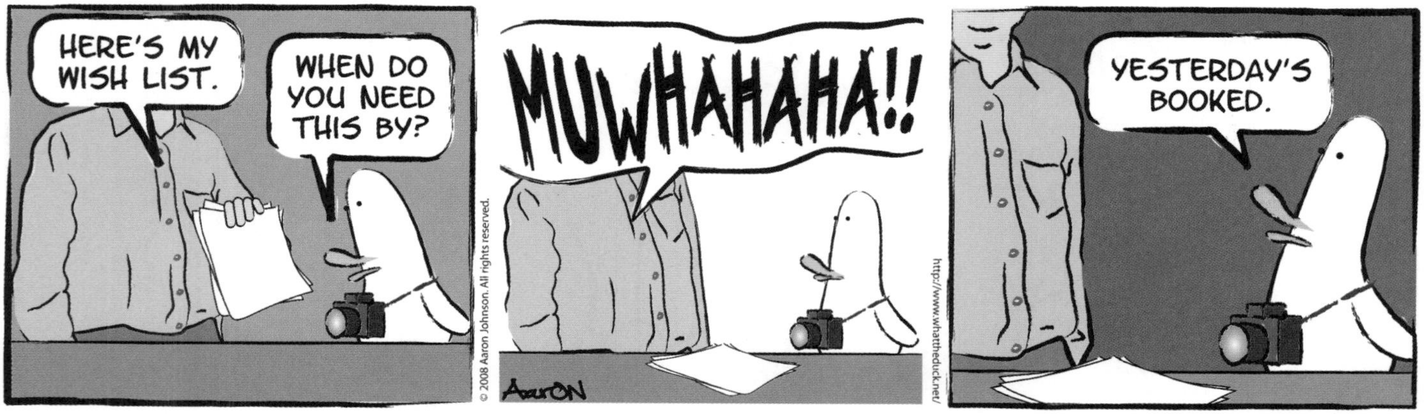
HERE'S MY WISH LIST.
WHEN DO YOU NEED THIS BY?
© 2008 Aaron Johnson. All rights reserved.
MUWHAHAHA!!
AarON
http://www.whattheduck.net/
YESTERDAY'S BOOKED.

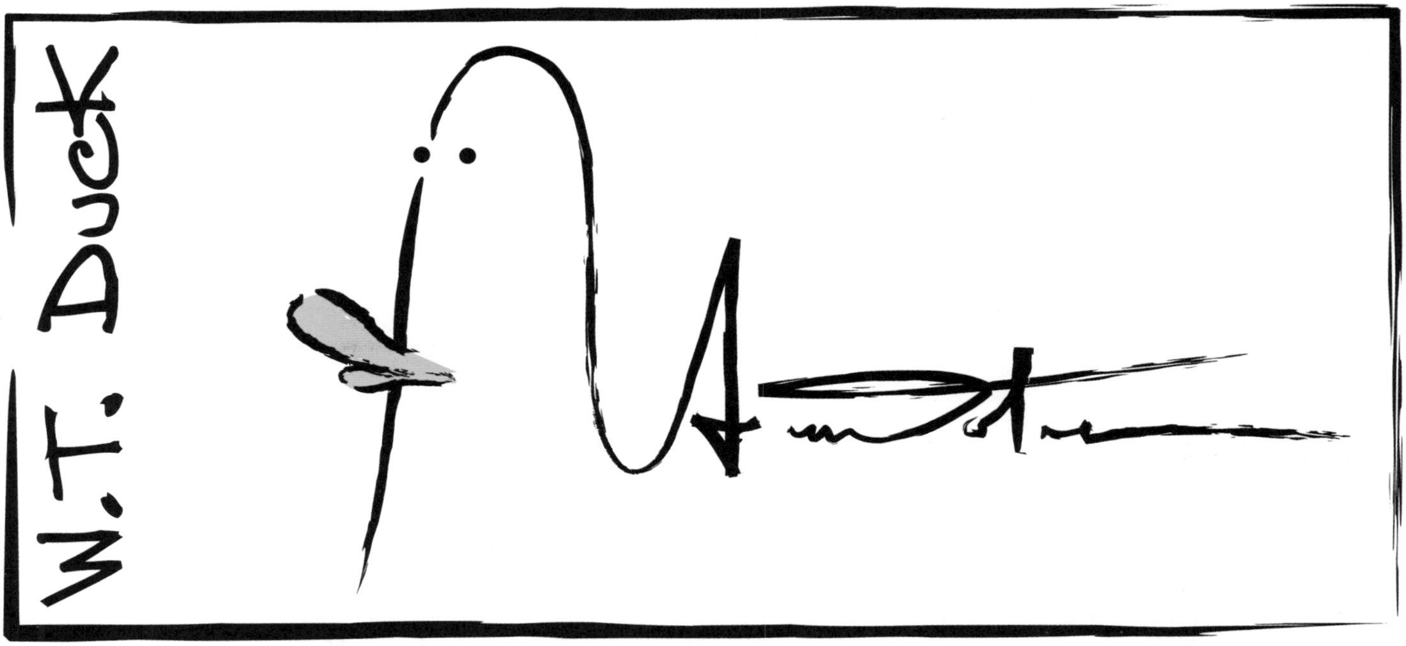
W.T. Duck

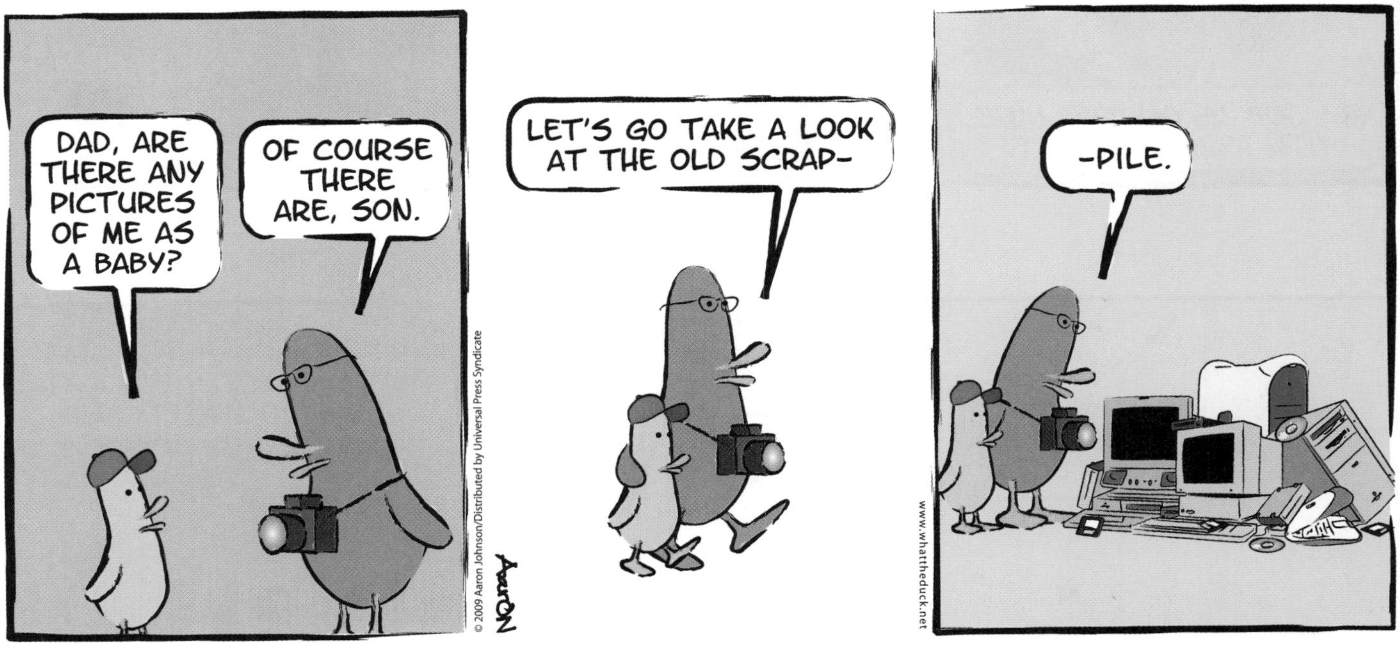
DAD, ARE THERE ANY PICTURES OF ME AS A BABY?
OF COURSE THERE ARE, SON.
© 2009 Aaron Johnson/Distributed by Universal Press Syndicate
LET'S GO TAKE A LOOK AT THE OLD SCRAP-
-PILE.
www.whattheduck.net

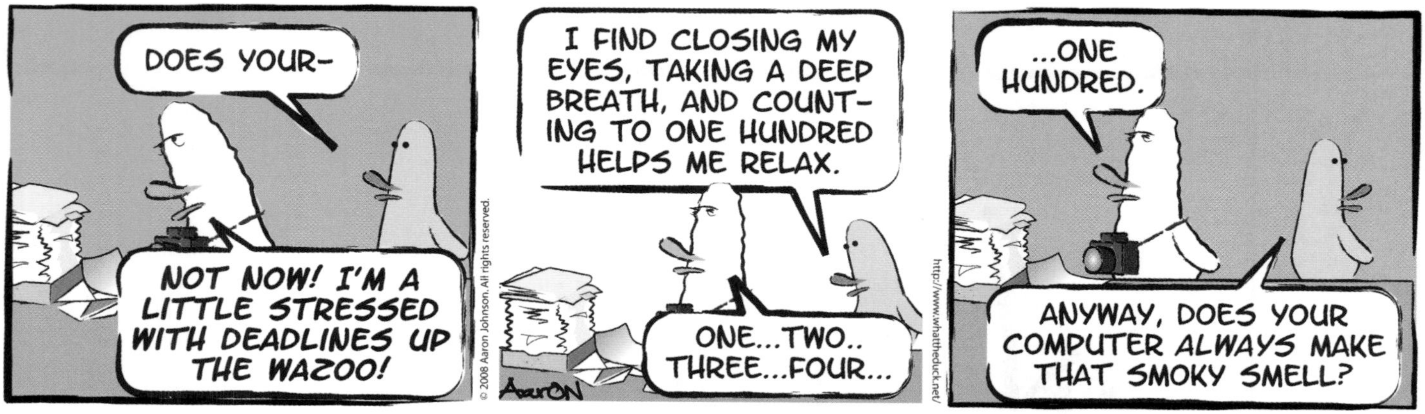
DOES YOUR-
NOT NOW! I'M A LITTLE STRESSED WITH DEADLINES UP THE WAZOO!
I FIND CLOSING MY EYES, TAKING A DEEP BREATH, AND COUNTING TO ONE HUNDRED HELPS ME RELAX.
ONE...TWO.. THREE...FOUR...
...ONE HUNDRED.
ANYWAY, DOES YOUR COMPUTER ALWAYS MAKE THAT SMOKY SMELL?
© 2008 Aaron Johnson. All rights reserved.
http://www.whattheduck.net/

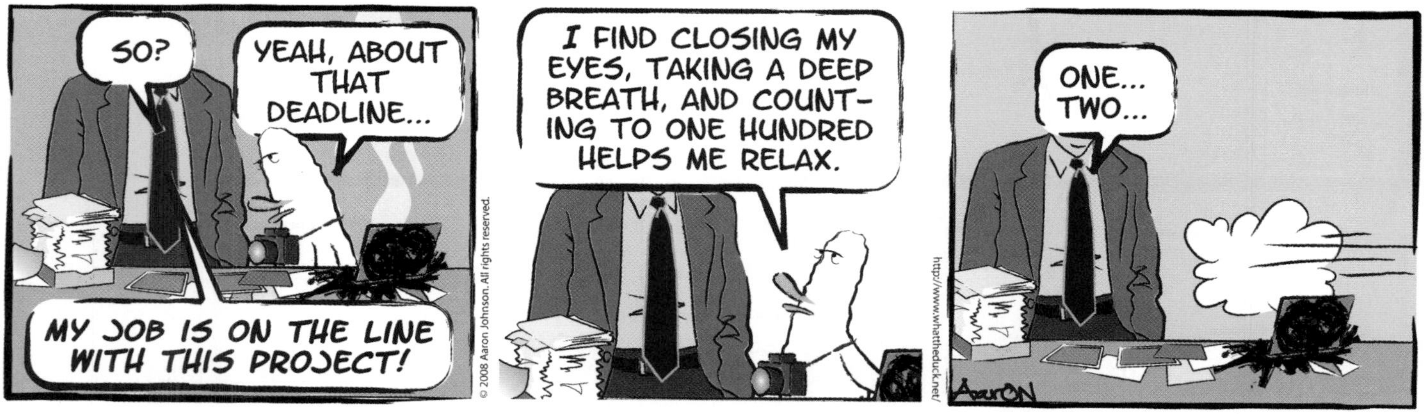
SO?
YEAH, ABOUT THAT DEADLINE...
MY JOB IS ON THE LINE WITH THIS PROJECT!
I FIND CLOSING MY EYES, TAKING A DEEP BREATH, AND COUNTING TO ONE HUNDRED HELPS ME RELAX.
ONE... TWO...
© 2008 Aaron Johnson. All rights reserved.
http://www.whattheduck.net/

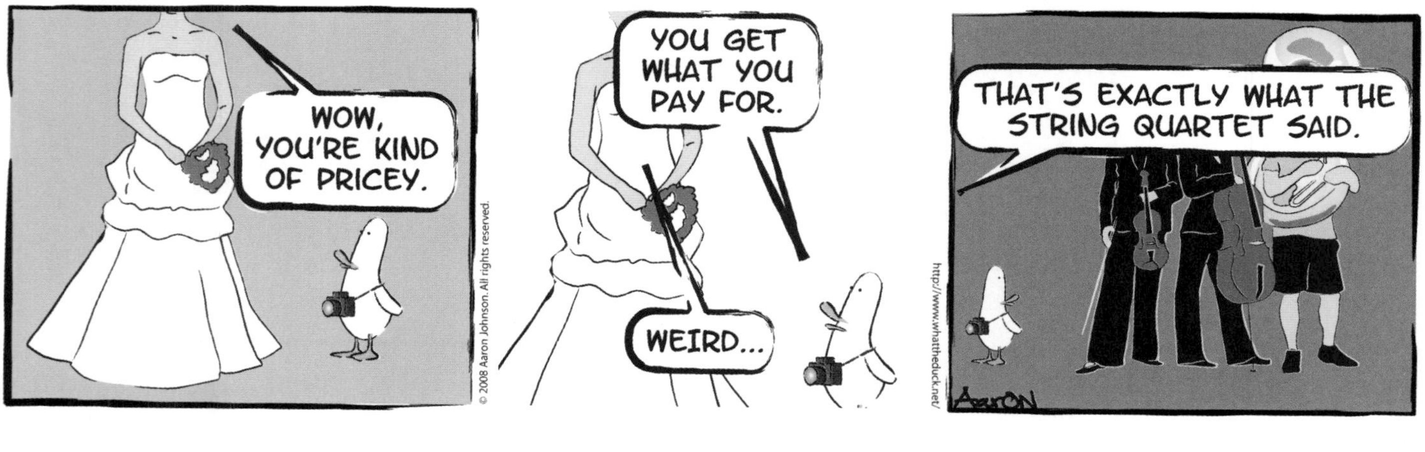
WOW, YOU'RE KIND OF PRICEY.
YOU GET WHAT YOU PAY FOR.
WEIRD...
THAT'S EXACTLY WHAT THE STRING QUARTET SAID.
© 2008 Aaron Johnson. All rights reserved.
http://www.whattheduck.net/

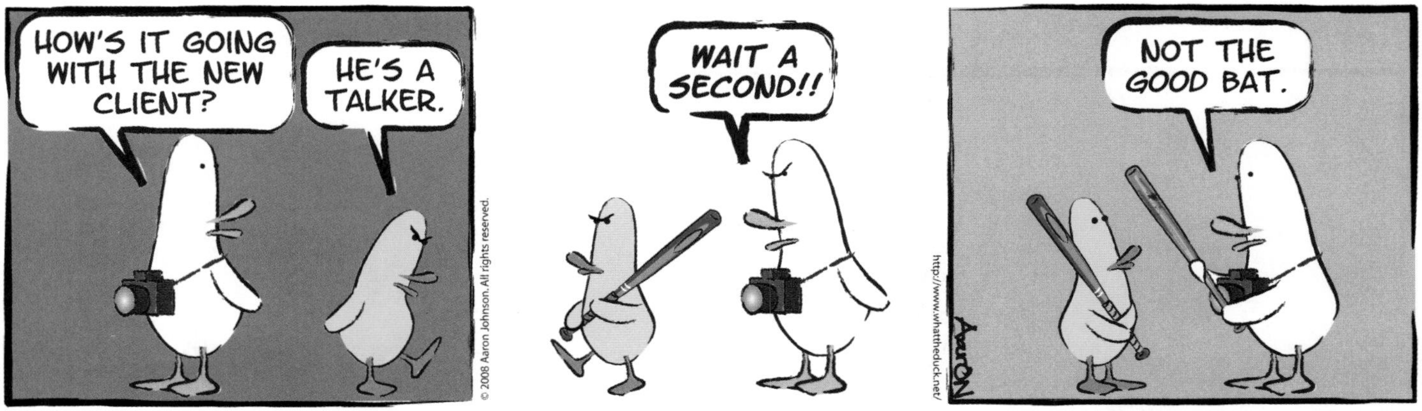
HOW'S IT GOING WITH THE NEW CLIENT?
HE'S A TALKER.
WAIT A SECOND!!
NOT THE GOOD BAT.
© 2008 Aaron Johnson. All rights reserved.
http://www.whattheduck.net/

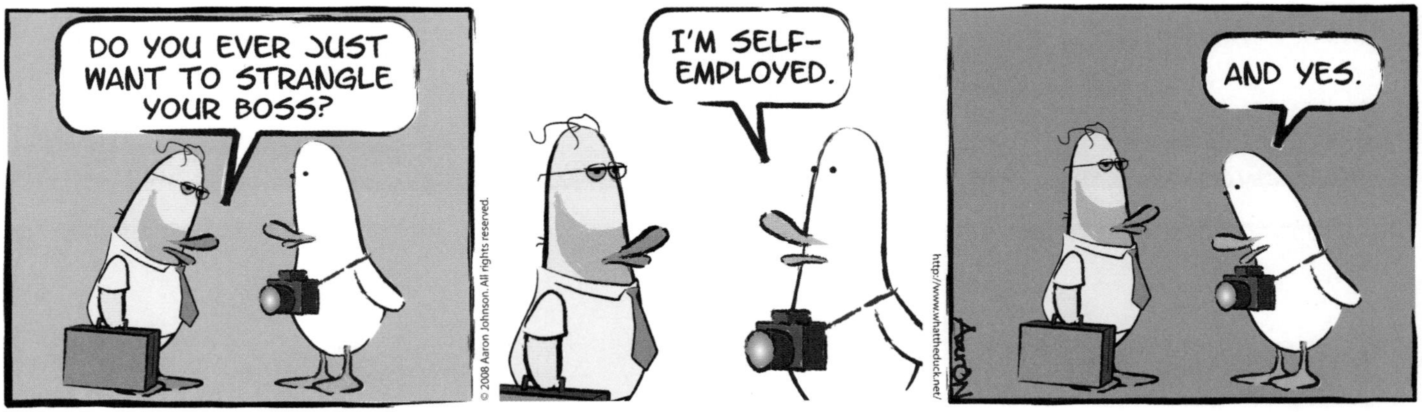
DO YOU EVER JUST WANT TO STRANGLE YOUR BOSS?
I'M SELF-EMPLOYED.
AND YES.
© 2008 Aaron Johnson. All rights reserved.
http://www.whattheduck.net/

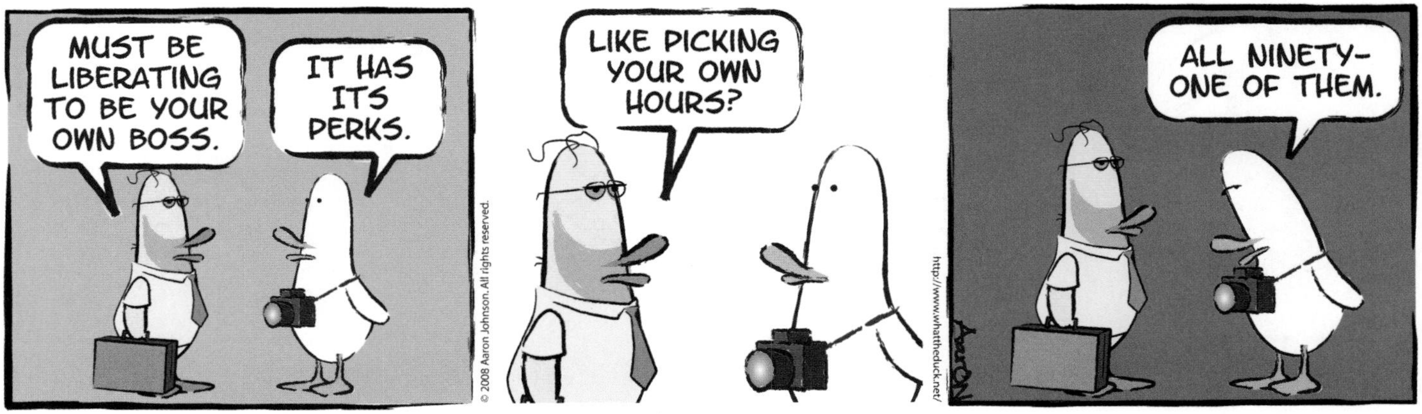
MUST BE LIBERATING TO BE YOUR OWN BOSS.
IT HAS ITS PERKS.
LIKE PICKING YOUR OWN HOURS?
ALL NINETY-ONE OF THEM.
© 2008 Aaron Johnson. All rights reserved.
http://www.whattheduck.net/

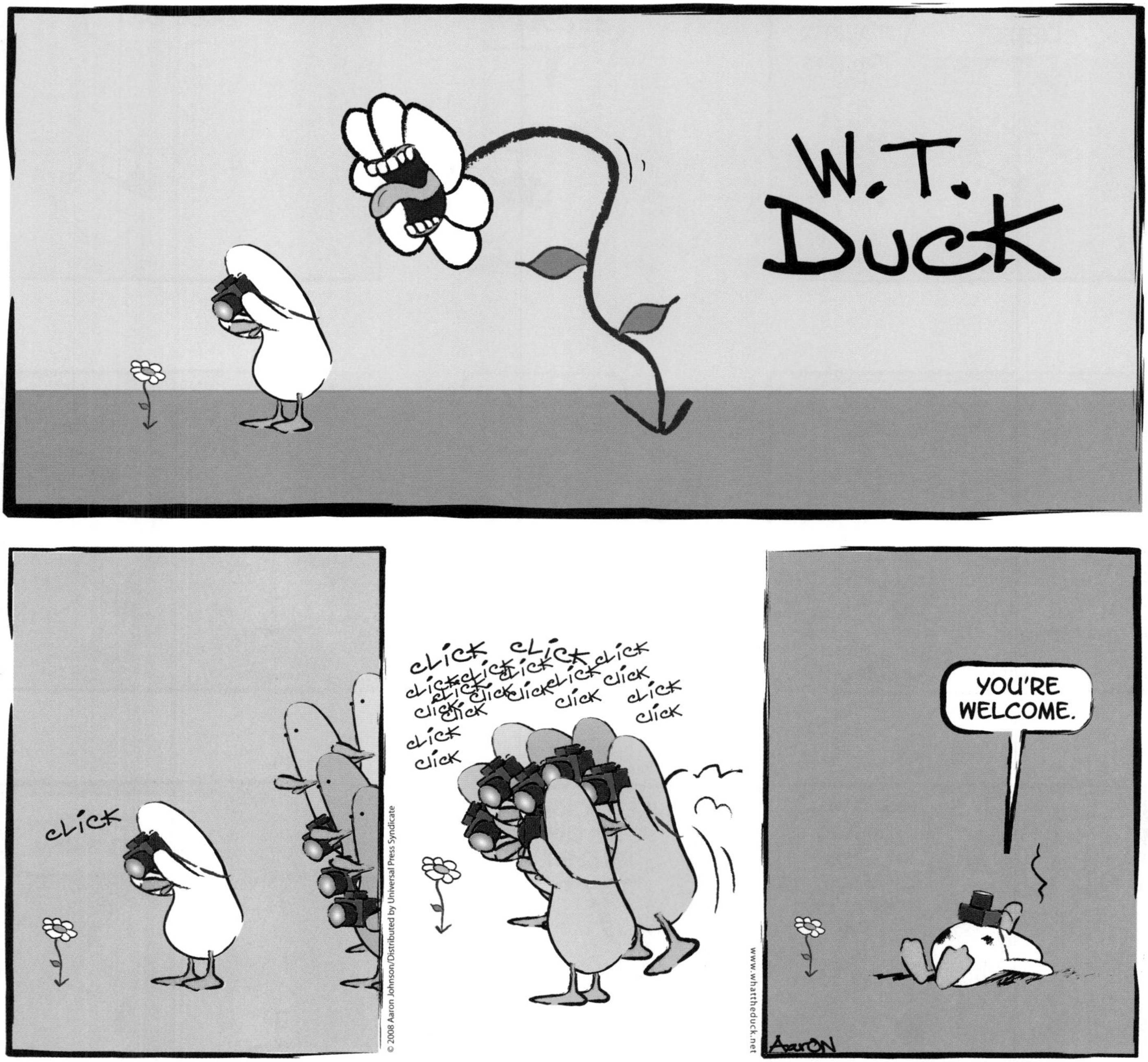
W.T. Duck
click
click
© 2008 Aaron Johnson/Distributed by Universal Press Syndicate
www.whattheduck.net
YOU'RE WELCOME.
AarON

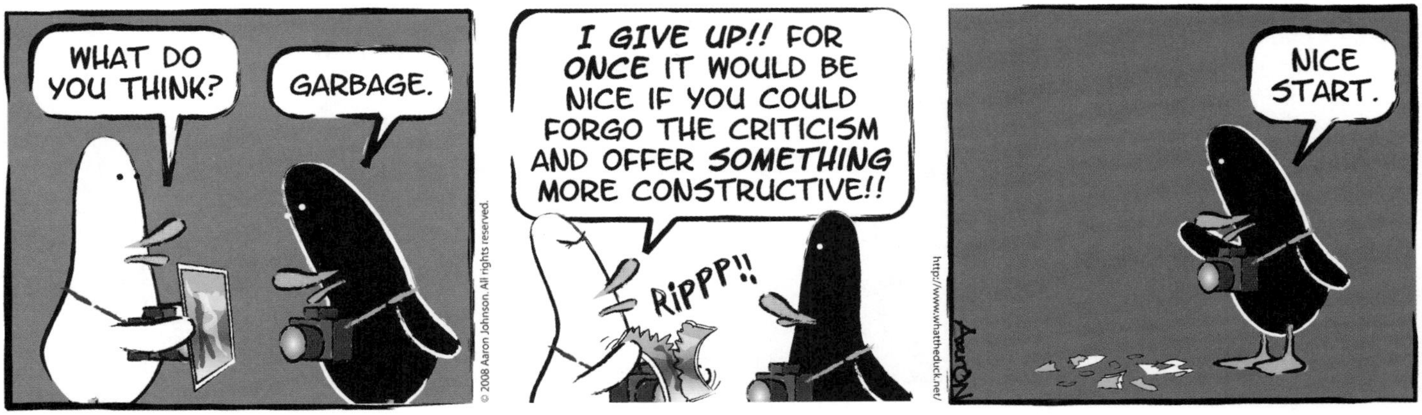
WHAT DO YOU THINK?
GARBAGE.
© 2008 Aaron Johnson. All rights reserved.
I GIVE UP!! FOR ONCE IT WOULD BE NICE IF YOU COULD FORGO THE CRITICISM AND OFFER SOMETHING MORE CONSTRUCTIVE!!
RIPPP!!
http://www.whattheduck.net/
NICE START.
AARON

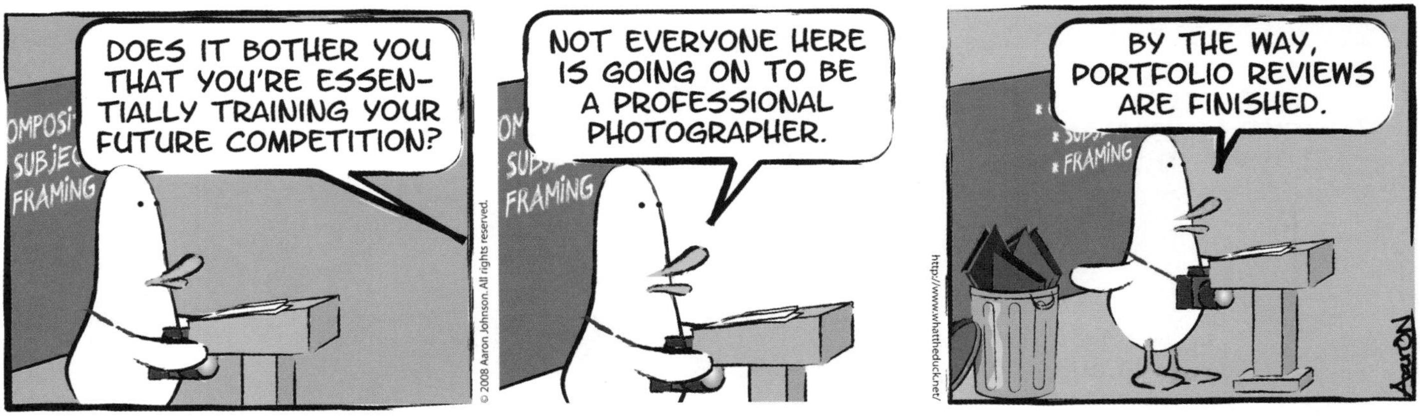
DOES IT BOTHER YOU THAT YOU'RE ESSEN-TIALLY TRAINING YOUR FUTURE COMPETITION?
FRAMING
© 2008 Aaron Johnson. All rights reserved.
NOT EVERYONE HERE IS GOING ON TO BE A PROFESSIONAL PHOTOGRAPHER.
http://www.whattheduck.net/
BY THE WAY, PORTFOLIO REVIEWS ARE FINISHED.
FRAMING
AARON

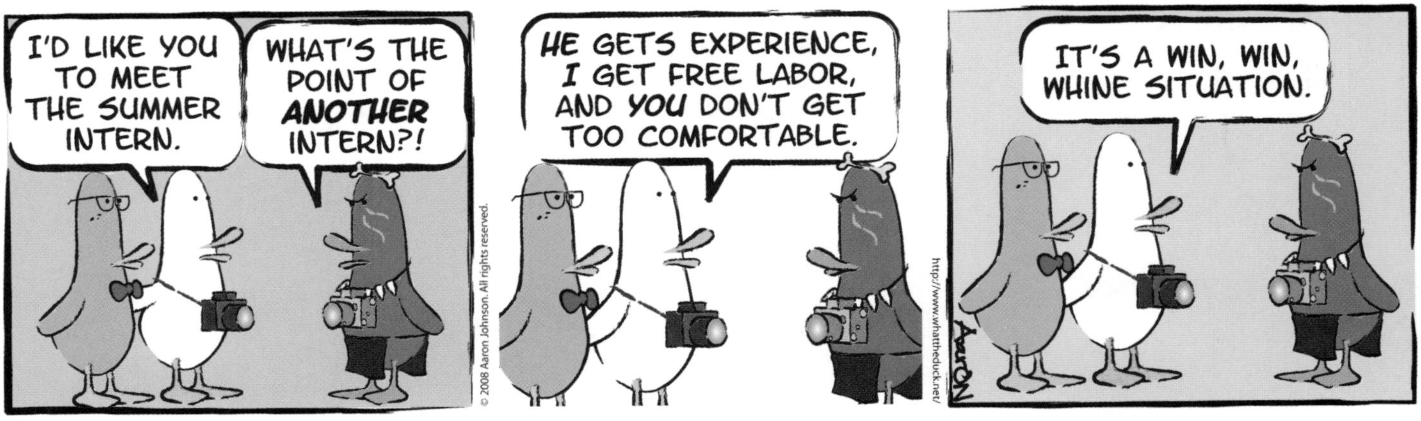
I'D LIKE YOU TO MEET THE SUMMER INTERN.
WHAT'S THE POINT OF ANOTHER INTERN?!
© 2008 Aaron Johnson. All rights reserved.
HE GETS EXPERIENCE, I GET FREE LABOR, AND YOU DON'T GET TOO COMFORTABLE.
http://www.whattheduck.net/
IT'S A WIN, WIN, WHINE SITUATION.
AARON

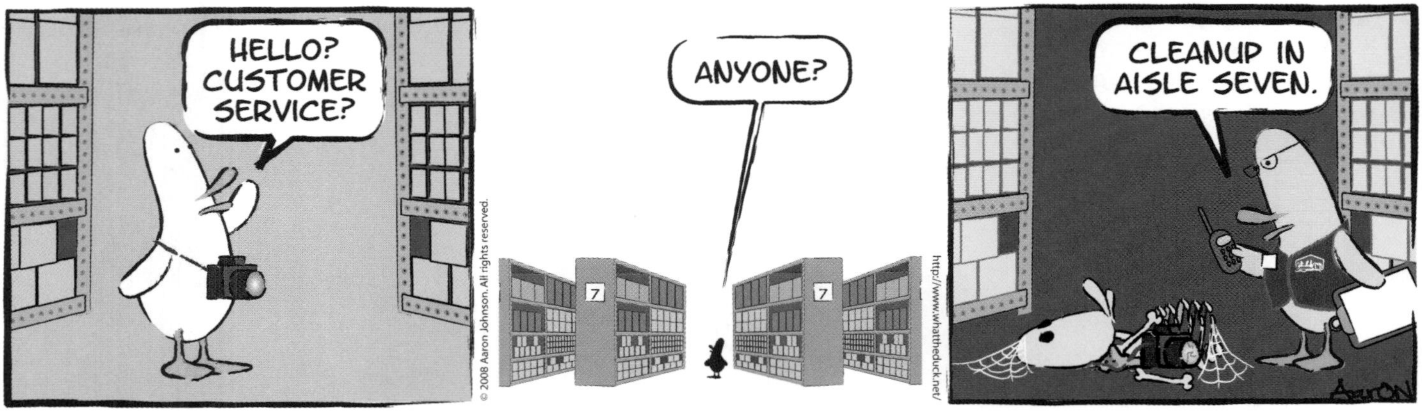
HELLO? CUSTOMER SERVICE?
ANYONE?
CLEANUP IN AISLE SEVEN.
© 2008 Aaron Johnson. All rights reserved.
http://www.whattheduck.net/

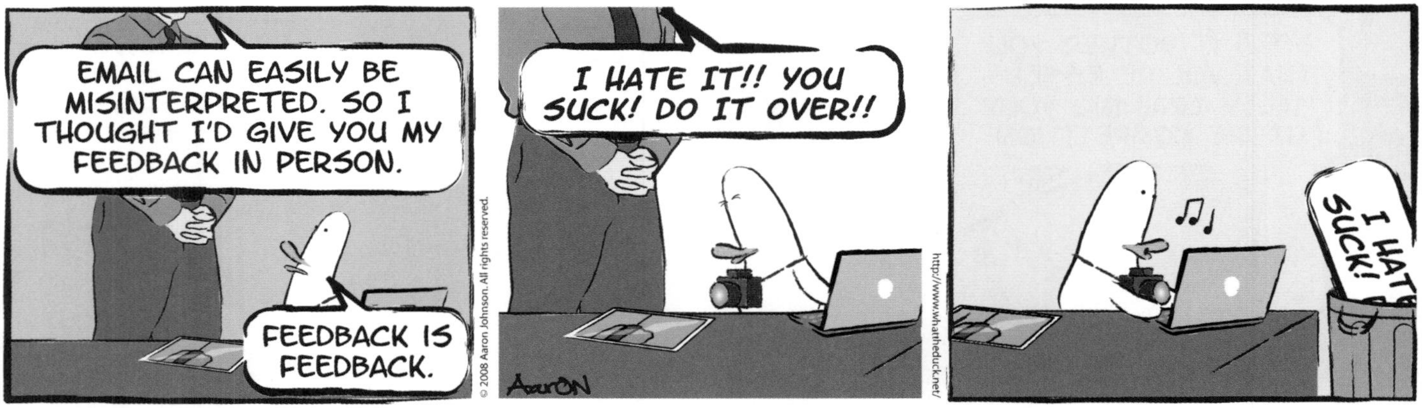
EMAIL CAN EASILY BE MISINTERPRETED. SO I THOUGHT I'D GIVE YOU MY FEEDBACK IN PERSON.
FEEDBACK IS FEEDBACK.
I HATE IT!! YOU SUCK! DO IT OVER!!
© 2008 Aaron Johnson. All rights reserved.
http://www.whattheduck.net/

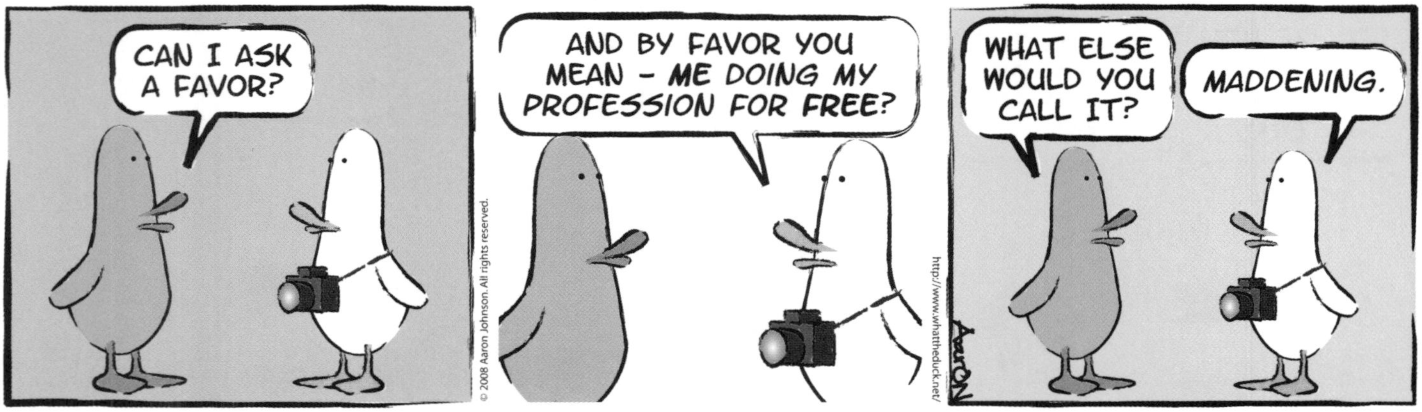
CAN I ASK A FAVOR?
AND BY FAVOR YOU MEAN – ME DOING MY PROFESSION FOR FREE?
WHAT ELSE WOULD YOU CALL IT?
MADDENING.
© 2008 Aaron Johnson. All rights reserved.
http://www.whattheduck.net/

DUCK
U
SCHOOL OF PHOTOGRAPHY
W.T. DUCK
I JUST WASTED MY MORNING WEEDING OUT EMAILS FOR ROLEX WATCHES, WEIGHT LOSS PILLS, AND VIAGRA.
WHO'S STILL GETTING SUCKERED INTO THESE SPAM MESSAGES?!
DON'T LOOK AT ME.
I'M TRYING NOT TO.
© 2008 Aaron Johnson/Distributed by Universal Press Syndicate
AARON
www.whattheduck.net

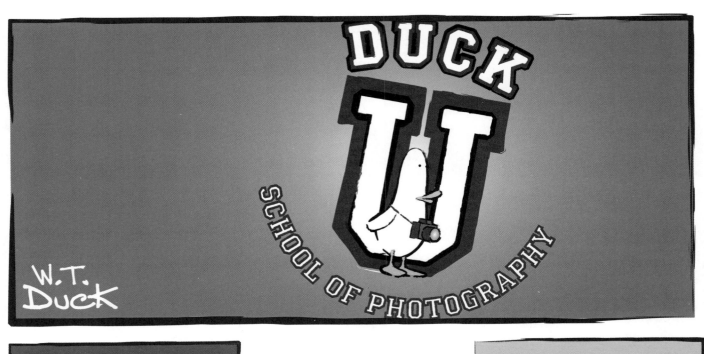

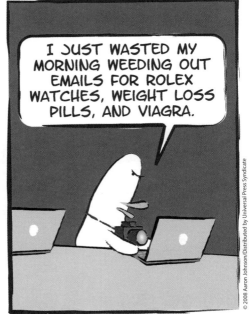

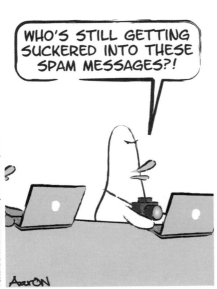

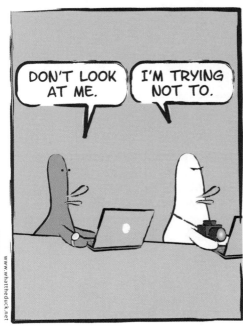

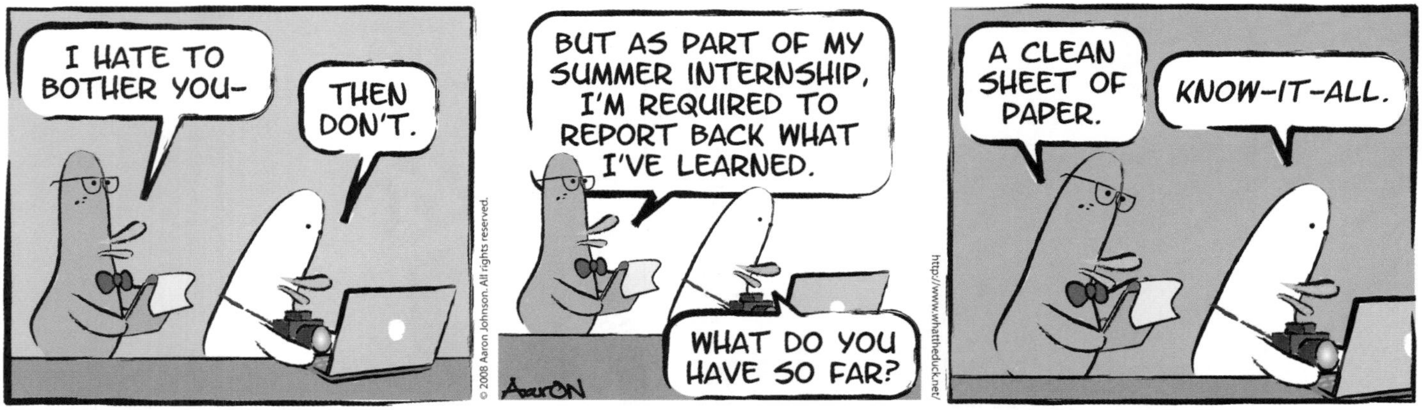
I HATE TO BOTHER YOU-
THEN DON'T.
BUT AS PART OF MY SUMMER INTERNSHIP, I'M REQUIRED TO REPORT BACK WHAT I'VE LEARNED.
WHAT DO YOU HAVE SO FAR?
A CLEAN SHEET OF PAPER.
KNOW-IT-ALL.
© 2008 Aaron Johnson. All rights reserved.
AARON
http://www.whattheduck.net/

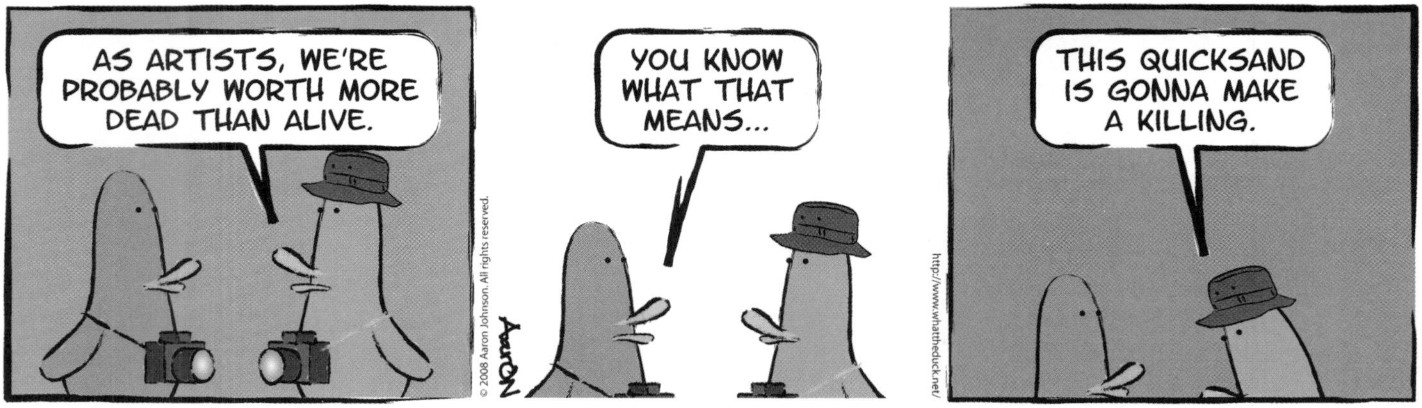
AS ARTISTS, WE'RE PROBABLY WORTH MORE DEAD THAN ALIVE.
YOU KNOW WHAT THAT MEANS...
THIS QUICKSAND IS GONNA MAKE A KILLING.
© 2008 Aaron Johnson. All rights reserved.
AARON
http://www.whattheduck.net/

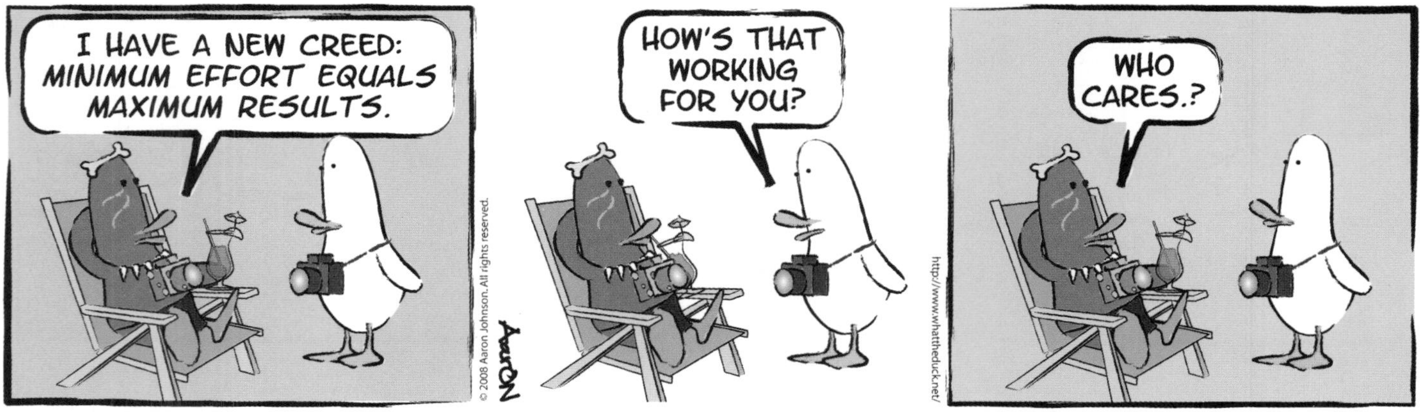
I HAVE A NEW CREED: MINIMUM EFFORT EQUALS MAXIMUM RESULTS.
HOW'S THAT WORKING FOR YOU?
WHO CARES.?
© 2008 Aaron Johnson. All rights reserved.
AARON
http://www.whattheduck.net/

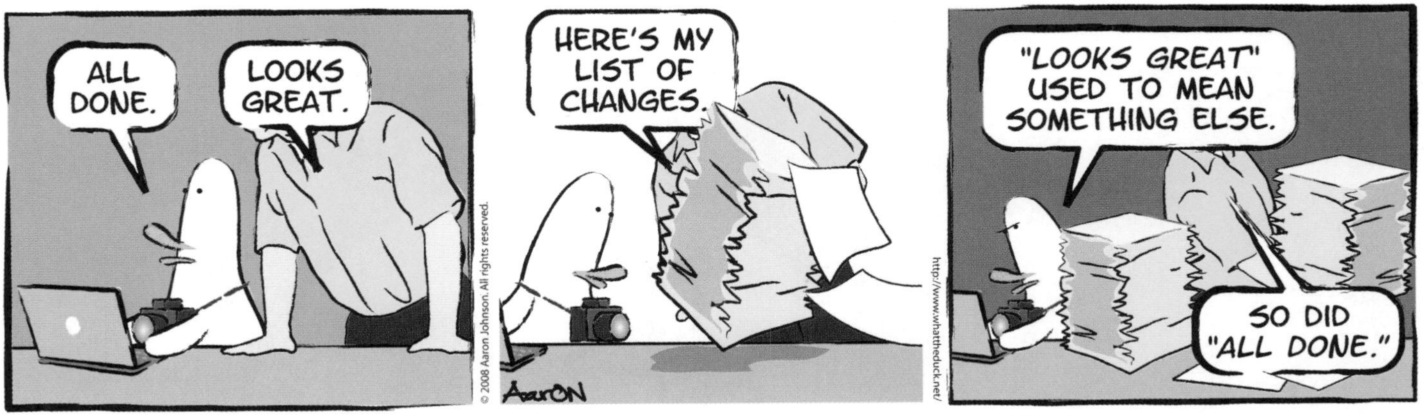
ALL DONE.
LOOKS GREAT.
HERE'S MY LIST OF CHANGES.
"LOOKS GREAT" USED TO MEAN SOMETHING ELSE.
SO DID "ALL DONE."
© 2008 Aaron Johnson. All rights reserved.
http://www.whattheduck.net/
AarON

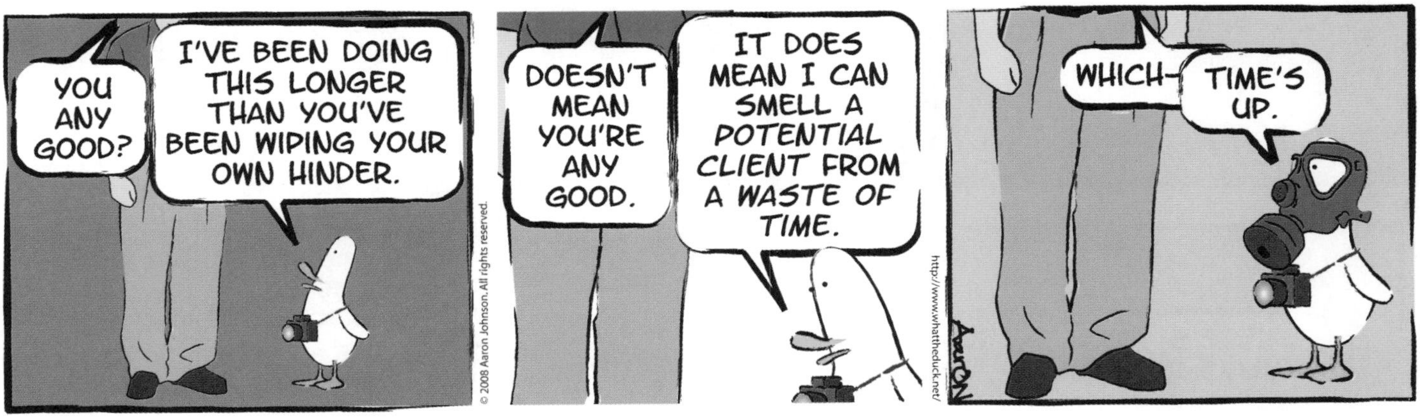
YOU ANY GOOD?
I'VE BEEN DOING THIS LONGER THAN YOU'VE BEEN WIPING YOUR OWN HINDER.
DOESN'T MEAN YOU'RE ANY GOOD.
IT DOES MEAN I CAN SMELL A POTENTIAL CLIENT FROM A WASTE OF TIME.
WHICH-
TIME'S UP.
© 2008 Aaron Johnson. All rights reserved.
http://www.whattheduck.net/
AarON

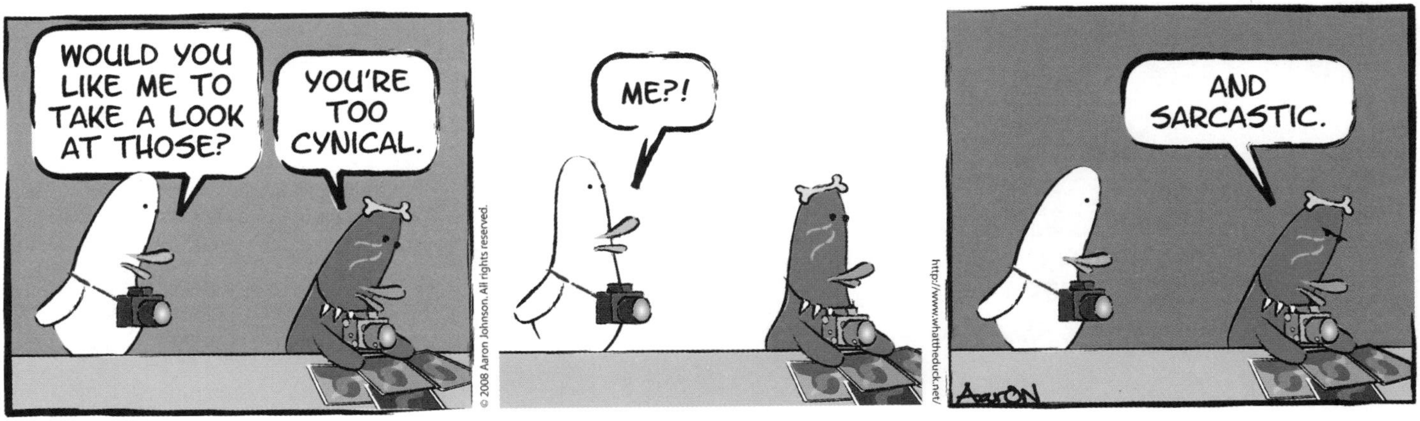
WOULD YOU LIKE ME TO TAKE A LOOK AT THOSE?
YOU'RE TOO CYNICAL.
ME?!
AND SARCASTIC.
© 2008 Aaron Johnson. All rights reserved.
http://www.whattheduck.net/
AarON

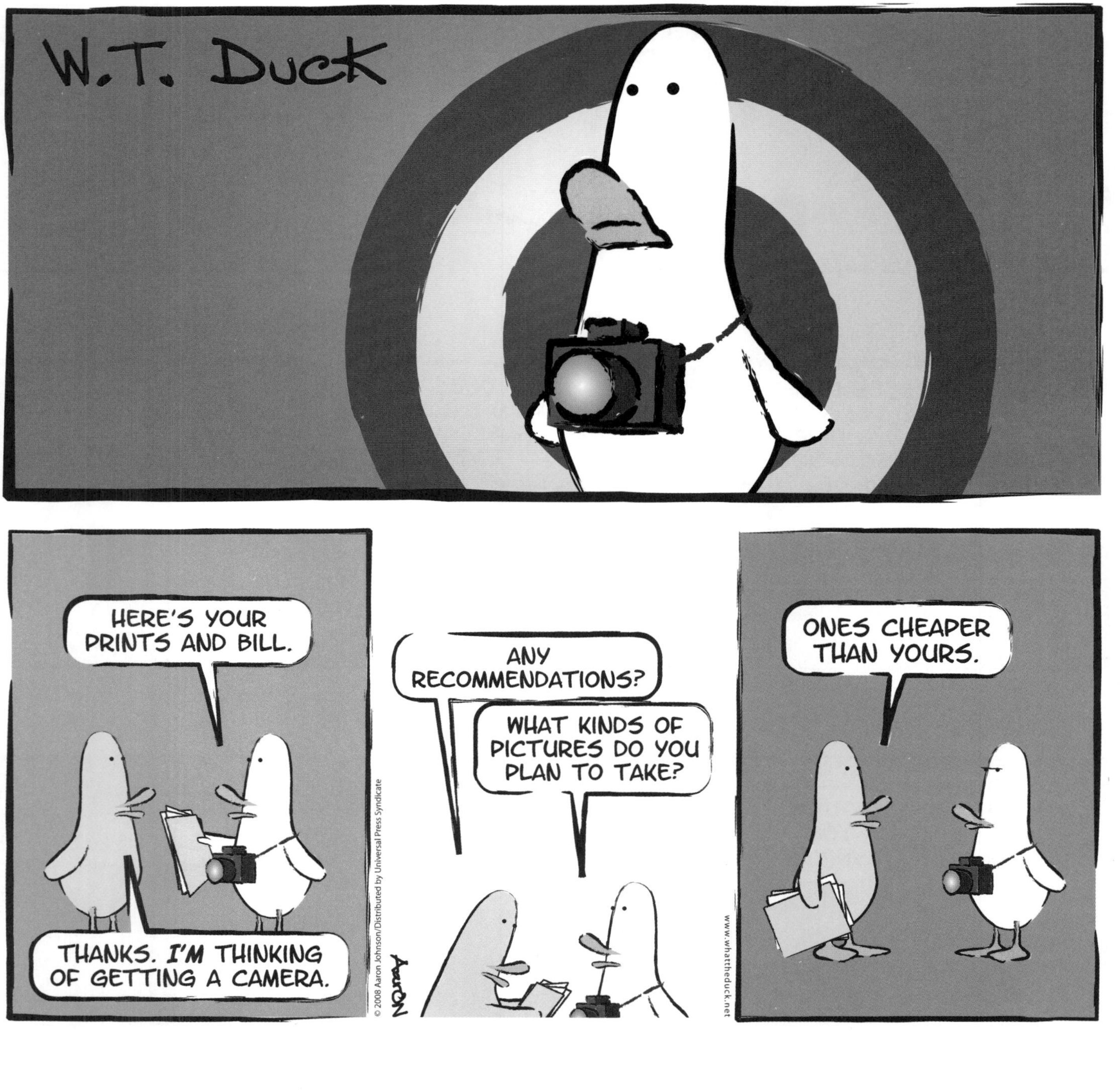
W.T. Duck
HERE'S YOUR PRINTS AND BILL.
THANKS. I'M THINKING OF GETTING A CAMERA.
ANY RECOMMENDATIONS?
WHAT KINDS OF PICTURES DO YOU PLAN TO TAKE?
ONES CHEAPER THAN YOURS.
© 2008 Aaron Johnson/Distributed by Universal Press Syndicate
AARON
www.whattheduck.net

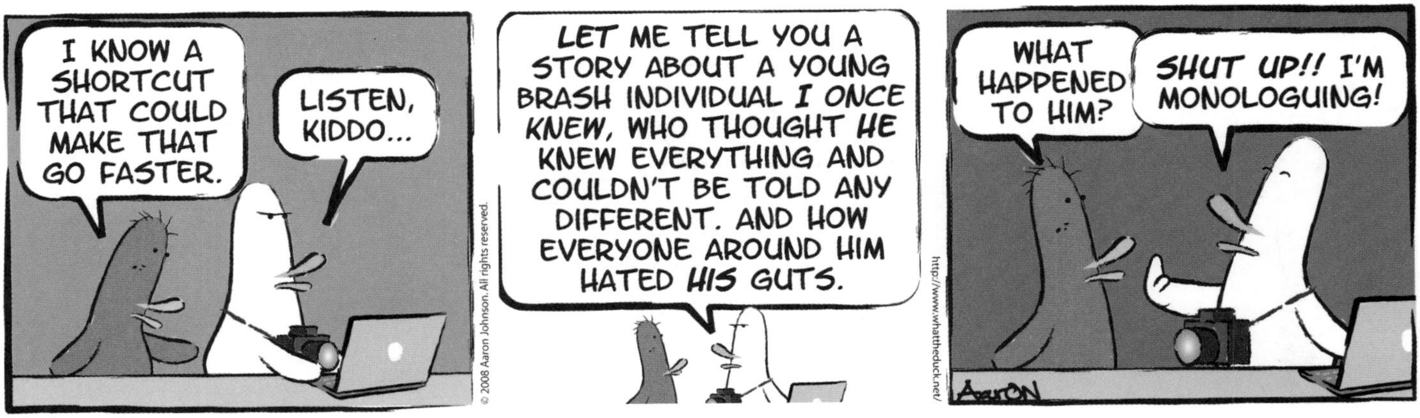
I KNOW A SHORTCUT THAT COULD MAKE THAT GO FASTER.
LISTEN, KIDDO...
© 2008 Aaron Johnson. All rights reserved.
LET ME TELL YOU A STORY ABOUT A YOUNG BRASH INDIVIDUAL I ONCE KNEW, WHO THOUGHT HE KNEW EVERYTHING AND COULDN'T BE TOLD ANY DIFFERENT. AND HOW EVERYONE AROUND HIM HATED HIS GUTS.
http://www.whattheduck.net/
WHAT HAPPENED TO HIM?
SHUT UP!! I'M MONOLOGUING!
AARON

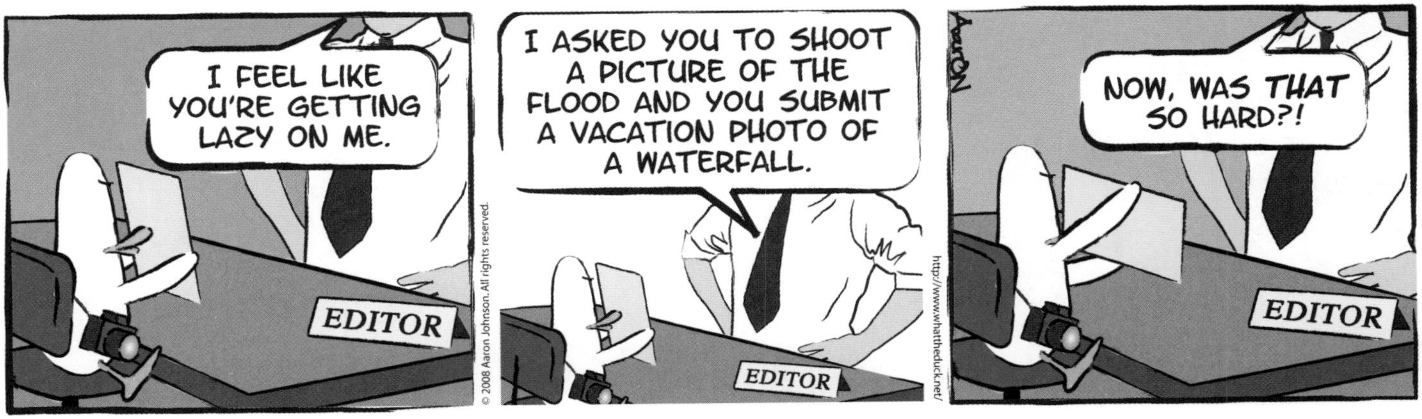
I FEEL LIKE YOU'RE GETTING LAZY ON ME.
EDITOR
© 2008 Aaron Johnson. All rights reserved.
I ASKED YOU TO SHOOT A PICTURE OF THE FLOOD AND YOU SUBMIT A VACATION PHOTO OF A WATERFALL.
EDITOR
http://www.whattheduck.net/
AARON
NOW, WAS THAT SO HARD?!
EDITOR

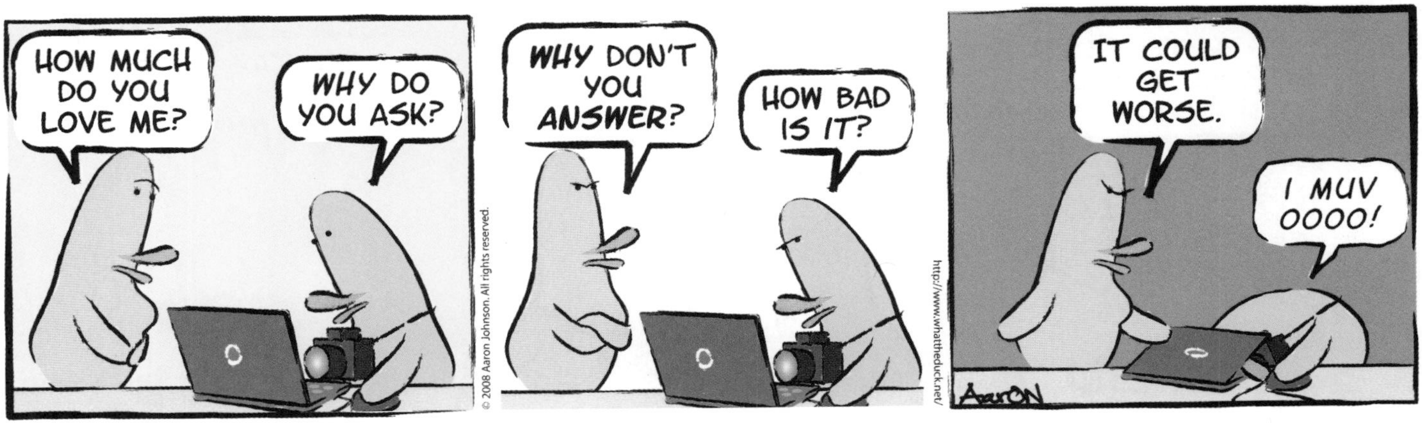
HOW MUCH DO YOU LOVE ME?
WHY DO YOU ASK?
© 2008 Aaron Johnson. All rights reserved.
WHY DON'T YOU ANSWER?
HOW BAD IS IT?
http://www.whattheduck.net/
IT COULD GET WORSE.
I MUV OOOO!
AARON

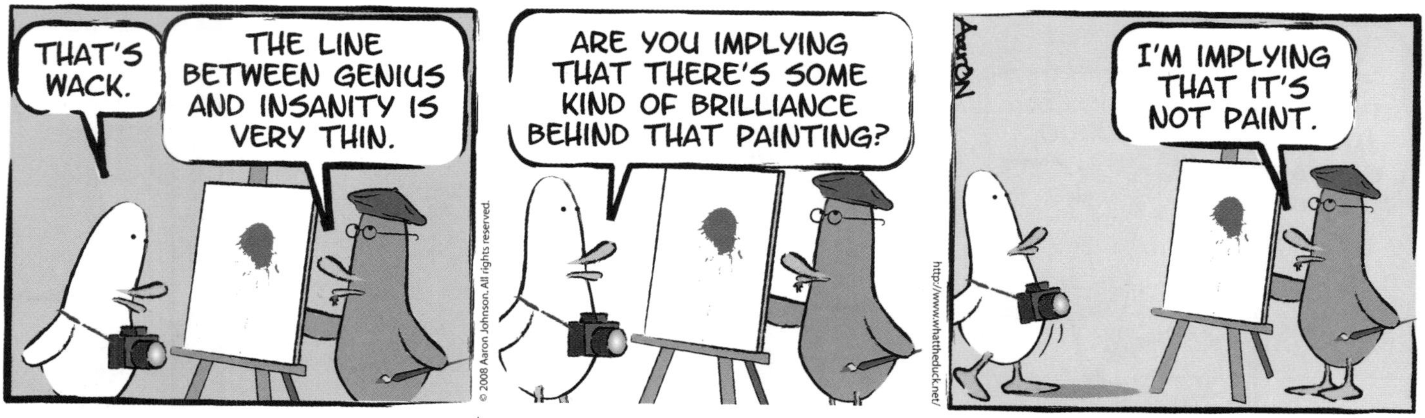
THAT'S WACK.
THE LINE BETWEEN GENIUS AND INSANITY IS VERY THIN.
ARE YOU IMPLYING THAT THERE'S SOME KIND OF BRILLIANCE BEHIND THAT PAINTING?
I'M IMPLYING THAT IT'S NOT PAINT.
© 2008 Aaron Johnson. All rights reserved.
http://www.whattheduck.net/
AARON

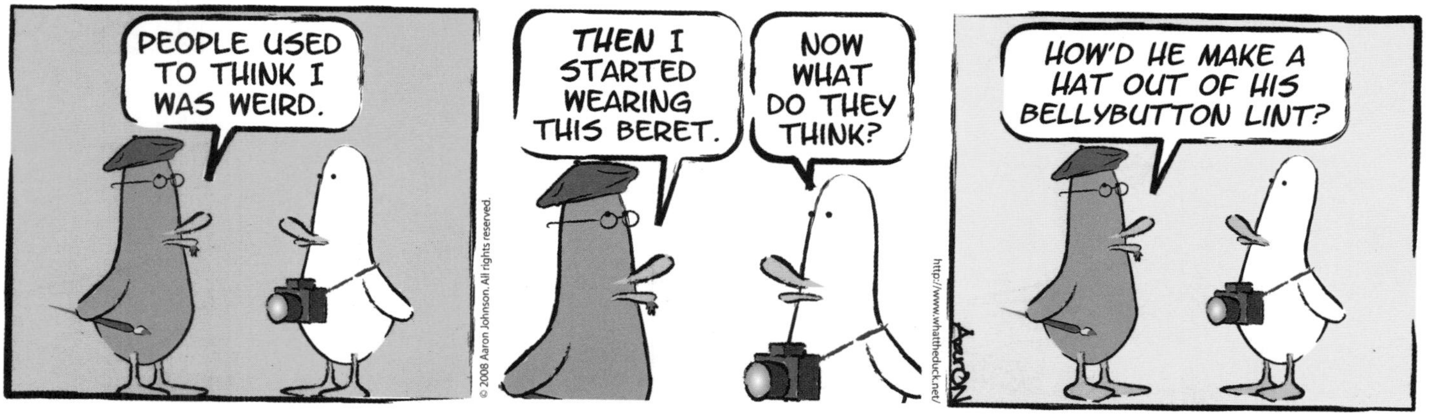
PEOPLE USED TO THINK I WAS WEIRD.
THEN I STARTED WEARING THIS BERET.
NOW WHAT DO THEY THINK?
HOW'D HE MAKE A HAT OUT OF HIS BELLYBUTTON LINT?
© 2008 Aaron Johnson. All rights reserved.
http://www.whattheduck.net/
AARON

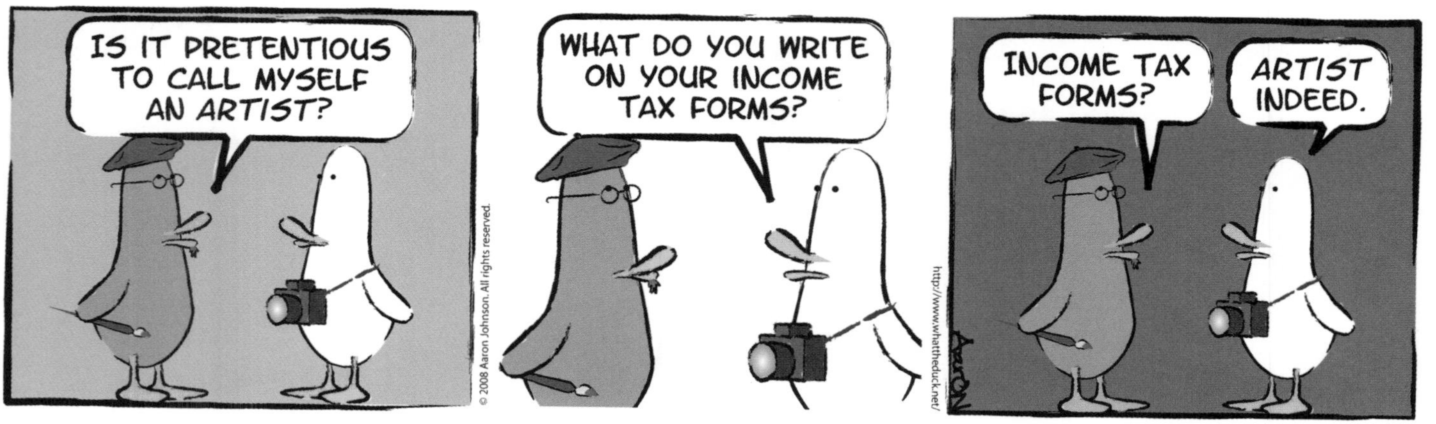
IS IT PRETENTIOUS TO CALL MYSELF AN *ARTIST?*
WHAT DO YOU WRITE ON YOUR INCOME TAX FORMS?
INCOME TAX FORMS?
ARTIST INDEED.
© 2008 Aaron Johnson. All rights reserved.
http://www.whattheduck.net/
AARON

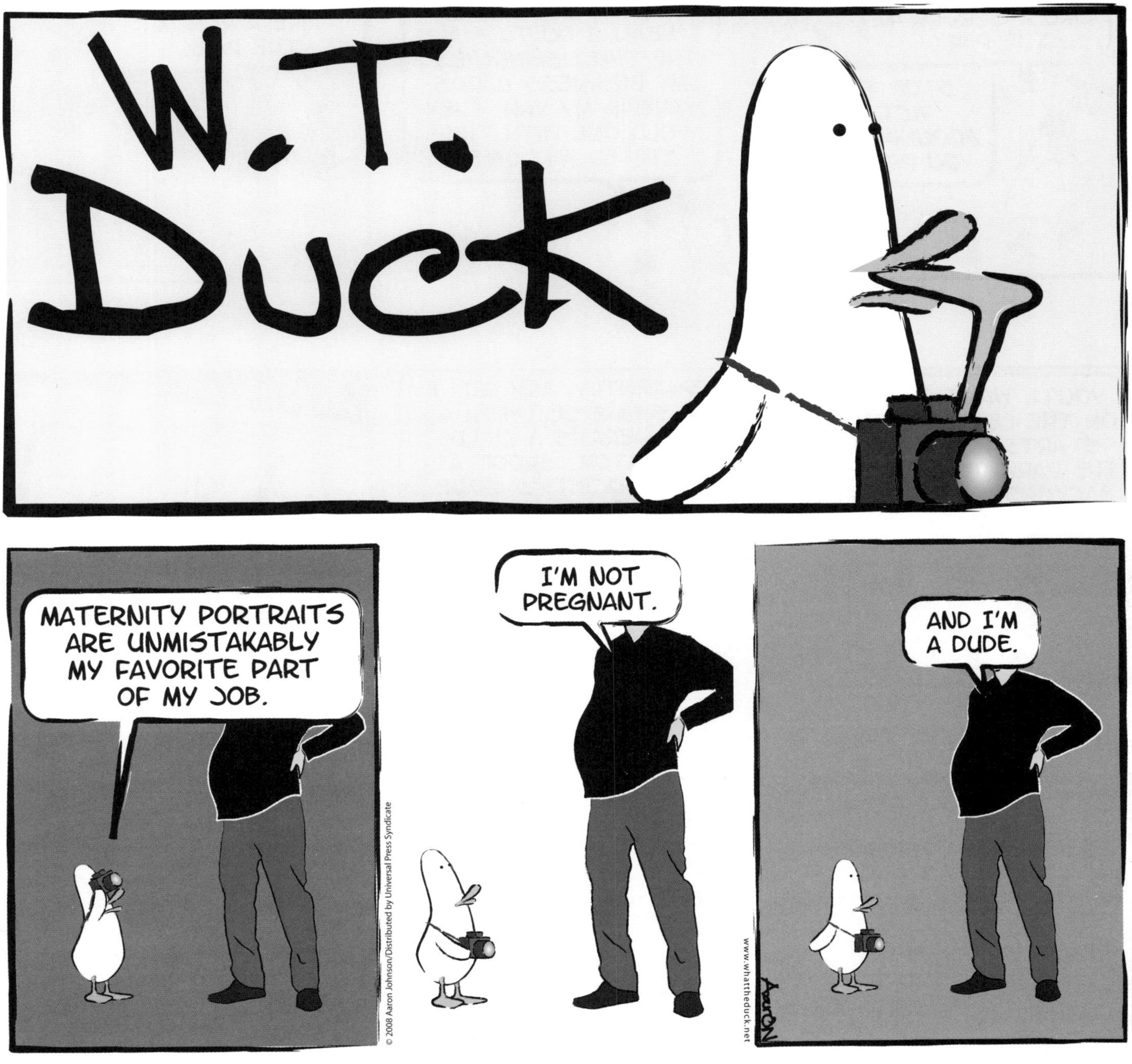
W.T. Duck
MATERNITY PORTRAITS ARE UNMISTAKABLY MY FAVORITE PART OF MY JOB.
I'M NOT PREGNANT.
AND I'M A DUDE.
© 2008 Aaron Johnson/Distributed by Universal Press Syndicate
www.whattheduck.net

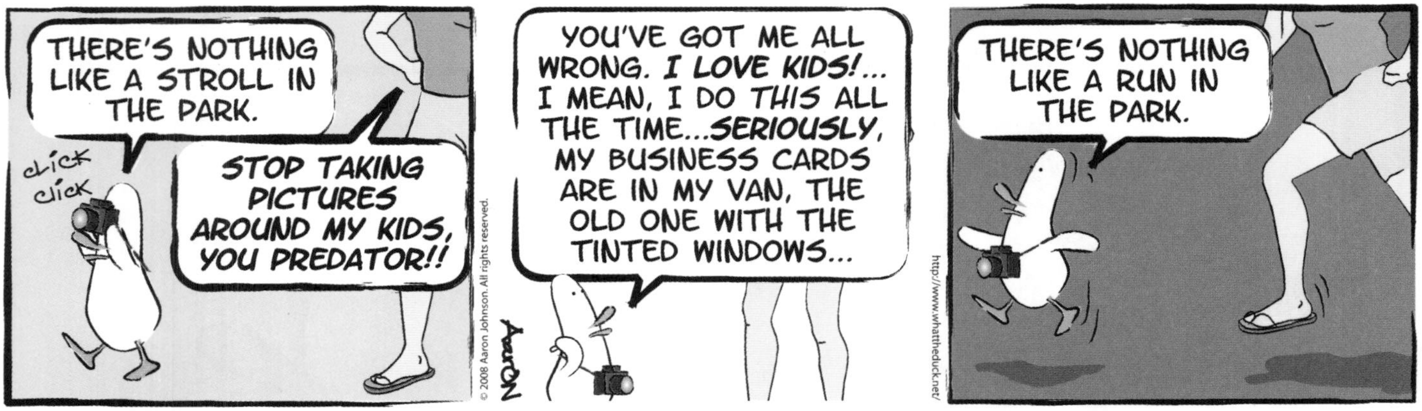
click
click
THERE'S NOTHING LIKE A STROLL IN THE PARK.
STOP TAKING PICTURES AROUND MY KIDS, YOU PREDATOR!!
© 2008 Aaron Johnson. All rights reserved.
AARON
YOU'VE GOT ME ALL WRONG. I LOVE KIDS!... I MEAN, I DO THIS ALL THE TIME...SERIOUSLY, MY BUSINESS CARDS ARE IN MY VAN, THE OLD ONE WITH THE TINTED WINDOWS...
http://www.whattheduck.net/
THERE'S NOTHING LIKE A RUN IN THE PARK.

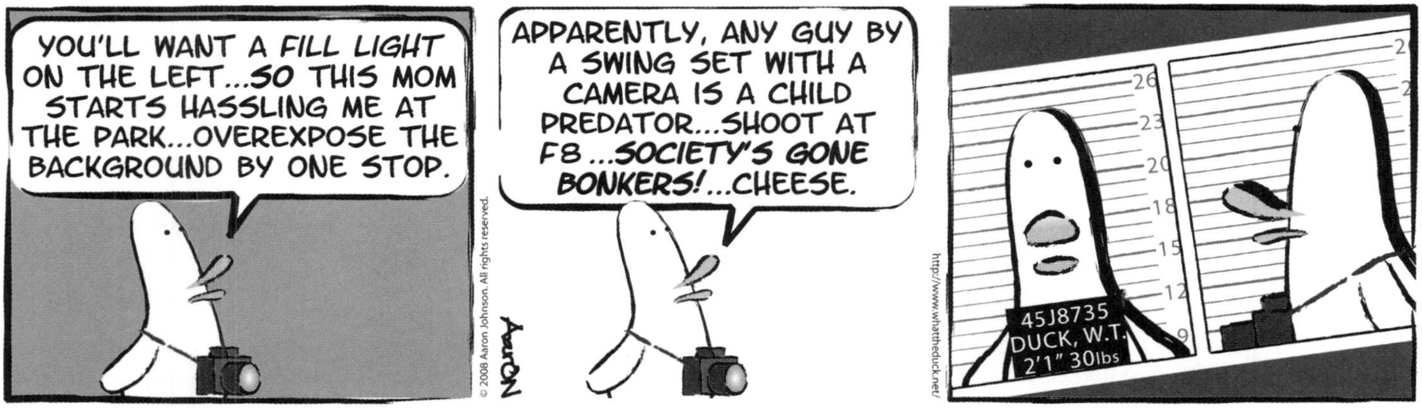
YOU'LL WANT A FILL LIGHT ON THE LEFT...SO THIS MOM STARTS HASSLING ME AT THE PARK...OVEREXPOSE THE BACKGROUND BY ONE STOP.
© 2008 Aaron Johnson. All rights reserved.
AARON
APPARENTLY, ANY GUY BY A SWING SET WITH A CAMERA IS A CHILD PREDATOR...SHOOT AT F8 ...SOCIETY'S GONE BONKERS!...CHEESE.
http://www.whattheduck.net/
45J8735
DUCK, W.T.
2'1" 30lbs

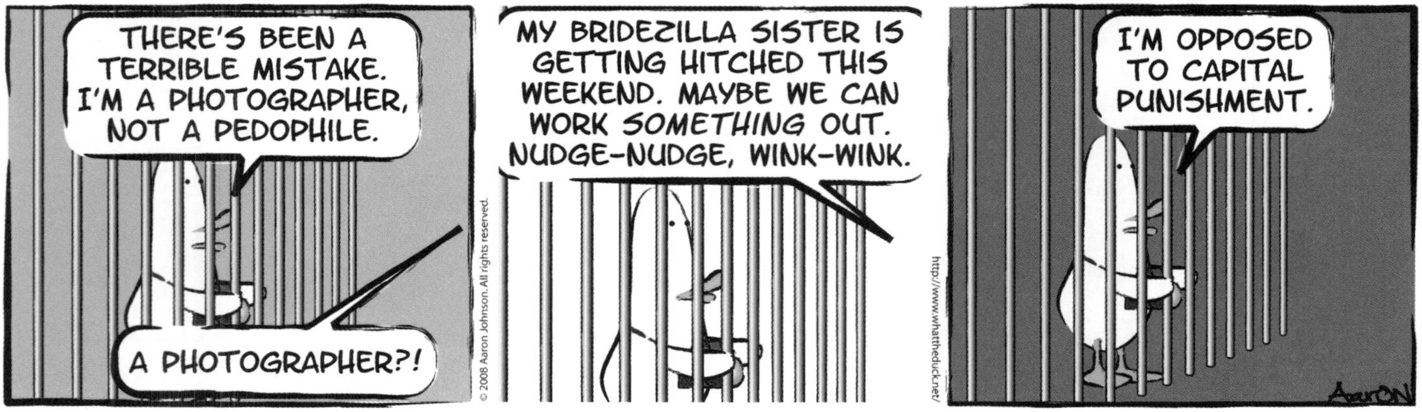
THERE'S BEEN A TERRIBLE MISTAKE. I'M A PHOTOGRAPHER, NOT A PEDOPHILE.
A PHOTOGRAPHER?!
© 2008 Aaron Johnson. All rights reserved.
MY BRIDEZILLA SISTER IS GETTING HITCHED THIS WEEKEND. MAYBE WE CAN WORK SOMETHING OUT. NUDGE-NUDGE, WINK-WINK.
http://www.whattheduck.net/
I'M OPPOSED TO CAPITAL PUNISHMENT.
AARON

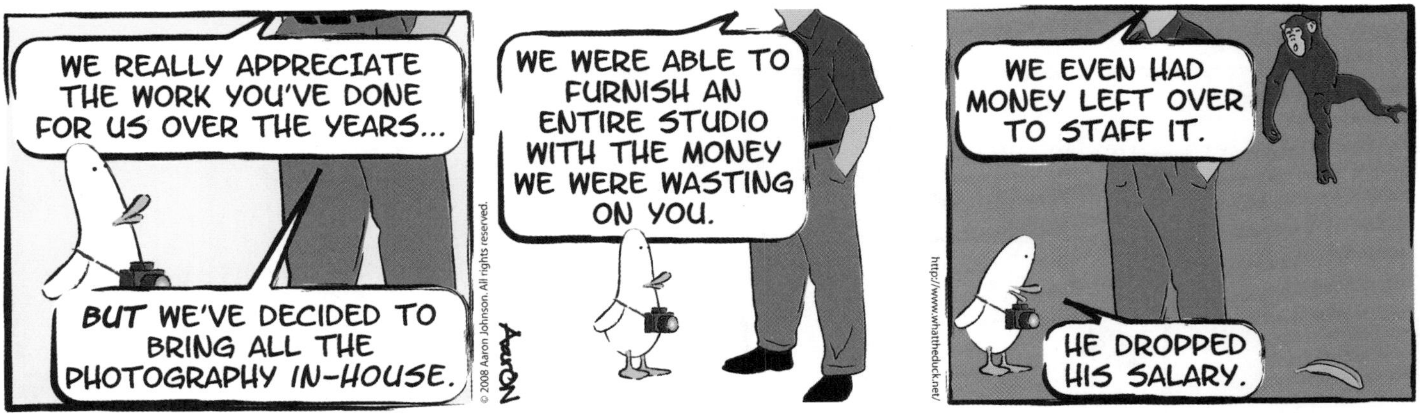
WE REALLY APPRECIATE THE WORK YOU'VE DONE FOR US OVER THE YEARS...
BUT WE'VE DECIDED TO BRING ALL THE PHOTOGRAPHY IN-HOUSE.
WE WERE ABLE TO FURNISH AN ENTIRE STUDIO WITH THE MONEY WE WERE WASTING ON YOU.
WE EVEN HAD MONEY LEFT OVER TO STAFF IT.
HE DROPPED HIS SALARY.
AARON

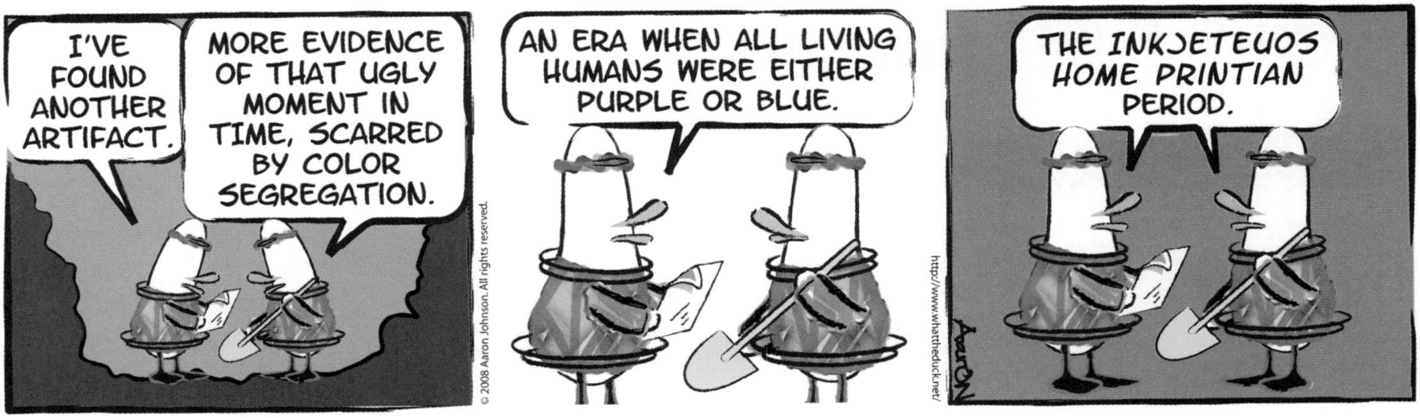
I'VE FOUND ANOTHER ARTIFACT.
MORE EVIDENCE OF THAT UGLY MOMENT IN TIME, SCARRED BY COLOR SEGREGATION.
AN ERA WHEN ALL LIVING HUMANS WERE EITHER PURPLE OR BLUE.
THE INKJETEUOS HOME PRINTIAN PERIOD.
AARON

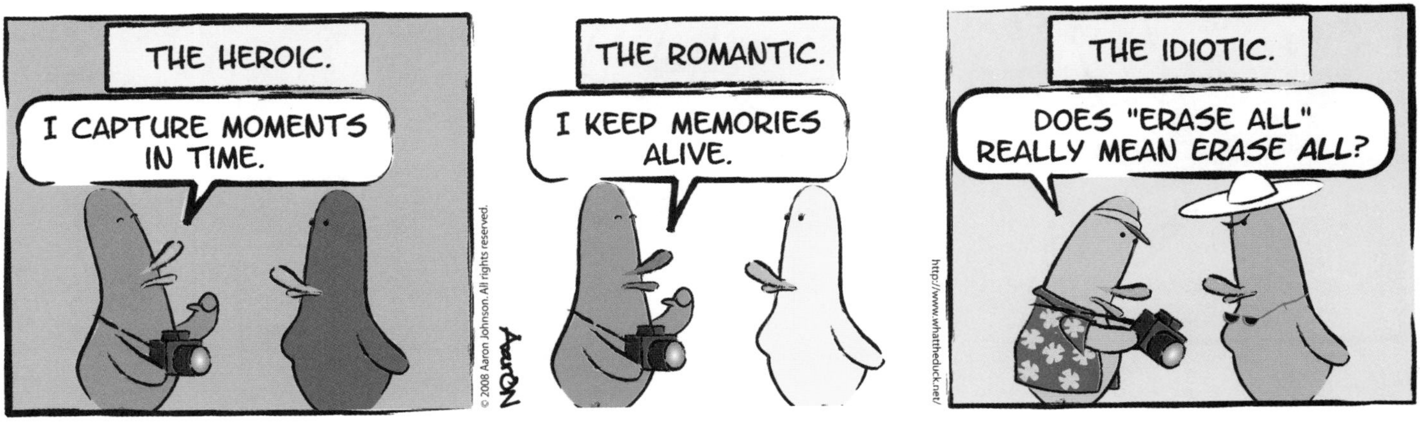
THE HEROIC.
I CAPTURE MOMENTS IN TIME.
THE ROMANTIC.
I KEEP MEMORIES ALIVE.
THE IDIOTIC.
DOES "ERASE ALL" REALLY MEAN ERASE ALL?
AARON

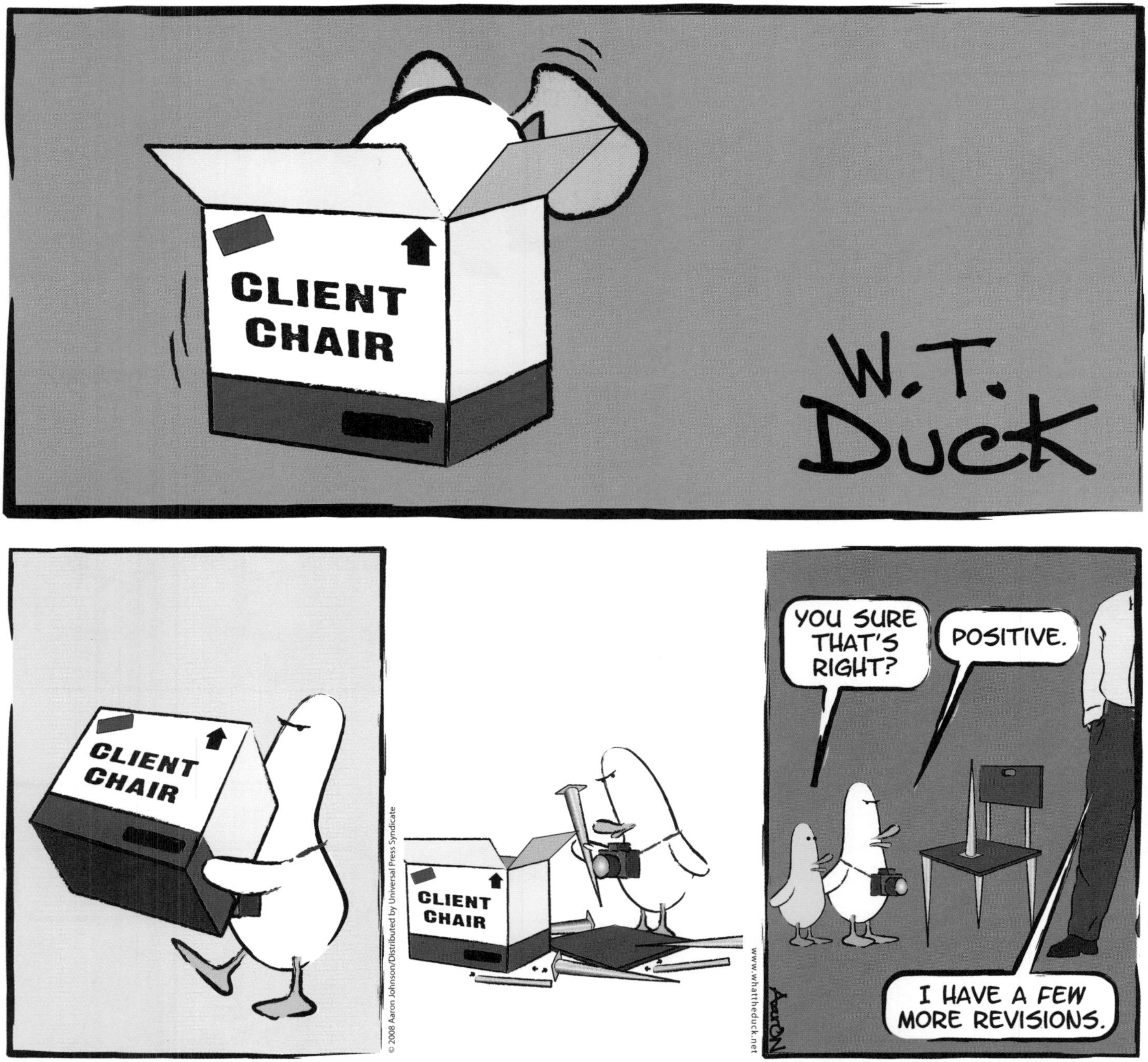

W.T. Duck
CLIENT CHAIR
CLIENT CHAIR
© 2008 Aaron Johnson/Distributed by Universal Press Syndicate
CLIENT CHAIR
YOU SURE THAT'S RIGHT?
POSITIVE.
I HAVE A FEW MORE REVISIONS.
www.whattheduck.net
AARON

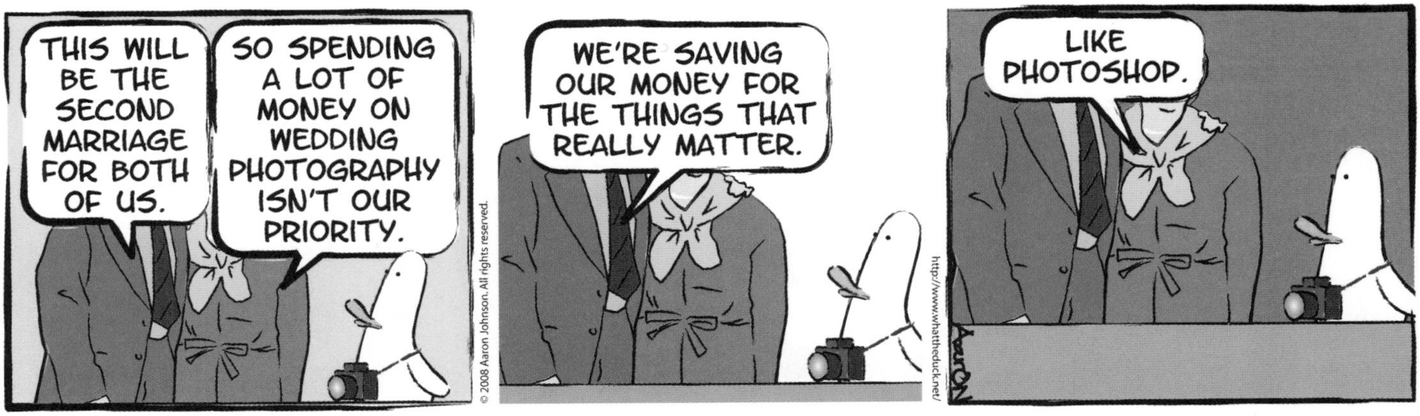
THIS WILL BE THE SECOND MARRIAGE FOR BOTH OF US.
SO SPENDING A LOT OF MONEY ON WEDDING PHOTOGRAPHY ISN'T OUR PRIORITY.
© 2008 Aaron Johnson. All rights reserved.
WE'RE SAVING OUR MONEY FOR THE THINGS THAT REALLY MATTER.
http://www.whattheduck.net/
LIKE PHOTOSHOP.
AARON

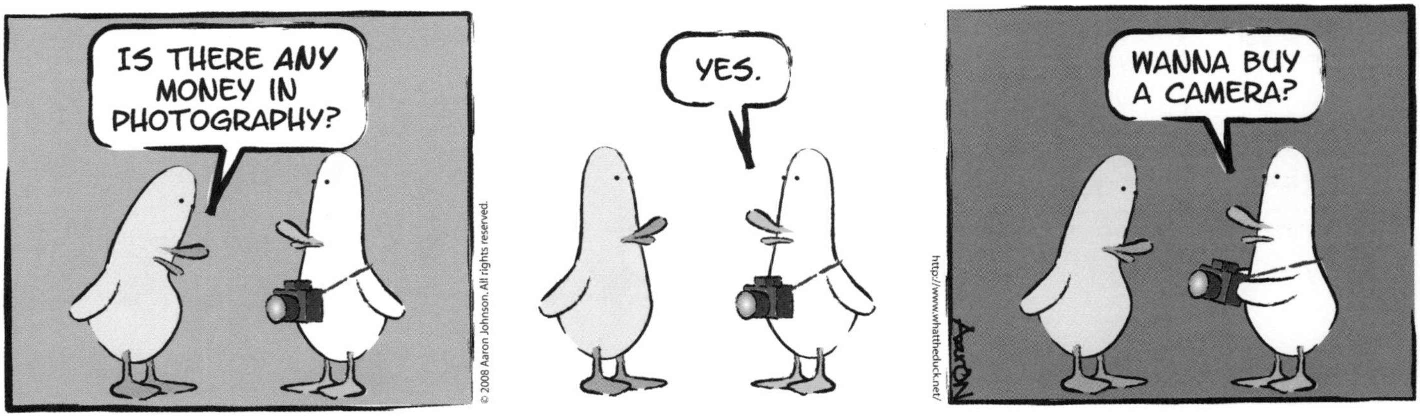
IS THERE ANY MONEY IN PHOTOGRAPHY?
© 2008 Aaron Johnson. All rights reserved.
YES.
http://www.whattheduck.net/
WANNA BUY A CAMERA?
AARON

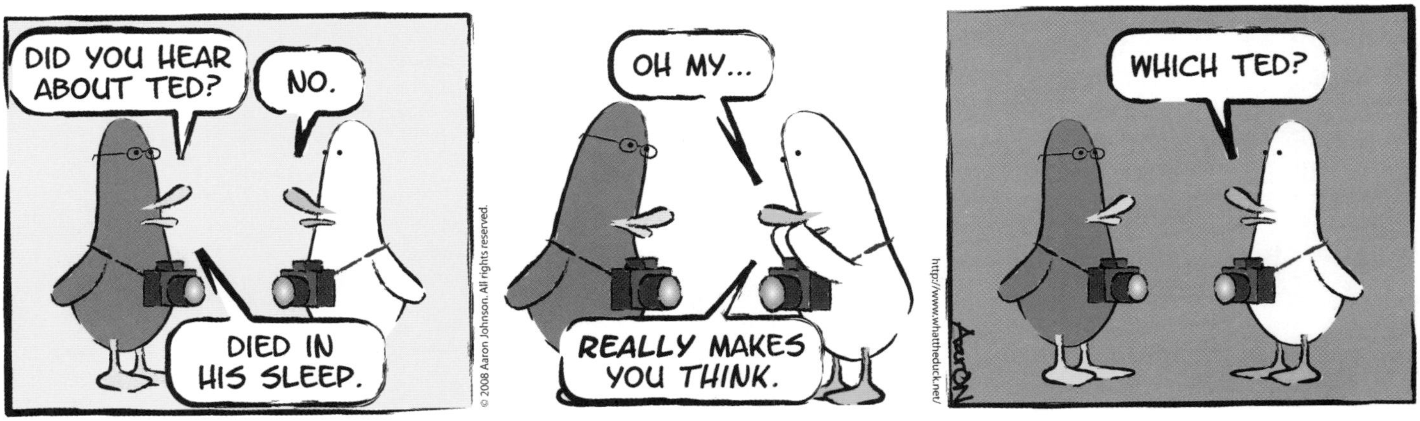
DID YOU HEAR ABOUT TED?
NO.
DIED IN HIS SLEEP.
© 2008 Aaron Johnson. All rights reserved.
OH MY...
REALLY MAKES YOU THINK.
http://www.whattheduck.net/
WHICH TED?
AARON

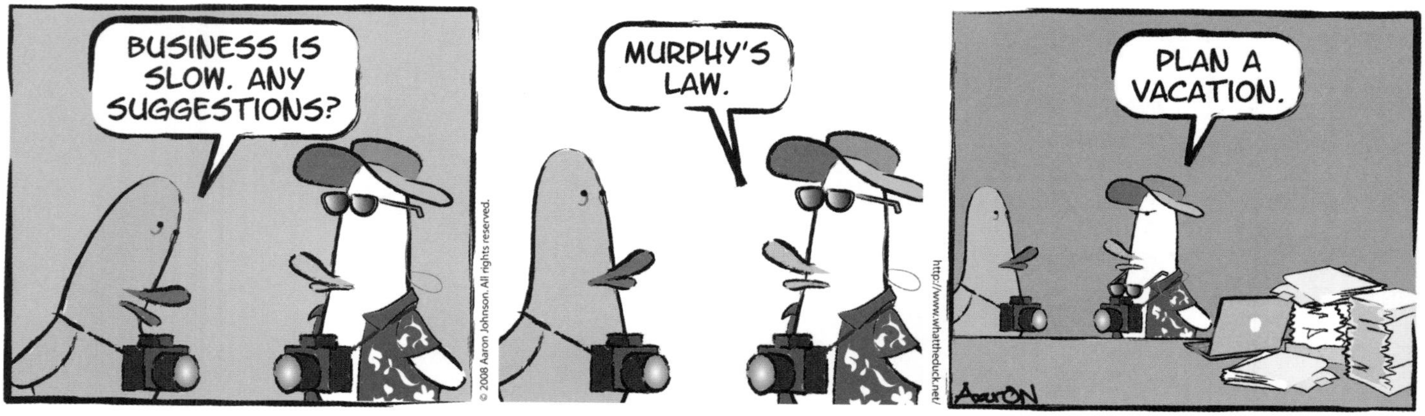
BUSINESS IS SLOW. ANY SUGGESTIONS?
MURPHY'S LAW.
PLAN A VACATION.
© 2008 Aaron Johnson. All rights reserved.
http://www.whattheduck.net/
AarON

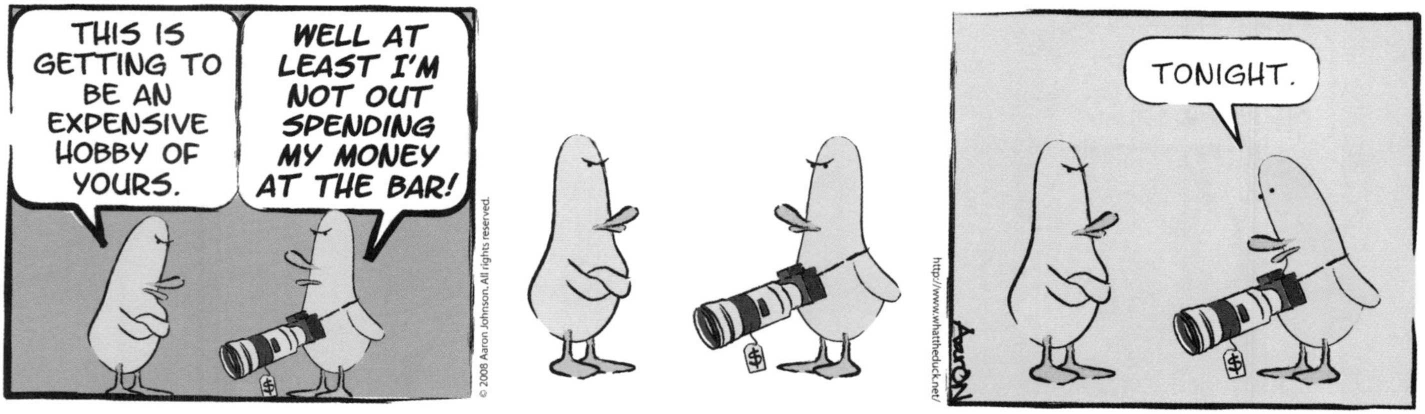
THIS IS GETTING TO BE AN EXPENSIVE HOBBY OF YOURS.
WELL AT LEAST I'M NOT OUT SPENDING MY MONEY AT THE BAR!
TONIGHT.
© 2008 Aaron Johnson. All rights reserved.
http://www.whattheduck.net/
AarON

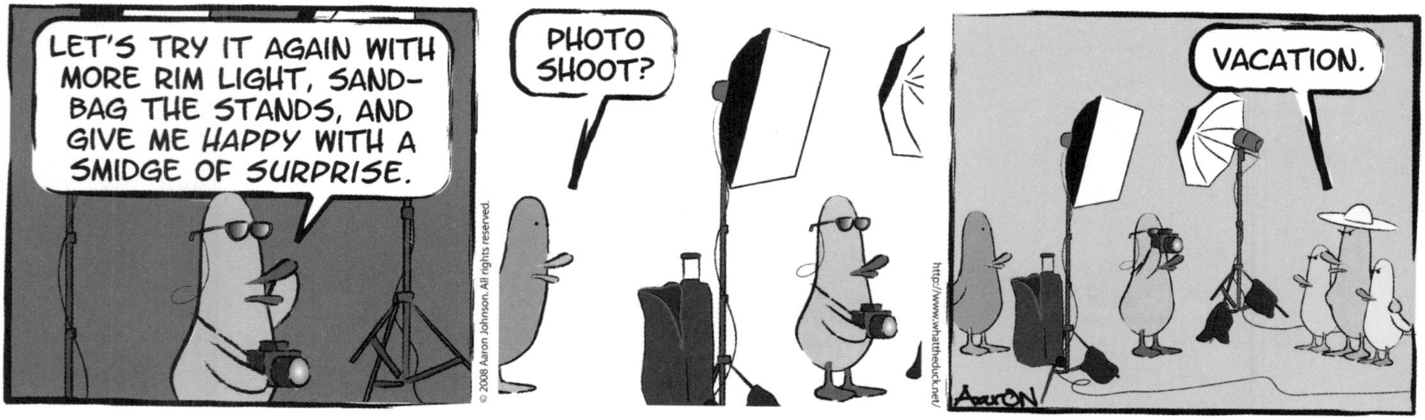
LET'S TRY IT AGAIN WITH MORE RIM LIGHT, SAND-BAG THE STANDS, AND GIVE ME HAPPY WITH A SMIDGE OF SURPRISE.
PHOTO SHOOT?
VACATION.
© 2008 Aaron Johnson. All rights reserved.
http://www.whattheduck.net/
AarON

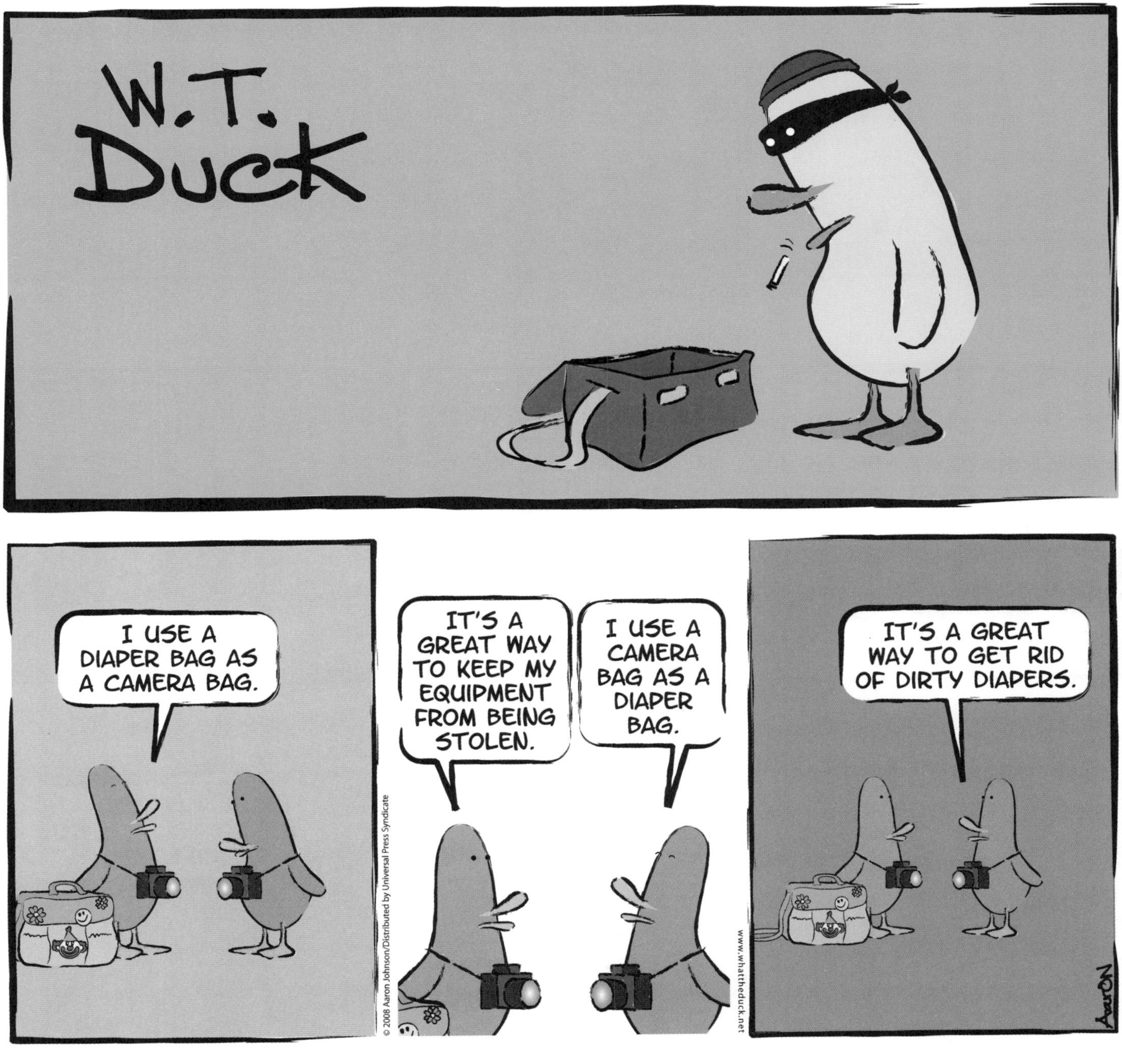
W.T. DUCK
I USE A DIAPER BAG AS A CAMERA BAG.
IT'S A GREAT WAY TO KEEP MY EQUIPMENT FROM BEING STOLEN.
I USE A CAMERA BAG AS A DIAPER BAG.
IT'S A GREAT WAY TO GET RID OF DIRTY DIAPERS.
© 2008 Aaron Johnson/Distributed by Universal Press Syndicate
www.whattheduck.net
AARON

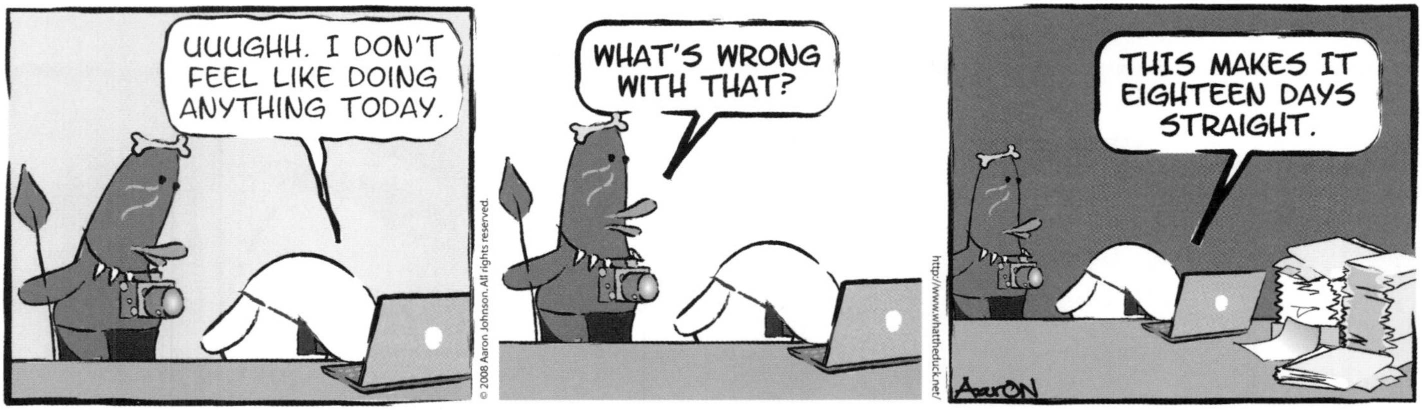
UUUGHH. I DON'T FEEL LIKE DOING ANYTHING TODAY.
WHAT'S WRONG WITH THAT?
THIS MAKES IT EIGHTEEN DAYS STRAIGHT.
© 2008 Aaron Johnson. All rights reserved.
http://www.whattheduck.net/
AarON

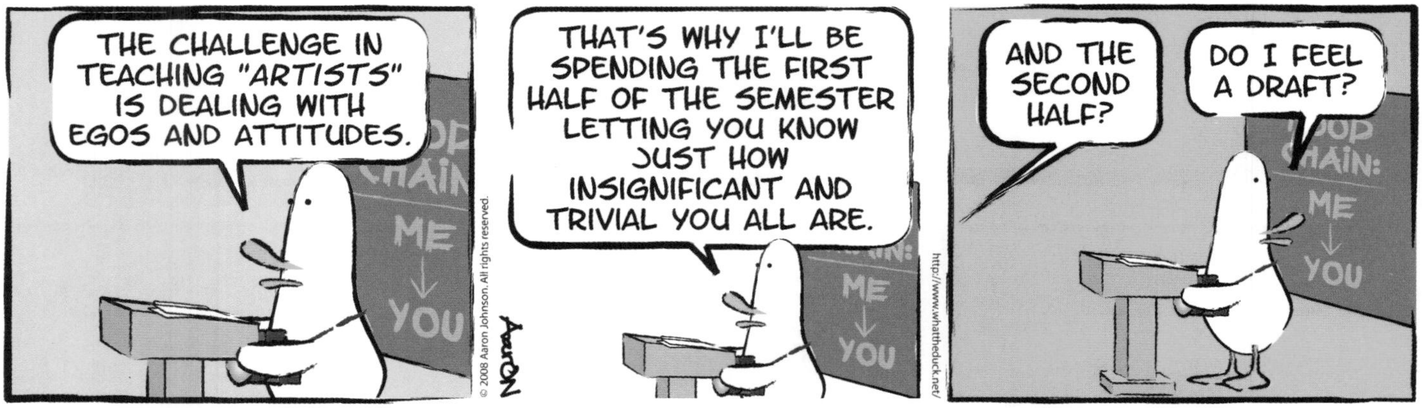
THE CHALLENGE IN TEACHING "ARTISTS" IS DEALING WITH EGOS AND ATTITUDES.
ME → YOU
THAT'S WHY I'LL BE SPENDING THE FIRST HALF OF THE SEMESTER LETTING YOU KNOW JUST HOW INSIGNIFICANT AND TRIVIAL YOU ALL ARE.
AND THE SECOND HALF?
DO I FEEL A DRAFT?
© 2008 Aaron Johnson. All rights reserved.
http://www.whattheduck.net/
AarON

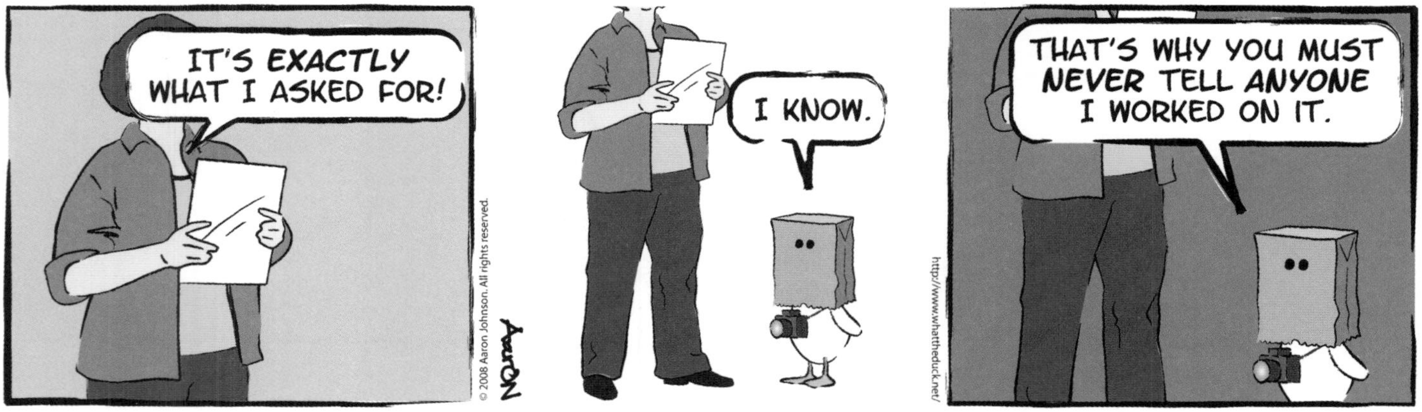
IT'S EXACTLY WHAT I ASKED FOR!
I KNOW.
THAT'S WHY YOU MUST NEVER TELL ANYONE I WORKED ON IT.
© 2008 Aaron Johnson. All rights reserved.
http://www.whattheduck.net/
AarON

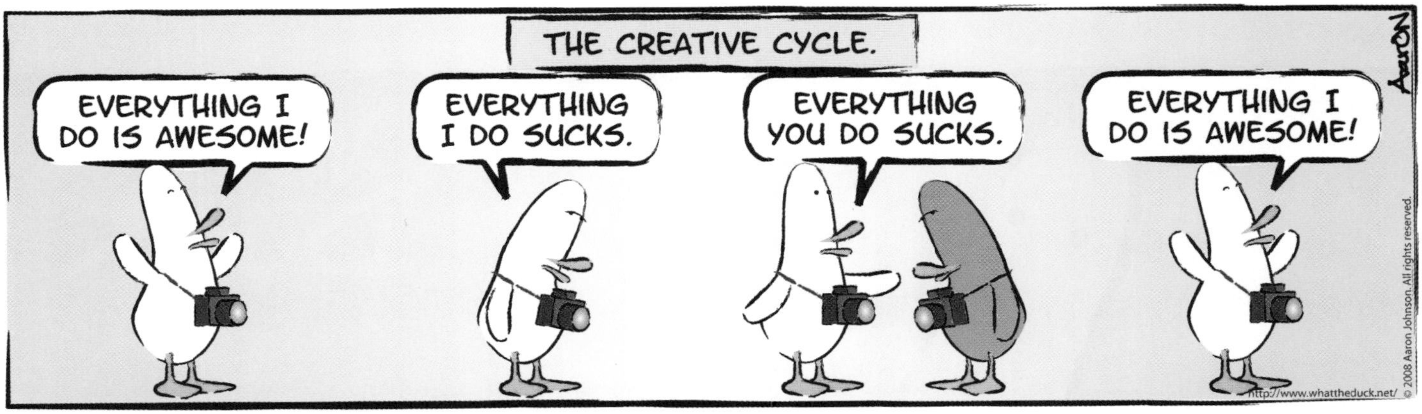
THE CREATIVE CYCLE.
EVERYTHING I DO IS AWESOME!
EVERYTHING I DO SUCKS.
EVERYTHING YOU DO SUCKS.
EVERYTHING I DO IS AWESOME!
AARON
http://www.whattheduck.net/
© 2008 Aaron Johnson. All rights reserved.

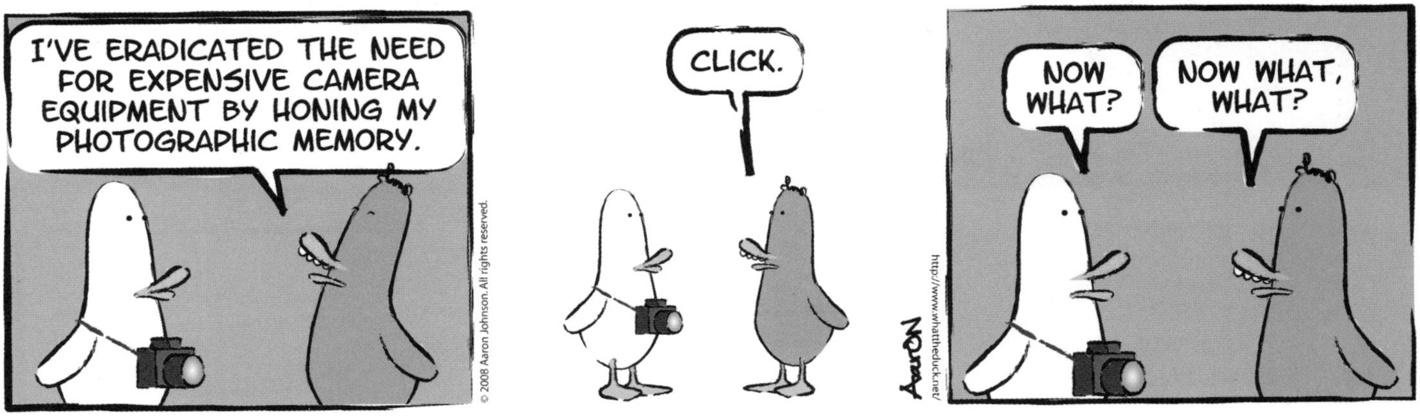
I'VE ERADICATED THE NEED FOR EXPENSIVE CAMERA EQUIPMENT BY HONING MY PHOTOGRAPHIC MEMORY.
CLICK.
NOW WHAT?
NOW WHAT, WHAT?
© 2008 Aaron Johnson. All rights reserved.
AARON
http://www.whattheduck.net/

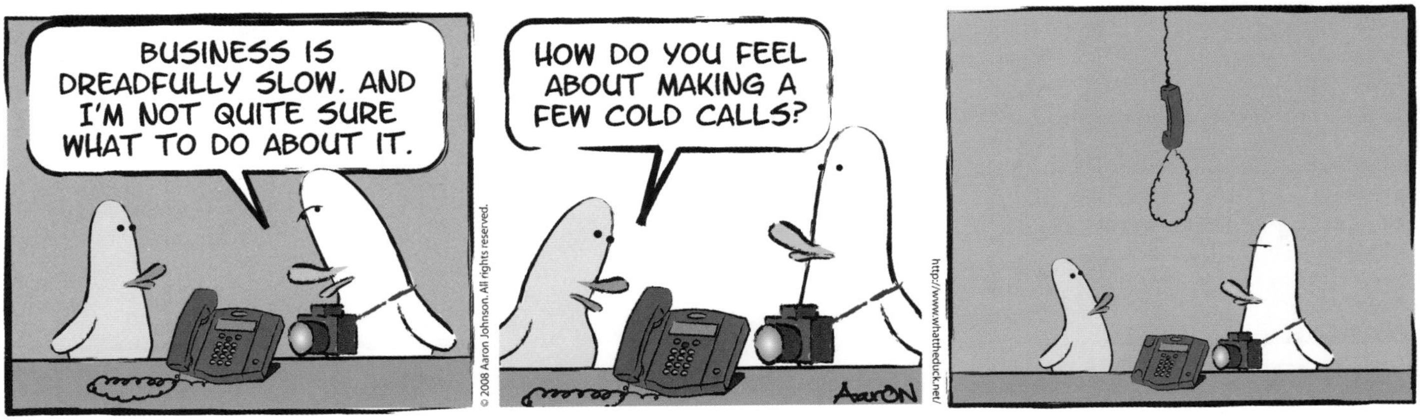
BUSINESS IS DREADFULLY SLOW. AND I'M NOT QUITE SURE WHAT TO DO ABOUT IT.
HOW DO YOU FEEL ABOUT MAKING A FEW COLD CALLS?
AARON
© 2008 Aaron Johnson. All rights reserved.
http://www.whattheduck.net/

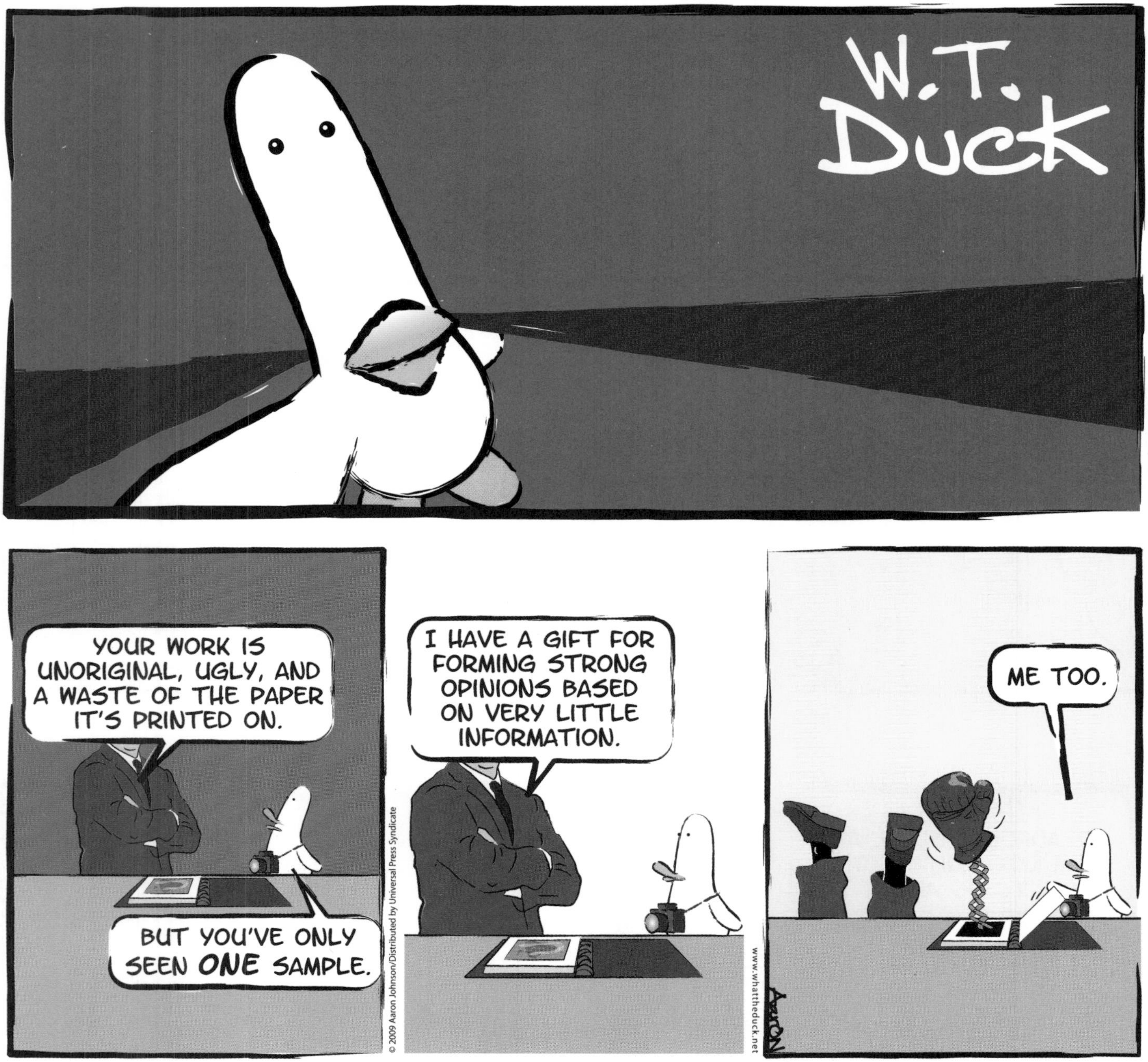

W.T. DUCK
YOUR WORK IS UNORIGINAL, UGLY, AND A WASTE OF THE PAPER IT'S PRINTED ON.
BUT YOU'VE ONLY SEEN **ONE** SAMPLE.
© 2009 Aaron Johnson/Distributed by Universal Press Syndicate
I HAVE A GIFT FOR FORMING STRONG OPINIONS BASED ON VERY LITTLE INFORMATION.
www.whattheduck.net
ME TOO.
AARON

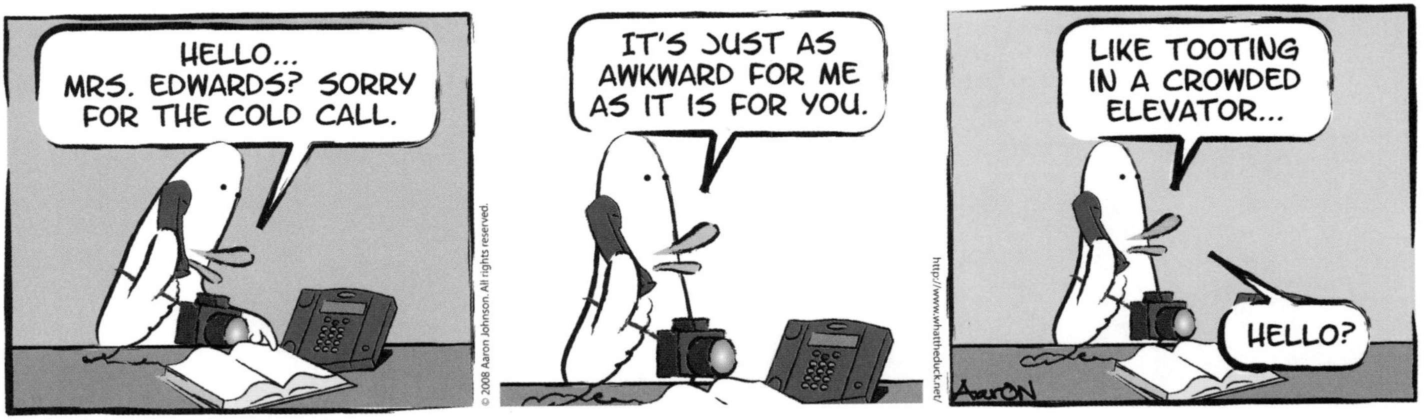
HELLO... MRS. EDWARDS? SORRY FOR THE COLD CALL.
IT'S JUST AS AWKWARD FOR ME AS IT IS FOR YOU.
LIKE TOOTING IN A CROWDED ELEVATOR...
HELLO?
© 2008 Aaron Johnson. All rights reserved.
http://www.whattheduck.net/
AarON

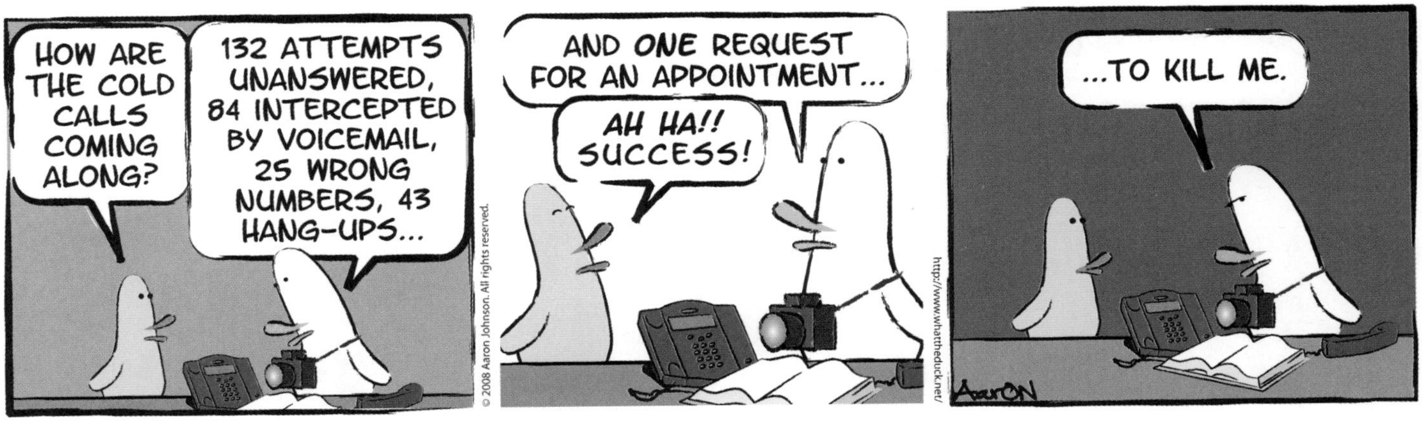
HOW ARE THE COLD CALLS COMING ALONG?
132 ATTEMPTS UNANSWERED, 84 INTERCEPTED BY VOICEMAIL, 25 WRONG NUMBERS, 43 HANG-UPS...
AND ONE REQUEST FOR AN APPOINTMENT...
AH HA!! SUCCESS!
...TO KILL ME.
© 2008 Aaron Johnson. All rights reserved.
http://www.whattheduck.net/
AarON

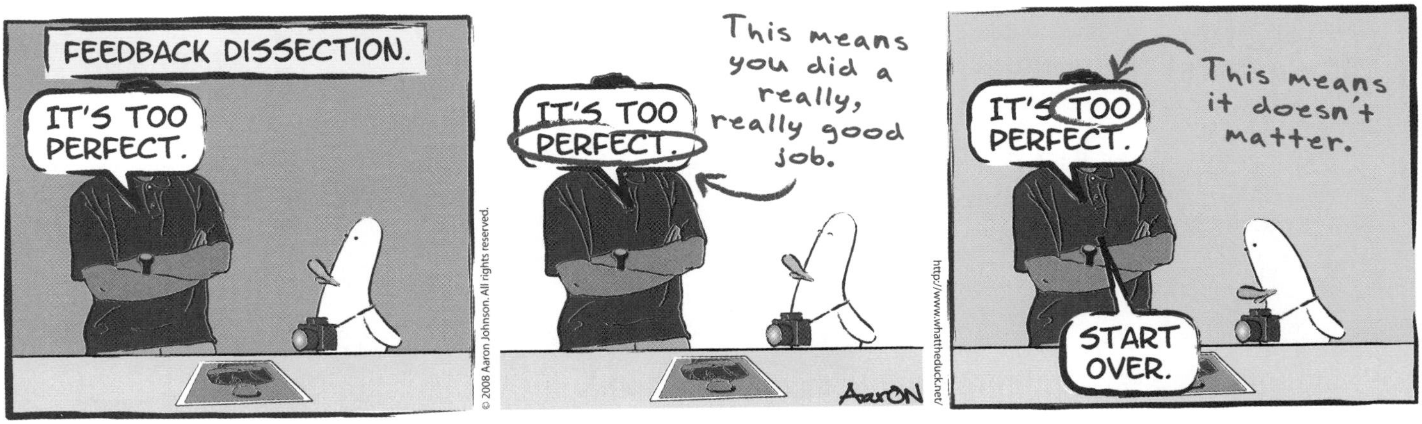
FEEDBACK DISSECTION.
IT'S TOO PERFECT.
IT'S TOO PERFECT.
This means you did a really, really good job.
IT'S TOO PERFECT.
This means it doesn't matter.
START OVER.
© 2008 Aaron Johnson. All rights reserved.
http://www.whattheduck.net/
AarON

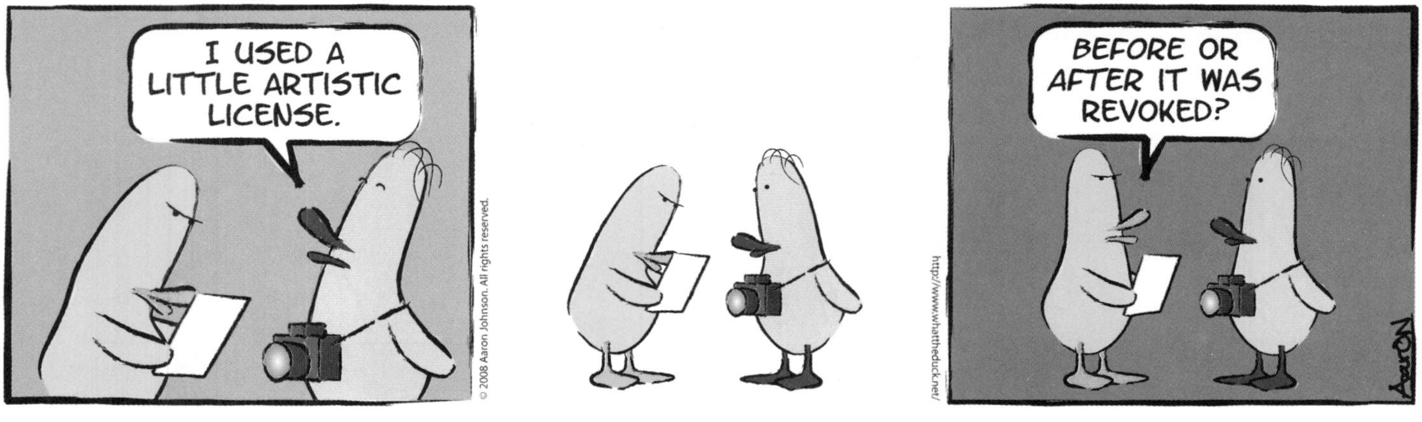
I USED A LITTLE ARTISTIC LICENSE.
BEFORE OR AFTER IT WAS REVOKED?
© 2008 Aaron Johnson. All rights reserved.
http://www.whattheduck.net/
AARON

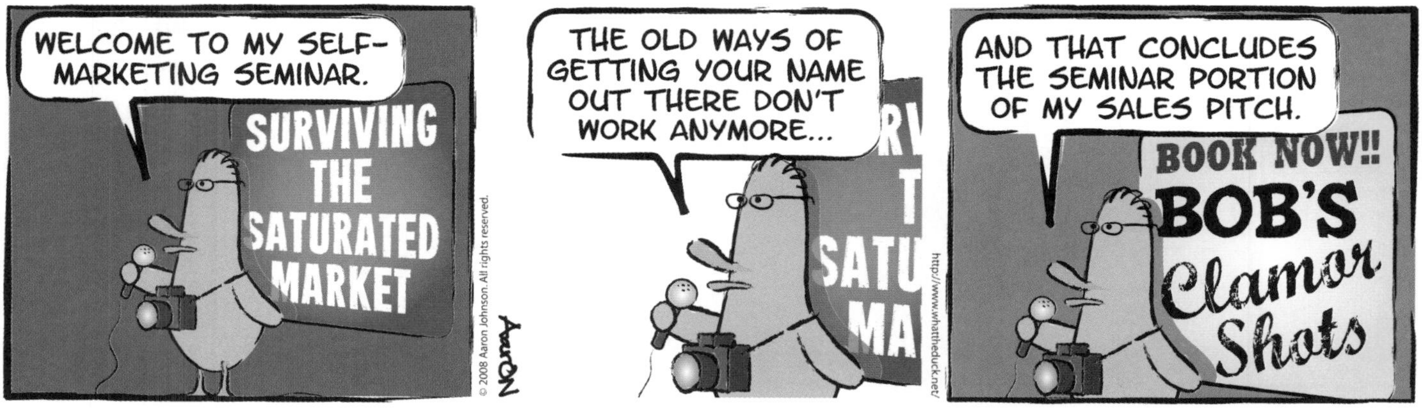
WELCOME TO MY SELF-MARKETING SEMINAR.
SURVIVING THE SATURATED MARKET
THE OLD WAYS OF GETTING YOUR NAME OUT THERE DON'T WORK ANYMORE...
AND THAT CONCLUDES THE SEMINAR PORTION OF MY SALES PITCH.
BOOK NOW!!
BOB'S Clamor Shots
© 2008 Aaron Johnson. All rights reserved.
http://www.whattheduck.net/
AARON

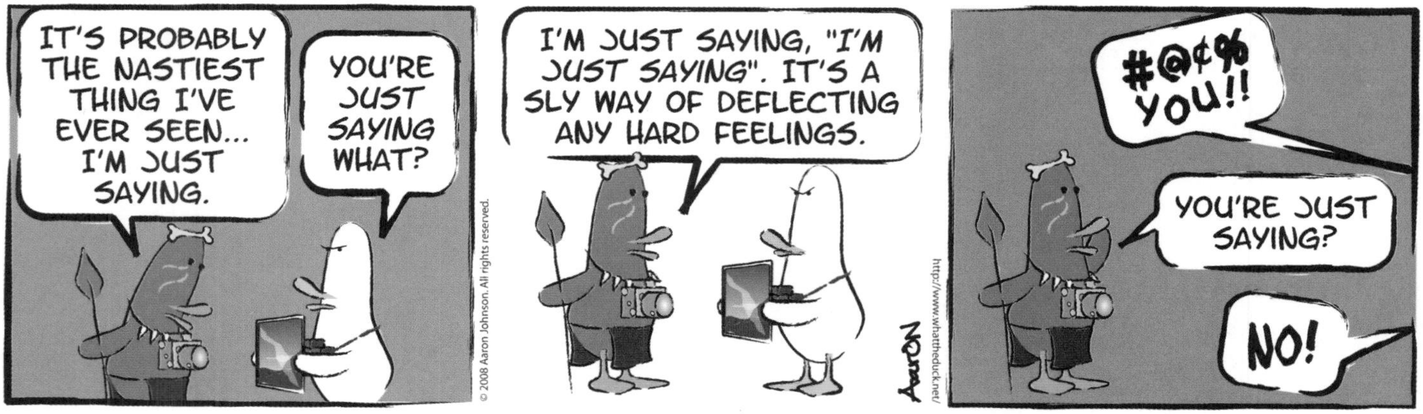
IT'S PROBABLY THE NASTIEST THING I'VE EVER SEEN... I'M JUST SAYING.
YOU'RE JUST SAYING WHAT?
I'M JUST SAYING, "I'M JUST SAYING". IT'S A SLY WAY OF DEFLECTING ANY HARD FEELINGS.
#@¢% YOU!!
YOU'RE JUST SAYING?
NO!
© 2008 Aaron Johnson. All rights reserved.
http://www.whattheduck.net/
AARON

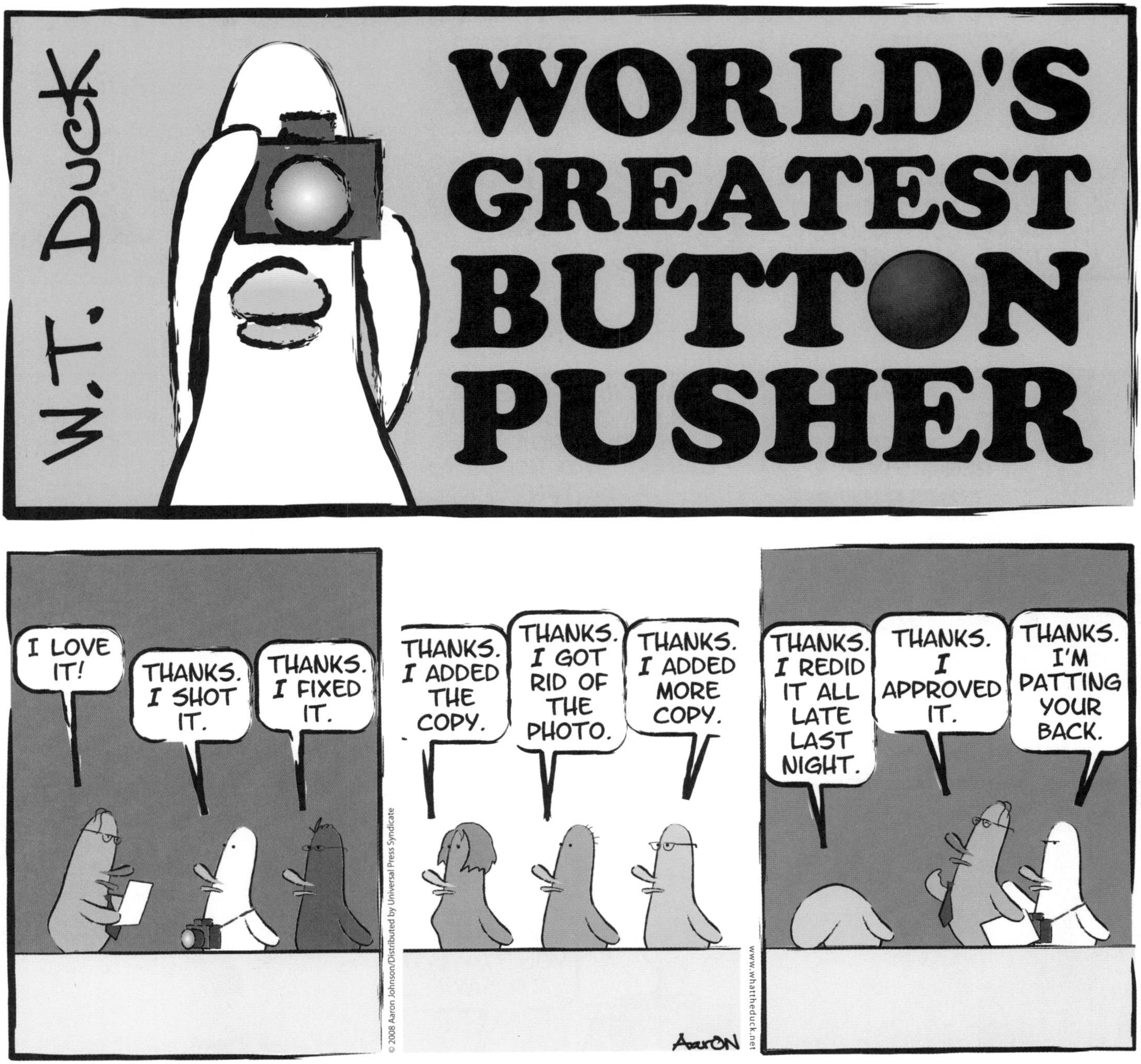
W.T. Duck
WORLD'S GREATEST BUTTON PUSHER
I LOVE IT!
THANKS. I SHOT IT.
THANKS. I FIXED IT.
THANKS. I ADDED THE COPY.
THANKS. I GOT RID OF THE PHOTO.
THANKS. I ADDED MORE COPY.
THANKS. I REDID IT ALL LATE LAST NIGHT.
THANKS. I APPROVED IT.
THANKS. I'M PATTING YOUR BACK.
© 2008 Aaron Johnson/Distributed by Universal Press Syndicate
www.whattheduck.net
AARON

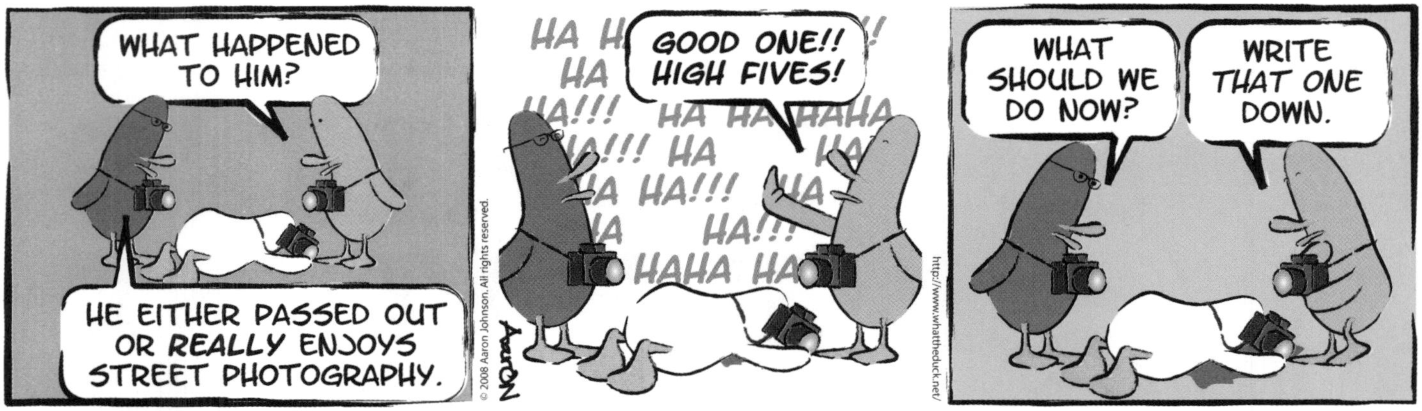
WHAT HAPPENED TO HIM?
HE EITHER PASSED OUT OR REALLY ENJOYS STREET PHOTOGRAPHY.
© 2008 Aaron Johnson. All rights reserved.
AARON
HA H
HA
HA!!!
HA HA HAHA
HA!!! HA
HA HA!!!
HA HA!!!
HAHA HA
GOOD ONE!! HIGH FIVES!
http://www.whattheduck.net/
WHAT SHOULD WE DO NOW?
WRITE THAT ONE DOWN.

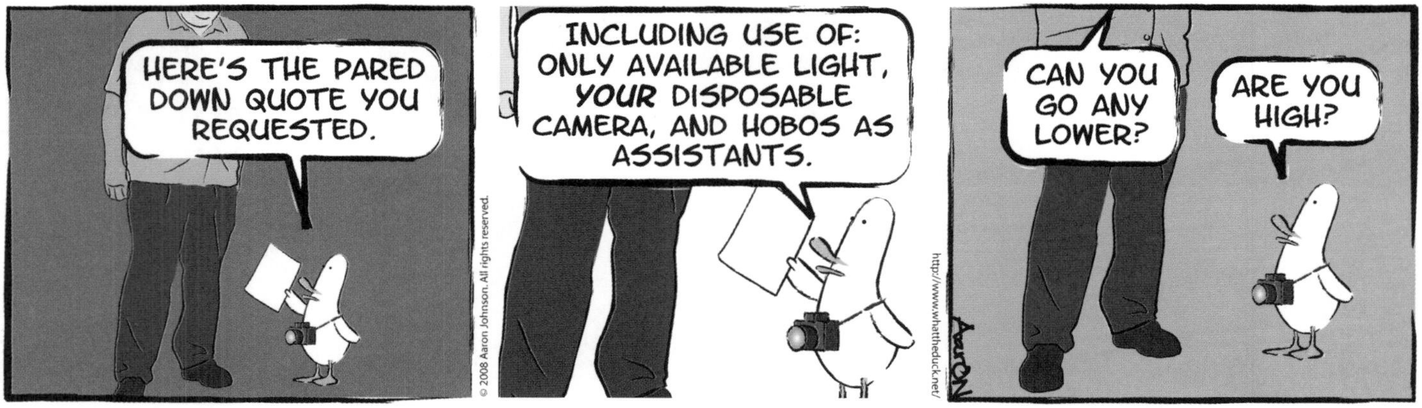
HERE'S THE PARED DOWN QUOTE YOU REQUESTED.
© 2008 Aaron Johnson. All rights reserved.
INCLUDING USE OF: ONLY AVAILABLE LIGHT, YOUR DISPOSABLE CAMERA, AND HOBOS AS ASSISTANTS.
http://www.whattheduck.net/
AARON
CAN YOU GO ANY LOWER?
ARE YOU HIGH?

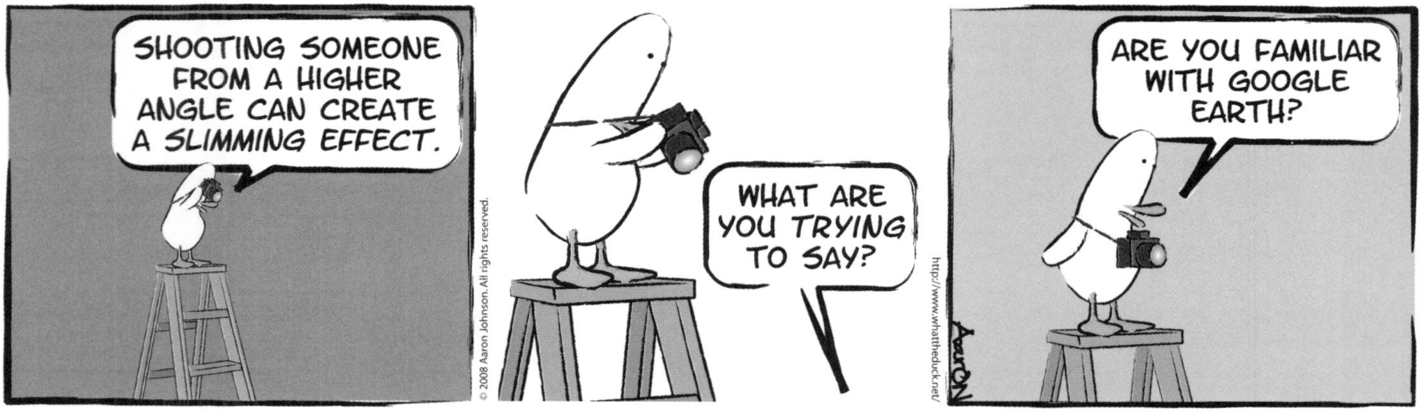
SHOOTING SOMEONE FROM A HIGHER ANGLE CAN CREATE A SLIMMING EFFECT.
© 2008 Aaron Johnson. All rights reserved.
WHAT ARE YOU TRYING TO SAY?
http://www.whattheduck.net/
AARON
ARE YOU FAMILIAR WITH GOOGLE EARTH?

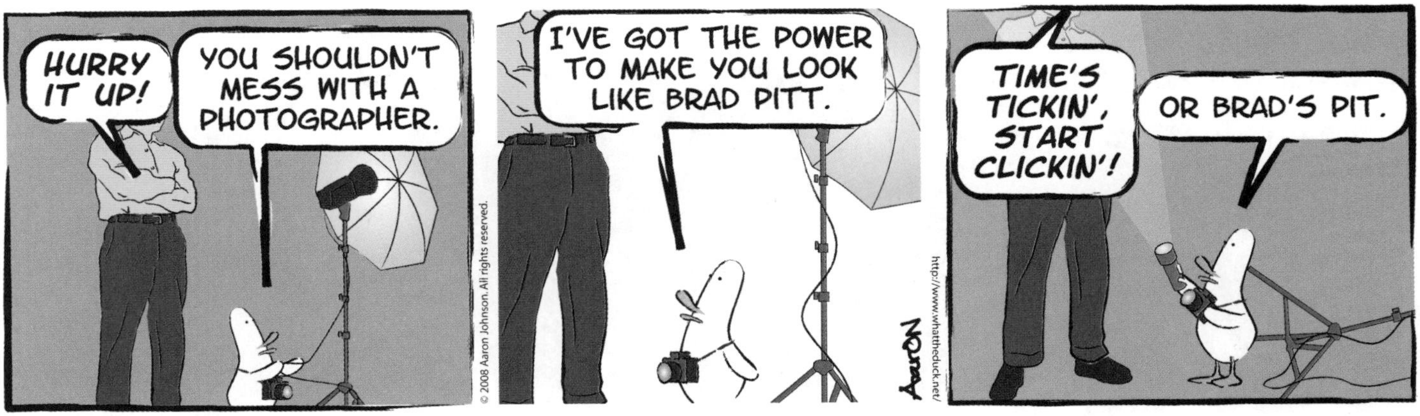
HURRY IT UP!
YOU SHOULDN'T MESS WITH A PHOTOGRAPHER.
I'VE GOT THE POWER TO MAKE YOU LOOK LIKE BRAD PITT.
TIME'S TICKIN', START CLICKIN'!
OR BRAD'S PIT.
AARON

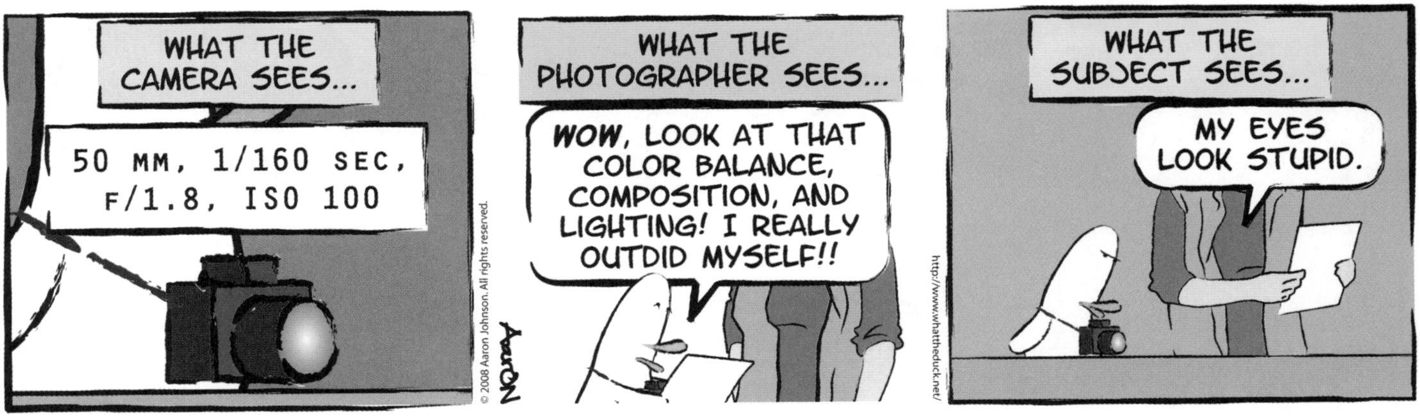
WHAT THE CAMERA SEES...
50 MM, 1/160 SEC, F/1.8, ISO 100
WHAT THE PHOTOGRAPHER SEES...
WOW, LOOK AT THAT COLOR BALANCE, COMPOSITION, AND LIGHTING! I REALLY OUTDID MYSELF!!
WHAT THE SUBJECT SEES...
MY EYES LOOK STUPID.
AARON

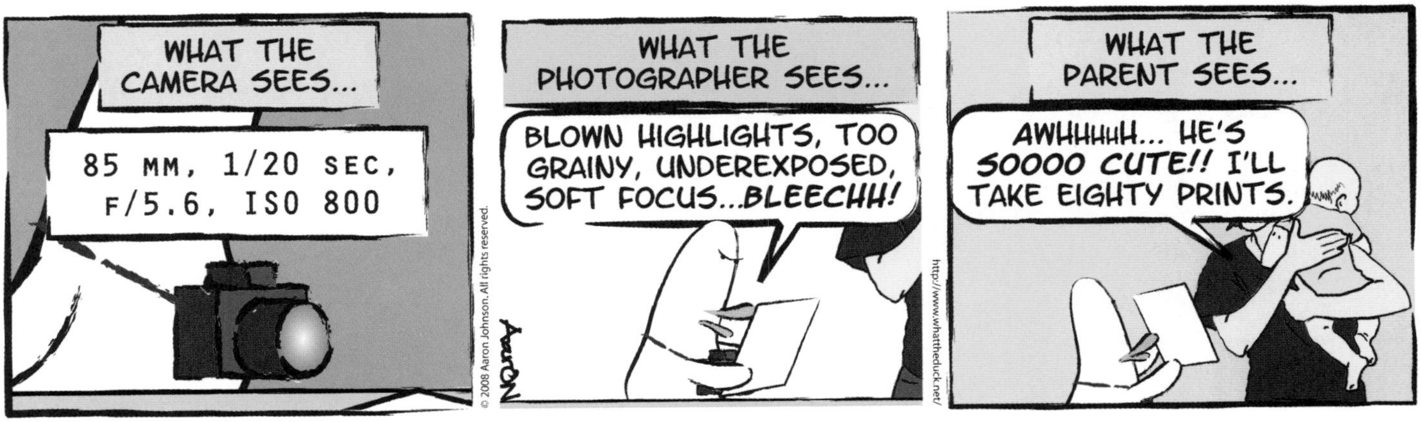
WHAT THE CAMERA SEES...
85 MM, 1/20 SEC, F/5.6, ISO 800
WHAT THE PHOTOGRAPHER SEES...
BLOWN HIGHLIGHTS, TOO GRAINY, UNDEREXPOSED, SOFT FOCUS...BLEECHH!
WHAT THE PARENT SEES...
AWHHHHH... HE'S SOOOO CUTE!! I'LL TAKE EIGHTY PRINTS.
AARON

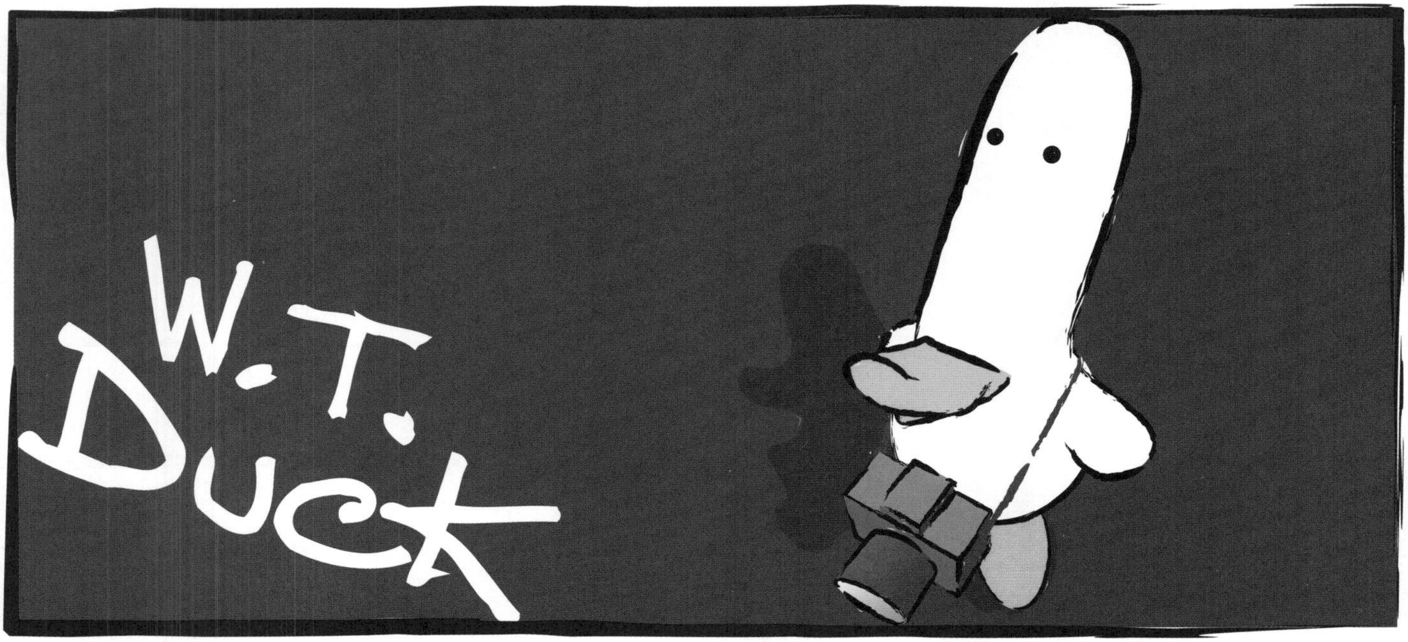
W.T. Duck

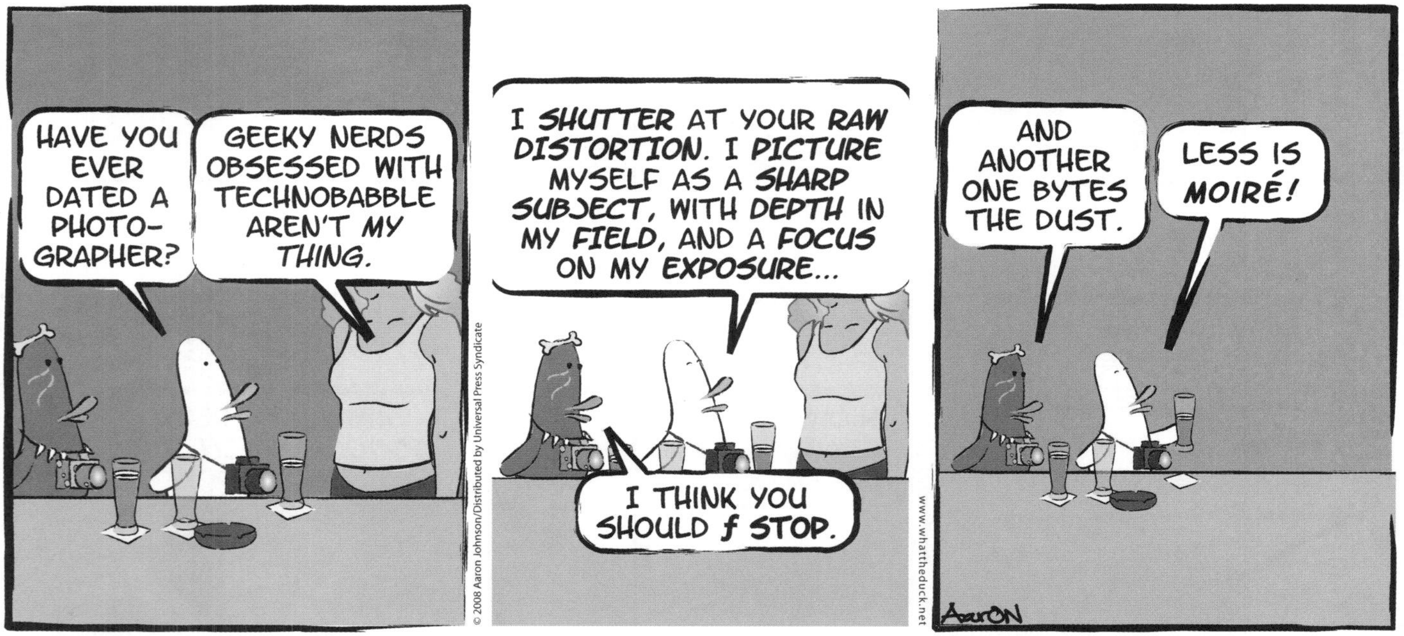
HAVE YOU EVER DATED A PHOTO-GRAPHER?
GEEKY NERDS OBSESSED WITH TECHNOBABBLE AREN'T MY THING.
© 2008 Aaron Johnson/Distributed by Universal Press Syndicate
I SHUTTER AT YOUR RAW DISTORTION. I PICTURE MYSELF AS A SHARP SUBJECT, WITH DEPTH IN MY FIELD, AND A FOCUS ON MY EXPOSURE...
I THINK YOU SHOULD f STOP.
www.whattheduck.net
AND ANOTHER ONE BYTES THE DUST.
LESS IS MOIRÉ!
AARON

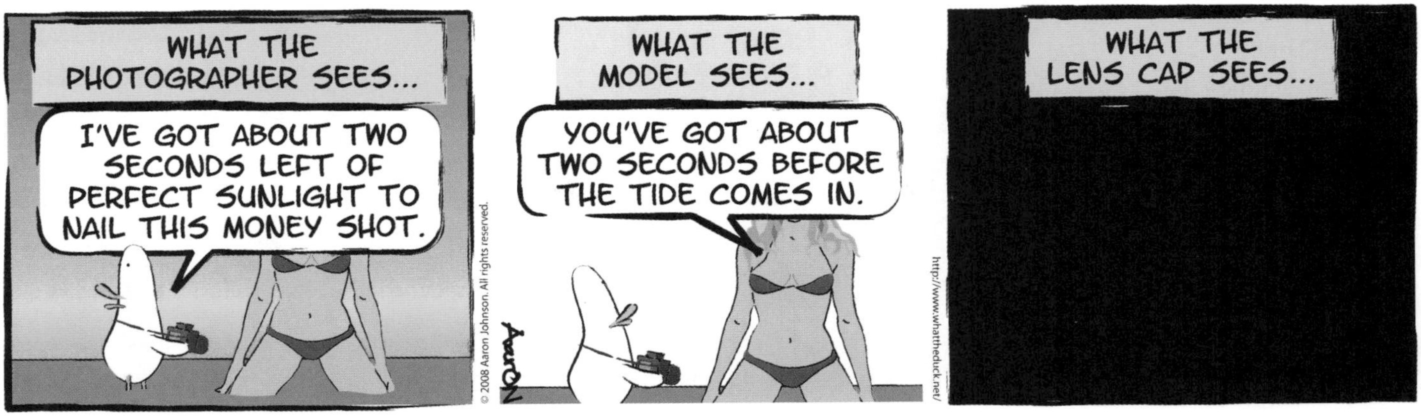
WHAT THE PHOTOGRAPHER SEES...
I'VE GOT ABOUT TWO SECONDS LEFT OF PERFECT SUNLIGHT TO NAIL THIS MONEY SHOT.
© 2008 Aaron Johnson. All rights reserved.
AARON
WHAT THE MODEL SEES...
YOU'VE GOT ABOUT TWO SECONDS BEFORE THE TIDE COMES IN.
http://www.whattheduck.net/
WHAT THE LENS CAP SEES...

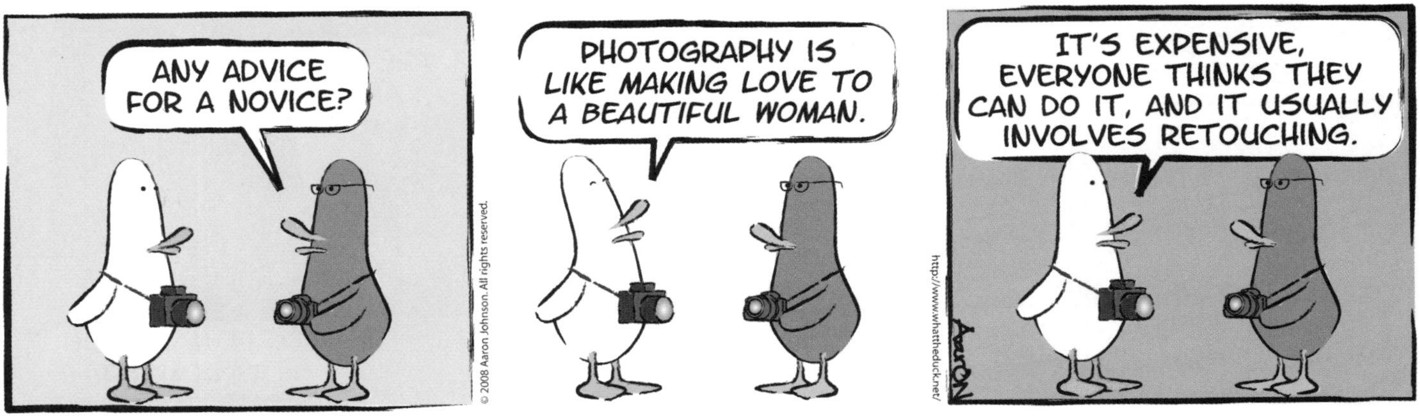
ANY ADVICE FOR A NOVICE?
© 2008 Aaron Johnson. All rights reserved.
PHOTOGRAPHY IS LIKE MAKING LOVE TO A BEAUTIFUL WOMAN.
http://www.whattheduck.net/
AARON
IT'S EXPENSIVE, EVERYONE THINKS THEY CAN DO IT, AND IT USUALLY INVOLVES RETOUCHING.

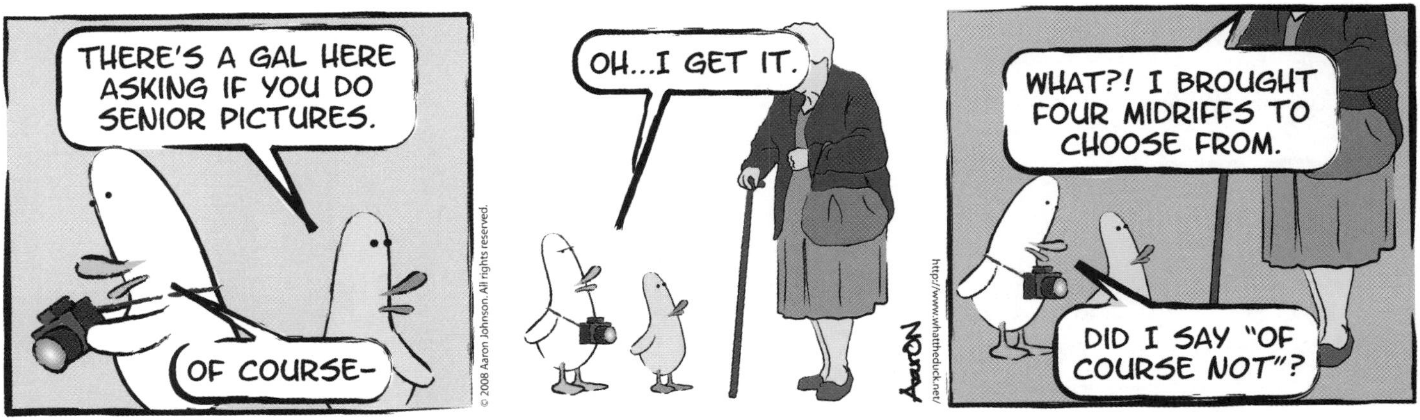
THERE'S A GAL HERE ASKING IF YOU DO SENIOR PICTURES.
OF COURSE-
© 2008 Aaron Johnson. All rights reserved.
OH...I GET IT.
AARON
http://www.whattheduck.net/
WHAT?! I BROUGHT FOUR MIDRIFFS TO CHOOSE FROM.
DID I SAY "OF COURSE NOT"?

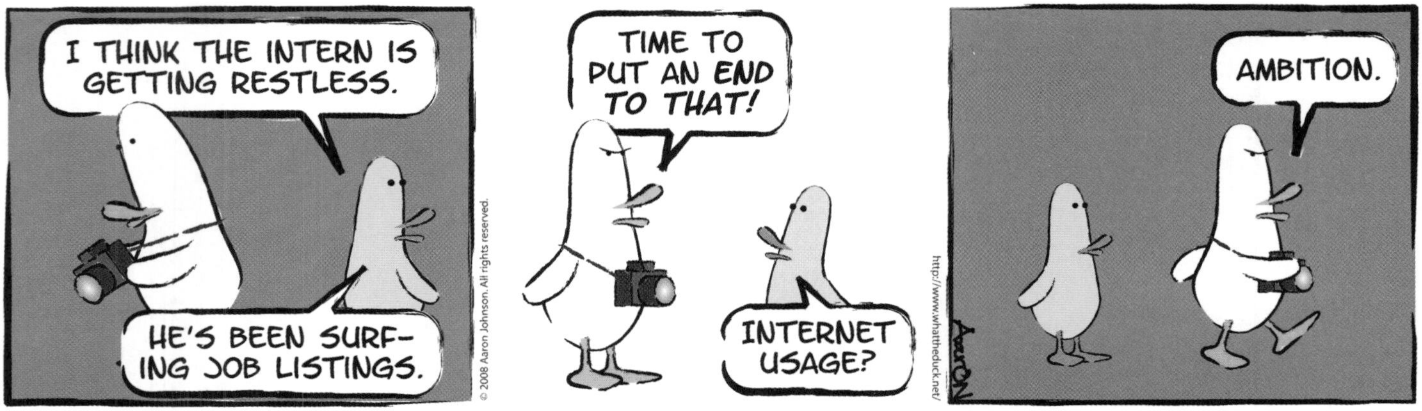
I THINK THE INTERN IS GETTING RESTLESS.
HE'S BEEN SURFING JOB LISTINGS.
© 2008 Aaron Johnson. All rights reserved.
TIME TO PUT AN END TO THAT!
INTERNET USAGE?
http://www.whattheduck.net/
AMBITION.
AaronN

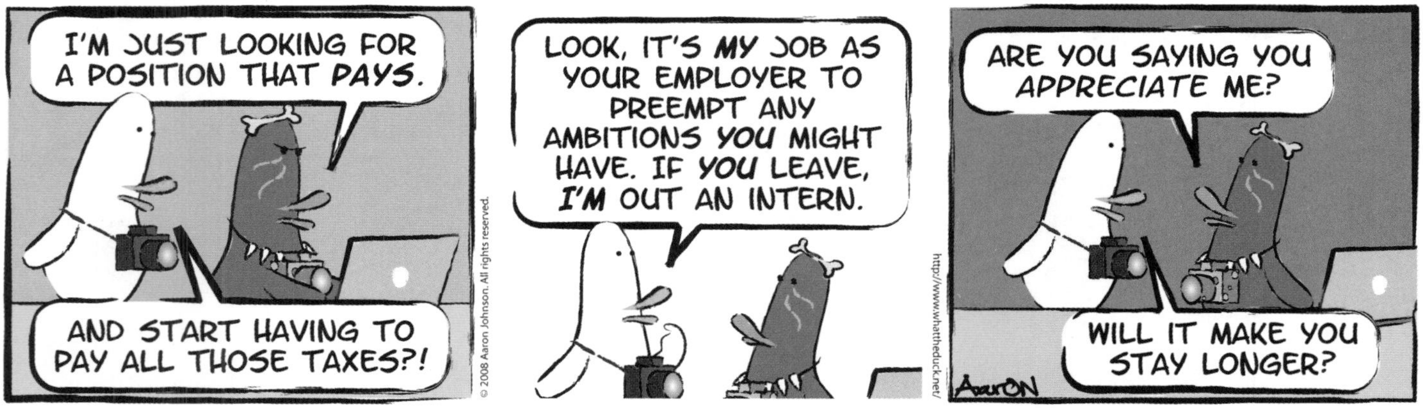
I'M JUST LOOKING FOR A POSITION THAT PAYS.
AND START HAVING TO PAY ALL THOSE TAXES?!
© 2008 Aaron Johnson. All rights reserved.
LOOK, IT'S MY JOB AS YOUR EMPLOYER TO PREEMPT ANY AMBITIONS YOU MIGHT HAVE. IF YOU LEAVE, I'M OUT AN INTERN.
http://www.whattheduck.net/
ARE YOU SAYING YOU APPRECIATE ME?
WILL IT MAKE YOU STAY LONGER?
AaronN

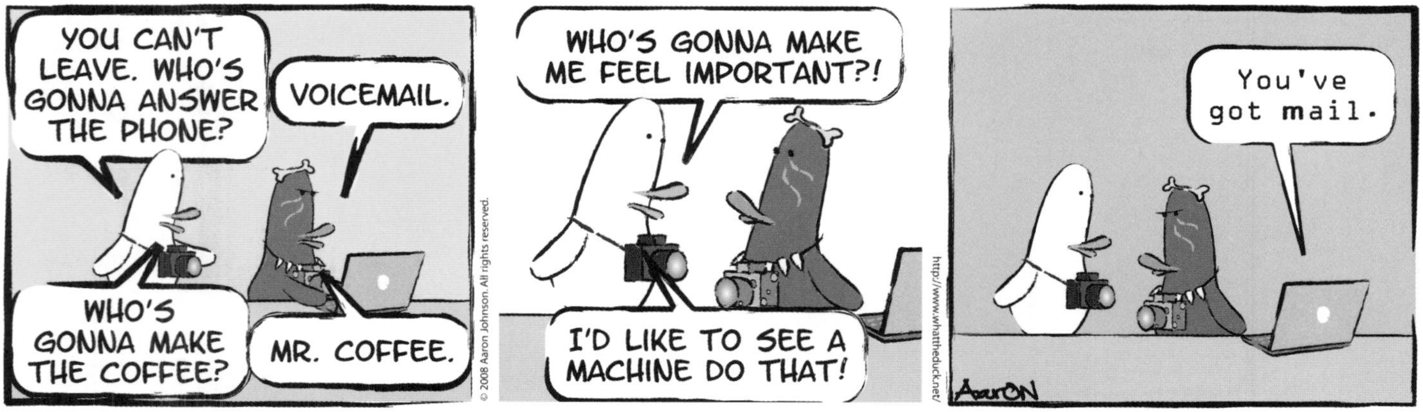
YOU CAN'T LEAVE. WHO'S GONNA ANSWER THE PHONE?
VOICEMAIL.
WHO'S GONNA MAKE THE COFFEE?
MR. COFFEE.
© 2008 Aaron Johnson. All rights reserved.
WHO'S GONNA MAKE ME FEEL IMPORTANT?!
I'D LIKE TO SEE A MACHINE DO THAT!
http://www.whattheduck.net/
You've got mail.
AaronN

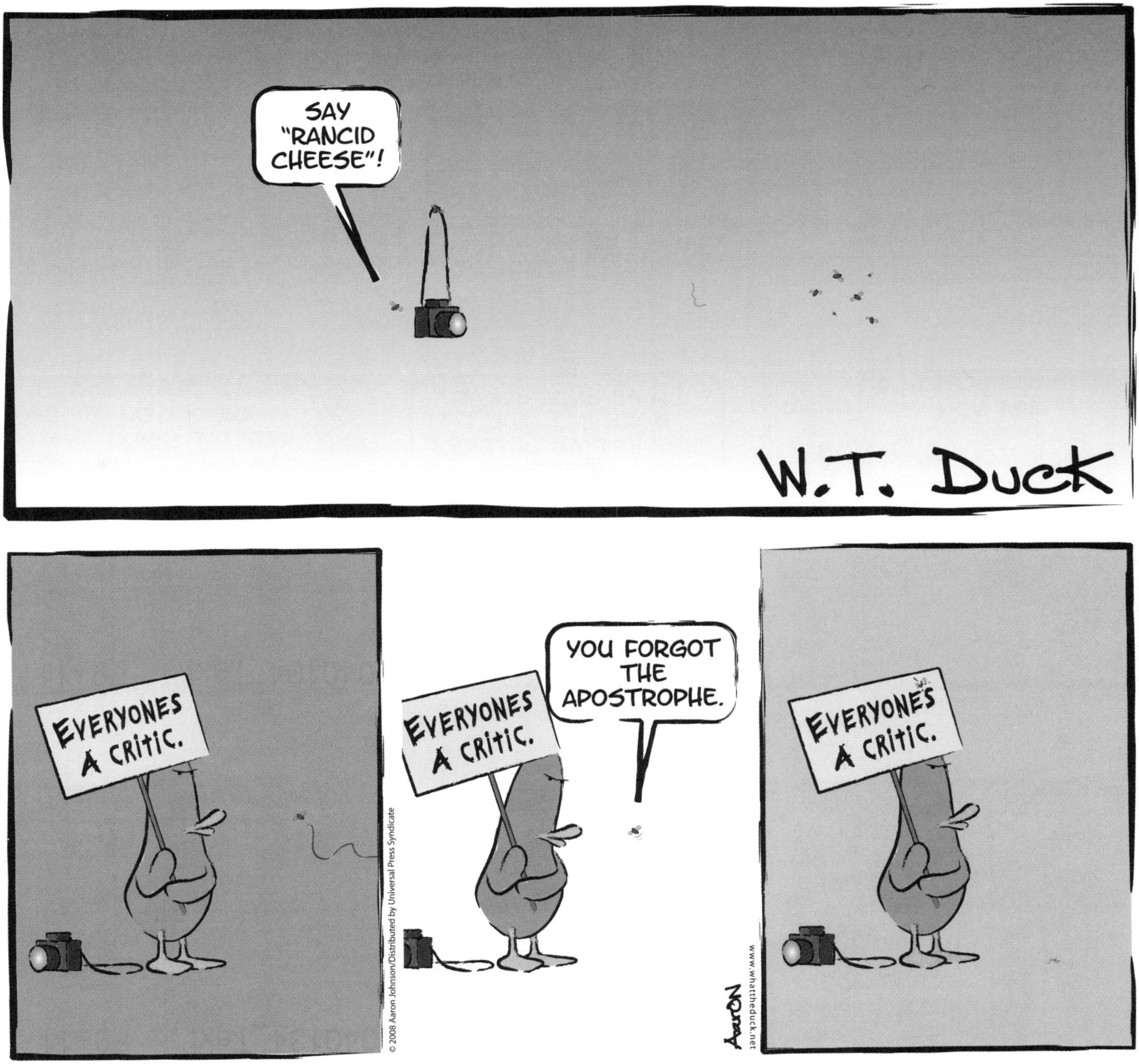
SAY "RANCID CHEESE"!
W.T. DUCK
EVERYONES A CRITIC.
EVERYONES A CRITIC.
YOU FORGOT THE APOSTROPHE.
EVERYONES A CRITIC.
© 2008 Aaron Johnson/Distributed by Universal Press Syndicate
AARON
www.whattheduck.net

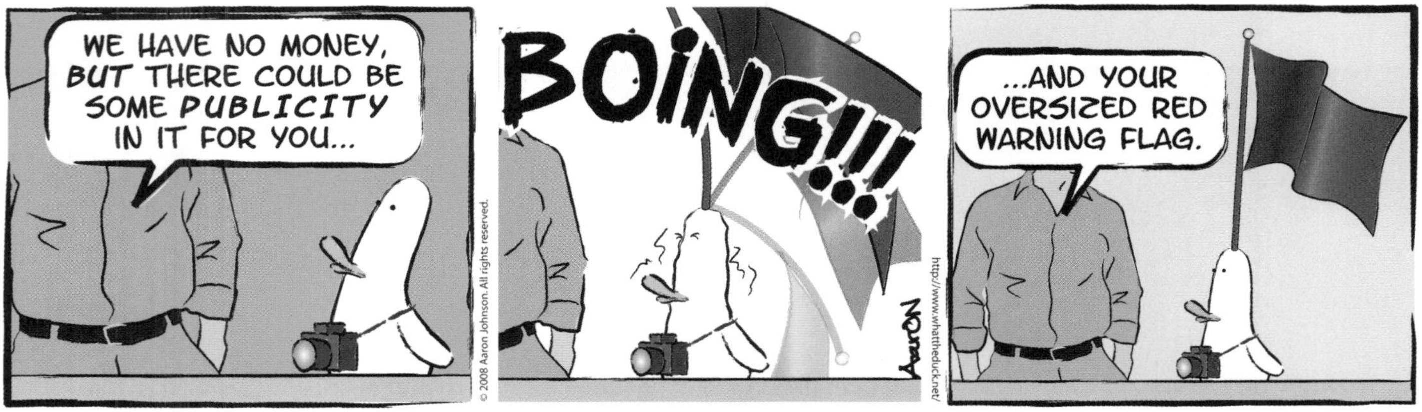
WE HAVE NO MONEY, *BUT* THERE COULD BE SOME *PUBLICITY* IN IT FOR YOU...
BOING!!!
...AND YOUR OVERSIZED RED WARNING FLAG.
© 2008 Aaron Johnson. All rights reserved.
http://www.whattheduck.net/
AarON

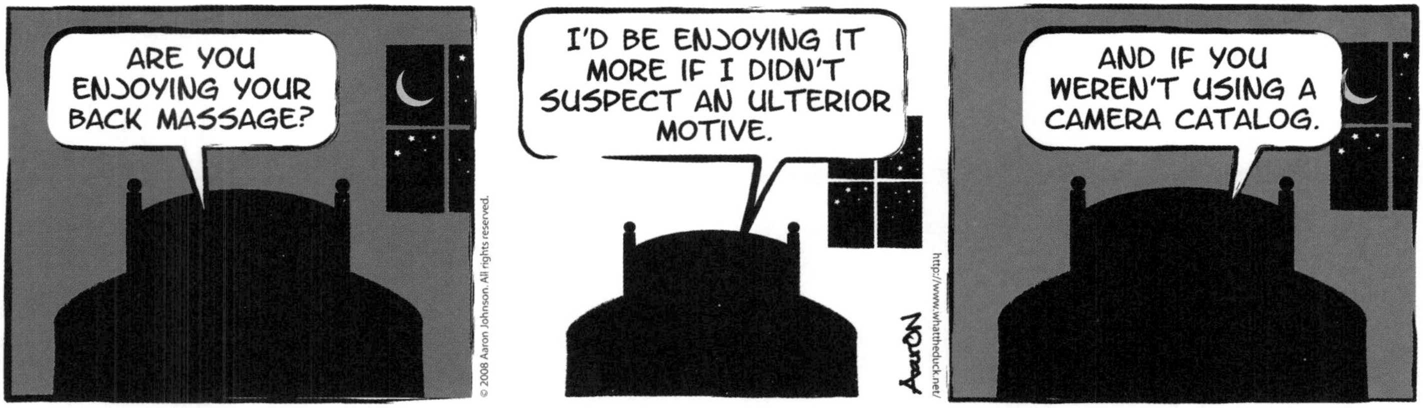
ARE YOU ENJOYING YOUR BACK MASSAGE?
I'D BE ENJOYING IT MORE IF I DIDN'T SUSPECT AN ULTERIOR MOTIVE.
AND IF YOU WEREN'T USING A CAMERA CATALOG.
© 2008 Aaron Johnson. All rights reserved.
http://www.whattheduck.net/
AarON

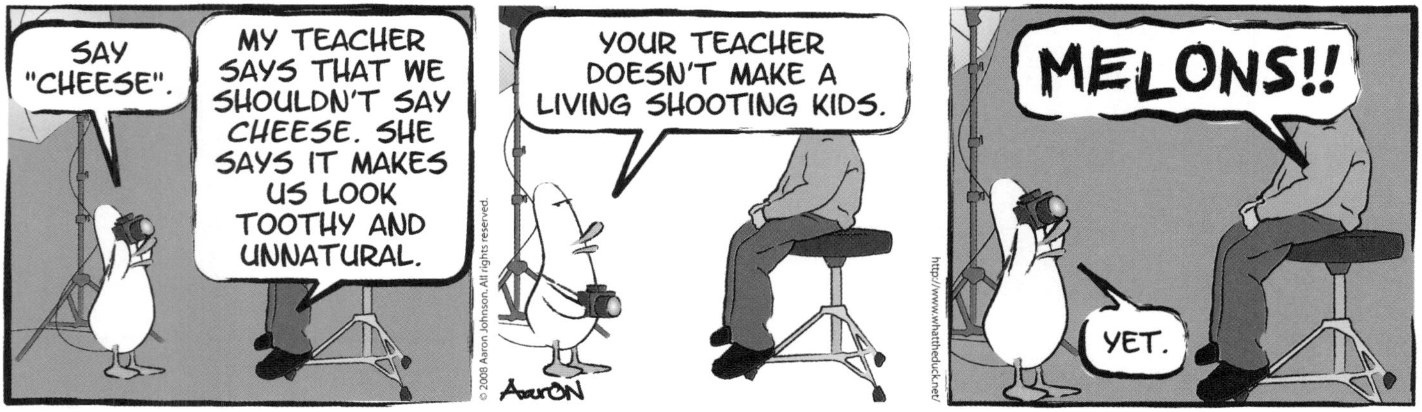
SAY "CHEESE".
MY TEACHER SAYS THAT WE SHOULDN'T SAY *CHEESE*. SHE SAYS IT MAKES US LOOK TOOTHY AND UNNATURAL.
YOUR TEACHER DOESN'T MAKE A LIVING SHOOTING KIDS.
MELONS!!
YET.
© 2008 Aaron Johnson. All rights reserved.
http://www.whattheduck.net/
AarON

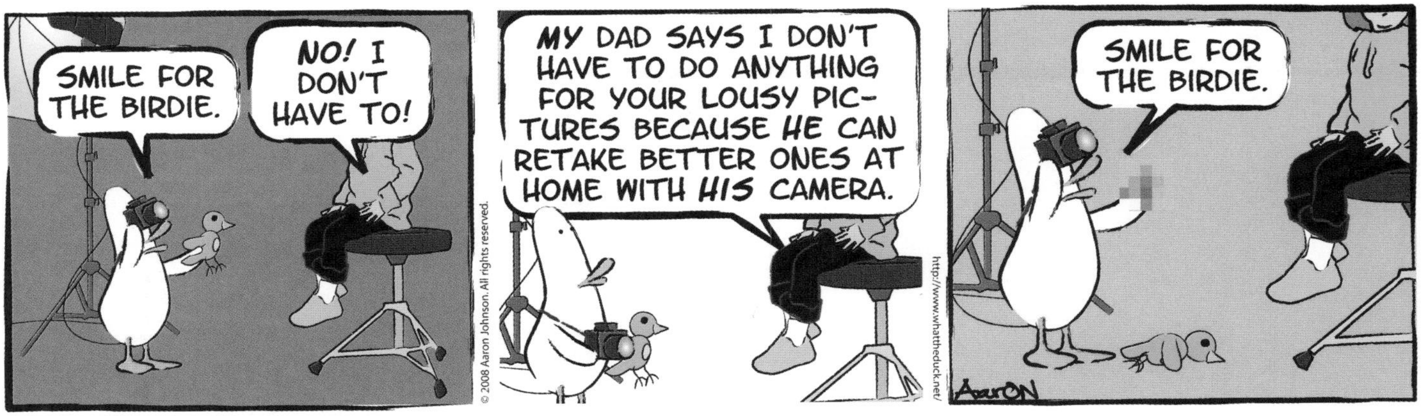
SMILE FOR THE BIRDIE.
NO! I DON'T HAVE TO!
MY DAD SAYS I DON'T HAVE TO DO ANYTHING FOR YOUR LOUSY PICTURES BECAUSE HE CAN RETAKE BETTER ONES AT HOME WITH HIS CAMERA.
SMILE FOR THE BIRDIE.
AARON

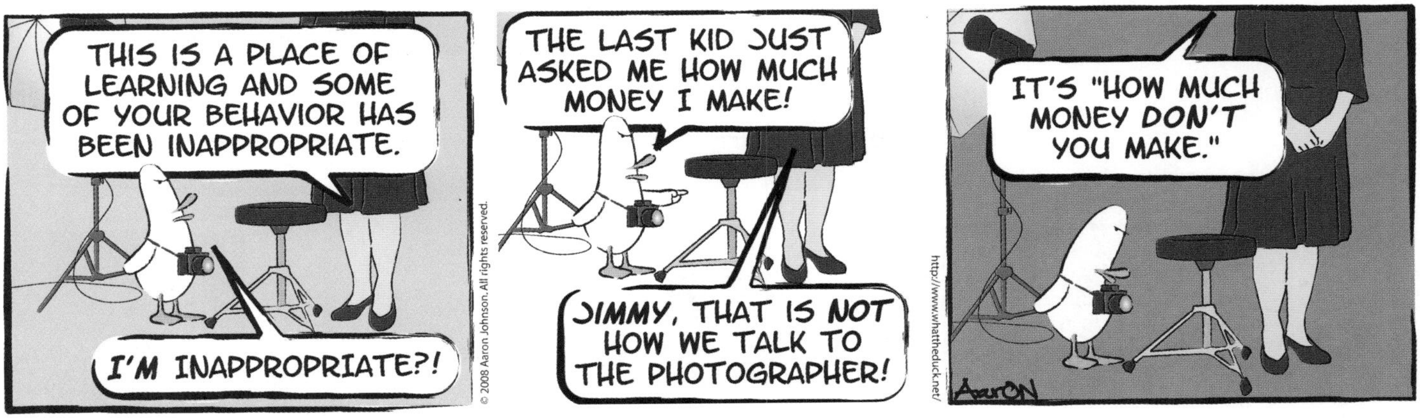
THIS IS A PLACE OF LEARNING AND SOME OF YOUR BEHAVIOR HAS BEEN INAPPROPRIATE.
I'M INAPPROPRIATE?!
THE LAST KID JUST ASKED ME HOW MUCH MONEY I MAKE!
JIMMY, THAT IS NOT HOW WE TALK TO THE PHOTOGRAPHER!
IT'S "HOW MUCH MONEY DON'T YOU MAKE."
AARON

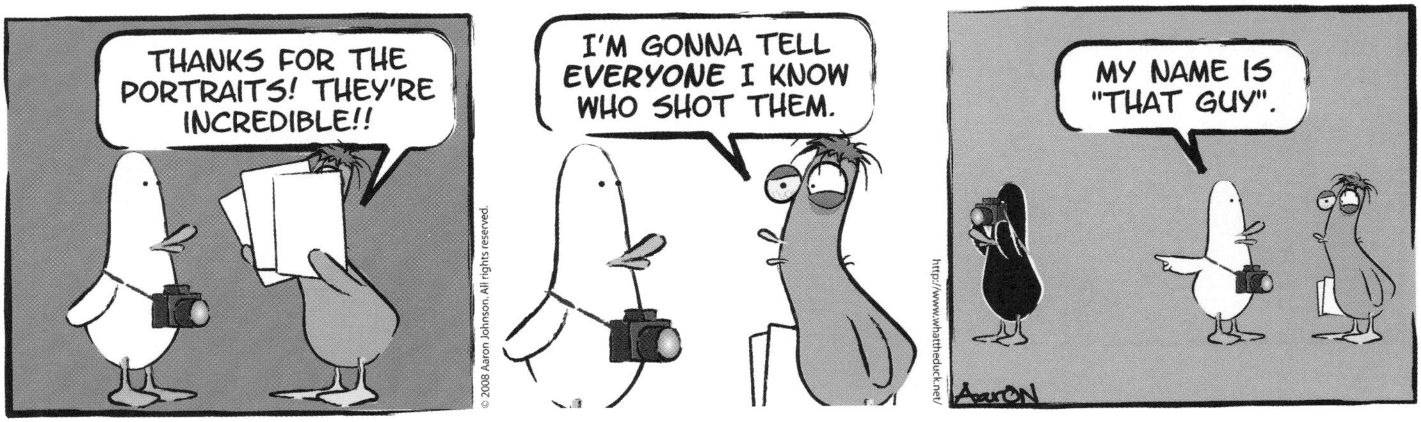
THANKS FOR THE PORTRAITS! THEY'RE INCREDIBLE!!
I'M GONNA TELL EVERYONE I KNOW WHO SHOT THEM.
MY NAME IS "THAT GUY".
AARON

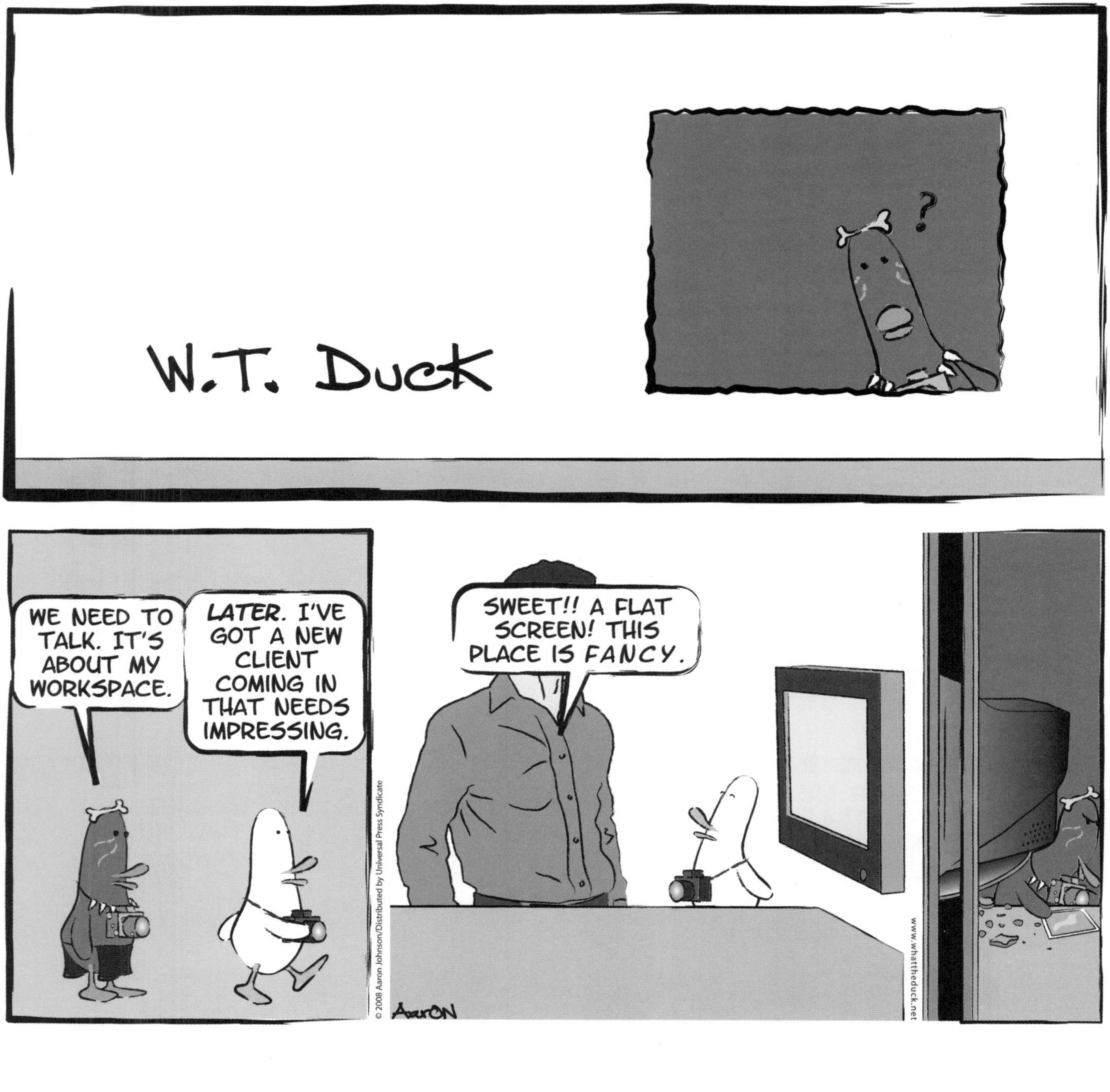
W.T. Duck
?
WE NEED TO TALK. IT'S ABOUT MY WORKSPACE.
LATER. I'VE GOT A NEW CLIENT COMING IN THAT NEEDS IMPRESSING.
SWEET!! A FLAT SCREEN! THIS PLACE IS FANCY.
© 2008 Aaron Johnson/Distributed by Universal Press Syndicate
AarON
www.whattheduck.net

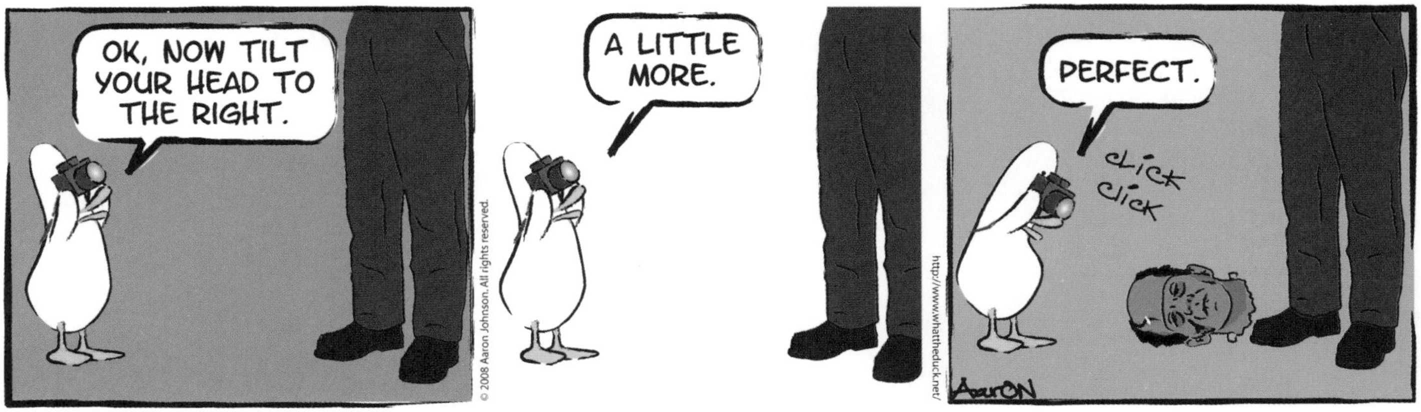
OK, NOW TILT YOUR HEAD TO THE RIGHT.
A LITTLE MORE.
PERFECT.
CLICK CLICK
© 2008 Aaron Johnson. All rights reserved.
http://www.whattheduck.net/

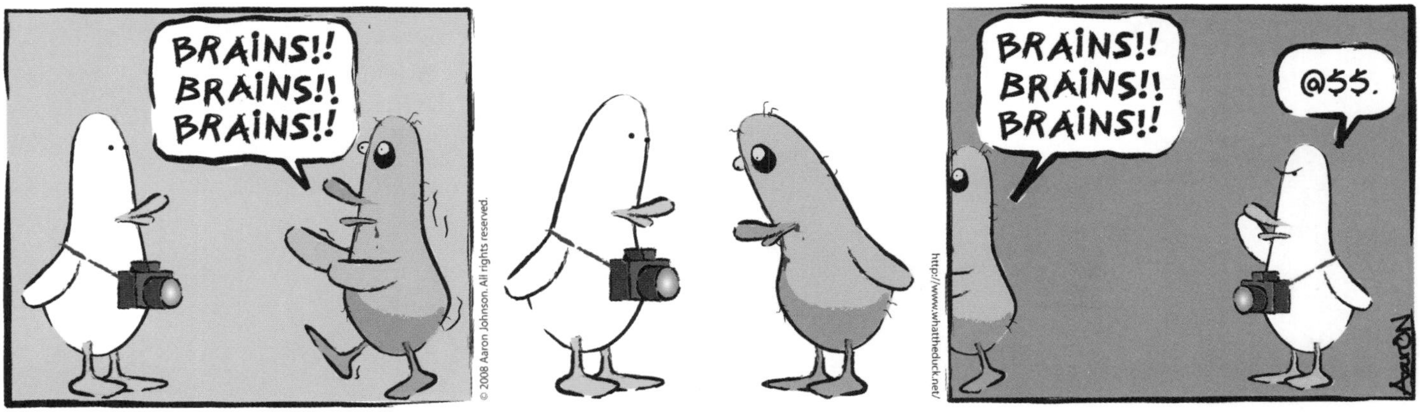
BRAINS!! BRAINS!! BRAINS!!
BRAINS!! BRAINS!! BRAINS!!
@$$.
© 2008 Aaron Johnson. All rights reserved.
http://www.whattheduck.net/

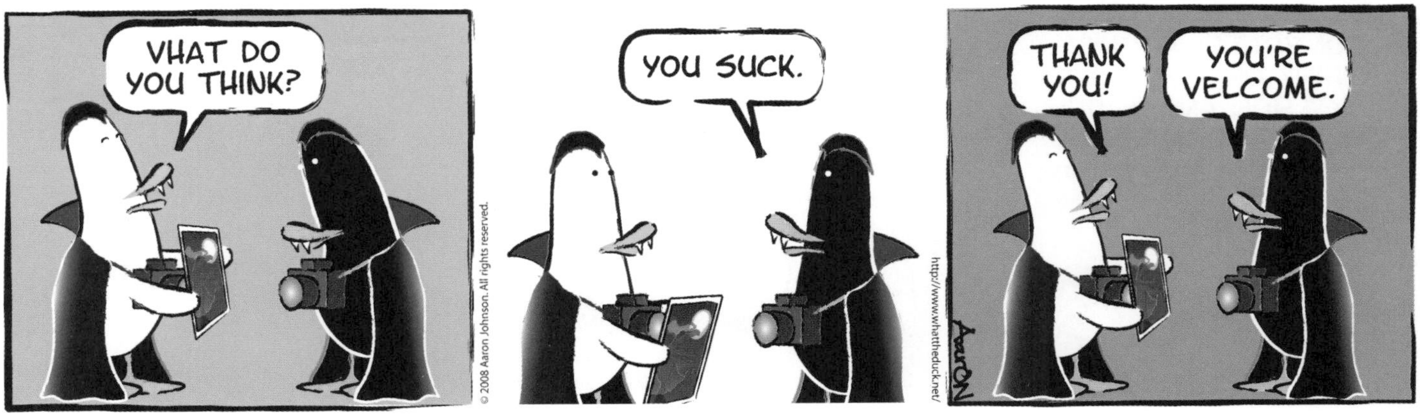
VHAT DO YOU THINK?
YOU SUCK.
THANK YOU!
YOU'RE VELCOME.
© 2008 Aaron Johnson. All rights reserved.
http://www.whattheduck.net/

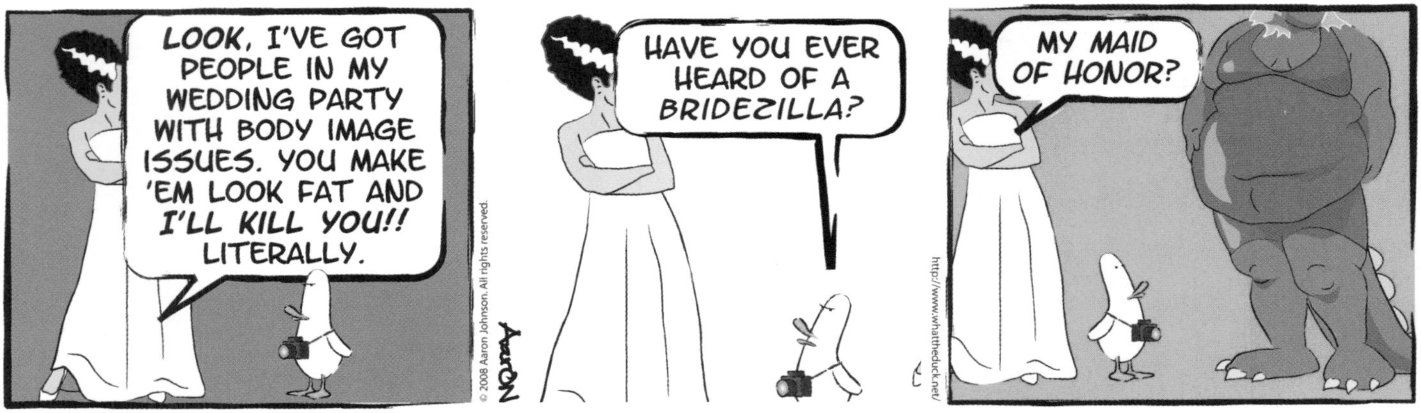
LOOK, I'VE GOT PEOPLE IN MY WEDDING PARTY WITH BODY IMAGE ISSUES. YOU MAKE 'EM LOOK FAT AND I'LL KILL YOU!! LITERALLY.
© 2008 Aaron Johnson. All rights reserved.
AARON
HAVE YOU EVER HEARD OF A BRIDEZILLA?
http://www.whattheduck.net/
MY MAID OF HONOR?

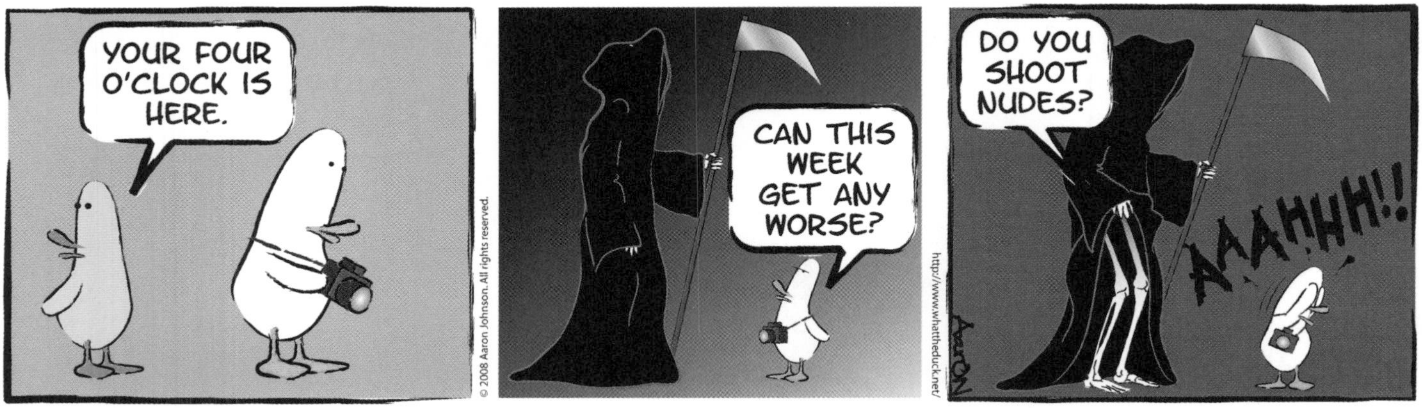
YOUR FOUR O'CLOCK IS HERE.
© 2008 Aaron Johnson. All rights reserved.
CAN THIS WEEK GET ANY WORSE?
http://www.whattheduck.net/
AARON
DO YOU SHOOT NUDES?
AAAHHH!!

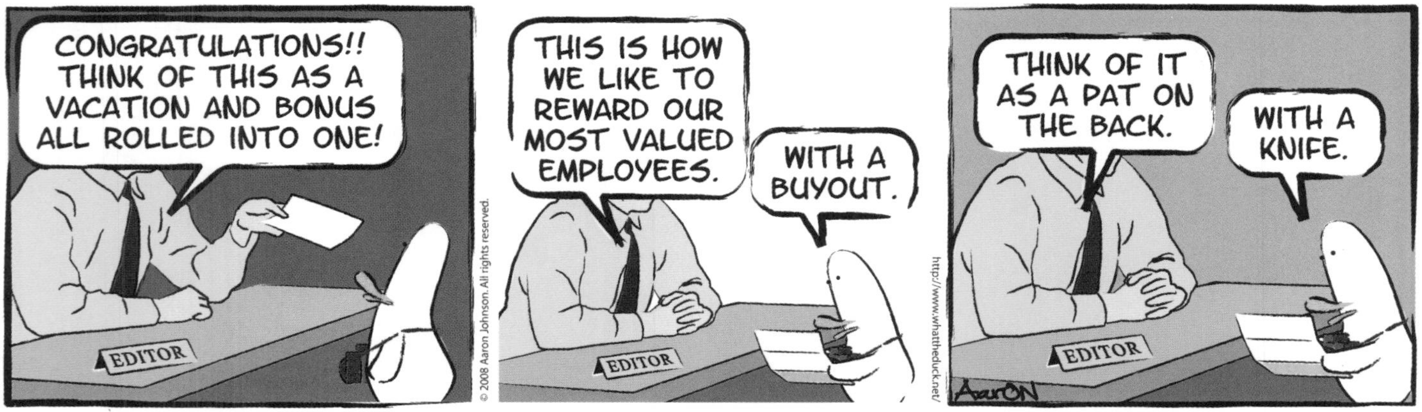
CONGRATULATIONS!! THINK OF THIS AS A VACATION AND BONUS ALL ROLLED INTO ONE!
EDITOR
© 2008 Aaron Johnson. All rights reserved.
THIS IS HOW WE LIKE TO REWARD OUR MOST VALUED EMPLOYEES.
WITH A BUYOUT.
EDITOR
http://www.whattheduck.net/
THINK OF IT AS A PAT ON THE BACK.
WITH A KNIFE.
EDITOR
AARON

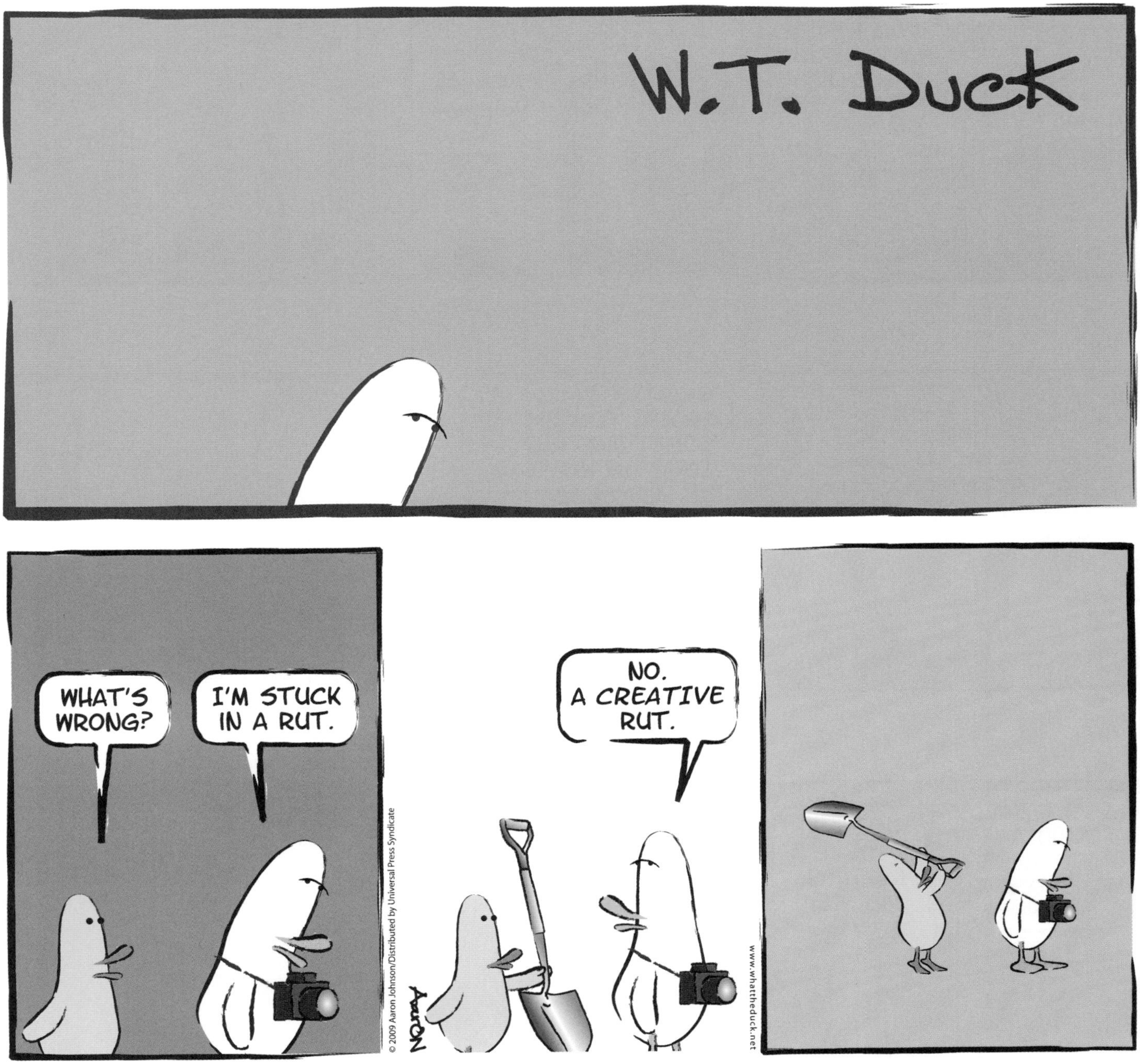
W.T. Duck
WHAT'S WRONG?
I'M STUCK IN A RUT.
NO. A CREATIVE RUT.
© 2009 Aaron Johnson/Distributed by Universal Press Syndicate
AARON
www.whattheduck.net

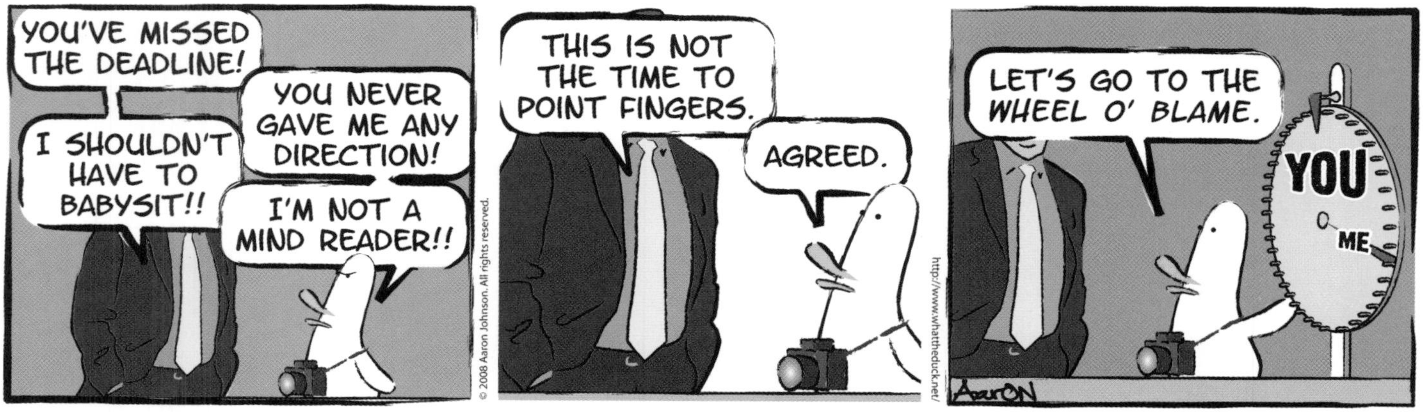
YOU'VE MISSED THE DEADLINE!
I SHOULDN'T HAVE TO BABYSIT!!
YOU NEVER GAVE ME ANY DIRECTION!
I'M NOT A MIND READER!!
© 2008 Aaron Johnson. All rights reserved.
THIS IS NOT THE TIME TO POINT FINGERS.
AGREED.
http://www.whattheduck.net/
LET'S GO TO THE WHEEL O' BLAME.
YOU
ME

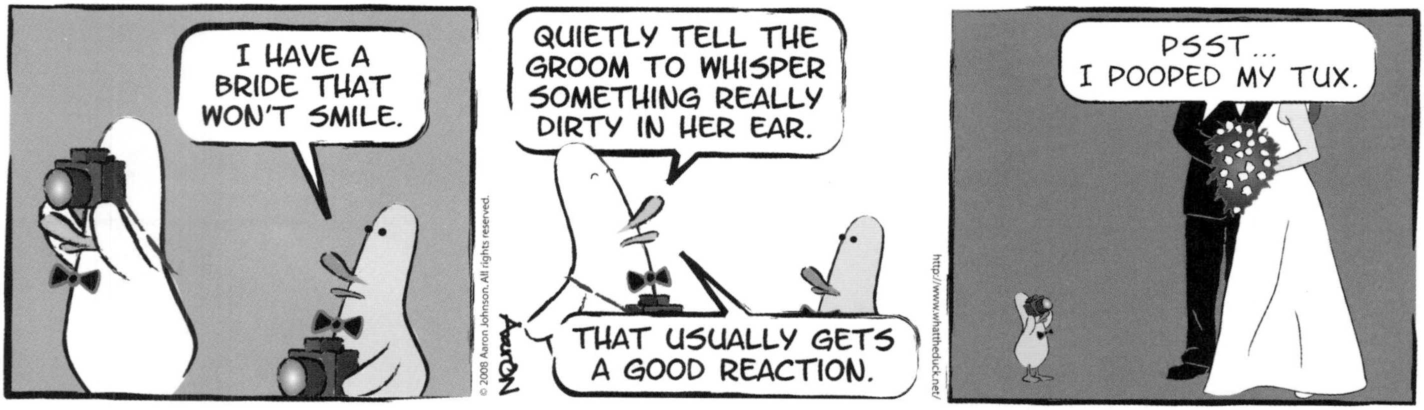
I HAVE A BRIDE THAT WON'T SMILE.
© 2008 Aaron Johnson. All rights reserved.
QUIETLY TELL THE GROOM TO WHISPER SOMETHING REALLY DIRTY IN HER EAR.
THAT USUALLY GETS A GOOD REACTION.
http://www.whattheduck.net/
PSST... I POOPED MY TUX.

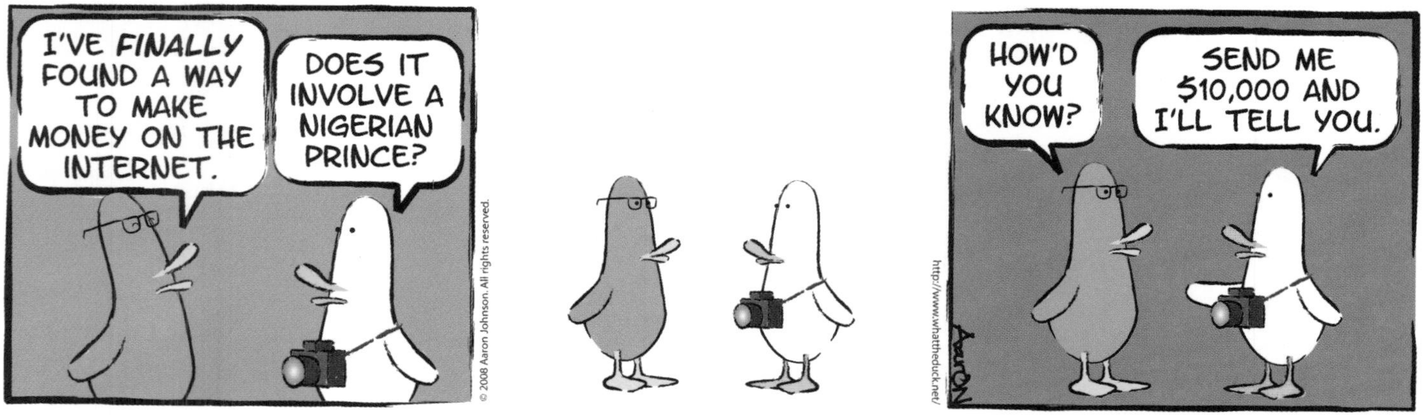
I'VE FINALLY FOUND A WAY TO MAKE MONEY ON THE INTERNET.
DOES IT INVOLVE A NIGERIAN PRINCE?
© 2008 Aaron Johnson. All rights reserved.
http://www.whattheduck.net/
HOW'D YOU KNOW?
SEND ME $10,000 AND I'LL TELL YOU.

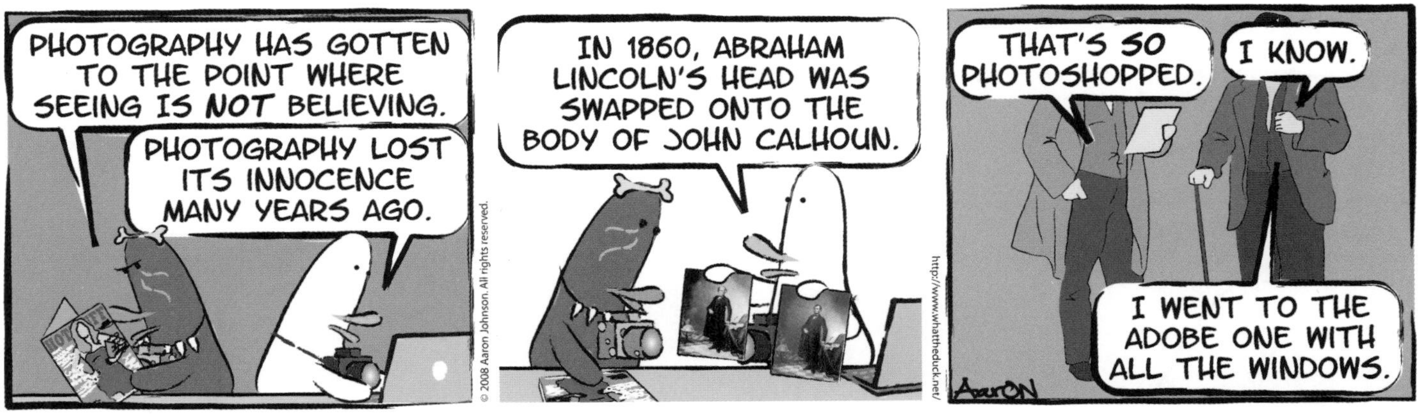
PHOTOGRAPHY HAS GOTTEN TO THE POINT WHERE SEEING IS NOT BELIEVING.
PHOTOGRAPHY LOST ITS INNOCENCE MANY YEARS AGO.
© 2008 Aaron Johnson. All rights reserved.
IN 1860, ABRAHAM LINCOLN'S HEAD WAS SWAPPED ONTO THE BODY OF JOHN CALHOUN.
http://www.whattheduck.net/
THAT'S SO PHOTOSHOPPED.
I KNOW.
I WENT TO THE ADOBE ONE WITH ALL THE WINDOWS.
AARON

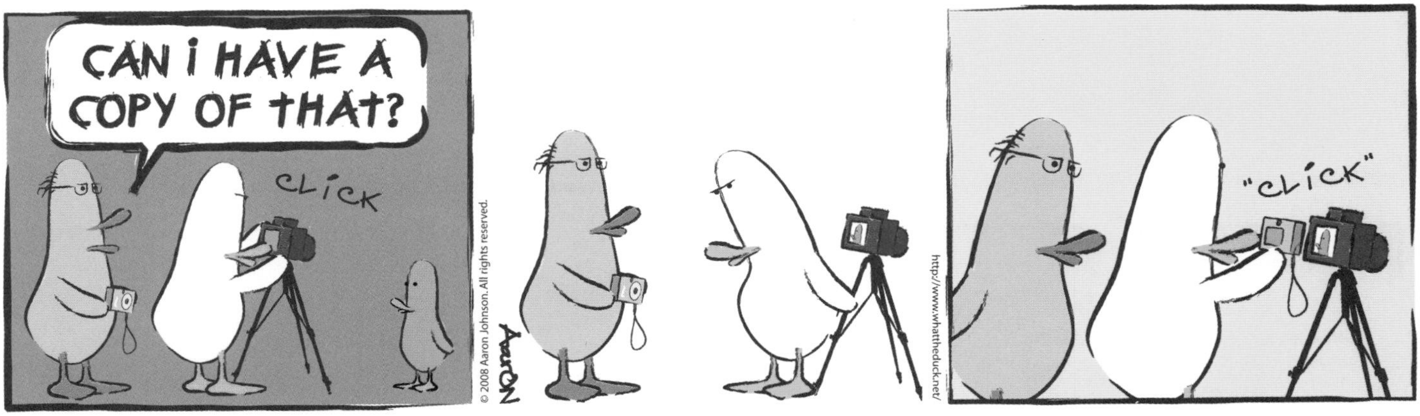
CAN I HAVE A COPY OF THAT?
CLICK
© 2008 Aaron Johnson. All rights reserved.
AARON
http://www.whattheduck.net/
"CLICK"

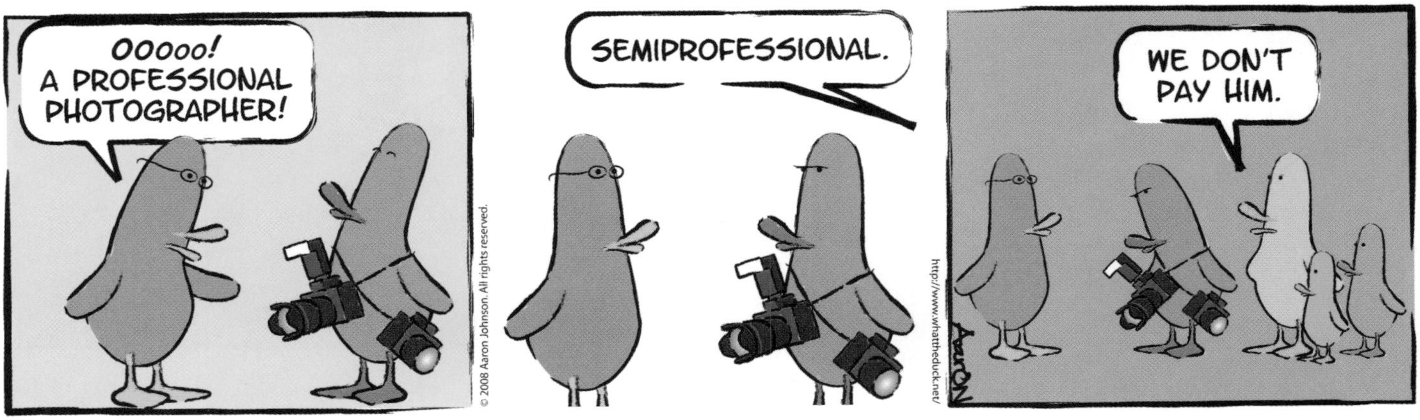
OOOOO! A PROFESSIONAL PHOTOGRAPHER!
© 2008 Aaron Johnson. All rights reserved.
SEMIPROFESSIONAL.
http://www.whattheduck.net/
WE DON'T PAY HIM.
AARON

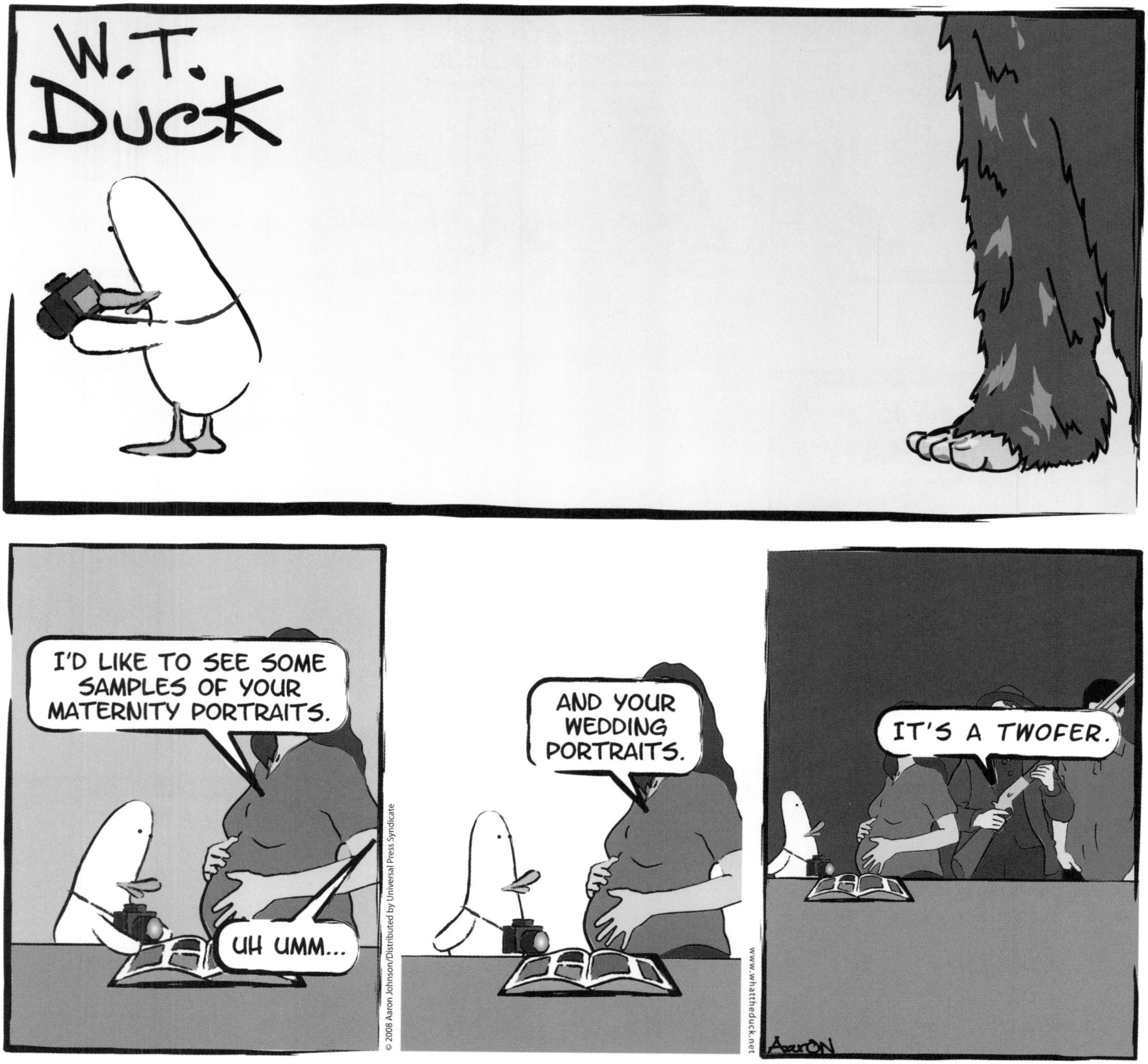
W.T. Duck
I'D LIKE TO SEE SOME SAMPLES OF YOUR MATERNITY PORTRAITS.
UH UMM...
AND YOUR WEDDING PORTRAITS.
IT'S A TWOFER.
© 2008 Aaron Johnson/Distributed by Universal Press Syndicate
www.whattheduck.net
AARON

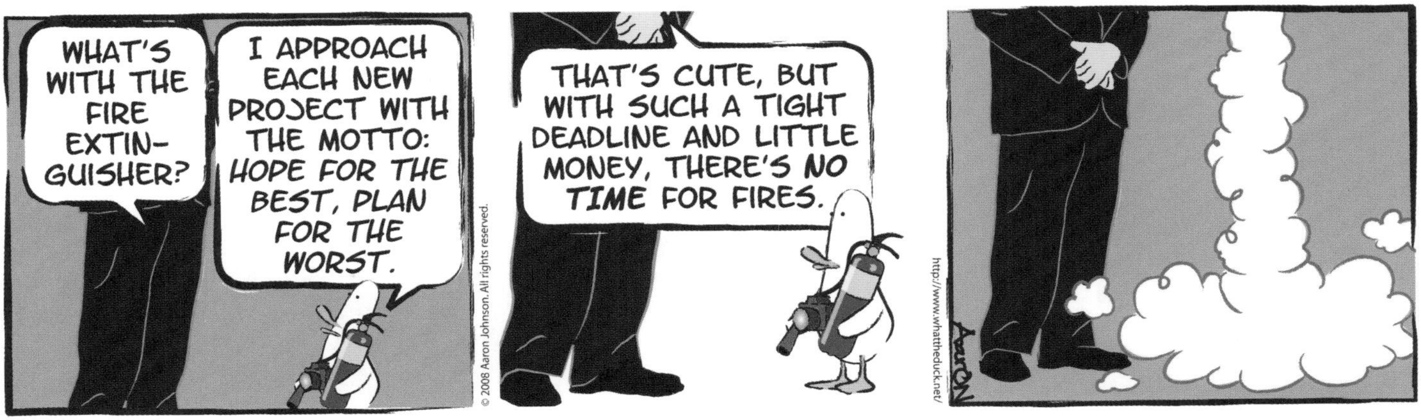
WHAT'S WITH THE FIRE EXTIN-GUISHER?
I APPROACH EACH NEW PROJECT WITH THE MOTTO: HOPE FOR THE BEST, PLAN FOR THE WORST.
THAT'S CUTE, BUT WITH SUCH A TIGHT DEADLINE AND LITTLE MONEY, THERE'S NO TIME FOR FIRES.
AARON

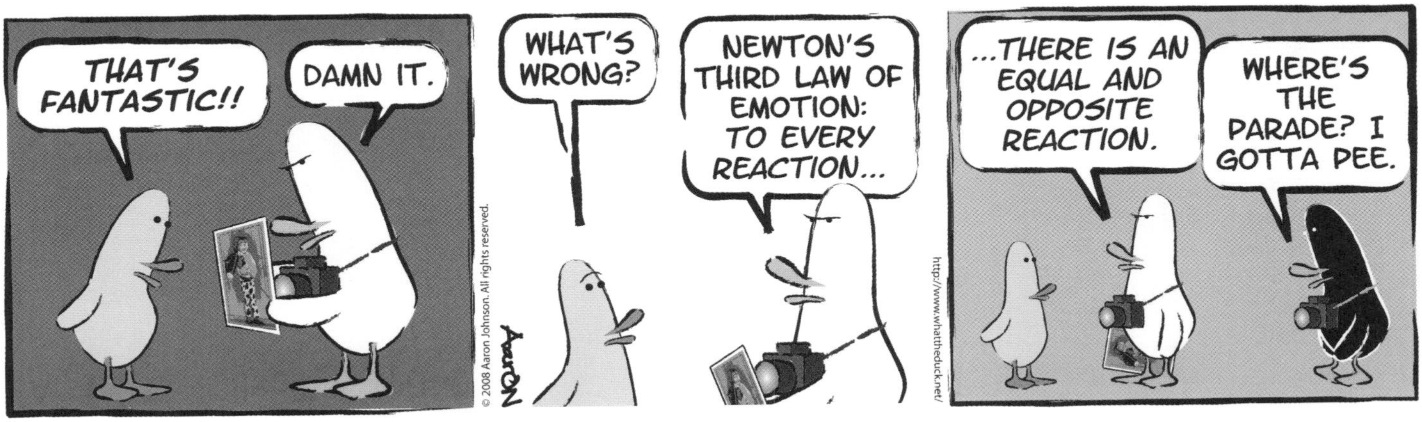
THAT'S FANTASTIC!!
DAMN IT.
WHAT'S WRONG?
NEWTON'S THIRD LAW OF EMOTION: TO EVERY REACTION...
...THERE IS AN EQUAL AND OPPOSITE REACTION.
WHERE'S THE PARADE? I GOTTA PEE.
AARON

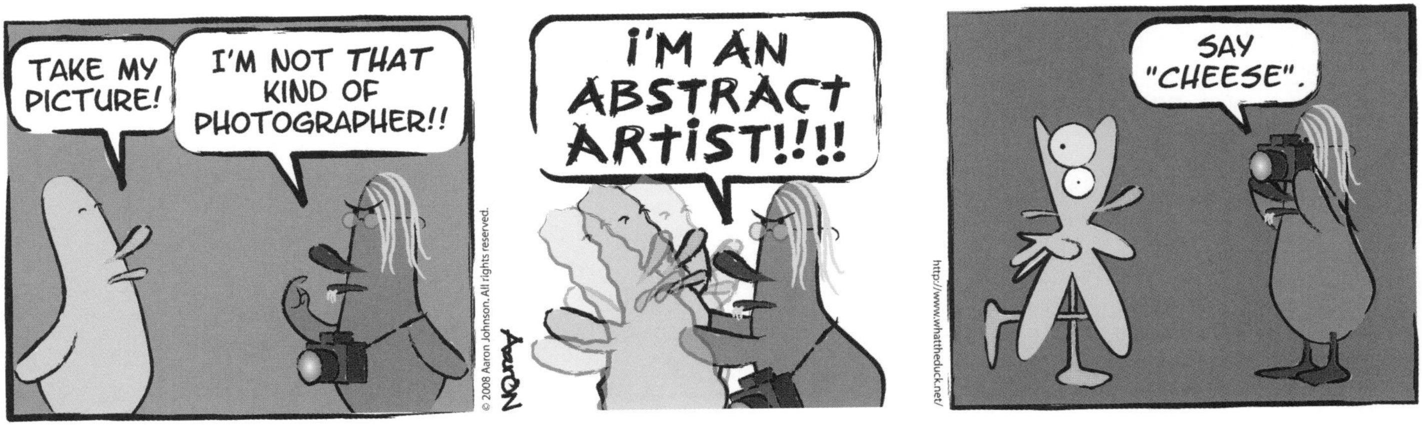
TAKE MY PICTURE!
I'M NOT THAT KIND OF PHOTOGRAPHER!!
I'M AN ABSTRACT ARTIST!!!!
SAY "CHEESE".
AARON

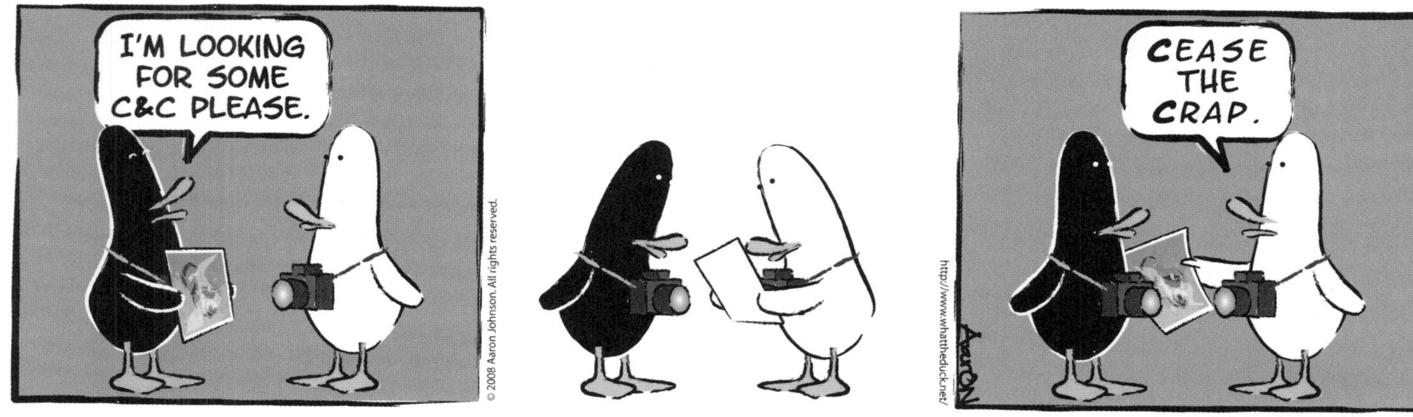
I'M LOOKING FOR SOME C&C PLEASE.
CEASE THE CRAP.
© 2008 Aaron Johnson. All rights reserved.
http://www.whattheduck.net/
AARON

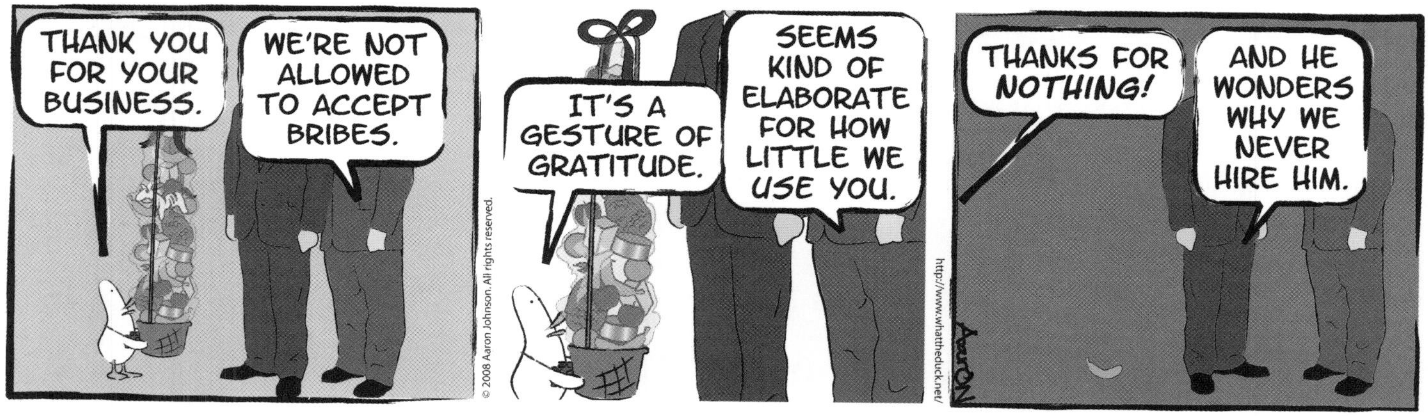
THANK YOU FOR YOUR BUSINESS.
WE'RE NOT ALLOWED TO ACCEPT BRIBES.
IT'S A GESTURE OF GRATITUDE.
SEEMS KIND OF ELABORATE FOR HOW LITTLE WE USE YOU.
THANKS FOR NOTHING!
AND HE WONDERS WHY WE NEVER HIRE HIM.
© 2008 Aaron Johnson. All rights reserved.
http://www.whattheduck.net/
AARON

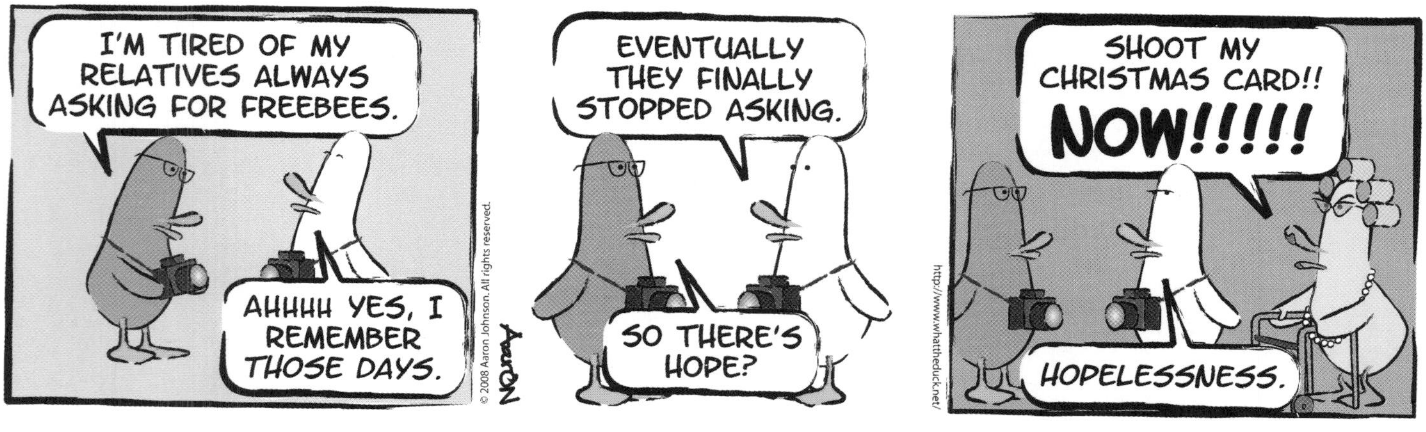
I'M TIRED OF MY RELATIVES ALWAYS ASKING FOR FREEBEES.
AHHHH YES, I REMEMBER THOSE DAYS.
EVENTUALLY THEY FINALLY STOPPED ASKING.
SO THERE'S HOPE?
SHOOT MY CHRISTMAS CARD!! NOW!!!!!
HOPELESSNESS.
© 2008 Aaron Johnson. All rights reserved.
http://www.whattheduck.net/
AARON

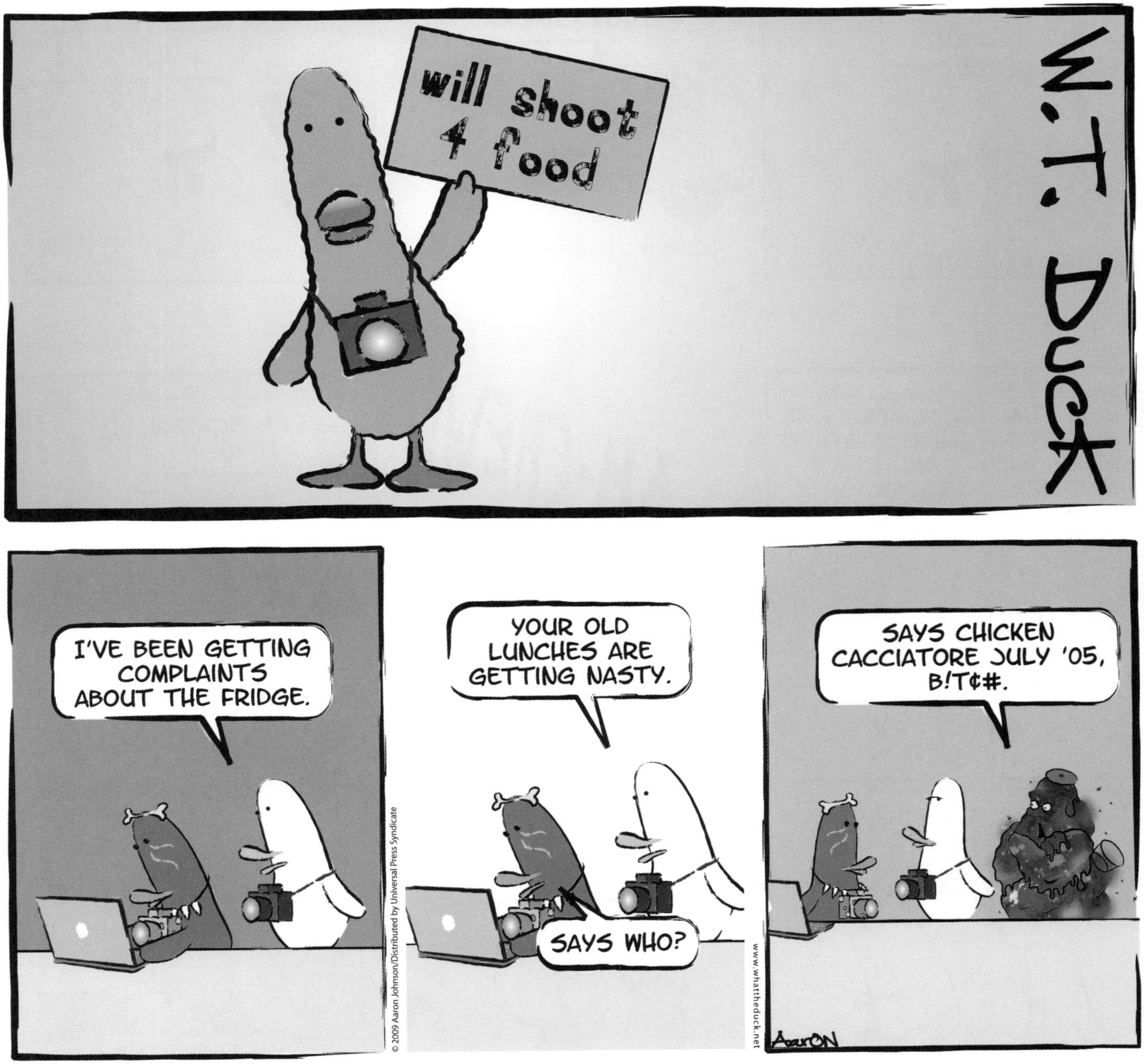
W.T. DUCK
will shoot 4 food
I'VE BEEN GETTING COMPLAINTS ABOUT THE FRIDGE.
YOUR OLD LUNCHES ARE GETTING NASTY.
SAYS WHO?
SAYS CHICKEN CACCIATORE JULY '05, B!T¢#.
© 2009 Aaron Johnson/Distributed by Universal Press Syndicate
www.whattheduck.net
AARON

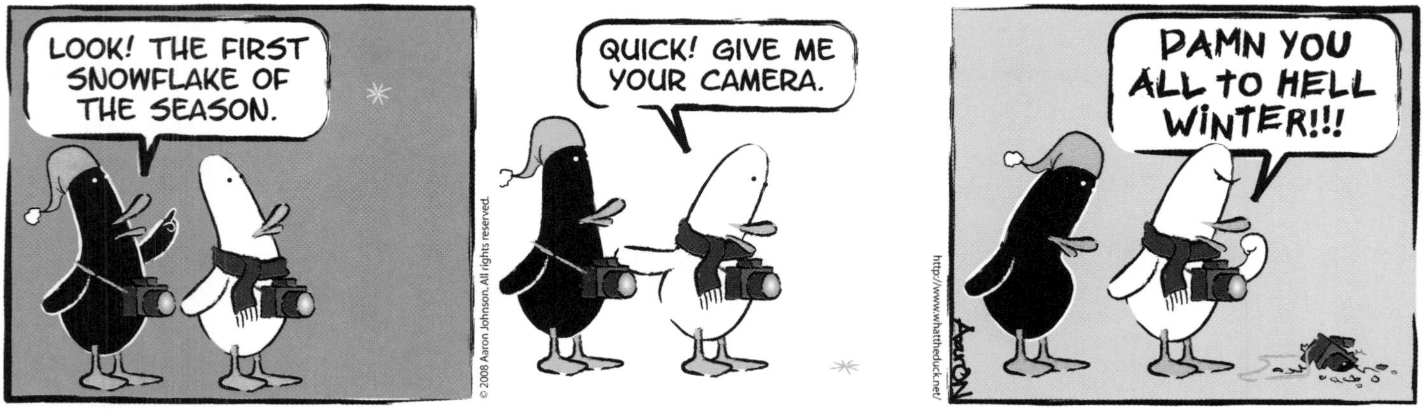
LOOK! THE FIRST SNOWFLAKE OF THE SEASON.
QUICK! GIVE ME YOUR CAMERA.
DAMN YOU ALL TO HELL WINTER!!!
© 2008 Aaron Johnson. All rights reserved.
http://www.whattheduck.net/
AARON

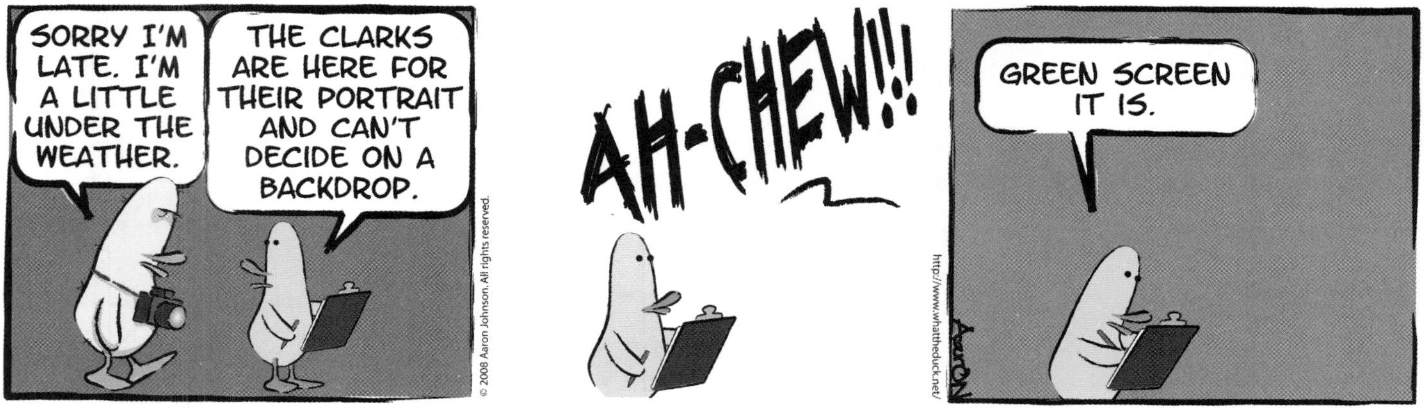
SORRY I'M LATE. I'M A LITTLE UNDER THE WEATHER.
THE CLARKS ARE HERE FOR THEIR PORTRAIT AND CAN'T DECIDE ON A BACKDROP.
AH-CHEW!!!
GREEN SCREEN IT IS.
© 2008 Aaron Johnson. All rights reserved.
http://www.whattheduck.net/
AARON

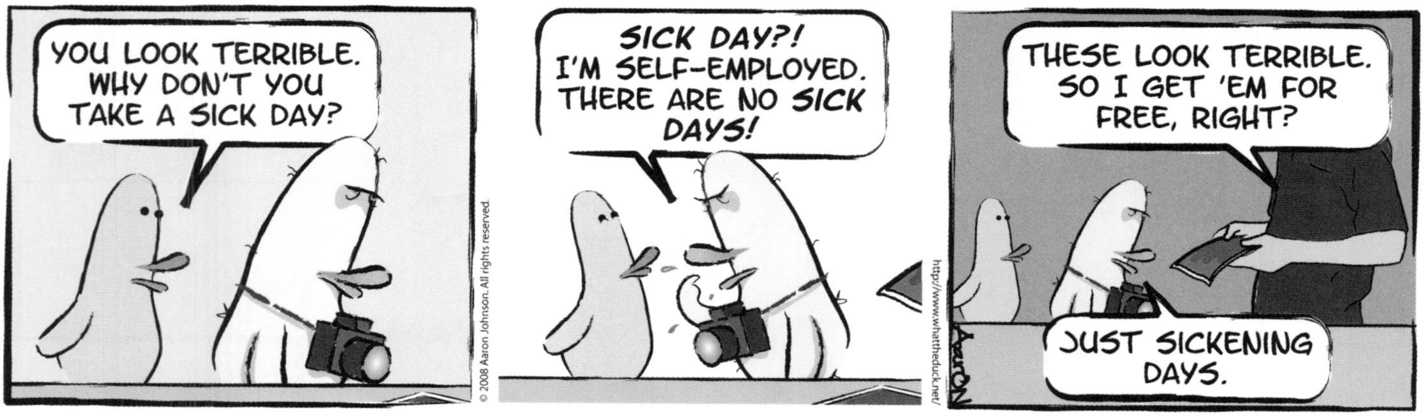
YOU LOOK TERRIBLE. WHY DON'T YOU TAKE A SICK DAY?
SICK DAY?! I'M SELF-EMPLOYED. THERE ARE NO SICK DAYS!
THESE LOOK TERRIBLE. SO I GET 'EM FOR FREE, RIGHT?
JUST SICKENING DAYS.
© 2008 Aaron Johnson. All rights reserved.
http://www.whattheduck.net/
AARON

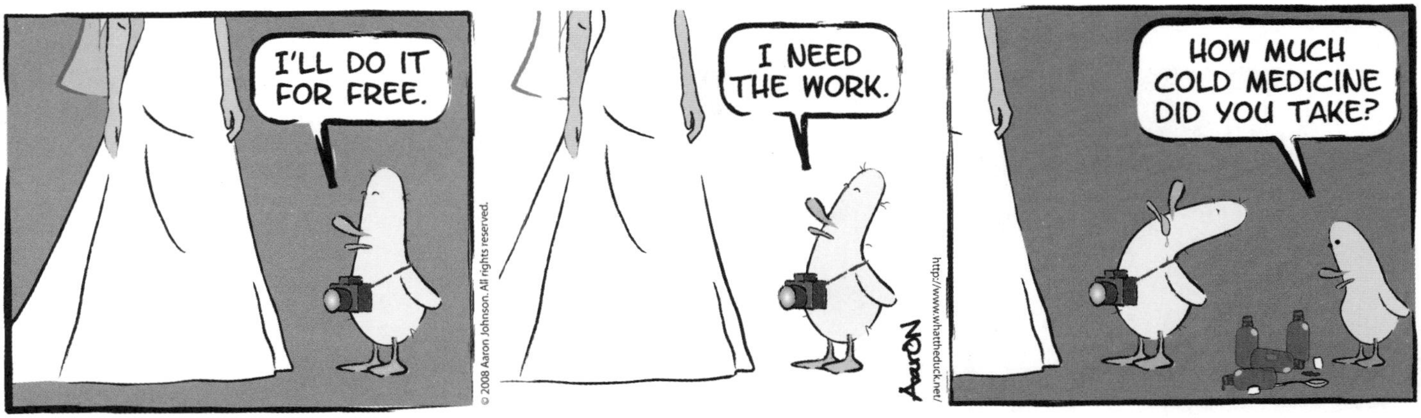
I'LL DO IT FOR FREE.
I NEED THE WORK.
HOW MUCH COLD MEDICINE DID YOU TAKE?
© 2008 Aaron Johnson. All rights reserved.
http://www.whattheduck.net/

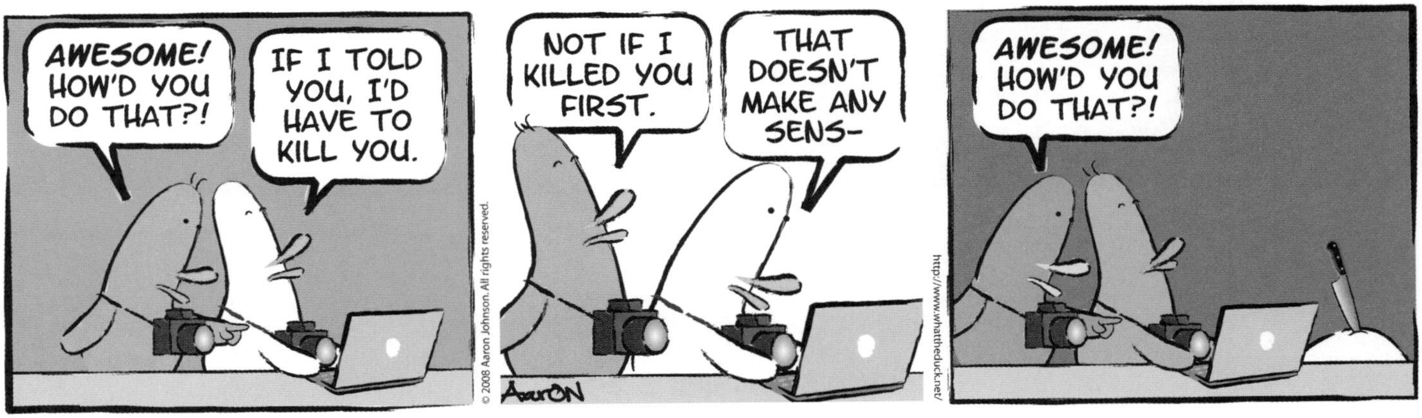
AWESOME! HOW'D YOU DO THAT?!
IF I TOLD YOU, I'D HAVE TO KILL YOU.
NOT IF I KILLED YOU FIRST.
THAT DOESN'T MAKE ANY SENS-
AWESOME! HOW'D YOU DO THAT?!
© 2008 Aaron Johnson. All rights reserved.
http://www.whattheduck.net/

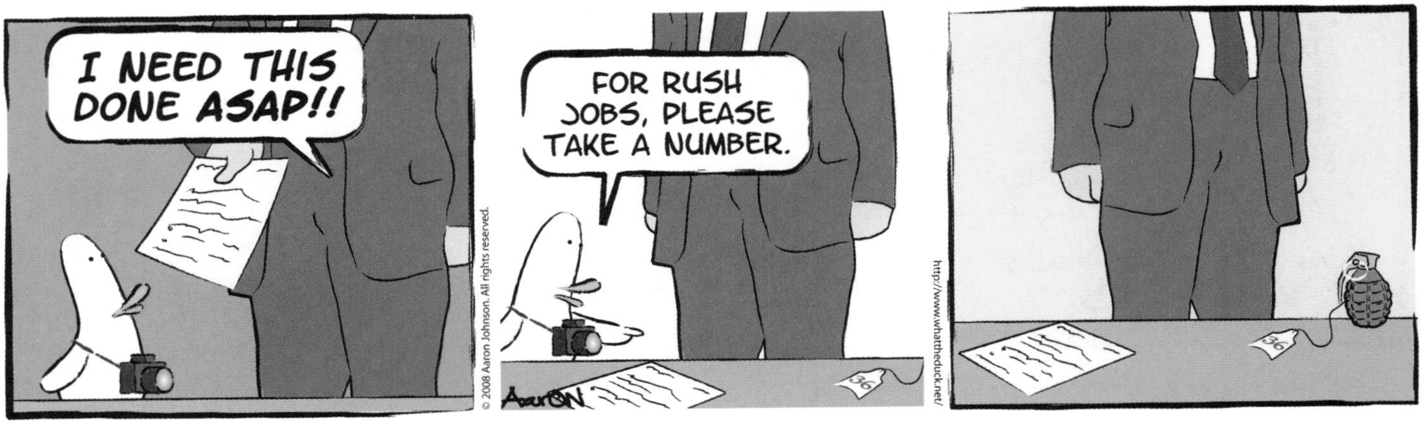
I NEED THIS DONE ASAP!!
FOR RUSH JOBS, PLEASE TAKE A NUMBER.
36
© 2008 Aaron Johnson. All rights reserved.
http://www.whattheduck.net/

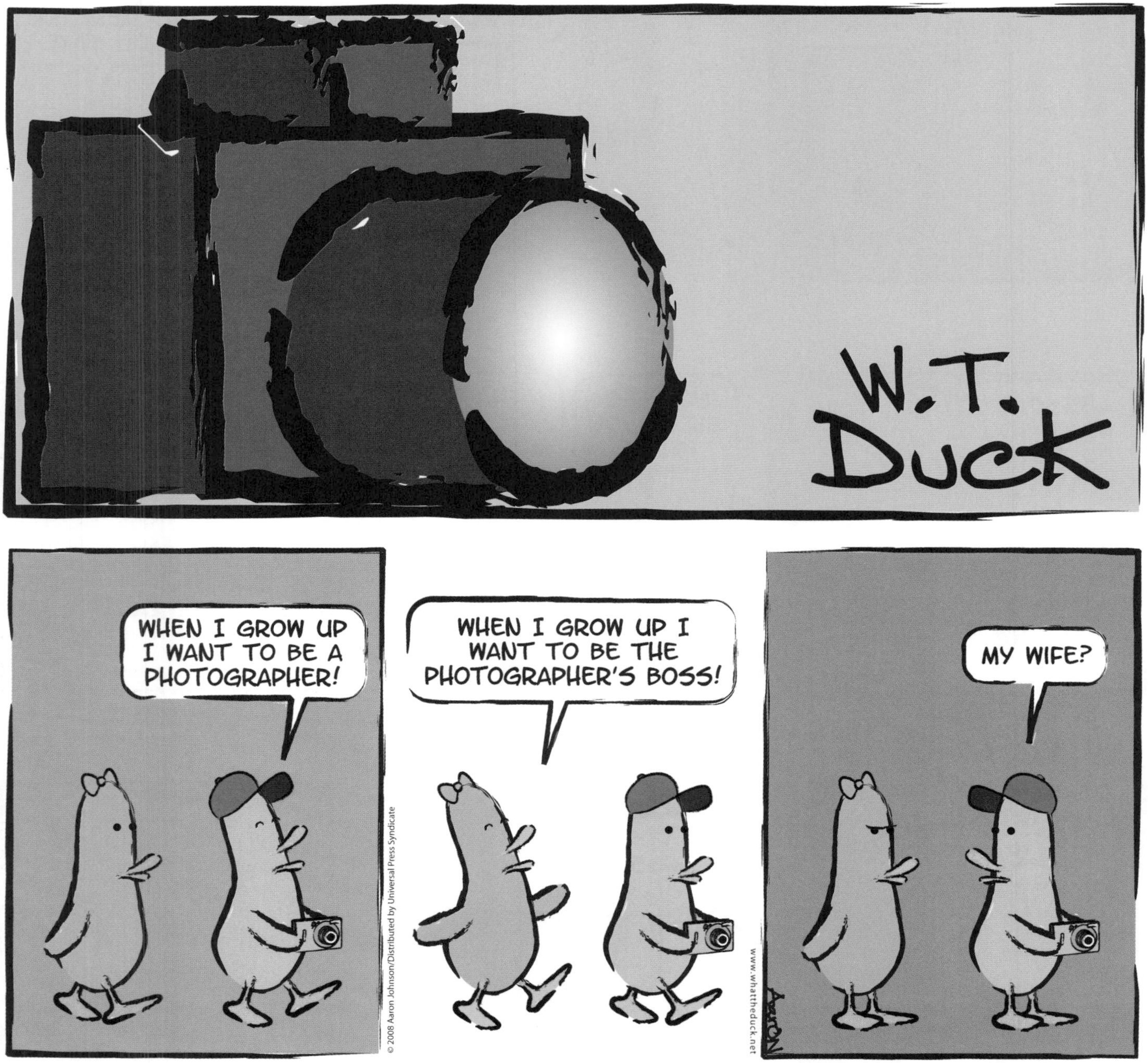
W.T. Duck
WHEN I GROW UP I WANT TO BE A PHOTOGRAPHER!
WHEN I GROW UP I WANT TO BE THE PHOTOGRAPHER'S BOSS!
MY WIFE?
© 2008 Aaron Johnson/Distributed by Universal Press Syndicate
www.whattheduck.net
AARON

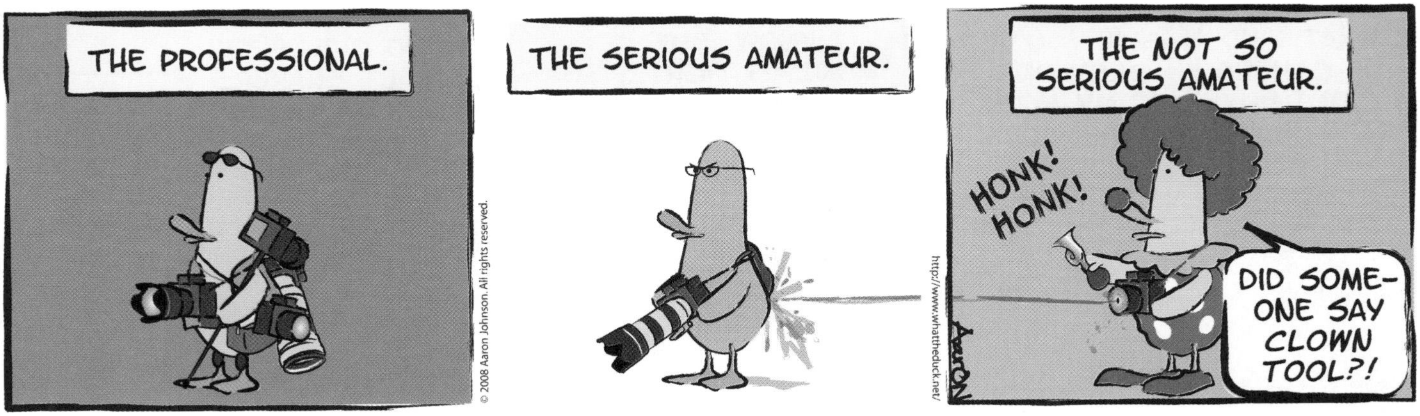
THE PROFESSIONAL.
© 2008 Aaron Johnson. All rights reserved.
THE SERIOUS AMATEUR.
http://www.whattheduck.net/
THE NOT SO SERIOUS AMATEUR.
HONK! HONK!
DID SOME-ONE SAY CLOWN TOOL?!
AARON

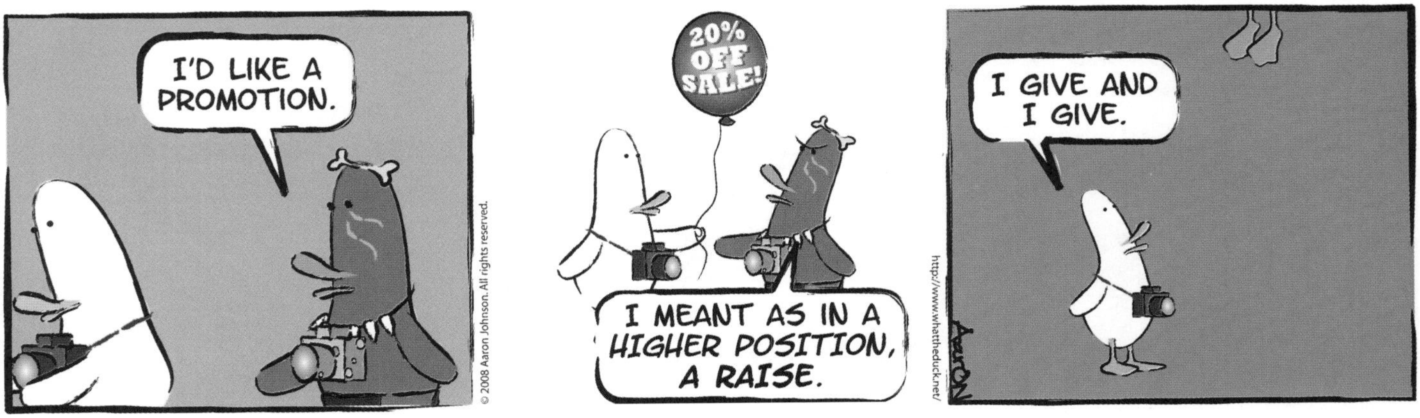
I'D LIKE A PROMOTION.
© 2008 Aaron Johnson. All rights reserved.
20% OFF SALE!
I MEANT AS IN A HIGHER POSITION, A RAISE.
http://www.whattheduck.net/
I GIVE AND I GIVE.
AARON

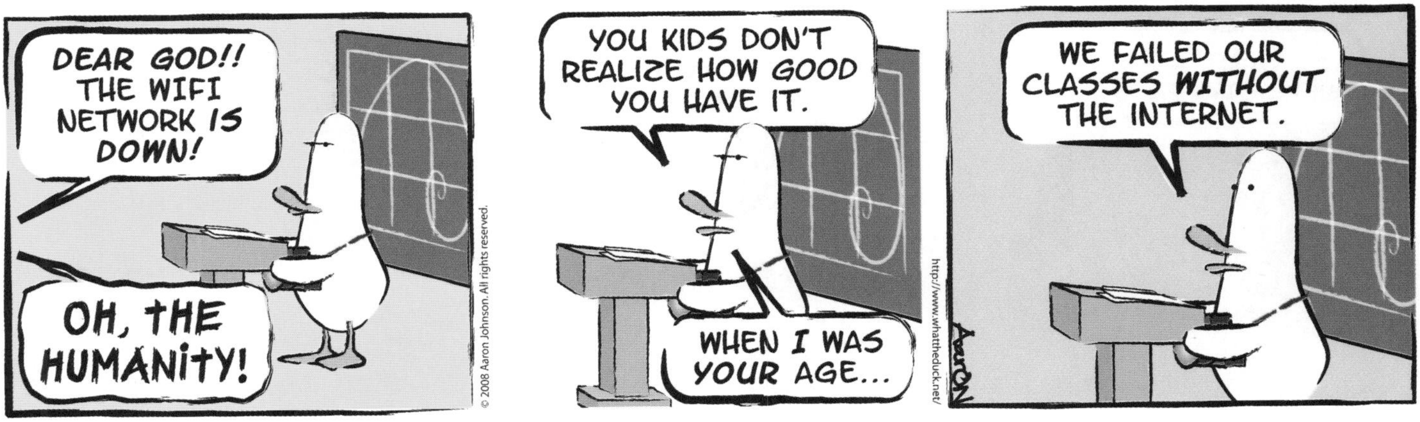
DEAR GOD!! THE WIFI NETWORK IS DOWN!
OH, THE HUMANITY!
© 2008 Aaron Johnson. All rights reserved.
YOU KIDS DON'T REALIZE HOW GOOD YOU HAVE IT.
WHEN I WAS YOUR AGE...
http://www.whattheduck.net/
WE FAILED OUR CLASSES WITHOUT THE INTERNET.
AARON

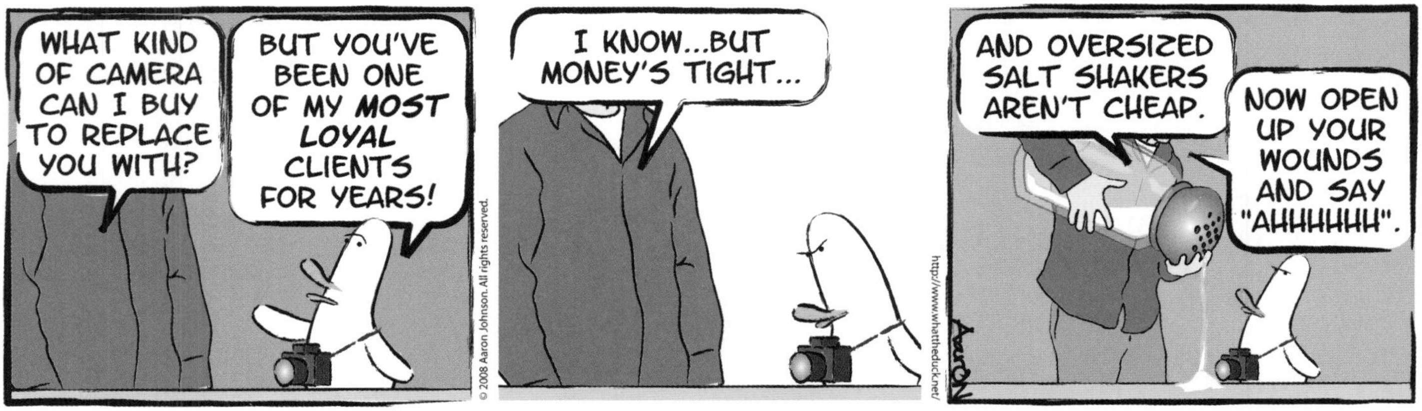
WHAT KIND OF CAMERA CAN I BUY TO REPLACE YOU WITH?
BUT YOU'VE BEEN ONE OF MY MOST LOYAL CLIENTS FOR YEARS!
© 2008 Aaron Johnson. All rights reserved.
I KNOW...BUT MONEY'S TIGHT...
http://www.whattheduck.net/
AND OVERSIZED SALT SHAKERS AREN'T CHEAP.
NOW OPEN UP YOUR WOUNDS AND SAY "AHHHHHH".
AARON

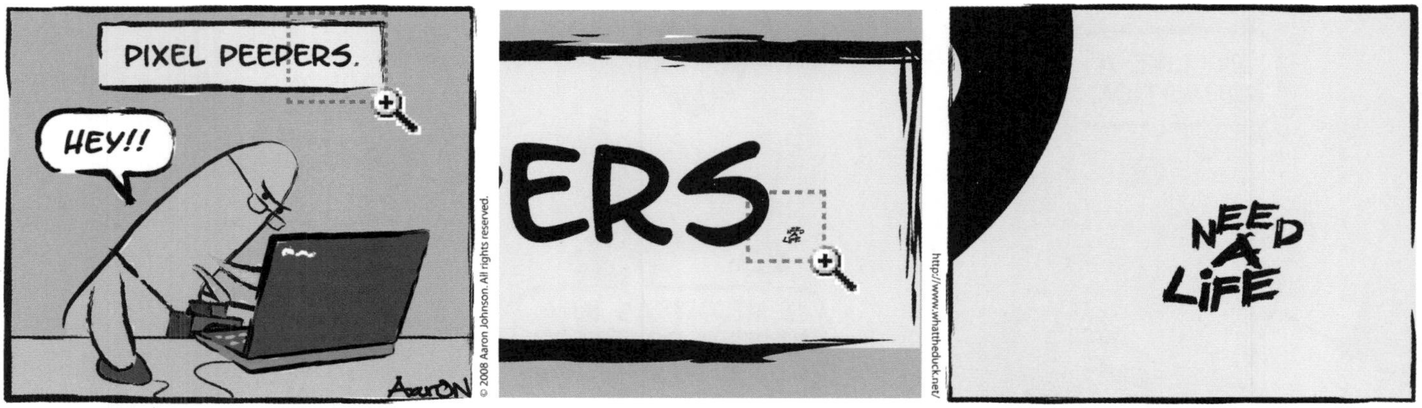
PIXEL PEEPERS.
HEY!!
AARON
© 2008 Aaron Johnson. All rights reserved.
ERS
http://www.whattheduck.net/
NEED A LIFE

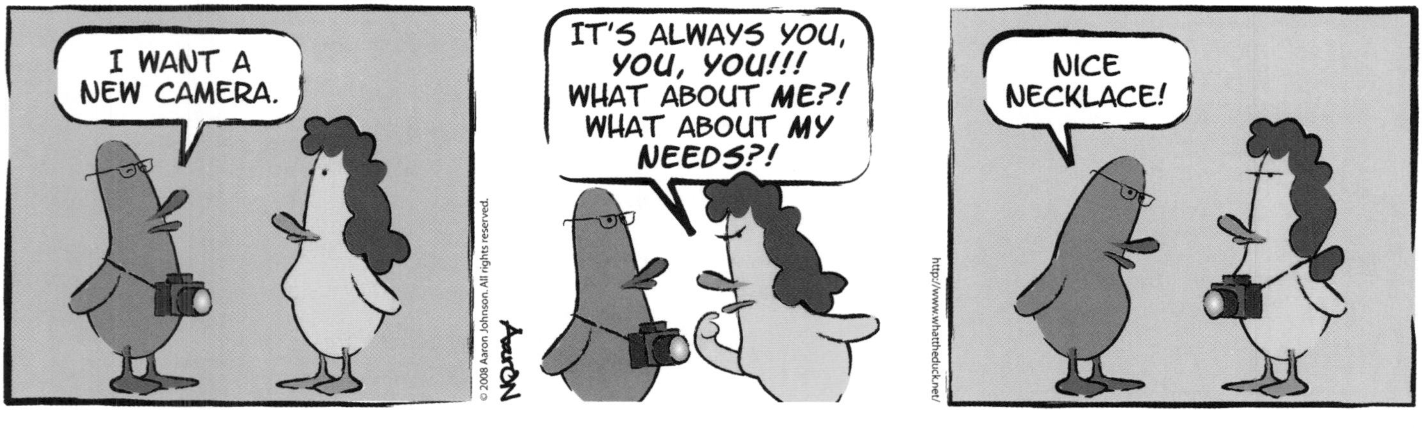
I WANT A NEW CAMERA.
© 2008 Aaron Johnson. All rights reserved.
AARON
IT'S ALWAYS YOU, YOU, YOU!!! WHAT ABOUT ME?! WHAT ABOUT MY NEEDS?!
http://www.whattheduck.net/
NICE NECKLACE!

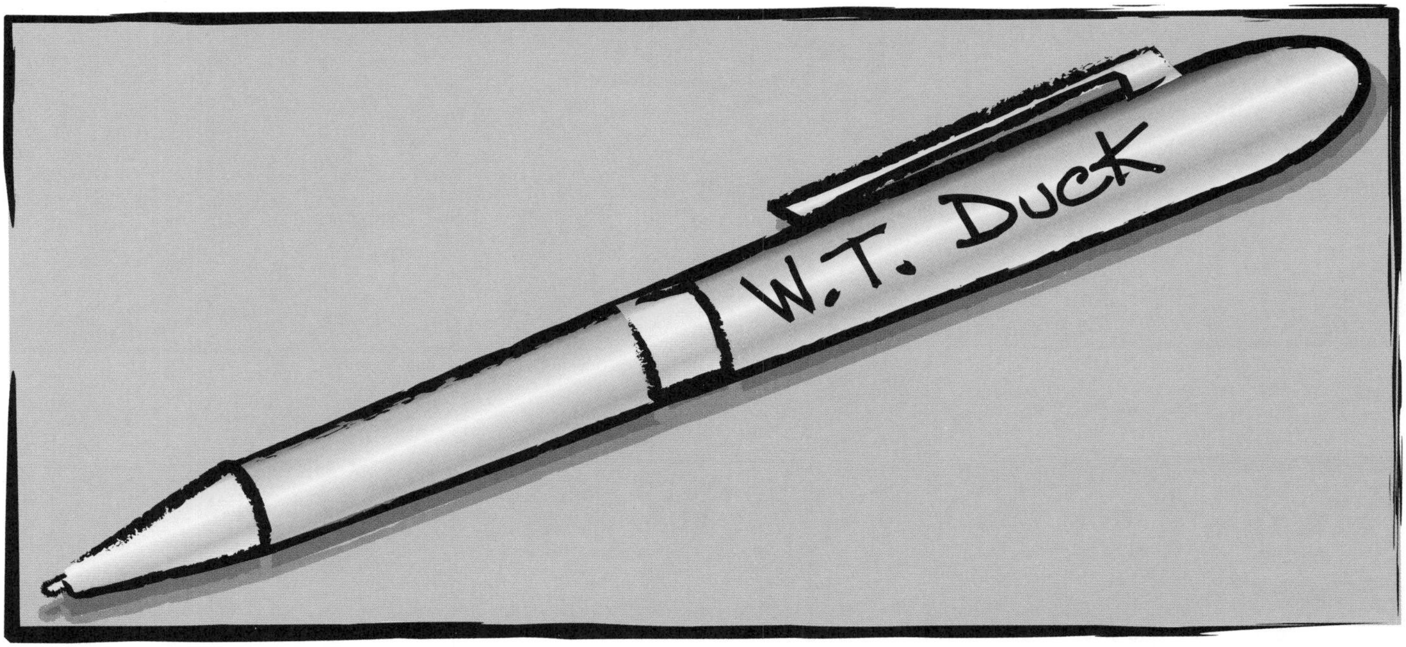
W.T. Duck

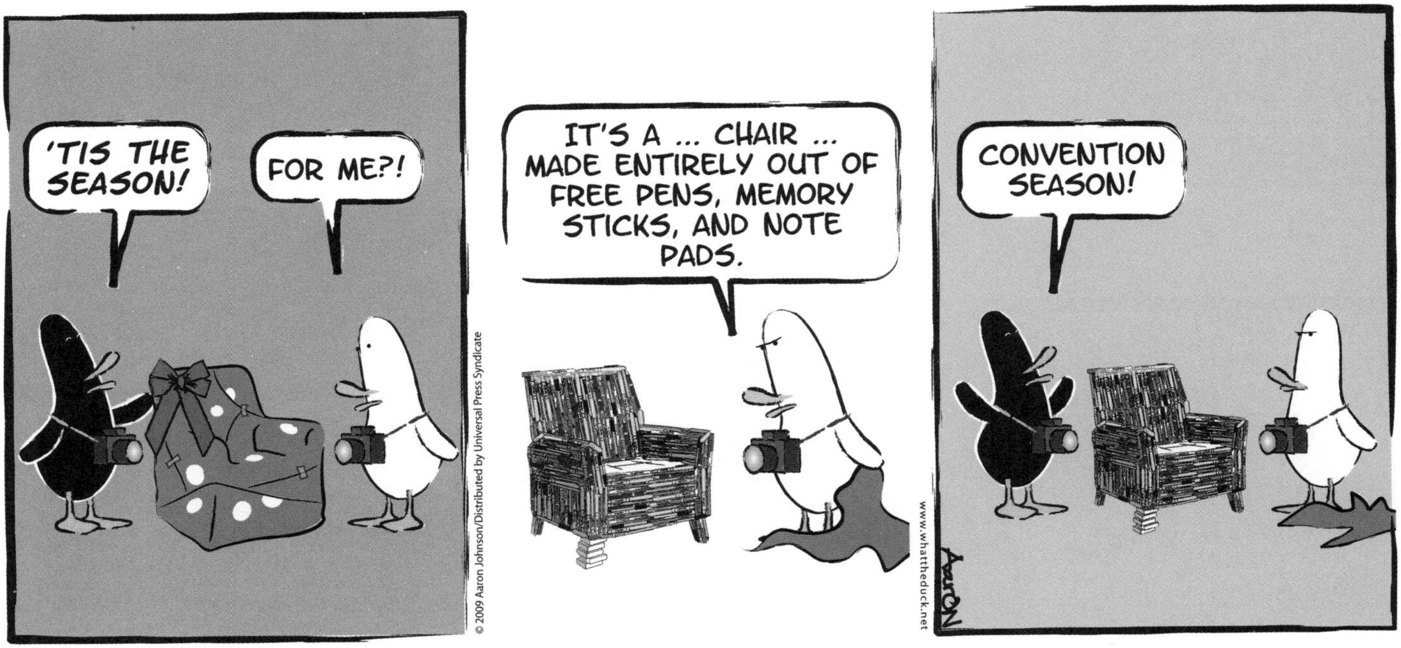
'TIS THE SEASON!
FOR ME?!
IT'S A ... CHAIR ... MADE ENTIRELY OUT OF FREE PENS, MEMORY STICKS, AND NOTE PADS.
CONVENTION SEASON!
© 2009 Aaron Johnson/Distributed by Universal Press Syndicate
www.whattheduck.net
AARON

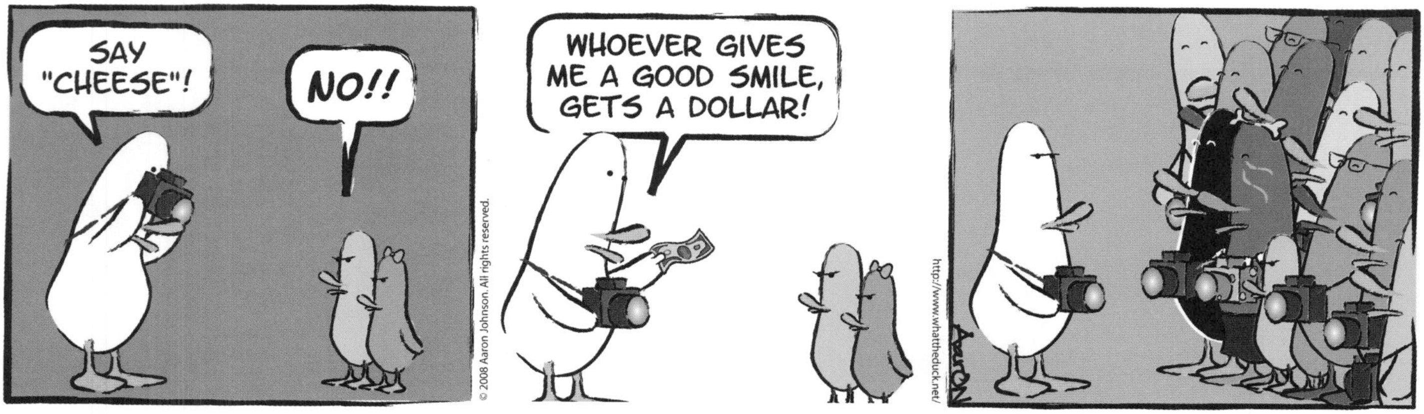
SAY "CHEESE"!
NO!!
WHOEVER GIVES ME A GOOD SMILE, GETS A DOLLAR!
© 2008 Aaron Johnson. All rights reserved.
http://www.whattheduck.net/
AARON

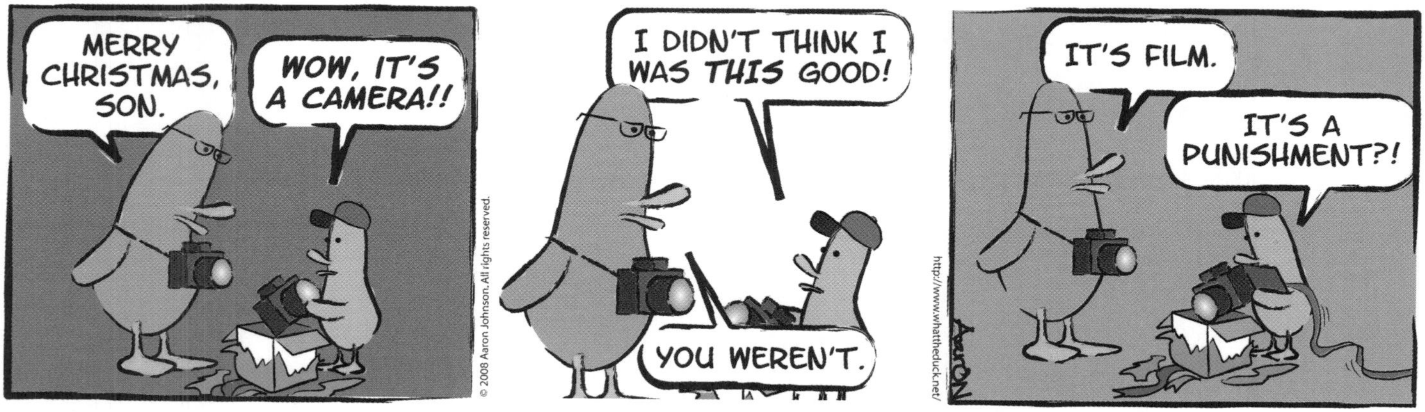
MERRY CHRISTMAS, SON.
WOW, IT'S A CAMERA!!
I DIDN'T THINK I WAS THIS GOOD!
YOU WEREN'T.
IT'S FILM.
IT'S A PUNISHMENT?!
© 2008 Aaron Johnson. All rights reserved.
http://www.whattheduck.net/
AARON

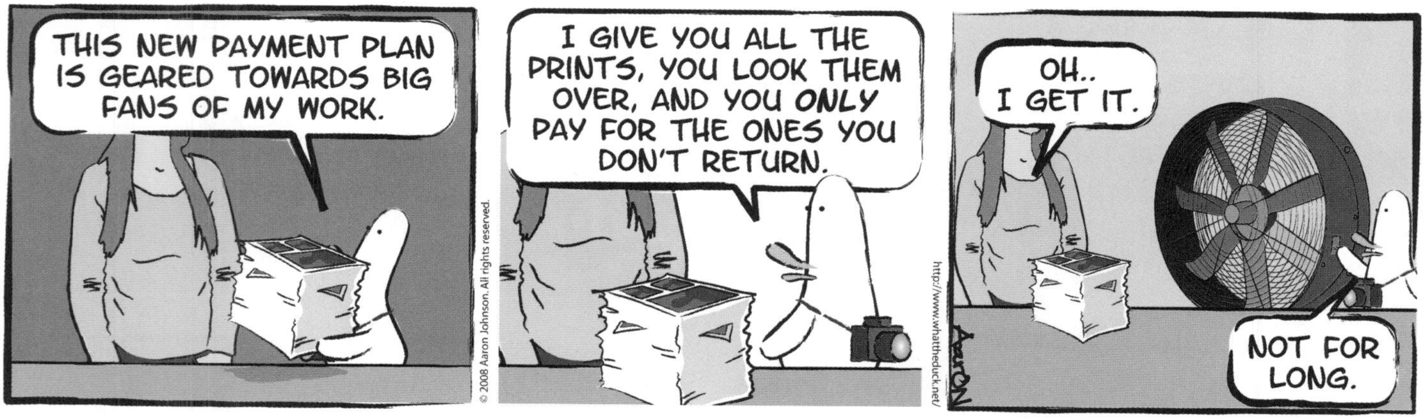
THIS NEW PAYMENT PLAN IS GEARED TOWARDS BIG FANS OF MY WORK.
I GIVE YOU ALL THE PRINTS, YOU LOOK THEM OVER, AND YOU ONLY PAY FOR THE ONES YOU DON'T RETURN.
OH.. I GET IT.
NOT FOR LONG.
© 2008 Aaron Johnson. All rights reserved.
http://www.whattheduck.net/
AARON

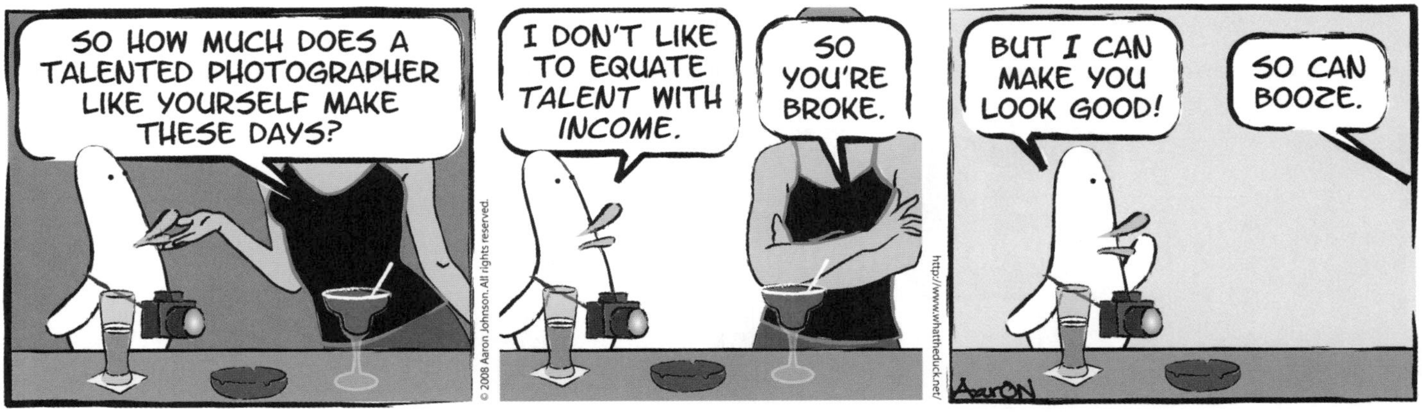
SO HOW MUCH DOES A TALENTED PHOTOGRAPHER LIKE YOURSELF MAKE THESE DAYS?
© 2008 Aaron Johnson. All rights reserved.
I DON'T LIKE TO EQUATE *TALENT* WITH *INCOME*.
SO YOU'RE BROKE.
http://www.whattheduck.net/
BUT *I* CAN MAKE YOU LOOK GOOD!
SO CAN BOOZE.
AARON

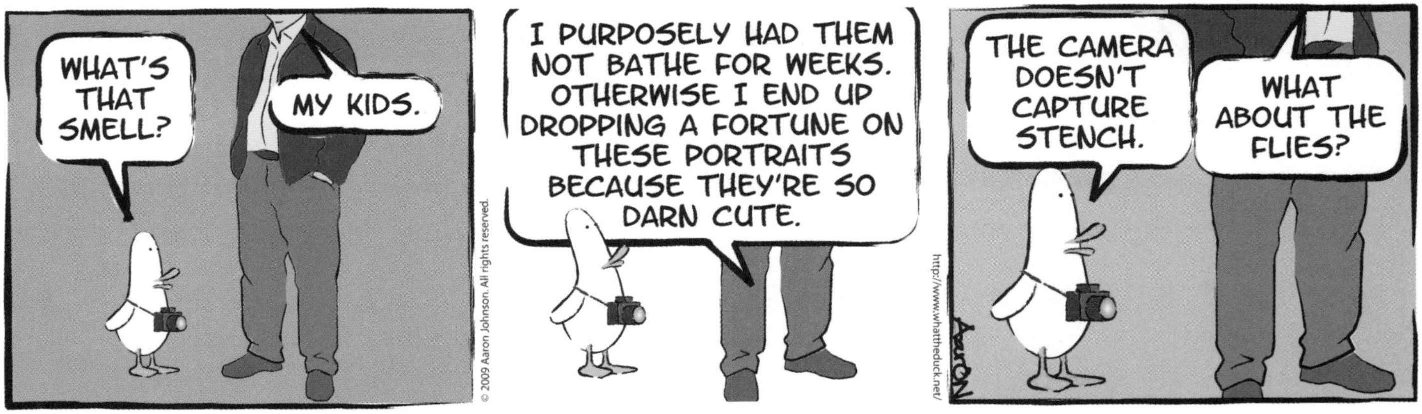
WHAT'S THAT SMELL?
MY KIDS.
© 2009 Aaron Johnson. All rights reserved.
I PURPOSELY HAD THEM NOT BATHE FOR WEEKS. OTHERWISE I END UP DROPPING A FORTUNE ON THESE PORTRAITS BECAUSE THEY'RE SO DARN CUTE.
http://www.whattheduck.net/
THE CAMERA DOESN'T CAPTURE STENCH.
WHAT ABOUT THE FLIES?
AARON

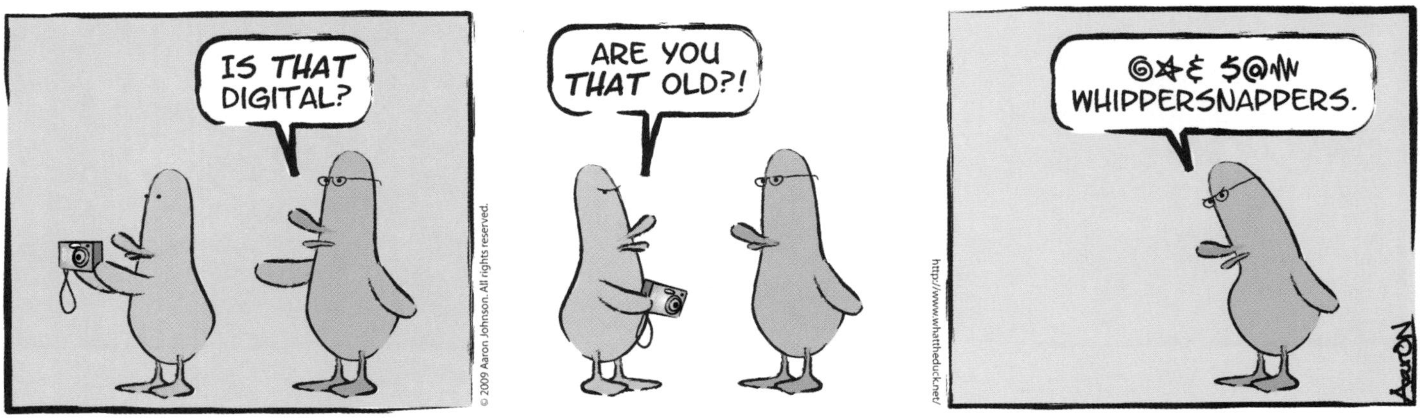
IS *THAT* DIGITAL?
© 2009 Aaron Johnson. All rights reserved.
ARE YOU *THAT* OLD?!
http://www.whattheduck.net/
WHIPPERSNAPPERS.
AARON

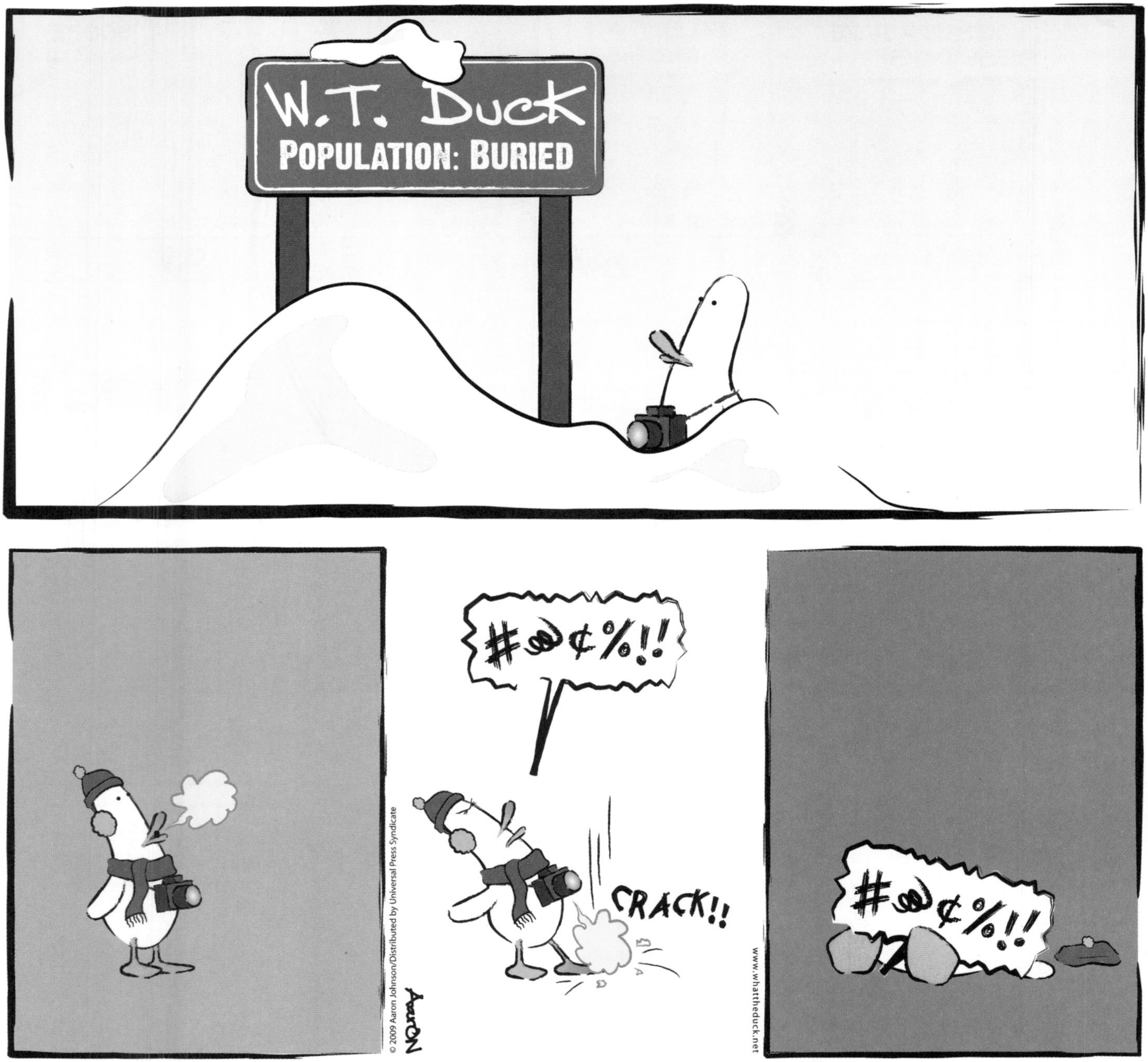
W.T. Duck
POPULATION: BURIED
#@¢%!!
CRACK!!
#@¢%!!
© 2009 Aaron Johnson/Distributed by Universal Press Syndicate
AARON
www.whattheduck.net